# Interdisciplinary Studies of the Market Order

# Economy, Polity, and Society

The foundations of political economy—from Adam Smith to the Austrian school of economics, to contemporary research in public choice and institutional analysis—are sturdy and well established, but far from calcified. On the contrary, the boundaries of the research built on this foundation are ever expanding. One approach to political economy that has gained considerable traction in recent years combines the insights and methods of three distinct but related subfields within economics and political science: the Austrian, Virginia and Bloomington schools of political economy. The vision of this book series is to capitalize on the intellectual gains from the interactions between these approaches in order to both feed the growing interest in this approach and advance social scientists' understanding of economy, polity, and society.

This series seeks to publish works that combine the Austrian school's insights on knowledge, the Virginia school's insights into incentives in nonmarket contexts, and the Bloomington school's multiple-method, real-world approach to institutional design as a powerful tool for understanding social behavior in a diversity of contexts.

## Series Editors

Virgil Henry Storr, Research Associate Professor of Economics and Senior Fellow,
    F. A. Hayek Program for Advanced Study in Philosophy, Politics and Economics,
    George Mason University.
Jayme S. Lemke, Senior Research Fellow, the Mercatus Center, George Mason University.

## Titles in the Series

*Interdisciplinary Studies of the Market Order: New Applications of Market Process Theory*,
    edited by Peter J. Boettke, Christopher J. Coyne, and Virgil Henry Storr.
*Knowledge and Incentives in Policy: Using Public Choice and Market Process Theory to
    Analyze Public Policy Issues*, edited by Stefanie Haeffele-Balch (forthcoming).

# Interdisciplinary Studies of the Market Order

## New Applications of Market Process Theory

Edited by
Peter J. Boettke, Christopher J. Coyne,
and Virgil Henry Storr

ROWMAN & LITTLEFIELD
INTERNATIONAL

London • New York

Published by Rowman & Littlefield International Ltd
Unit A, Whitacre Mews, 26-34 Stannary Street, London SE11 4AB
www.rowmaninternational.com

Rowman & Littlefield International Ltd.is an affiliate of Rowman & Littlefield
4501 Forbes Boulevard, Suite 200, Lanham, Maryland 20706, USA
With additional offices in Boulder, New York, Toronto (Canada), and Plymouth (UK)
www.rowman.com

**British Library Cataloguing in Publication Data**
A catalogue record for this book is available from the British Library

ISBN: HB 978-1-7866-0200-8
       PB 978-1-7866-0201-5

**Library of Congress Cataloging-in-Publication Data**

ISBN 978-1-78660-200-8 (cloth: alk. paper)
ISBN 978-1-78660-201-5 (pbk: alk. paper)
ISBN 978-1-78660-202-2 (electronic)

♾™ The paper used in this publication meets the minimum requirements of American
National Standard for Information Sciences—Permanence of Paper for Printed Library
Materials, ANSI/NISO Z39.48-1992.

Printed in the United States of America

# Contents

# Introduction

## New Approaches to Market Process: Interdisciplinary Studies of the Market Order

### Peter J. Boettke, Christopher J. Coyne, and Virgil Henry Storr

The chapters in this volume explore and engage market process theory from an interdisciplinary perspective. Market process theory explains the sequence through which the knowledge and expectations of economic actors lead toward coordination and cooperation. Our purpose in this introductory chapter is twofold. First, we provide a general overview of market process theory with the goal of providing context to the subsequent chapters. Second, we provide an overview of each of the subsequent chapters. Each chapter contains original research that explores or applies various aspects of market process theory and, in doing so, demonstrates the continuing relevance of this framework and approach within a wide variety of disciplines.

## MARKET PROCESS THEORY: AN OVERVIEW

A market refers to interactions between buyers and sellers. These interactions could take place in a physical marketplace (e.g., the local shopping plaza, bazaar, or stock exchange) or in a conceptual marketplace (e.g. the domestic market for automobiles or the global financial market). Potential buyers enter the market hoping to acquire goods or services. Potential sellers enter the market hoping to find buyers for the goods and services they can provide. If a potential buyer and seller cannot come to terms (i.e., the seller wants more than the buyer is willing to pay), then both parties may leave the market without having traded; both parties may leave the market frustrated. However, if a potential buyer and seller are able to agree on terms (i.e., on a particular price for a particular quantity of a good or service), then a market exchange takes place. If an exchange occurs, the buyer leaves the market with the good or service he wanted having paid a price for that good or service that he was willing to pay. The seller, likewise, leaves the market having obtained a price that she was willing to accept for the good or service she was offering.

Market process theory is an attempt to understand how prices emerge and how economic actors respond when prices change. It was most fully developed by three economists—Ludwig von Mises (1920, 1949), F. A. Hayek (1948), and Israel Kirzner (1973, 1992, 1997).[1] Mises (1949, 257) captured the essence of the theory when he wrote that "[t]he market is not a place, a thing, or a collective entity. The market is a process, actuated by the interplay of the actions of the various individuals cooperating under the division of labor." Similarly, Hayek (1948, 86–87) highlighted the important role of the price system, noting,

> It is more than a metaphor to describe the price system as a kind of machinery for registering change, or a system of telecommunications which enables individual producers to watch merely the movement of a few pointers, as an engineer might watch the hands of a few dials, in order to adjust their activities to changes of which they may never know more than is reflected in the price movement.

Additionally, Kirzner (1973, 73) stressed the key role that entrepreneurship plays in driving the market process, emphasizing that "[w]hat drives the market process is entrepreneurial boldness and imagination; what constitutes that process is the series of discoveries generated by that entrepreneurial boldness and alertness." It is this analytical focus on process that sets Mises, Hayek, and Kirzner apart from their peers in economics.

Market process theory seeks to understand how the knowledge and expectations of dispersed individuals are coordinated through an ongoing process of mutual discovery and learning. This theory has five defining and related characteristics: (1) markets depend on the existence of a particular set of institutions, (2) the market process is a cultural process, (3) markets are driven by entrepreneurial discovery in the face of sheer ignorance, (4) the process of discovery takes place in an open-ended system and is therefore ongoing, and (5) the market is a spontaneous order that emerges from the interactions of individuals pursuing their own ends. We will consider each of these characteristics in turn.

In order for markets to emerge and operate effectively, certain institutions must exist (see Boettke and Coyne 2003, 2009). Perhaps the most important institution is a regime of private property rights that delineate how resources are owned or used. Property rights, although often formally codified, are themselves emergent orders based on a complex, centuries-old set of moral traditions and experiences that no one planned or can fully understand (see Hayek 1973, 1983).

Property rights are crucial for the market process because they allow economic actors to engage in economic calculation, which refers to their ability to determine which of a range of technologically feasible alternatives is the most economically suitable to adopt (see Mises 1920; Vaughn 1980; Lavoie 1985; Boettke 1998).

Economic calculation operates as follows. Property rights over the means of production allow for competition and exchange between market participants. Because property owners will reap the economic benefits from their activities, they have an incentive to pay as little as they can for the goods and services they desire and to charge as much as they can for the goods and services that they are able to supply. As such, they have an incentive to compete with one another for the best deals.

Competition and exchange, in turn, lead to the emergence of market prices. These market prices capture information regarding the relative value of resources, which can then be used by economic actors to determine the expected value of alternative, technologically feasible uses of those resources. These spontaneously generated market prices allow economic actors to both evaluate past decisions and plan for the future because they effectively communicate information and tacit knowledge from throughout the economic system (see Hayek 1948, 77–91; Kirzner 1992, 139–51; Thomsen 1992). As Hayek writes, "In a system in which the knowledge of relevant facts is dispersed among many people, prices can act to co-ordinate the separate actions of different people in the same way as subjective values help the individual co-ordinate the part of his plan" (Hayek 1948, 85).

Changes in prices, thus, communicate that something about the world has changed. A price increase means that a good or service has become more scarce. If, for example, there is a natural disaster in a distant area that adversely affects the availability of an economic resource, the price of that resource will rise accordingly. Likewise, a decrease in the price means that a good or service has become more readily abundant. For instance, the price of a scarce resource like diamonds would fall if a new mine was discovered that dramatically increased the availability of diamonds. Even if market actors throughout the economic system have no idea about the fundamental cause of the price change, they will respond to the price change when making their plans. In this manner, market prices communicate local information and knowledge to other market actors, allowing them to adjust their plans accordingly.

Although market prices effectively communicate information, they do not contain all relevant information and are, therefore, necessarily imperfect knowledge surrogates (see Thomsen 1992). These imperfect prices are the result of sheer ignorance and are central to the market process because they represent profit opportunities for alert entrepreneurs to reallocate resources to new and better uses.

In order to fully appreciate the institutional environment of markets, it is important to recognize that the market process, like all social processes, is unavoidably a cultural process (Grube and Storr 2015). Culture can be defined as a historically transmitted pattern of meanings that is shared by a group of people and learned by new members as they become a part of the group (Geertz 1973; Chamlee-Wright 1997; Storr 2013). Rather than being a tool or resource (like a capital good), culture is the environment against, within, and through which individuals act in and experience the world. It is the lens through which individuals process reality.

In the context of the market process, an appreciation of the role of culture is important for several reasons. First, culture (partly) determines which formal institutions are feasible and sustainable (see Boettke, Coyne, and Leeson 2008). Second, culture (partly) determines how individuals understand the formal and informal rules that govern their market activities, including the property rights regimes discussed earlier. Third, culture also (partly) determines who can buy and sell, which items can legitimately be bought and sold, and when a deal between market participants has been properly consummated. Fourth, culture (partly) determines how market participants will view and respond to market signals like price changes as well as profits and losses. Finally, culture (partly) determines which profit opportunities entrepreneurs notice and which they ignore as well as the strategies entrepreneurs pursue as they attempt to exploit the opportunities that they perceive (Lavoie 1991).

Situated within a broader institutional and cultural environment, the market process is driven by entrepreneurial discovery in the face of sheer ignorance. Kirzner emphasizes the important difference between ignorance and sheer ignorance (see Kirzner 1992, 46–49). Ignorance refers to a known lack of knowledge that one can remedy by seeking out the requisite knowledge. For example, a person may lack the knowledge of foreign business regulations because possessing this information is not necessary to their domestic operations. This is an example of ignorance as commonly understood, which could be resolved by seeking out available information on foreign regulations.

Sheer ignorance, in contrast, refers to not only lacking knowledge, but also lacking knowledge that the information exists in the first place. In the context of markets, sheer ignorance entails a lack of knowledge about potential opportunities for profit. It is the existence of sheer ignorance and the subsequent imperfect prices that create the profit opportunities that attract alert entrepreneurs to relocate resources.

The conjectures of these alert entrepreneurs, who, in turn, believe they have identified a profit-yielding opportunity, are subjected to the profit-and-loss test. A profit reveals that the entrepreneur's conjecture was accurate—resources were previously misallocated and were in fact rearranged to generate greater value. A loss reveals the converse—the entrepreneur has reallocated resources in a manner that yields less value as compared to alternative uses. Taken together, the market process can be seen as pulling back the curtain of sheer ignorance as economic actors become aware of opportunities to which they were previously unaware. The result is, thus, improved coordination across the economic system.

The market process, as described above, is an open-ended system. It is a continuous process of discovery and resource reallocation. The complete reconciliation among individual plans is never achieved (see Kirzner 1992, 39–41). The alignment of individual plans with the constellation of individuals' preferences as well as available technologies and resources in the economic system never occurs. There is, instead, often a conflict between the plans of some market participants. Moreover, there is often a disjoint between individual preferences, technologies, and resource allocations. Through an ongoing competitive process of discovery, past inconsistencies are removed while new ones are introduced (Hayek 1948, 92–106; Kirzner 1992, 46–49).

The market process, thus, results in a spontaneous order—that is, an arrangement that is the result of purposive individual action but not design (see Hayek 2013). In this context, order refers to an integration or coordination of activities between individual elements embedded in a system characterized by certain rules and patterns of behavior.

Spontaneous orders have several defining characteristics. The market process satisfies all of them. First, spontaneous orders emerge from human action but not from intentional design. That is, in purposefully pursuing their particular and diverse goals, individuals contribute to a broader order or integration of activities. In the context of the market process, each individual participant is pursuing his or her own ends. In doing so, each one must interact and coordinate with others who are simultaneously pursuing their own goals. These interactions tend to produce mutually beneficial outcomes for the immediate participants to the interactions. At the same time, they contribute to the broader market order that we observe when we step back and take a broader view of the market at any point in time. Ludwig von Mises (1949, 338) captured this point when he wrote:

> The pricing process is a social process. It is consummated by an interaction of all members of the society. All collaborate and cooperate, each in the particular role he has chosen for himself in the framework of the division of labor. . . . All people are instrumental in bringing about the result, viz., the price structure of the market, the allocation of the factors of production to the various lines of want-satisfaction, and the determination of the share of each individual. These three events are not three different matters. They are only different aspects of

one indivisible phenomenon which our analytical scrutiny separates into three parts. In the market process they are accomplished *uno actu*.

As Mises emphasizes, the interactions of dispersed individuals bring about the broader allocation of resources that we refer to as "the market." On a daily basis, each and every market participant contributes to the broader market order without even realizing it. In fact, one of the most stunning aspects of the market process is that it functions to achieve desirable outcomes without anyone needing to understand exactly how it operates.

Second, spontaneous orders can meaningfully be described as orders meaning there is an identifiable pattern emerging from the interaction of the individuals in the system. As Hayek (1973, 36) writes, an emergent order is "a state of affairs in which a multiplicity of elements of various kinds are so related to each other that we may learn from our acquaintance with . . . part of the whole to form correct expectations concerning the rest." The market process satisfies this condition because clear relationships, tendencies, and patterns emerge through interaction in markets. For example, prices will tend to correspond to opportunity costs through the entrepreneurial process described earlier. Similarly, through that same process resources tend to be reallocated to their highest valued uses.

Third, spontaneous orders require mechanisms to provide both positive and negative feedback to the individual actors so that they can adjust their behaviors accordingly to achieve coordination. These feedback mechanisms enable the order to be self-enforcing. In markets, the profit-and-loss mechanism serves this function. Entrepreneurs are alert to potential profit opportunities. The profit-and-loss mechanism provides feedback as to whether these perceived opportunities were accurate or inaccurate. Economic actors are incentivized to adjust their behavior to feedback received through the profit-and-loss mechanism. For example, a business earning a loss will be incentivized to adjust its behavior because if it fails to do so it will be unable to survive.

The fourth characteristic of spontaneous orders is that the actors in the system follow general rules of conduct. These rules, which are informal or formal in nature, are embedded in a cultural environment and govern the interactions between actors, and hence the kind of order that emerges. In the context of markets, there is an array of rules that govern the behaviors of participants. As discussed, private property rights delineate what can be owned and the range of permissible activities by property owners. Private property rights also allow for economic calculation and provide an incentive to act on that knowledge through the feedback mechanisms just discussed. In addition to property rights, there is an array of other institutions that allow markets to function. For example, social relationships and norms of trust and etiquette facilitate coordination and cooperation between people (see Granovetter 1974; Storr 2008, 2013).

Finally, spontaneous orders are abstract, meaning they cannot be fully grasped using human reason. This has two implications. First, since spontaneous orders are not the result of human design, the participants in the system do not need to understand, or even be aware of, the broader order and their contribution to the order. This is clearly the case with markets. Each participant pursues particular goals and, in doing so, contributes to the broader "economy" without realizing that he or she is doing so. Second, and related, the abstract nature of spontaneous orders means that they are able to extend beyond the limits that human reason can imagine as a potential state of affairs. No person, or group of people, can centrally plan the markets necessary for advanced material production and, historically, efforts to do so have led to devastating consequences precisely because the abstract nature of the order generated by the market process was ignored.

In sum, market outcomes are a spontaneous order. This order emerges from an institutional setting of private property that allows for the emergence of market prices and the operation of the profit-and-loss mechanism. Property rights, prices, and profit and loss are embedded in a broader cultural environment that influences how these variables are interpreted and acted upon. The entrepreneur who is alert to profit opportunities resulting from past ignorance and error is the central driver of the market process. Through an open-ended discovery process, these errors are corrected and adjustments are continually made as new knowledge becomes available. The result is social cooperation and coordination.

## AN OVERVIEW OF THE VOLUME

The remainder of the volume consists of eleven chapters, split into two parts. Part I of the volume, "Exploring and Extending the Theory of the Market Process," consists of four chapters. Part II, "Interdisciplinary Applications of Market Process Theory," consists of the remaining seven chapters.

The chapters in the first part of the volume explore and extend various aspects of market process theory from an interdisciplinary perspective. In chapter 1, Nathan Sawatzky argues that Plato's economic genius has largely been overlooked. His central claim is that a careful assessment of Socrates's economic analysis in the healthy, "early city" of Plato's *Republic* reveals that historians of economic thought, including Schumpeter, Finley, and Robbins, have missed many or most of Plato's contributions to economic theory. According to Sawatzky, Socrates's analytical approach and resulting economic theory in the early city contrast sharply with the approach and conclusions of his interlocutors Glaucon and Adeimantus later in the *Republic*. These differences, thus, call into question the common view that Plato is a sort of communist, fascist, or totalitarian.

Among other things, Plato has Socrates adopt an approach to social and political analysis, similar to those of Weber and Mises, that seeks to account for the experiences of acting individuals. Plato through Socrates also systematically builds a theory of why such individuals exchange with one another. He also advances a theory that includes three reasons for the division of labor that complement but go beyond those offered by Adam Smith. Finally, Plato appears to understand the role of fiat money and articulates much of the theory of comparative advantage.

In chapter 2, Brianne Wolf explores Adam Smith's writings on sympathy and the poor law. In the *Wealth of Nations*, Adam Smith provides a brief discussion of the English poor law as part of a larger discussion about labor markets. Smith argues that the law distorts the labor market in two ways: (1) by restricting the free circulation of labor and (2) by causing differences in price across labor markets. However, as Wolf notes, Smith spends a good deal more time talking about the moral consequences of the law. This chapter attempts to explain why Smith discusses the moral effects of the law rather than simply dismissing it on economic grounds by employing Smith's argument about the poor law in *Wealth of Nations* together with his arguments about the extent of sympathy in *Theory of Moral Sentiments*.

Wolf argues that focusing on the moral consequences of this policy shows how economic liberty is also tied to the development of healthy moral judgment and sympathetic relationships. As Wolf recounts, Smith highlights two key aspects of the law that harm the moral situation of the poor by exacerbating the problem of distance in sympathetic relationships. First, the poor law establishes a position of arbitrary power for its overseers relative to the rest of society. Second, the law positions the poor as objects to be administered rather than individuals with moral worth. Smith shows that interfering with the market makes it more likely that we enhance its negative potential for fostering selfishness to the detriment of sympathy.

In chapter 3, Nick Cowen asks: How can liberal political theorists combine their normative commitments with realistic assumptions of human behavior and capacities? This is an important question for scholars who wish to use their theories to evaluate existing political institutions and recommend practical alternatives. This chapter describes a particular approach to realism in political theory by using the notion of "robustness" from the Robust Political Economy framework. Robust institutions are those that perform well even when people are neither omniscient nor perfectly motivated to follow the common good. On this view, certain market institutions (e.g., private property and the rule of law) are certainly robust institutions.

Cowen argues that the problems of limited knowledge and self-interest emerge from three assumptions about the constitution of human beings commonly found in the liberal theoretical tradition: methodological individualism, subjectivism, and analytical egalitarianism. He proposes a combination of public choice and market process theory as being best suited for evaluating the robustness of normative political theories. Cowen argues that this combination allows us to apply these assumptions systematically to all domains of human activity. Compared to standard neo-classical methodology, this approach offers an enriched account of the epistemic challenge to social cooperation that individuals face and the role of institutions, including private property and voluntary exchange, in ameliorating this challenge. Cowen shows how this systematic evaluation of the motivational and epistemic properties of institutions can help critique and extend Rawls's contractarian theory of justice and offer a new perspective on the role of realism in political theory.

In the final chapter in part I (chapter 4), Dan Shahar examines the work of F. A. Hayek in the context of environmental political economy. Defenders of "free-market" environmentalism have often appealed to the writings of F. A. Hayek to support their favored approaches to environmental political economy. Yet Hayek's power to vindicate such perspectives is controversial. In fact, some writers have found in Hayek's writings an invitation to extensive political interventions in the environmental arena. Shahar explores three environmentally relevant themes in Hayek's writings in order to clarify his true legacy for environmental political economy.

The first theme emphasizes that natural resources represent just one subset of the productive capital available to society and thus seeks to address environmental problems through the coordinating power of the market. The second stresses the challenges created by "neighborhood effects" in many environmental contexts, generating a potential case for political interventions aimed at preventing undesirable outcomes. The third theme highlights the need for principled protection of the complex, self-organizing systems on which humanity relies, potentially including certain natural ecosystems.

Shahar concludes that the paradigm resulting from a synthesis of these themes leaves significant room for political action to address environmental problems, contrary to the characterizations of some free-market environmentalists. But, Shahar argues, a Hayekian approach to environmental policy making also demands that interventions respect certain constraints to preserve the functionality of economic markets. Shahar argues that Hayek's most important contributions to environmental debates can be found in his guidance for making public policies compatible with the functionality of the market order.

Part II, "Interdisciplinary Applications of Market Process Theory," consists of the remaining seven chapters. These chapters apply the insights of market process theory to a variety of topics, demonstrating its continuing relevance. In chapter 5, Crystal Dozier explores the role of competitive feasting in the establishment of long-range trading relationships in three societies. Dozier begins with the recognition that human cooperation has been the focus of many disciplines of social science. While people have lived in small, mobile groups for the majority of our existence (over one hundred fifty thousand years) the sudden development of more complex societies in the Holocene (about eleven thousand years ago) is a phenomenon worthy of exploration. The first archaeological evidence of people meeting in large groups is represented through feasting traditions worldwide. Dozier argues that competitive feasting represents one of the first mechanisms through which individuals could gain special social status through trade and cooperation. Her chapter explores evidence for feasting traditions in Anatolia (now Turkey), among the Bronze Age Celts (now northern Europe), and Toyah Phase (now Texas) as case studies. In all of these examples, the first evidence for long-distance trade in the area is limited to nonfunctional or ceremonial goods, with evidence that these goods played a crucial role in gatherings of large numbers of people.

Dozier notes that the social differentiation afforded by feasting, emerging from more egalitarian forms of social organization, only succeeds because the hosts of the feast can fulfill their own desires as well as that of their guests. Motivation for competitive feasting spurred long-distance trade for exotic, luxury items as well as for the creation of special foods. These fundamental changes in human society are reflected in the first evidence for social ranking, private property, and long-distance trade—in other words, this transition marks the first evidence for an emerging market process.

In chapter 6, Nicholas O'Neill explains why the conservative Catholic press in France invoked a liberal political economy during the 1848 Revolution. He argues that as political actors attempted to define the fledgling republic that year, they grounded their claims to authority on external sources of legitimacy and established regimes of truth that could justify competing policy positions. As unemployment spiked in Paris, the debate over whether there existed a right to work played a pivotal role in determining the path of the revolution. O'Neill's chapter reconstructs the moral economy rooted in Christian ethical teachings that radicals referenced to justify active state intervention in the economy to provide work to all in need. He highlights key elements of the era's prevailing political economic theories about how market processes generated a market order. O'Neill also traces shifts in the conservative Catholic press when it embraced and then abandoned a liberal political economy as a political rhetoric against the radical understanding of the revolution. By doing so, his chapter emphasizes the importance of considering the political and cultural context surrounding the adoption of ideologies.

In the subsequent chapter (chapter 7), Bryan Leonard explores private property and collective action in the context of natural resource management. The problem of natural resource management has traditionally been confronted with either "top-down" or "bottom-up" institutions to coordinate individual actions. Top-down institutions prescribe particular outcomes or impose restrictions on individual behavior with the goal of preventing socially costly behavior. Alternately, bottom-up solutions for resolving collective action problems include two broad categories of institutions: informal institutions, where norms guide behavior, and market-based institutions built around formal property rights.

Leonard's chapter focuses on how formal property rights can serve as a basis for coordination and explores the conditions under which property rights are a more effective solution to collective action problems than either political or informal institutions by exploring the development of the prior appropriation doctrine—a novel first-possession system of allocating water in the American West. First possession rights to water emerged as de facto claims because they made exclusion possible in a setting where agents arrived at different points in time and where land ownership—the traditional margin of demarcation for water rights—was in flux. The formal legal recognition of appropriative water rights made exclusion possible and allowed a market for irrigation clubs to form, generating information to help determine the efficient scope and size of irrigation works and governance. First possession property rights to water served as a basis for collective action in a setting where state provision of public goods and local informal arrangements built on cultural norms were equally infeasible.

Chapter 8, authored by Frank Garmon Jr., examines the logic behind Adam Smith's principles of taxation and their application in the early American republic. He argues that early-American policy makers applied theories proposed by Smith and others because these fiscal strategies proved less distortional to the market process than other forms of taxation. Garmon outlines Adam Smith's principles of taxation and investigates their relationship with other political theorists in the late eighteenth century. He then examines Smith's reception in the early American republic. The founding generation read Smith avidly and incorporated elements of his maxims into their tax systems when they installed new tax administrations after the American Revolution. The combined system of federal and state taxation owes almost as much to Adam Smith's principles as it does to Alexander Hamilton, who had read Smith closely and proposed a grand vision for concurrent tax powers. Hamilton articulated the benefits of constitutional limitations on taxing authority in the *Federalist* Papers. For Hamilton, the Constitution constrained the federal government's power to levy direct taxes but provided it with unlimited authority over indirect taxes. The combined federal and state system of taxation had the effect of minimizing distortions in the market process by limiting the burden of taxation on average Americans.

In chapter 9, Jason Douglas discusses how stories can narrate and enhance the reach of market process theory. His chapter answers the following question: What does an account of the market process for the masses look like? Douglas contends that unlike some forms of specialized knowledge, economics has its greatest impact when it becomes part of public knowledge. Therefore, fostering greater public understanding of the market as a process requires multidisciplinary collaborations that draw from cultural studies. Douglas argues that stories are an essential tool for communicating economic ideas. Because people understand the world they live in through stories, we need to understand how such stories can be used to narrate the market process. In order to understand how stories can be effective tools of teaching and communicating economic ideas, Douglas identifies formal similarities between narrative and the market process by analyzing Cameron Hawley's 1955 business novel, *Cash McCall*.

The subsequent chapter (chapter 10), authored by Jerrod Anderson, examines how market process theory offers insight into the operation of health care markets. Many economists argue that an unregulated health care market would be dysfunctional due to problems of high switching costs and asymmetric information, affecting both consumer and producer decision making. These critiques of the health care market often come with calls for more regulation in order to protect the consumer or increase transparency. Anderson provides an alternative analysis of the health care market and shows how expanding the scope of exchange relationships, rather than constraining them through regulation, can lead to an improved competitive environment. In order to illustrate his main points, Anderson uses the example of doctors hired by mutual aid societies in the early 1900s. In doing so, he shows how the problems of asymmetric information were mitigated through a mix of contracting and labor market competition. Anderson then examines the contemporary practice of medical tourism and describes how lessons from the mutual aid societies can be combined with medical tourism to improve domestic health care competition. Anderson's analysis shows that while market imperfections may seem endemic to the health care market, these issues can be mitigated over time if consumers and producers are allowed the freedom to contract and engage in mutually beneficial exchange.

Finally, in chapter 11, Audrey Redford explores the connection between market process theory and the government prohibition of drugs. Markets for prohibited goods, specifically illegal drugs, exist, despite extensive efforts to suppress them. The intention of prohibitionist policies is to eliminate the market for a particular good(s). Redford argues that in order to remain in the market, prohibition entrepreneurs have the incentive to figure out ways of minimizing the costs of doing illegal business—for example, the costs required to evade law enforcement and consideration of the cost and likelihood of punishment—as well as establishing and maintaining institutions that promote cooperation where formal property rights are not provided. Redford's analysis suggests that because illegal markets are forced outside of the traditional property rights–based institutional arrangements and must continually avoid law enforcement, entrepreneurial efforts within illegal markets will be channeled toward protective innovations that allow these entrepreneurs to remain in business. As entrepreneurs discover new methods by which to innovate, they will be shaped by the entrepreneur's knowledge and the environment within which the entrepreneur is acting. This helps to explain why illegal and legal drugs diverge on margins, including the use of violence and advances (or lack thereof) in product quality.

Taken together, the chapters in the volume demonstrate the interdisciplinary relevance of market process theory. Each chapter offers specific insights into different areas of this theoretical framework. There is much additional work to be done in exploring, extending, and applying the insights of this framework from a variety of disciplinary perspectives. Our hope is that this volume will encourage an ongoing interdisciplinary discussion that is sure to generate mutual gains from intellectual exchange.

## NOTE

1. For more on the history of market process theory, see Boettke and Prychitko (1998).

## REFERENCES

Boettke, Peter J. 1998. "Economic Calculation: The Austrian Contribution to Political Economy." *Advances in Austrian Economics* 5: 131–58.

Boettke, Peter J., and Christopher J. Coyne. 2003. "Entrepreneurship and Development: Cause or Consequence?" *Advances in Austrian Economics* 6: 67–88.

———. 2009. *Context Matters: Entrepreneurship and Institutions.* Hanover, MA: Now Publishers.

Boettke, Peter J., Christopher J. Coyne, and Peter T. Leeson. 2008. "Institutional Stickiness and the New Development Economics." *American Journal of Economics and Sociology* 67 (2): 331–58.

Boettke, Peter J., and David L. Prychitko (eds.). 1998. *Market Process Theories* (2 vols.). Cheltenham, UK: Edward Elgar Publishing.

Chamlee-Wright, Emily 1997. *The Cultural Foundations of Economic Development: Urban Female Entrepreneurship in Ghana.* New York: Routledge.

Geertz, Clifford. 1973. *The Interpretation of Cultures: Selected Essays*. New York: Basic Books.

Granovetter, Mark. 1974. *Getting a Job: A Study of Contracts and Careers*. Chicago: Chicago University Press.

Grube, Laura E., and Virgil Henry Storr (eds.) 2015. *Culture and Economic Action*. Cheltenham, UK: Edward Elgar Publishing.

Hayek, F. A. 1948. *Individualism and Economic Order*. Chicago: Chicago University Press.

———. 1973. *Law, Legislation, and Liberty, Volume 1: Rules and Order*. Chicago: Chicago University Press.

———. 1983. *Our Moral Heritage*. Washington, DC: Heritage Foundation.

———. 2013. *The Market and Other Orders. The Collected Works of F. A. Hayek, Volume 15*, edited by Bruce Caldwell. Chicago: Chicago University Press.

Kirzner, Israel M. 1973. *Competition and Entrepreneurship*. Chicago: Chicago University Press.

———. 1992. *The Meaning of the Market Process*. New York: Routledge.

———. 1997. "Entrepreneurial Discovery and the Competitive Market Process." *Journal of Economic Literature* 35 (1): 60–85.

Lavoie, Don. 1985. *Rivalry and Central Planning: The Socialist Calculation Debate Revisited*. Cambridge, MA: Cambridge University Press.

———. 1991. "The Discovery and Interpretation of Profit Opportunities: Culture and the Kirznerian Entrepreneur." In *The Culture of Entrepreneurship*, edited by Bridgette Berger, 33–51. San Francisco: Institute for Contemporary Studies.

Mises, Ludwig von. 1920 [1935]. "Economic Calculation in the Socialist Commonwealth." In *Collectivist Economic Planning*, edited by F. A. Hayek, 87–130. London: George Routledge & Sons.

———. 1949 [1996]. *Human Action: A Treatise on Economics*. Fourth edition. San Francisco: Fox & Wilkes.

Storr, Virgil Henry. 2008. "The Market as a Social Space: On the Meaningful Extraeconomic Conversations That Occur in Markets." *Review of Austrian Economics* 21 (2): 135–50.

———. 2013. *Understanding the Culture of Markets*. New York: Routledge.

Thomsen, Esteban F. 1992. *Prices and Knowledge: A Market-Process Perspective*. New York: Routledge.

Vaughn, Karen I. 1980. "Economic Calculation under Socialism: The Austrian Contribution." *Economic Inquiry* 18: 535–54.

*Part I*

# EXPLORING AND EXTENDING THE THEORY OF THE MARKET PROCESS

# Chapter 1

# Plato's Economic Genius

## Nathan Sawatzky

Based primarily on his reading of Plato's *Republic*, Karl Popper (1947, 76) famously insisted that Plato's "political demands are purely totalitarian and anti-humanitarian." In this chapter I argue that Popper and many other prominent authors, from Plato scholars (e.g., Julia Annas 1991, 73–79, 172–81; Malcolm Schofield 1999, 77–80 and 2006, 205) to historians of economic thought (e.g., M. I. Finley 1970, 4; Joseph Schumpeter 1959, 55–56; Lionel Robbins 2000, 11–12, 14, 16) to political theorists (e.g., Sheldon Wolin 1960, 41–44, 47–50; Wendy Brown 1994, 176) to Austrian economists (e.g., Ludwig von Mises 2007, 583; Friedrich Hayek 1992, 32, 52, 109–10),[1] have misidentified Plato as a proponent of extreme unity and control in politics because they have overlooked or misunderstood (i) the economic genius underlying the early stages of the city that Socrates and his young friend Adeimantus—Plato's literary characters—design at *Republic* 369b–372d,[2] along with (ii) the distinct roles that Plato has his different characters play in designing that city. Socrates's brief account of how exchanges between individuals build a city, I propose, when carefully analyzed and placed in its proper context within the *Republic*, constitutes evidence that Plato was not, as is commonly thought, a communist, a totalitarian, or a fascist.[3] Instead, Plato intends to *contrast* Socrates with his young friends Adeimantus and Glaucon—men who *are* enthusiastic supporters of thoroughgoing political unity and control and to whose education Socrates attempts to contribute—by making Socrates a consistent proponent of political and economic systems that as much as possible respect and respond to *individuals'* needs and aptitudes. If Popper had understood Plato, he would have embraced him.[4]

By providing a close reading of the "early city" (the name I adopt for what is generally but mistakenly, if not disparagingly, called the "city of pigs"[5] but which Socrates at 372e calls a "true" and "healthy" city) at *Republic*

*Nathan Sawatzky*

369b–372d, I argue that Plato thought deeply and analytically about market exchanges and the division of labor, discovering principles that go far beyond both the socially embedded and socially constrained economic structures of Ancient Greece and the aristocratic values and theories of his contemporary writers. In fact, Plato articulated principles that have become foundational for modern market economies and modern economics. His economic genius, expressed through Socrates, consists in (i) adopting, for social and political analysis, the basic perspective of individual decision makers who weigh the costs and benefits of alternative actions, assess the relative desirability of different ends for their relative contributions to a "better" condition, and, where needed, seek to discover new and better means and ends; (ii) systematically developing a theory of why such individuals come to cooperate and exchange with one another, a theory which features three apparently exhaustive reasons for the division of labor; (iii) separating out the variability of supply from the variability of demand; (iv) incorporating a normative claim—that individuals should only do what is needed/necessary—as an essential part of a descriptive analysis of why individuals engage in exchange; (v) distinguishing among, and systematically linking, demand for consumption goods and demands for labor, tools, materials, transportation, and other factors of production; (vi) identifying the part of the principle of supply and demand concerned with the effect of aggregate demand on supply; (vii) understanding that the foregoing principles governing exchange extend beyond state boundaries; (viii) proposing a fiat (as opposed to a commodity)[6] understanding of money, and (ix) articulating reasons for the employer-employee relationship that come remarkably close to a full theory of comparative advantage.

   Plato is the first to write about any of these, to the best of my knowledge. What is more, Plato accomplishes what he does in the space of only three pages, as part of a much larger project in which he portrays Socrates trying to educate his companions, who are optimistic regarding their abilities to design a city, about what is just and unjust in both public and private life. That Plato could write something of this nature is all the more extraordinary given S. Todd Lowry's otherwise true claim that ancient writings on economic matters were "framed in terms of personal and public administrative perspectives rather than in terms of commercial market analyses," since after all, "capitalist markets did not exist in ancient Greece" (Lowry 1987, 14, 18).

   I anticipate that the arguments I develop in this chapter will be of interest to four (overlapping) audiences. For historians of economic thought, I present evidence that Plato developed a surprisingly *general* and *analytic* theory of a market economy, contrary to the prevailing view. Intriguing for political philosophers, I imagine, will be the ways in which Socrates relies on the descriptive principle that *all human communities are built out of individuals seeking to fulfill their needs* and incorporates the normative principle that *one should always do what is most needed/necessary* into his economic analysis. For those scholars and lay readers with a general interest in either Plato or pedagogical literary devices, I intend my account of how he uses the dialogue form as a means of conveying his economic and political thought to yield provocative, interpretively consequential insights into Plato's politics and pedagogical strategies in the *Republic*. Finally, those with an interest in the themes of this volume—the market process and the kinds of order that emerge from that process—will find that the analytical approach Socrates uses to construct his entire account of a system of market exchanges shares fundamental similarities with the versatile, powerful methods of Max Weber and Ludwig von Mises.

As Boettke and Storr (2002, 161–76) have highlighted, Weber's method of "*Verstehen*" and Mises's methodological individualism both seek to explain social phenomena by accounting for the experience of the individual decision maker.[7] "[F]or the subjective interpretation of action in sociological work," Weber (1978, 13) writes, "collectivities must be treated as *solely* the resultants and modes of organization of the particular acts of individual persons, since these alone can be treated as agents in a course of subjectively understandable action." Mises's method is similar:

> If we scrutinize the meaning of the various actions performed by individuals we must necessarily learn everything about the actions of collective wholes. For a social collective has no existence and reality outside of the individual members' actions. The life of a collective is lived in the actions of the individuals constituting its body. . . . Thus the way to a cognition of collective wholes is through an analysis of the individuals' actions. (Mises 2007, 42)

An aim of this chapter is to show how Plato, more than two thousand years before Weber, portrays Socrates using a similar approach to construct a theory of how individuals cooperate and form communities and thereby constitute a city and an economic system. For although Plato did not use a modern economic or sociological vocabulary, the principles he discovered are in some cases similar to modern ones and may, with some care, be accurately represented in modern terms.[8]

In the first substantive section of this chapter, I identify what I see to be the main reasons why Plato's economic thought has long been overlooked and misunderstood. In the next section, I begin to address these reasons by explaining Socrates's investigative procedure, a grasp of which is essential for avoiding unfair criticisms of Plato. Over several subsequent sections I turn to an exegesis of the early city, analyzing the economic principles Socrates identifies and explains, and responding to previous scholarly views of the early city. In the final section, I respond to the objection that, for all

Plato's economic insight, he nevertheless advocates extreme political control over economic activities.

## WHY PLATO'S ECONOMIC THOUGHT IS USUALLY OVERLOOKED OR MISUNDERSTOOD

Plato's economic genius, as Weinstein (2009, 439–40) observes, is generally overlooked. There are several reasons for this. Perhaps the most significant is that his most developed ideas are presented concisely (in only three pages) and in informal terms as part of a wandering conversation between Socrates and Adeimantus about why and how cities come into being. It is easy to assume that Plato's informal style of presentation corresponds to a lack of rigorous analysis. To this is added the fact that, for various reasons, most Plato scholars dismiss the early city Socrates and Adeimantus construct as, at least in Plato's view, mistaken and inferior to the versions of the city developed later in the *Republic*[9]—if Plato did not consider the early city to be a serious political model, then why would one look there for any serious contributions to economic theory? Furthermore, that the later versions of the city exemplify a "rigid stationarity" in which "[a]ll economic and non-economic activity [is] strictly regulated" (Schumpeter 1959, 56, 55; see also Ekelund and Hébert 2007, 11–12) seems to suggest that the early city could not possibly contain any systematic insights about dynamic economic processes. Moreover, even in those cases when a scholar does study the early city in some detail (e.g., McNulty 1975, 373–74; Foley 1974, 228–34; 1975, 379; Greco 2009, 55), its interpretation is usually so conditioned by later versions of the city in the *Republic* that its economic principles are, as I will show, misrepresented and misunderstood.[10] In this chapter, I aim to assess the economic and ethical principles of the early city on their own merits. This is of both analytical and historical interest in itself; it is also interpretively significant as a precondition for any fair comparisons of the early city to later versions of the city in the *Republic*.

Among historians of economic thought, three voices have done the most to spread the view that Plato's works contain no rigorous economic thought. Joseph Schumpeter asserts that "[t]he essential difference [between Plato's and Aristotle's approaches to economics] is that an analytic *intention*, which may be said (in a sense) to be absent from Plato's mind, was the prime mover of Aristotle's. This is clear from the logical structure of his arguments" (Schumpeter 1959, 57). Schumpeter defines economic *analysis*, distinct from mere economic *thought* or *description*, as "intellectual efforts . . . to *understand* economic phenomena" (Schumpeter 1959, 3; see also Lowry 1979, 66–67). The eminent classicist Moses I. Finley concurs: "It is agreed on all sides that only Aristotle offered the rudiments of [economic] analysis"

(Finley 1970, 4). Lionel Robbins, too, thinks that Aristotle "is much more germane to technical analysis than Plato's remarks on the division of labour" (Robbins 2000, 15), and he adds that we "must not expect too much of Plato," since he was "backward looking" in (allegedly) preferring the harsh, regimented Spartan regime to Athenian democracy and commerce (Robbins 2000, 11). Unsurprisingly, in light of these three prominent voices, a recent popular reader in the history of economic thought skips over Plato and begins with Aristotle (Medema and Samuels 2013, 2–4). Moreover, Finley's influential thesis that in the ancient world economic interactions were governed by considerations of status and "embedded" in hierarchical social relationships to such an extent as to make modern economic models of little use for understanding those interactions (Finley [1973] 1999, 35–61) has made it still more unlikely that scholars would look for a systematic economic theory in Plato. Against these voices, I seek to show that Socrates's casual style masks an analytic intention,[11] and that he develops a systematic and far-reaching theory of market exchanges and the division of labor based on the interactions of thinking, decision-making individuals.

## SOCRATES' INVESTIGATIVE PROCEDURE AND PEDAGOGICAL STRATEGY

Socrates and Adeimantus begin to construct a "city in speech," a hypothetical or theoretical (as opposed to an actual) city, because they want to know what justice is and because they hope that, as the city develops, it will be easier for them to spot justice and injustice in it than in a person's soul, which is harder to observe (368c–369b). Socrates therefore sets out to build a realistic, "true" (372e6) city. Yet he attempts neither to narrate the *historical* development of a city[12]—accusations that the early city develops in a historically unrealistic way (e.g., Harris 2002, 72–74) are therefore unfair—nor to build a theoretical model of a city systematically from first principles, as Schofield's characterization of "a sort of transcendental deduction of the very existence of the market" suggests (Schofield 1999, 76; followed by Weinstein 2009, 440).[13] Rather, Socrates adopts what we might call an *investigative* procedure.

Presumably no one who is first discovering or inventing a theory articulates it fully and systematically *while* it is being discovered. Rather, in the process of discovery one moves back and forth between general and specific principles (if not also particular events), clarifying, extending, or correcting one's initial notions wherever one realizes that such activities are needed. In the same way, Plato portrays Socrates in the process of discovering a systematic theory with Adeimantus, alternately (i) *positing or clarifying general principles* (e.g., reasons for the division of labor) and (ii) *applying these by developing specific principles for specific kinds of cases* (e.g., applying the division of labor to the production of raw materials or transportation). This *alternating* investigative procedure gives the appearance of a wandering conversation, but this does not prevent Socrates from producing an economic theory surprisingly systematic in content.[14] Schumpeter does not notice that Plato's purpose is not only to communicate ideas; in addition, Plato seeks to model the process of discovering ideas, and to lead the reader through his or her own process of discovery.

A further aspect of Plato's writing has proven particularly difficult for modern interpreters to make sense of, as we will see—his use of different speakers in the dialogue. The most common mistake is to assume that all or most things Adeimantus, his brother Glaucon, or even Socrates says represent Plato's own view. But the brothers do *not* merely "help [Socrates] expound elaborate theoretical constructions by friendly encouragement and the occasional well-placed question" (Schofield 1999, 70). Plato portrays Adeimantus and Glaucon as distinct individuals with their own character traits and prejudices. We will observe instances in which these prejudices—not Socrates's (or Plato's) *own* convictions—begin to introduce regulatory, static, aristocratic regime features into the city in speech. By having Socrates develop the early city *before* Glaucon and Adeimantus start influencing the course of later versions of the city, Plato sets up a contrast. As Socrates then allows the brothers to introduce new regime features into the city and helps them work out the consequences of those features (securing their approval at every step) in his attempts to help them know themselves better and to educate them, the city comes to embody a *mix* of principles introduced by all three interlocutors. Socrates's pedagogical strategy requires that he allow his interlocutors to influence the course of their joint investigation.

In sum, Socrates, if not Plato, is usually indiscriminately held responsible for most of the features of the city introduced after the early city,[15] but this is a mistake. Very little of Socrates's pedagogy consists of simply telling Glaucon and Adeimantus what to believe. Distinguishing Socrates's views from the brothers' requires paying attention to which speaker introduces which principles as they jointly build the city, beginning with the early city and the subsequent turn to the city of luxury. It is these passages that are the focus of this chapter.

## THE FIRST PRINCIPLE, ELEMENTS, AND SOCIAL STRUCTURE OF COOPERATIVE HUMAN RELATIONS

Socrates' first step, before he and Adeimantus begin building the city proper, is to discuss which "beginning" or "principle" (the word *archê* can mean either or both of these depending on the context, which is often ambiguous) they will look to in order to build it, and their reasons for choosing that beginning/principle. Here is the passage in question:

"Now then," I said, "a city comes to be, as I believe, since each of us happens not to be self-sufficient but to be in need [*endeês*] of many [things]. Or do you believe that any other beginning/principle [*archê*] founds a city?" "None [other]," he said. "In *this* way, therefore, as one [of us] takes on one [person], and another [takes on] another—[each one of us taking on one] for one thing, and [another] for another thing—[and all this] because of need [*chreiai*], since we are needing [*deomenoi*] many [things]—[now then,] when we have gathered many people as partners and rescuers into one settlement, as a name for *this* shared-settlement we put[16] [down] 'city,' isn't that right?" "Very much so." "Does one [of us] *give a share* [of something] to one [person] and another [of us] to another, whenever he does give some share [of something]—or [again,] does one take a share [when one does take some share of something]—supposing that it is better for himself?" "Quite so." "Come on, then," I said, "let's make a city in speech from the beginning/principle; and our need [*chreia*], as seems likely, will make it." "Of course." (369b7–c11)[17]

There are several points here worth noting. In the second chapter of *An Inquiry into the Nature and Causes of the Wealth of Nations*, Adam Smith famously bases his theory of the division of labor on the simple "propensity in human nature . . . to truck, barter, and exchange one thing for another" (Smith 1904, 15). Socrates begins from a more fundamental principle that explains *why* people are inclined to exchange. He proposes that, even after they do what they can for themselves, individuals[18] are needy; it is this sort of "need" [*chreia*], or being "in need" [*endeês*], or "needing" [*deomenoi*], that founds a shared-settlement, or "city." The opposite of need is self-sufficiency—not needing anything from outside oneself to be complete.

Having identified this founding principle, Socrates explains that each needy person will look around for a variety of people who each have a specific product he needs, and he will seek to induce them to help him. These are individuals who think and make decisions for themselves. Their actions build a network of mutual assistance with no central coordination. Such assistance requires considerable proximity, so they will live near one another, producing a "shared-settlement." Like Weber and Mises, Socrates seeks to explain social phenomena, in this case cooperation, exchange, proximate habitation, and the formation of a city, by accounting for the experiences of individual decision makers.

Needy individuals do not "rescue" one another because they are generous, however; their own need motivates them to address others' needs through exchange (Strauss 1978, 94; Höffe 1997, 74; McKeen 2004, 84–85). Yet even here, Socrates does not refer simply to "exchange." Instead, he carefully breaks down the exchange relationship into its four component decisions: Person A decides to give Product $\alpha$ to Person B, B decides to take $\alpha$ from A, B decides to give Product $\beta$ to A, and A decides to take $\beta$ from B. Each decision is motivated by an actor's belief that the decision will contribute to a "better" outcome for himself than if he had not made that decision. In modern terms, rational actors engage in cost-benefit analyses in order to maximize their utility through trade. When both parties agree to the same set of four decisions—to a shared plan for exchange—they contract with one another and become "partners" (*koinônoi*) in fulfilling both of their needs.

This does not mean, however, that every actor, confronted by the scarcity of means at his disposal, can be understood to have a fixed set of specific, ranked, competing ends and to seek out only the particular means that will most satisfy those ends, as Lionel Robbins's influential theory of the nature of economics would have it (Robbins 1932, 12–16, 23–24). In critiquing Robbins on this point, Israel M. Kirzner draws on the "Misesian notion of *human action*":

> The human-action concept, unlike that of allocation and economizing, does not confine the decision-maker (or the economic analysis of his decisions) to a framework of *given* ends and means. Human action, in the sense developed by Mises, involves courses of action taken by the human being "to remove uneasiness" and to make himself "better off". . . . Human action treats both tasks—that of identifying the relevant ends-means framework and that of seeking efficiency with respect to it—as a single, integrated human activity. (Kirzner 2013, 26–27)

Socrates similarly identifies only the most *general* of goals toward which the citizens are pushed by their need: achieving a "better" condition and avoiding worse ones (369c), "being and living" (369d), and relative ease in productive work (370a, c). Citizens in Socrates's city evaluate their actions and other goals with reference to these, and they seek and discover both new actions and new, more specific goals that would allow these most general goals to be achieved, as we will see in the following sections.

Let us also note that, by reducing exchange to its constituent parts, Socrates isolates what we would call the demand side and the supply side of any exchange. He draws attention to the fact that supply and demand are both *variable* and *independently* variable (at least at this level of analysis), conditional on the needs and decisions of individuals.


## THE MOST NECESSARY CITY


Equipped with a founding principle of human motivation (need), with a basic theory of the social organization of individuals who act on that principle, and with an account of the components of a single exchange between such autonomous actors, Socrates starts to construct a city. He begins by specifying needs: "Okay then, the *first*, at least, and the greatest of needs is the provision of nourishment for the sake of both being and living" (369d1–2). The second need is for the provision of a dwelling, and the third is for the provision "of clothing and these sorts of things" (369d4). To fulfill these needs requires certain means: "a farmer [will be] one [of the citizens], another a house-builder, and some other a weaver" (369d7–8), and there will be a shoemaker and perhaps "someone else of those [who are all] about the care of the body" (369d8–9). Socrates concludes their first stage of city building thus: "But the most necessary [*anangkaiotatê*] city would be composed of four or five men." (369d11–e1)

There are several matters worthy of note in this tiny "city." First, Socrates has no interest, as a city founder, in making detailed prescriptions for the citizens. He is deliberately vague about the category of products similar to clothing, about what roles exactly may be needed to care for the body, and about how many producers the city will have. The reason he avoids any systematic or definite list of needs and citizens is that his concern is simply that the inhabitants' greatest needs be provided for, whatever they happen to be, and he has already explained how the city's inhabitants will fulfill these needs through exchange, motivated by their own awareness of their needs.[19]

Second, this city illuminates several features of "need" and "necessity" (*anangkê*). The city of four or five producers is needed as the *means* to the *ends* of providing nourishment, dwellings, and clothing. These ends are also the greatest needs. This is because they are in turn the most indispensable *means* to the greater *ends* of "being and living." A chain of means is thus formed. In "the most necessary city" we can see that "necessary" therefore has the same meaning as "needed." The city of four or five is the most needed/necessary for providing for basic needs because providing for basic needs is in turn most needed/necessary for being and living. What is necessary/needed is that without which a certain end cannot come to be.[20] Conversely, that for the sake of which something is needed is what makes the needed thing needed, what makes fulfilling it worthwhile and imperative, given certain conditions. It is only *because* we aim at being and living that we need the provision of nourishment—that it is necessary. Whenever we say we need something or that something is necessary, we can always ask *why, for the sake of which greater end*. What is necessary is always conditional on an end, never an end in itself.

In any chain of necessity, the end that justifies the whole chain is not itself something necessary. It is simply good. This is not to say that such an end is *unnecessary*, however, since what is unnecessary, just like what is necessary, is defined in relation to an end beyond itself. Given a certain end, what is unnecessary is whatever is *not* necessary for that end. We will return to the role of necessity in Socrates's moral and economic thought in the early city below, after investigating the reasons he gives for the division of labor.

## JUSTIFYING THE DIVISION OF LABOR

Socrates's economic analysis so far is rudimentary. Upon reflection, he is not satisfied with it himself. What bothers him about the city of four or five men is that its foundational principles are unexplained and now appear to him uncertain. He and Adeimantus have assumed (i) the neediness of individuals, (ii) the need for the division of labor, and (iii) that one person will specialize in a single job. They therefore next question whether these assumptions are justified (369e–370a): Is it actually worth the trouble to partner with others? Is it necessary? Why not simply spend the "time" (*chronos*) and "effort" (literally "toil," *ponos*)—Socrates recognizes both of these as limited resources—that one would have to spend on a single activity (e.g., farming) if one were to produce enough for several people so as to trade with them, on a variety of productive activities for oneself (e.g., making a house, cloak, and shoes, as well as farming)? Adeimantus supposes that it would be easier to exchange one's products with others than to go it alone (370a). Socrates finds nothing strange about this hunch, and, more importantly, he offers three reasons why.

First, no one is "extremely similar" to anyone else, "but one [of us] excels with respect to his nature at making one product, and another [naturally excels] at making another" (370b1–3). Second, "as an individual [*lit.* being one], someone would act more finely [*kallion*] in working [in] one [art]" than in working in many arts (370b5–6). Third, in all working it is necessary to have adequate "free time" (*scholê*) to follow the emerging product closely through the process of production, watching at each stage for the "crucial moments" (*kairoi*) to act upon it, if the product is to come out as desired (370b–c). In other words, specialization is justified because of (i) variation in individuals' *natural* aptitudes (by "aptitude," I include both ability and inclination),[21] (ii) the conduciveness of focused experience to individuals' *acquired* aptitudes, and (iii) the need for attentiveness to *the right moment for acting according to* one's aptitudes. Within a limited group of potential trade partners, individuals will specialize *to the extent that* variation in any of these three conditions exists. Where no variation exists, there is no reason to specialize and exchange, and individuals will produce a variety of things for themselves. The division of labor thus described yields certain results: "the amount of each of the products increases, and they come into being more finely and more easily" (370c4–5).[22] In the words of Robbins (1932, 14), "There are the sum of the principles, more or less correctly stated, of the division of labour."

The analytical comprehensiveness of Socrates's theory of the division of labor can be brought to light by a comparison to that of Adam Smith. Smith famously proposes that the division of labor arises due to three beneficial outcomes: "first, to the increase of dexterity in every particular workman; secondly, to the saving of time which is commonly lost in passing from one species of work to another; and lastly, to the invention of a great number of machines which facilitate and abridge labour" (Smith 1904, 9). Smith's first reason for the division of labor corresponds to Socrates's second. Smith's second reason Socrates does not identify, but it would properly fall under the general category of Socrates's second stated reason, that one works more finely when practicing one art than several. Smith's third reason, too, may be classed as part of Socrates's second reason, if we consider the development of tools to be (an unstated) part of the mastery of an art. As regards Socrates's first reason for specialization, Smith's theory is lacking. As Robbins observes, "there is a great difference between the principles of the division of labour" in Plato and Smith, since the latter, in his famous explanation of what makes one person a philosopher and another a street porter, "dwells all, or nearly all, on education" instead of also on differences in nature (Robbins 2000, 14; see Smith 1904, 17–18). Moreover, Smith's theory omits Socrates's third reason altogether, the crucial variable of availability to be attentive to particular events.

Nevertheless, many scholars have criticized Plato for his theory of the division of labor.[23] Schumpeter (1959, 56) claims that he "puts the emphasis not upon the increase of efficiency that results from division of labor per se but upon the increase of efficiency that results from allowing everyone to specialize in what he is by nature best fitted for," and that his "caste system" rests upon this basis. Lowry (1987, 16) takes a similar view. Yet Schumpeter and Lowry inaccurately read the "caste system" introduced later in the *Republic* back in the early city. In fact, as Joshua I. Weinstein notes (2009, 442–43) and as we have just seen, in the early city Socrates offers natural differences as only one of *three* reasons for the division of labor. Similar to Schumpeter and Lowry, Paul J. McNulty places "natural differences" at the center of Plato's theory of the division of labor, which he says Plato uses as a "justification for occupational stratification and labor immobility" (McNulty 1975, 373, 372, and see 372–74; see also Devereux 1979, 36, 38). In doing so, however, he quotes only from the first of Socrates's reasons for the division of labor, ignoring the others. He also relies heavily on a later passage, where Socrates seems to recall with Glaucon that

we were thoroughly preventing the shoemaker from attempting at the same time to be a farmer, weaver, or house builder, but [he was only allowed to be] a shoemaker, . . . and in the same way we were assigning one [work] to each one of the others, [the work] for which each [person] was naturally suited and in which, by remaining at leisure from other things and working at it throughout his life and not passing up the crucial moments, he was going to produce in a fine way. (374b6–c3)

I must highlight, however, that this passage comes two pages after the early city in a context whose significance McNulty overlooks. The early, "healthy" city Socrates is building with Adeimantus is cut off at 372c–e when Glaucon interrupts and demands that the city have luxuries—by definition, *unnecessary* products—instead of the simple, necessary food and possessions so far described. As the inhabitants subsequently begin to pursue unlimited pleasure, Socrates notes ways in which they, and the city as a whole, become unhealthy. Of relevance to us is that Glaucon, in making his demand, insists metaphorically that, "if you were furnishing a city of sows"—an animal proverbially contrasted in intelligence with human beings[24]—it would be necessary to "fatten" such inhabitants with all manner of contemporary Greek pleasures (fine food, furniture, etc.). Glaucon assumes for himself and Socrates a managerial project akin to that of managing unthinking livestock. His characteristic, sanguine inclination to manage others[25] contrasts sharply with Socrates's previous treatment of the inhabitants as individuals who choose to specialize in their work so as to exchange with one another and so best fulfill their needs. Socrates and Adeimantus "made" (369c9, 371b6–7) and "founded" (371b7) the early city merely as observers, as it were, of the ways in which "our [human] need" (369c10) truly structures the cooperative interactions of individuals, which they described. Following Glaucon's interruption, by contrast, Glaucon and Socrates become *members* of the city who directly intervene in the citizens' lives by leading them to wage war on neighboring cities (373d–e).

Keeping this in mind, we must also account for the fact that the block quote above (374b6–c3) is preceded by a statement in which Socrates tests Glaucon's memory; he proposes that the city will need specialized soldiers "'if *you*, at least, and all of us, agreed in a fine way when we were forming the city,' I said, 'and presumably we agreed, if you remember, that it is impossible for one [person] to work at many arts in a fine way.' 'That's true,' he said" (374a4–7). Throughout Plato's Socratic dialogues, Socrates uses the word "presumably" (*pou*) to introduce a premise that he thinks his interlocutor might take for granted, whether or not he believes it himself.[26] In fact, Socrates and Adeimantus never agreed that one person could *never* do many arts well; rather, they said that focusing on a single art would allow one to practice that art better than one would if one also had to practice others, and they implied that one person could not do many arts well *to the extent that* his nature was ill-suited for them or he could not devote adequate time to them, which hardly applies to *all* sets of multiple arts.

Yet even this is not the most important difference between what Glaucon "remembers" and what actually happened. The primary and explicit concern for Socrates and Adeimantus in the early city was whether an individual has a productive *advantage* over others—whether specializing and exchanging would lead to more and better products, with less effort, for each actor. This is what determines whether someone chooses to specialize in a certain task. What Glaucon has "agreed" to is something simpler and more rigid, though, and it is on this new basis, and on the basis of Glaucon's crude managerial involvement in the city, that Socrates proceeds in the block quote above to remember, "presumably," that "we were assigning" one job to each inhabitant and "were thoroughly preventing" him from ever deviating from his task throughout his whole life—even though this is *not* what he and Adeimantus actually did. When we pay attention in this way to the speaker and the context of what is said, we cannot assume as Schumpeter and McNulty do that later descriptions of the city in the *Republic* represent Socrates's (or Plato's) own convictions in a straightforward way. I do not intend to present a full theory here about why or how Plato makes the speakers of the *Republic* develop the city in speech in different directions at different stages. I wish only to represent and explain the analysis of the early city in its own terms, and on this basis to point out certain ways in which it is distinct from and *incompatible* with later passages commonly cited to explain it.

Another criticism of Plato's explanation of the division of labor focuses on Socrates's wish to promote the mastery of "arts." Drawing from both the early city and later passages in the *Republic* (including the block quote we have just discussed),[27] Anna Greco argues at length that for Plato the division of labor is driven not by a pursuit of economic efficiency but by a conventional Greek concern to promote "excellence" (*aretê*) through the mastery of "arts" (or "crafts," *technai*)—for example, the arts of farming, of house building, or of weaving (Greco 2009, 53, 56–57, 59, 61–66). As a consequence, "[u]nlike what happens in Adam Smith's model, for Plato it is not the case that division of labour requires specialization . . . [but] the other way around," as specialization in specific arts for the sake of improving quality drives the division of labor (Greco 2009, 61; see Finley 1970, 4). Plato is not concerned, on this reading, with *efficiency* either from an individual or from a systemic point of view; whereas art aims at quality, efficiency of production is also concerned with quantity. Moreover, Greco proposes, efficiency is achieved not only by making the most of workers' "natural abilities, talents, skills or knowledge"—resources to which Plato does pay attention—but also by reducing costs in "materials and time," which in her view are not Plato's concern (Greco 2009, 58; see also 62–64).

Let us first address the question of time: Socrates is explicitly aware that time constraints constitute an independent reason for the division of labor. We have already seen that at 369e–370a Socrates identified time along with effort as a limited resource requiring the most beneficial allocation. Of more analytical significance, his third reason for the division of labor specifies that one must be free enough from other activities to be able to carry out a needed productive task. In other words, *regardless of one's natural aptitudes or the benefits of focused work*, there may be situations in which one person will specialize in a certain job simply because no one else is as available to do that job at the time it is needed.[28]

As regards productive efficiency, Greco fails to give Socrates's *concluding* statement about the results of the division of labor its deserved weight (Greco 2009, 52); Socrates says that the *amount* of the products will *increase*, and that the *process* of their coming into being will occur "more finely and more easily" (*kallion kai rhaion*), as Weinstein (2009, 443) also insists. Moreover, Socrates does not bother to repeat here either that mastery of the arts will increase or that products will be of higher quality; instead, we hear only of (i) the increase in their *quantity*, (ii) the "fineness" of the productive process—in the context, perhaps this vague term even refers to the efficiency of resource use—and (iii) the reduced *effort* required for production. In other words, as Schofield (1999, 74–76) similarly concludes, Socrates thinks that the division of labor is justified at least in part because it increases *efficiency*.

Greco also offers evidence that the ancient Greek economy did not feature significant competition that could have spurred the pursuit of efficiency— and this helps to explain, she suggests, why Plato did not come up with such a theory (Greco 2009, 62–63). I find her historical conclusions some-what doubtful,[29] but even if they were not, they are irrelevant in the face of Socrates's clear statements demonstrating that Plato indeed did have a theory of the division of labor driven by concerns for efficiency. Moreover, Socrates's original, foundational theory that individuals will exchange with one another for *mutual* benefits—a theory in which the goals of developing an art or improving product quality play no part—makes clear that he seeks efficiency from both the individual and the *systemic* points of view, and that it is in fact the division of labor that drives specialization, not the other way around.

Greco insightfully notes "a tension in Plato between (i) the recognition of the fundamental economic forces originating and sustaining political associa-tions [in the early city] and (ii) the construction of an ideal city which ends up obliterating such economic forces" (Greco 2009, 67). I agree that there is a real tension between the principles of the early city and those of the city that emerges by the end of Book 3, where rulers use an extreme, propagan-distic "noble lie" to increase patriotism and ensure obedience, classifying citizens crudely into three classes (414b–415d)—and between the early city and the city of Book 5, where rulers and soldiers own virtually no private property and may not touch money (see 416c–417b), are forbidden private families, and are assigned their sexual partners every night in a lottery rigged for eugenic purposes, with any children they bear quickly taken away to be raised in a communal pen (457c–464c). I insist that none of this takes away from the insights present in the early city. As Robbins (1932, 12) observes, "Plato is the first man, or first famous writer, . . . to enunciate the principle of the division of labour."

## NECESSITY AS A NORMATIVE PRINCIPLE AND AN OBJECT OF DESCRIPTIVE ANALYSIS

Socrates's emphasis on efficiency in the previous section raises questions about the meaning of "need/necessity" (*chreia/anangkê*). First, although we might have assumed that "need" originally meant "need if one is to survive," since the greatest needs were for nourishment, shelter, and clothing, it is now clear that seeking for greater output and less effort in production does not always, or even often, mean seeking to survive. After all, Socrates seems to think it might be *possible* to live without exchanging at all (369e–370a). Does he still suppose that the city's inhabitants are entirely motivated by desires to fulfill their *needs*, then? He does, in fact; he will soon distinguish the entire early, "true," "healthy" city of 369b–372d from Glaucon's unhealthy city of luxury, identifying instances of "stepping beyond the boundary of the necessary things" (373e1) as "the things from which bad things especially come to be for cities, both privately and publicly, whenever they do come to be" (373e7–8). The early city is built entirely by individuals seeking what is needed/necessary.

We may notice a normative judgment present in these claims: individuals *should* limit themselves to doing only what is necessary. We might wonder, then: To what extent is Socrates's emphasis on the contrast between what is necessary and what is unnecessary, between fulfilling needs and pursuing luxuries, essential to his economic analysis? Does his economic theory need this normative element? If we turn to the popular economics textbooks by, for example, Samuelson and Nordhaus, Varian, or Mankiw, we find that they study "preferences" at the level of the consumer and "demand" at the level of the market or society (Samuelson and Nordhaus 2001, 45–51; Varian 2010, 3–11, 33–44; Mankiw 2012, 65–71, 441–52), but they do not study the difference between needs and wants at either level. Samuelson and Nordhaus do mention "wants and needs" and "needs and desires" (Samuelson and Nordhaus 2001, 4, 13), thus acknowledging a difference between needs and wants, but by treating them as indistinguishable within their analysis they show that they "have chosen not to dwell on the differences" (Raiklin and Uyar 1996). If this is a common practice in economics, in public policy, by contrast, the distinction between wants and needs is essential; as Raiklin and Uyar (1996) point out, all public assistance programs, and the very concept of a "social safety net," which helps those who have difficulty meeting their needs, are based on the distinction. The distinction is far from devoid of analytical relevance or application in the modern world.[30] How and why, then, does Socrates integrate normative claims about need/necessity into his economic analysis?

Let us first clarify what Socrates means by "needs." Just before Glaucon demands the turn to the city of luxury, Socrates proposes that

> setting before themselves noble barley cakes and [wheat] loaves on some reeds or clean leaves [and then] lying down on beds of straw scattered with yew and myrtle, they [i.e., the citizens in the early city] will entertain [*or* feast] themselves well, both they and their children—drinking their wine afterward, crowned with wreaths and extolling the gods in song, interacting with one another with pleasure." (372b3–c1)

In their feasts, Socrates continues, they will have "flavorful side dishes" (*opson*), and he lists salt, olives, cheese, root vegetables boiled with garden herbs, desserts (figs, chickpeas, and beans), and roasted myrtle berries and acorns, all to be enjoyed "as they moderately drink a little" (372c–d). Most of these activities and much of this food are necessary neither for survival nor for increased or easier production. In what sense, then, are all these activities and foods *necessary*?

It would seem that Socrates thinks his citizens will do what is necessary not only for living but for living *well*, as their quest for what would be better for themselves suggests (369c), as well as the moderately pleasurable foods and activities of the citizens' "way of life" (373a1) just described. This is confirmed when Socrates much later, long after he and his interlocutors have finished constructing all versions of the city in speech, explains what he understands to be "necessary desires." He proposes that such desires must meet at least one of two criteria: they are those desires "that we are not able to turn away . . . and as many as help us when they are fulfilled[.] For by our nature there is a necessity [for us] to desire both of these" (558d11–e3). Correspondingly, unnecessary desires are those "that someone could get rid of if he trains himself from youth, and [also those that] when they are present contribute to nothing good—and some of them even [contribute to] the opposite" (559a3–4). As examples, Socrates then specifically identifies the desire for bread as necessary for "both health and a good condition," and the desire for "flavorful side dishes" as necessary for a good condition simply (559a–c). Socrates is not, then, as Stanley Rosen has accused him of being, a proponent of "extreme austerity" in the early city (Rosen 2005, 72; see also Taylor 1997, 49). Its citizens experience a "need" for food, but also for tasty food, for feasting together, for enjoying one another, and for moderate drinking, since all of these contribute to a good condition.

As examples of "unnecessary things" in the city of luxury, Socrates imagines "couches and tables and the rest of the furniture, and [yes,] *flavorful side dishes*, perfumes, incense, courtesans, and cakes—all sorts of each of these" (373a2–4). From this list and the context of 372c–373e, it is clear that Socrates has no interest in composing two exhaustive, black-and-white lists of needs vs. luxuries that apply to everyone at all times and allow no exceptions. Some flavorful side dishes are necessary, as we have seen, but some are not. What concerns him is that some people uncritically follow certain desires and pursuits that feel necessary without having ascertained *why* they are necessary; this amounts to treating what is necessary as what is good, as an end in itself (see 493b–c). But something can be necessary for a bad end as well as a good one; insisting *that* a certain action is necessary is therefore not justification enough. Certain questions should be asked: How will following the desire one is currently experiencing improve one's condition overall more than competing desires could? And if it will not, then to what extent can one get rid of it? How does a desire fit (or not fit) into one's *most* necessary plan of action overall?[31] Answering these questions enables individuals to better fulfill the needs they experience, and this is a, if not the, aim of the healthy city.

Socrates is not only interested in analyzing the types of goals that people generally find better or worse, however; he also thinks that it is possible to discover and analyze certain things that *are* good or bad for individuals and cities. It is not difficult to see that individuals experience a difference between necessary and unnecessary desires, or that they see different potential courses of action as more or less necessary for a better condition overall. Some people decide to stop smoking, watching television, or eating unhealthy foods, for example, even though they enjoy those activities. Just as Socrates implies that one could help another discover the fact that a certain means does not, as the other believes, contribute to a certain goal (for example, that producing both food and clothes for oneself will not, in fact, yield more or better food and clothes for oneself than specializing in the one and trading for the other), so he thinks that one could help another discover that a certain goal does not in fact contribute to the general goal of a better condition. A friend could help another see that regularly enjoying a great deal of meat leads to serious health risks of which the other has not been aware, for example.[32] To help another in this way would involve bringing a conflict in the other's goals to his or her attention and prompting him or her to rank those goals (or look for a new goal) in a way he or she previously has not. The aim is presumably to pursue a condition that accommodates one's most necessary desires in the least contradictory way possible.

Similarly, someone who cares about the good of a city could notice that certain prevalent behaviors lead to bad outcomes for the city and its inhabitants—to use Socrates's examples, that patterns of indulgent diets lead to widespread ill health and the need to spend significantly more on doctors (372d–373d), or that widespread demands to seize land from citizens of neighboring cities will lead the city as a whole to do so and consequently to go to war (373d–e). Discerning what would be better for individuals and cities is an essential part of analyzing systems of exchange, for Socrates, because it concerns what would actually best fulfill the particular needs experienced by, and motivating, the various individual citizens. This in no way means that Socrates thinks he (or others) can discover *everything* that would be best for each person or for all people, or for each city or for all cities. What it does mean is that he believes it is important to discover as much as one can, and that he is committed to helping others discover such things for themselves, whether in talking with them one on one (as he does with Glaucon and Adeimantus) or, it would seem, in designing institutions that foster discoveries of better conditions (such as a system of exchange).

Socrates treats necessity as an inextricable part of economic analysis precisely because he believes that individuals' happiness objectively depends on their adherence to necessity as a normative principle. He wants to know not only why they do what they currently do but what they would readily do if they knew better. Whether it is Socrates's analytical approach or those of Samuelson and Nordhaus, Varian, or Mankiw that more seriously undertake to explain social phenomena by accounting for the experiences of individuals would therefore be an interesting matter for debate.[33]

## SPECIALIZED SUPPORT OF THE MOST NECESSARY ROLES

When Socrates returns from articulating reasons for the division of labor and continues building the city in speech, every addition he proposes has an analytical significance. He proceeds by discovering not only new needs but new *kinds* of needs, and he proposes a variety of specialized productive roles necessary for addressing them. Having specialized four or five productive roles on the supply side of the economy (farming, house building, etc.) in order to address the basic consumer needs of all, Socrates notes that each of these productive roles will itself involve needs for things that it would be inefficient for that producer to make. As Greco observes, by differentiating between the original set of producers and the subsequent set addressing the production needs of the first set, "Plato implicitly anticipates the distinction between those that are nowadays seen as the two major types of production: of consumer products and of products for the industry, respectively" (Greco 2009, 60).

Some of these needs are for *tools*. A farmer will not make his own plow, hoe, or other tools, if they are going to be of high quality, since he does not have the time to learn all those arts well (370c–d). For the same reason, a house builder will not make the many tools he requires either, and the same is true for a weaver and shoemaker (370d). Carpenters, smiths, and many other craftsmen are therefore needed as partners in the city (370d). The farmer's and builder's needs for *pulling power* will also yield cowherds, since oxen are needed for pulling plows and hauling loads (370d–e). Weavers and shoe-makers will also require such *raw materials* as wool and hides on which to work, and this will lead to the specialization of shepherds and other kinds of herdsmen (370d–e). Socrates also notes that some producers will produce products that address multiple needs simultaneously: the cowherd's oxen can both haul and supply hides. This could complicate such a producer's cost-benefit calculations in making plans to exchange. In sum, Socrates identifies a variety of what we may call factors of production, distinguishes them as a class from consumption goods, and shows how the need for them is derived from the need for consumption goods.[34]

## MERCHANTS AS FACILITATORS OF EXCHANGE, AND MARKET DYNAMICS IN INTERCITY TRADE

Yet just as individuals are not self-sufficient, neither is one city. Even though the city was formed because individuals could help one another satisfy each other's needs and could do so better when they lived in close proximity, the location-specific resources available to them will still to some extent be insufficient for their needs (370e). Therefore, they will need to trade with people in other cities. It is therefore impossible that for Plato the aim of a city is *self-sufficiency*, as Weinstein (2009, 441, 443–44, 449) and Gordon (1975, 28) claim, and as it is for Aristotle (1999, 1:2.1252b27–1253a1); an aim of the early city is *interdependence* with other cities. Socrates breaks down intercity trade into its component needs and roles. There will need to be "merchants" (371d7), whom Socrates classifies as "agents" (or "servants," *diakonoi*, 370e12, 371a10), to bring what is needed from another city. For the first time, Socrates introduces a specialized productive role that does not produce a material object but rather renders a service that others need.

Yet if the merchants have nothing to give foreign producers in return for what the first city's inhabitants need, they will be given nothing; therefore certain inhabitants (for example, farmers and craftsmen) will have to produce more of the products that those foreigners need than is needed at home—that is, more than domestic consumption demands, a surplus (370e–371a). In addition, to the extent that the inhabitants continue to need what the foreign-ers produce, they must produce whatever kind and quantity of surplus product will be *sufficient* for the foreign exchange partners' needs (371a). Merchants must therefore specialize in both importing and exporting as needed. Their work will in turn make use of sea travel, which will require "multitudes of others who have knowledge of the work related to the sea" (371b1–3). The general insight that seems to lie behind this new role is that distances and physical barriers can themselves be hindrances to exchange and can increase the effort required to obtain what is needed. Certain inhabitants must therefore reduce those costs by specializing in *transportation* roles (previously, farmers did their own hauling). In sum, the service that merchants, aided by experts in sea travel, have to offer is to facilitate exchanges between distant exchange partners (371a).

In Plato's time the "art of household management" (*oikonomia*) was much discussed, taught, and written about, but as Lowry (1987, 12) notes, "[i]t was an administrative, not a market approach, to economic phenomena." By contrast, Lowry claims, "there is no general discussion of supply and demand in response to impersonal market forces in ancient Greek writings." Socrates's analysis of intercity trade, I propose, must be the one exception. Those who consider buying and transporting foreign products for domestic resale must make calculations about aggregate, and therefore *impersonal*, domestic demand for those products. Similarly, domestic producers and merchants who consider which goods to produce and sell to foreigners must assess aggregate, impersonal demand for a variety of products in another city. Moreover, by breaking intercity trade into its component needs and corresponding productive roles, Socrates explains *that* and *why* both the kind and quantity of domestic production vary in response to foreign demand. He even notes the limit on *increasing* domestic production; once foreigners are satisfied with the "sufficient" amount of a specific import, producers in the early city will produce no more than that and an equilibrium between supply and demand will have been reached, to use the modern terms. This constitutes the first formulation of the part of the law of supply-and-demand concerned with the effect of demand on supply.[35] And in all of this, Socrates continues to speak not of their own city or of foreign cities as actors, but only of local and foreign *individuals* engaging in exchanges where that would be beneficial to both parties.

## OTHER MEANS OF FACILITATING EXCHANGE: CURRENCY, A MARKETPLACE, AND "DEALERS"

Next, having dealt with transportation, Socrates finally turns to address other great challenges to citywide and intercity systems of *exchange*. He reminds Adeimantus that the entire purpose of the original partnership that holds the city together is the exchange of products, and asks him how this will occur

(371b). Adeimantus says the inhabitants will clearly do so "by buying and selling" (371b8). In addition to the transportation of material products, then, other aspects of exchange also need to be improved, other transaction costs reduced: "a marketplace, then, and a currency as a token for the sake of exchange will come into being for us" (371b9–10). Lowry (1987, 21) collects evidence that Aristotle's monetary theory already identifies "the four functions of money which modern economists recognize: as a medium of exchange, as a measure of value, . . . as a store of value . . . [, and] as a standard of deferred payment." Socrates identifies at least the first two of these. Given the context of interstate trade just discussed, it seems likely that Socrates also appreciates how portable it is (see Aristotle 1999, 1:9.1257a30–41).

Remarkably, given the historical dominance of commodity theories of money, Socrates here prescribes fiat money (Gordon 1961, 611–12; Weinstein 2009, 439, 454n30). With regard to his portrayal of money, Schumpeter (1959, 56) says that "such an occasional saying means very little and does not justify the attribution to Plato of any definite view on the nature of money."[36] Yet as Aristotle observes (1984, 5:5.1133a30–31), *nomisma* (the word for "currency") stems from *nomos* (law, convention). Socrates, in contrast to Adeimantus shortly afterward (371d1, d2), does not use either of the more common words for "money" (*chrêmata* and *argyrion*, which literally means "piece of silver"). More importantly, he identifies the currency only as a "token" (*symbolon*) of value useful for exchange. Moreover, the existence of fiat money in the ancient world was known to Greek writers, including Plato,[37] and Gordon (1961) has convincingly argued (against the claims of A. E. Monroe 2001, 8–9 and Schumpeter 1959, 63) that Aristotle, Plato's student, had a fiat understanding of money.

Socrates does not explicitly analyze why—he only states that—a marketplace is necessary, but perhaps he is thinking that having a single place in which one can both deliver one's own products all at once and acquire a wide variety of needed products saves considerable time and effort by reducing travel and transportation among numerous exchange partners. What he does go on to analyze is why there will be a need for "dealers" (*kapêloi*, 371d4) in the marketplace: so as to reduce the time that a craftsman (such as a farmer) has to spend waiting around for others who need what he has to exchange, which prevents him from doing his own work (371c). A purpose of these "agents" (see 371c6, d6) is thus to save everyone else time, to reduce the opportunity costs (due to transaction costs) of everyone else's exchanges.

It is at this point that Adeimantus displays a little of his own character by adding an explanation of his own: "[T]hose who in seeing this [need] set themselves up for this service are, in correctly managed cities, pretty much the weakest with respect to their bodies and useless for doing any other work" (371c5–8). He scorns the dealers, assuming that strong bodies are required to do more important work, that being a dealer in the market requires little skill beyond the ability to wait around, and that, as he implies (371c–d), it is shameful to have a job whose sole aim is the acquisition of money. These thoughts constitute the only substantive contribution Adeimantus makes to the construction of the early city.

Some scholars attribute these views to Plato (McNulty 1975, 375; Hayek 1992, 90; Cohen 2002, 101).[38] What they have not noticed is that Socrates completely ignores what Adeimantus says about the dealers' qualifications and skills, and he affirms only Adeimantus's claim that "there is a need" (*dei*, 371c8) for the dealers to stay in the market in order to exchange with "as many as need" (*hosoi . . . deontai*, 371d3) to buy or sell. Socrates simply thinks the city needs specialists in market exchanges to address the needs citizens have for easy buying and selling.

## SPECIALIZATION DUE TO INTELLIGENCE:
## EMPLOYERS AND EMPLOYEES

We may furthermore observe that, despite Adeimantus's dismissive assessment, the dealers' work requires a significant aptitude for working with numbers. At this stage of the city's construction, those who resolve most of the city's enormous information and coordination problems, who (to the extent that needs in the city are fulfilled through *monetary* exchanges in the marketplace) are the mind of the city, as it were, gauging and keeping track of how much certain goods are collectively needed, and setting prices accordingly that encourage or discourage other citizens' production of various goods, are the dealers. As they sit in the marketplace, they collect, analyze, and disseminate information about collective supply and demand.[39] Yet do any such thoughts occur to Socrates? Or is he more likely of Adeimantus's persuasion? The next roles he introduces offer us a clue.

The new producers Socrates next finds to be necessary are the "wage earners" (371e4). We might wonder why he identifies this kind of "agent" (371d9), since other citizens (such as smiths or herdsmen) have already been introduced whose sole purpose is supporting the work of another craft (such as farming), and still others (importers, exporters, and dealers) have equally been called "agents." He describes the wage earners as "whoever with regard to the [activities] of thinking [*dianoia*] are not very worthy of partnership, but with regard to the strength of their body have sufficient [strength] for labor" (371d9–e2). They trade their strength for a wage and take orders from an employer.

It is curious that Socrates describes workers who have physical strength but have relatively little ability to think immediately after Adeimantus has praised physical strength and ignored the calculative work of the dealers.

As an experienced young soldier and a member of an aristocratic, landowning family, Adeimantus despises the self-appointed dealers who appear to make their fortune without physical exertion. Socrates then immediately if unobtrusively points out that strong bodies and the work they produce are no great matter for pride and should in fact be subordinate to a superior capacity for thinking.[40] His introduction of wage earners does not prove beyond a doubt that he understands dealers to play a crucial intellectual role in the city. What it does prove is that, if Socrates *were* to perceive that they play this role (and he likely does), he would favor it, unlike Adeimantus.

Yet the introduction of wage earners is of profound analytic significance for Socrates's economic theory in three further ways. First, although "thinking" (*dianoia*) is not the same as "knowledge" (*epistêmê*)—elsewhere thinking appears to be the deductive activity by which one either *seeks* or *applies* knowledge, which is itself the *grasping* of principles (see 510b–511e, 533c–534a)—it does seem to be linked. This would mean that wage earners are the first instance, in the stages of the city in the *Republic*, of the principle that *those who know should rule those who do not*. This principle, which Socrates appears wholeheartedly to endorse in Books 5 and 6 (see 473c–e, 484b–d, 488a–489c), does not in itself make necessary the totalitarian regime of the *Republic*. For that, one would have to add the premises that a particular person actually does know, and can as a ruler achieve, everything that is best for everyone else, and that he or she should do so even without the consent of the ruled. Such premises do not begin to be introduced until Glaucon begins to treat the citizens of the city as animals to be managed, as we have seen. In the context of the early city, the principle that those who know more will direct those less able to discern the truth emerges entirely within the framework of market exchanges. Employer and employee choose to contract with one another to the extent that they both believe the partnership will be better for them.

Second, it is significant that the role of the employee who contributes labor is unique in that it is not a specific sort of role. An employee could farm, shepherd, weave, or make shoes, for example. One can be a shepherd and an employed laborer at the same time.

Third, wage earners are not introduced, as all previous roles have been, because a certain *role* is needed; there are already people in the city, such as farmers or house builders, who are strong enough to labor, and who do labor (371c–d, 370c–e). Rather, the existence of *less intelligent* people in the city is taken as a new given, and such people are *accommodated* in exchanges between unequals by the new institution of employment. This is the other consequence of the first reason for the division of labor, variation in natures: not only must those relatively better at certain jobs do those jobs, but the simple jobs that most people could do equally well should be left to those *relatively unable* to do complex ones. Such a discovery comes startlingly close to the full principle of comparative advantage. The early city is not a city only for people who are better at one art than anyone else, who have an absolute advantage; an intelligent employer may be stronger than his employee, but this does not mean the former will do manual labor. Socrates constructs the city by making the *most* of the resources, including the human resources, at his disposal.

## WHETHER PLATO ENDORSES SEVERELY LIMITING THE EARLY CITY AND ITS ECONOMIC PRINCIPLES

Yet is it the case that Plato first has Socrates develop a theory of "economic activity and the production of wealth as fundamental to society" only so that he can take drastic, totalitarian measures, as Schofield argues, to address "the social and moral dangers within it" by depriving rulers and soldiers of all private property and family (Schofield 1999, 80; see 77–80, and Taylor 1997, 49–50)? For several reasons, the answer is no. For one thing, Socrates never even hints that the exchanges and partnerships in the early city are dangerous; to the contrary, he only portrays them as fulfilling needs, and he calls the early city "true" and "healthy." Similarly, Socrates explicitly criticizes abandoning the principle that structures the entire early city—the principle that individuals should seek to do only what is necessary—because abandoning this is the source of many bad things for cities. Those commentators who argue that citizens of the early city only pursue money or desires and so, in Plato's view, require others to rule and moderate them (e.g., Reeve 1988, 171; Wallach 2001, 251–52; Barney 2002, 218–20; Schofield 2006, 204; Weinstein 2009, 441n5, 455–58) unfairly attribute claims made later in the *Republic* about the city's money-making class (e.g., 431c–e, 434a–c; see also 442a–b, 581c–d) to the early city. As Catherine McKeen (2004, 79, 85, 87) and Mark E. Jonas, Yoshiaki M. Nakazawa, and James Braun (2012, 347–51) have shown, the citizens of the early city use their *calculating faculty* as they discover and pursue their enlightened self-interest and choose to avoid such excesses as harmful drinking and producing too many children (372b–d).[41]

Just as importantly, Schofield does not account for how Glaucon abandons the point of view of the individual thinker and actor when he proposes fattening citizens like sows. It is this Glauconian analytical approach that later on, immediately after Glaucon mistakenly declares the rulers to be "entirely perfect and complete" (414b; compare to 522a–b and 543c–544a), frames the propagandistic noble lie for all citizens, which is explicitly designed to stop them from reflecting on the nature of their education (414d) and which divides them crudely into three classes (415a–c) so as to assure their ultimate devotion to the city. It similarly frames the abolition of private property (see especially 415e–416c) and of private families for the rulers and soldiers.

Glaucon's analytical approach prevents the one who uses it from even noticing the perceived needs and choices of individuals—those needs and choices to which Socrates, like Weber and Mises, pays such assiduous attention.

In the early city citizens unite with others only in those cases where, and to the extent that, they see it would lead to a better condition for themselves; in all other cases, they are content to do their own thing. They seek only to improve their conditions, not to achieve what Weinstein calls "collective self-sufficiency" or "autarky" at the city level, as we have seen (Weinstein 2009, 441, 443). A mix of unity and independence is portrayed to be the best means of fulfilling needs. As the perspective of individual decision makers is later gradually eclipsed by the perspective of managers whose primary aim is to promote what is advantageous for the city (especially its unity and strength) *without concern for what is advantageous for its members* (see, for example, 412c–e, 419a–421c, 519c–520e), the scope for the application of Socrates's three principles of specialization, along with all of the fulfillment of needs that they enable, is ever more severely curtailed. This extends not only to the rulers but to the whole city; with Adeimantus's approval, the happiness of *all* citizens is subordinated to the "happiness" of the city (421b–c), and rulers are given the responsibility of regulating the citizens' wealth, preventing them from becoming either wealthy or poor (421c–422a). Under Glaucon's oversight, similarly, citizens are relieved of their ability to choose their own work, are assigned their work by the rulers, and are forbidden to deviate from that work over the whole course of their life (374a–c, 406c–407a).

## CONCLUSION

I have argued that Socrates's development of the early city offers no evidence that Plato favors communism, totalitarianism, or fascism and that (i) Socrates's principles governing exchange and cooperation and (ii) his analytical approach of beginning from the experiences of *individual* decision makers jointly provide evidence that Plato's Socrates favors economic systems and political regimes that accommodate the needs and aptitudes of individuals. Since Plato contrasts these principles and this approach with those of Adeimantus and Glaucon, whose eagerness to manage others like unthinking livestock leads to violent, crude, inflexible arrangements that are incompatible with arrangements in the early city, it seems reasonable to conclude that, as regards the early city at least, Plato agrees with Socrates.

I have proposed that historians of economic thought and scholars in the fields of ancient philosophy, political theory, and Austrian economics have underappreciated the genius of Plato's economic analysis, of his analytical approach, or of both, because they have misrepresented or understudied the early city. This has happened because too little attention has been paid to Plato's manner of writing. He does not offer a treatise but shows Socrates, Adeimantus, and Glaucon interacting informally in a dialogue. He portrays Socrates conducting an *investigative* procedure, not a historical or purely deductive one, and this procedure is in turn part of a larger pedagogical strategy in which Socrates seeks to educate the brothers by allowing them to introduce various features of the city and by helping them work out the consequences of their assumptions.

We have seen that in many instances Socrates's economic analysis compares favorably with that of several modern economic theorists. Beginning like Weber and Mises from the crucial point of view of a needy, thinking, decision-making individual, Socrates builds a *systemic* account of how a set of such individuals will choose to exchange with one another, settle in proximity, and form a city. In the process, he distinguishes supply and demand as independent variables. He goes on to identify three variables determining the extent to which citizens will specialize and exchange with one another: variation in natural inclination and ability, in acquirable inclination and ability, and in availability for particular tasks. These three reasons for the division of labor are more comprehensive than the three famously offered by Adam Smith.

Equipped with these reasons, Socrates identifies the need for a division of labor in supplying a variety of factors of production (raw materials, tools, animal power, and the transportation of materials). Socrates then explains why cities are not self-sufficient and why their inhabitants must engage in intercity trade. As he breaks this process down into its component parts, he describes the effect that the impersonal forces of aggregate demand have on supply in a market economy—and this despite the fact that a market economy did not exist in the ancient world. Having identified various means of facilitating production, he then develops means for facilitating exchange itself, proposing the need for a fiat currency and a marketplace, and explaining the need for specialized roles facilitating long-distance transportation, buying, and selling. In the process, he never endorses the elements of Adeimantus's analysis of "dealers" that despise physical weakness, immobility, and moneymaking. Finally, Socrates introduces the principle that variation in intelligence is responsible for specializing employers and employees. In doing so, he explains why even those with no absolute advantage will engage in partnerships.

A single question has guided Socrates's entire process of city building: *Given individuals' needs and resources*, what arrangements for and developments of those resources is necessary in order for their needs to be met in the best way possible? His aim, like the aim of each citizen, is to avoid in actuality every potential end that would be worse. His understanding of a true city, and of every step of its construction, centers on enabling autonomous individuals to be the primary engines of cooperation and exchange. This contrasts with Glaucon's approach to managing citizens as unthinking beings by means of a rigid division of labor, by the noble lie and abolition of private property in Book 3, and by the arrangements for a single communal family of rulers and soldiers in Book 5. For Socrates, determining what is truly most necessary appears to require paying close attention to the balance of needs present in current conditions and questioning *why* attractive plans and theories that at first seem necessary are really necessary.

In explaining the economic analysis and promotion of individual autonomy in the early city, I do not mean to argue that Socrates, or Plato, is opposed to all forms of central government or all politically sanctioned use of force, since (as many have pointed out) these are not present in the early city. Such a conclusion would be unwarranted. As we have seen, Socrates is simply cut off, in the middle of an incomplete investigative procedure, from developing the city in speech as he thought necessary. Nor do I mean to suggest that Socrates or Plato thinks *every* sort of unwanted intervention in the lives of individuals who think and make decisions for themselves should be avoided. It is conceivable that, had Glaucon not interrupted, Socrates would have discovered some threat to the city's citizens that would require a centrally coordinated or even coercive response in certain limited ways. Yet had he done so, his analytical approach would have remained fundamentally grounded in and attentive to the needs and aptitudes of individual actors choosing to engage in exchanges of all kinds. In any case, whatever Socrates's or Plato's preferred form of regime might turn out to be upon further investigation, we ought at least to hold that the true ethical, economic, and political principles of the *Republic* as a whole can only emerge to the extent that we pay attention to the distinct personalities, beliefs, and contributions to the city that Plato attributes to Socrates, Adeimantus, and Glaucon, and to the extent that we account for the genius of the economic analysis and of the analytical approach that are present in Plato's portrayal of the early city.

## NOTES

1. Patrick C. Tinsley (2011, 1–3) identifies Carl Menger and Murray Rothbard, as well as a number of "proto-Austrian libertarians," as holding similar views.

2. The prevailing system for referencing passages in Plato uses "Stephanus numbers," which refer to the pagination in the 1578 edition of Plato's complete works edited by Henri Estienne (Henricus Stephanus, in Latin). Stephanus numbers are printed in most recent editions and translations. In this chapter, I accordingly refer

to the Stephanus page(s), section(s), and (when giving quotations) line(s) in S. R. Slings's Greek edition of the *Republic* (Plato 2003).

3. Robbins (2000, 12) says Plato was a communist when he wrote the *Republic* and a fascist by the time he wrote the *Laws*. Popper (1947, 28, 47, 76–81, 93–95, 105) accuses him of being a totalitarian, and Schumpeter (1959, 55–56) concludes that he is a fascist.

4. My reading of the text is not based on the premise that Socrates's views represent Plato's; any responsible interpretation of Plato must distinguish between the author and the literary characters he portrays (e.g., Socrates, Glaucon, and Adeimantus). When I mention Plato or Socrates in this chapter, then, I do so deliberately, as author or literary character, respectively. In the end, I find reasons to conclude that Plato *does* agree with Socrates, as we will see, but this cannot be assumed at the outset. What Socrates says must be evaluated on its own merits in its context within the *Republic*.

5. "City of pigs" is a name that Glaucon, Socrates's young interlocutor, introduces immediately after the discussion of the early city. Beginning with a counterfactual—that is, with a hypothetical statement of what is *not* currently the case ("if you were . . . would you fatten")—Glaucon proposes an improvement on and departure from the preceding city, and he calls *this improved city* "a city of sows." The vast majority of scholarship and teaching on the *Republic* thus wrongly attributes the name "city of sows" (or more commonly but less accurately, "city of pigs") to the *preceding* stages of the city instead of to the modified city that follows (see, e.g., Gadamer 1980, 54; Strauss 1978, 93, 95; Robbins 2000, 14; Devereux 1979, 36; Bloom 1991, 346; Annas 1991, 76; Janke 1999, 13; Cooper 2000, 13; Barney 2002, 212; McKeen 2004, 70–71; Rosen 2005, 75, 79–80; Zuckert 2009, 346; Jonas, Nakazawa, and Braun 2012, 333). This overlooks not only (i) the existence of the counterfactual, but also the fact that, when Glaucon goes on to explain himself, (ii) he clearly wants "to fatten" the citizens on richer side dishes and desserts than previously, and (iii) he thinks the citizens should not endure hardship. This is the way to fatten up livestock. Glaucon is not proposing an alternative to a city of sows, but the city of sows as itself an alternative to the preceding city. Wallach (2001, 251) correctly identifies the "city of pigs" as "the now lavishly endowed city."

6. By contrasting fiat with commodity money, I do not mean to imply that Socrates thinks the former is necessarily assigned its value, or is otherwise regulated, by a single political authority. He does not specify who can or must declare the value of money, only that its value lies solely in its function as an accepted *token*. For a narrower use of the term "fiat," see Gordon (1975, 43), who uses the term "non-metallist" for what I am calling "fiat" money.

7. Boettke and Storr also show that that both Weber and Mises avoid the analytical extremes of atomism, where an individual is without social and institutional influences, and of naive holism, where an individual is entirely determined by his or her social environment. This is also true of Socrates in the *Republic*, who gives extensive analyses of the ways in which individuals both make their own decisions (e.g., 369b–372d) and are prepared to have various dispositions by their environment (e.g., 400c–402a).

8. We must be careful not to attribute to Plato modern categories of thought inaccurately. Plato does not use terms that can be directly translated as "division of labor," "supply and demand," "consumption goods," "factors of production," "fiat money," "comparative advantage," or even "the economy" or "economics." I use these terms as convenient and familiar handles for discussing elements of the early city because they seem to me to correspond precisely to what Plato communicates in other words. For example, Plato portrays a system in which scarce products and services are produced, exchanged, and used, so we may meaningfully refer to this system as an "economy." Nevertheless, we must not assume that for Plato an "economic" subject matter can be treated separately from politics, as it often has been treated over the past one hundred fifty years; for him and for his contemporaries, what we call economics is part of the study of politics, which covers every human activity significantly affecting the condition of a city-state. To reduce the risks of mistakenly attributing a modern view to Plato, I conduct much of my analysis of Socrates's early city in the original terms Socrates uses before converting my findings into equivalent modern terms, where converting them seems likely to make the elements of his theory more recognizable to a modern audience.

9. Most interpreters hold that Plato thinks the early city needs to be improved by the communist, totalitarian institutions introduced in Books 3–5 (e.g., Reeve 1988, 171; Cooper 2000, 14–17; Wallach 2001, 251–52; Barney 2002, 218–20). German scholars and Straussians tend to argue that the early city is deficient because it lacks political and philosophical activities (e.g., Wilamowitz 1919–1920, 214–17; Gadamer [1934] 1980, 51–56; Strauss [1964] 1978, 93–97; Bloom [1968] 1991, 344–51; Rosen 2005, 79–82).

10. For an exception, see Schofield (1999, 74–80), whose mistaken (in my view) reliance on later versions of the city in developing his interpretation of Plato's overall views in the *Republic* does not hinder his assessment and appreciation of "Plato's model of the economy" in the early city, which he says is "a brilliant piece of theory," a "dazzling and dazzlingly original piece of theorizing" that "constitutes . . . the invention of the concept of an economy" (Schofield 1999, 80, 76). Weinstein (2009, 441–47, 455–58) follows Schofield in these matters.

11. Schofield similarly concludes that the economic theory of the early city "is evidently an *analysis*" (Schofield 1999, 76); on this point see also Taylor (1997, 49) and Weinstein (2009, 440).

12. Schofield (1999, 73–74) comes to the same conclusion, though he bases his arguments more on other passages in the *Republic* and on other Platonic texts than on the way in which the early city develops, as I do. See also Weinstein (2009, 443n13).

13. Weinstein nevertheless acknowledges that Socrates returns to reevaluate prior assumptions and seek justifications for them (Weinstein 2009, 442).

14. It is true that, while reading the passages in question for the first time, the reader is likely to feel uncertain about where the conversation is going. Socrates does not start out with an overview of the topics he will discuss; he, as Plato's literary character, does not yet have in mind what exactly they will be. In addition, Socrates develops some parts of his economic theory in detail before introducing other, more rudimentary parts. For example, his explanation of ways in which the principle of the division of labor would need to be applied leads him to distinguish between cowherds,

shepherds, and other kinds of herdsmen before he ever considers the needs for a marketplace or currency. Yet the fact that Plato uses an unfamiliar (to us) style of writing
does not keep him from having an analytic intention or achieving a systematic result.

15. Robbins's view of Plato is more generous and respectful than most, but even he
attributes the later stages of the city to Plato, who he says "gives quite a remarkable
account, since it's the first time in conspicuous literature at any rate, of the advantages so far as productivity is concerned of the division of labour. But he stops there"
(Robbins 1932, 16).

16. With "put" in the aorist (past) tense here, presumably Socrates is no longer
using "we" to refer to the human beings who form cities. Now "we" seems to refer to
him and Adeimantus first mentioning cities and deciding to build and examine one.
The sense, then, is: "back then, we had this sort of shared-settlement in mind when
we referred to a city, isn't that right?" In his next sentence Socrates returns to the first
sense of "we."

17. I translate fairly literally so as to let the reader track Plato's uses of the same
words. I add implied words, as well as the Greek for key terms, in brackets.

18. I adopt the term "individual" because it reflects Socrates's thorough emphasis
on single actors in 369b–370c.

19. Weinstein claims that this city of four or five "is organized communally, much
as a single household might be," and that, when other craftsmen are added a page
later, this "communal policy is overturned and replaced with one" in which "citizens
are to exchange their products in the marketplace through buying and selling," which
in turn leads to "a veritable revolution" in economic institutions (Weinstein 2009,
439). I find no textual evidence whatsoever for the assertion that the city of four or five
is centrally, communally organized. Weinstein overlooks the fact that, in the elemental
interactions that build the city at 369b–c (and ever after that in the early city), Socrates
does not describe "communalism" (Weinstein 2009, 443) but individuals choosing to
give certain products in return for others—that is, to "exchange" with one another,
even though Socrates does not use the word itself (*allagê*, 371b9) until a little later, as
Weinstein (2009, 446) observes. At every stage of the early city, individual producers
make their products "common" (*koina*, 369e4) to all simply by making them available
to all for exchange.

20. Although the Greek "*chreia*," like the English "need," can be used to mean
either *a lack* or *the thing lacked*, it is clear from the context which meaning is meant.
For Socrates's usual use of "need" (*chreia*) as the former, see 371a1, 372a2, and
373d1; an exception appears at 369d1.

21. C. D. C. Reeve also chooses "aptitude" (Reeve 1988, 172).

22. Since *pleiô* (more) is neuter plural, I take it as a predicate adjective modifying
*hekasta* (each [of the products]), and I take the neuter singular words *kallion* (finely)
and *rhaion* (easily) as adverbs modifying *gignetai* (they come into being).

23. Schofield (1999) is a notable exception, remarking that Socrates's account
of the early city "is focused on specialization" and is "an *analysis*, which by appeal
to the one principle of specialization . . . demonstrates a dynamic explaining the
development and expansion of a whole range of economic activities" (Schofield 1999,
75, 76).

24. See Plato's *Laches* 196d–e, *Rival Lovers* 134a, *Theaetetus* 161c, 166c, and *Laws* 819d.

25. For earlier examples, see 327b, c, 328b, 337d. For a Socratic theory about ruling that is critical of this approach, see 347a–d.

26. For example, Socrates cannot possibly believe that the "presumably" true statements at 331c5–7 and 332a1–2 are both true.

27. In addition to the *Republic*, Greco also draws on a myth from Plato's *Protagoras* (Greco 2009, 61). Yet this myth—which Plato puts in the mouth of Protagoras, the very person he has Socrates cross-examine and refute on a number of matters—is of no relevance for interpreting Socrates's theories in the *Republic*'s early city.

28. We therefore should not accept Greco's claim that Plato's "notion of specialization does not refer so much to the exclusivity of the worker's occupation (whatever it happens to be) as to the specialized knowledge that the occupation under discussion requires" (Greco 2009, 56). Greco does concede that Socrates's third reason for specialization deals with time but does not see how fundamentally this challenges her central contention that for Plato specialization is driven primarily by a concern for art, not for efficiency (Greco 2009, 63). Schofield (1999, 74–76) overlooks the third reason for specialization.

29. Greco argues that, since foreign markets are unlimited in scope, it is primarily foreign markets that drive the pursuit of efficiency, and she offers evidence that, apart from certain sorts of pottery, Greek intercity trade in Plato's time included large amounts of raw materials and slaves but few manufactured items. Nevertheless, it is hard to believe that (i) the great expansion of Athenian trade in the fifth and fourth centuries BCE did not introduce any significant competition, and therefore incentives for efficient production, in at least some manufactures; that (ii) manufactures were the only sort of productive activity likely to incentivize efficiency; and that (iii) local competition did not drive a significant quest for the efficiency of labor, given the existence of private, large-scale operations in mining and arms production. Moreover, Socrates specifically mentions manufacturers ("craftsmen," 371a7) as those who will need to produce a surplus for *intercity* trade.

30. Raiklin and Uyar (1996) also note that the distinction between wants and needs is important for philosophers, political scientists, sociologists, and psychologists.

31. It is curious that Socrates describes the city of four or five in superlative terms as "the most necessary city." This implies that there are in fact *degrees* of necessity, that a certain goal, and so a certain desire or decision, might be somewhat necessary but still less necessary than another. As the inhabitants weigh and select from a variety of possible courses of action, they must prioritize their desires according to how *relatively* necessary those desires are in any given situation. What is essential, in Socrates's view, is that we watch out that there is no *greater* necessity presenting itself to us at any given moment, and that we track and prioritize our needs (including our need to care for those who care for us through exchanges of any kind) from the simplest level up to the most comprehensive level of our "way of life."

32. I use this example because Socrates seems to be a vegetarian; see 372b–d, 373b–d. 370d–e and 338c–d are also pertinent.

33. As Barry Gordon reports, "Plato . . . would see the modern claim to autonomy for economics as most inhibiting for the progress of social enquiry. Economic analyses can only be conducted properly as aspects of a much broader study than that for which most modern economists seem content to settle" (Gordon 1975, 27).

34. For a similar but far less systematic account in Adam Smith, see Smith (1904, 357), in which Foley sees echoes of Plato (Foley 1974, 226–27).

35. Socrates does not discuss the effect of supply on demand. We may also note that he has not yet introduced money into his analysis, so he does not immediately make prices in monetary units the measure of need; what he wishes to point out is simply that production will increase to the extent that perceived need increases, however need is measured.

36. Yet even Schumpeter admits, in light of other passages (he seems to refer to 416e–417a and *Laws* 741e–742c), that Plato is "the first known sponsor of one of the two fundamental theories of money"—of fiat money (Schumpeter 1959, 56).

37. It is generally thought that fiat money did not appear until the eleventh century under the Sung dynasty in China (Selgin 2003, 163), but as Lowry (1987, 26n22) points out, there are several references in ancient Greek literature to instances of money with no intrinsic, but only conventional, worth. Pseudo-Plato's *Eryxias* (1997, 399e–400d) discusses the intrinsic uselessness of currencies such as Carthaginian small, sealed leather pouches, Spartan lead tokens, and Ethiopian engraved stones. Pseudo-Aristotle also reports in *Oeconomica* that Dionysius of Syracuse minted coins out of tin (1920, 2:2.1349a32–36) and that Timotheus the Athenian similarly minted coins from bronze (1920, 2:2.1350a23–30). For other passages in Plato demonstrating his theory of fiat money, see the previous endnote.

38. McNulty offers these views as evidence that Plato, in contrast to Adam Smith, saw the activity of exchange as belonging not to everyone but only to those unfit for other duties. Yet this view cannot be right, since it disregards not only (i) the entire basis of the city as constituted by exchanging individuals but also (ii) the fact that everyone with whom the dealers exchange, such as the farmer who goes to the marketplace, is still engaging in exchange.

39. For a similar argument, see Weinstein (2009, 453–55).

40. It therefore cannot be true that, as Dorter (2006, 65) claims, the early city "has no rational component." This ignores the abilities of the dealers and employers.

41. For an interpretation lying between those of Reeve and McKeen, but ultimately nearer the former, see Devereux (1979, 37–39).

# REFERENCES

Annas, Julia. 1991. *An Introduction to Plato's "Republic."* Oxford: Clarendon Press.
Aristotle. 1999. *Nicomachean Ethics*. Second edition. Translated by Terence Irwin. Indianapolis: Hackett Publishing Company.
———. 1984. *The Politics*. Translated by Carnes Lord. Chicago: University of Chicago Press.

Barney, Rachel. 2002. "Platonism, Moral Nostalgia, and the 'City of Pigs.'" *Proceedings of the Boston Area Colloquium in Ancient Philosophy* 17: 207–27.

Bloom, Allan. 1991. "Interpretive Essay." In *The Republic of Plato*. Second edition. Translated by Allan Bloom, 307–436. New York: Basic Books.

Boettke, Peter J., and Virgil Henry Storr. 2002. "Post-Classical Political Economy: Polity, Society and Economy in Weber, Mises and Hayek." *American Journal of Economics and Sociology* 61 (1): 161–91.

Brown, Wendy. 1994. "'Supposing Truth Were a Woman . . .': Plato's Subversion of Masculine Discourse." In *Feminist Interpretations of Plato*, edited by Nancy Tuana, 157–80. University Park: Pennsylvania State University Press.

Cohen, Edward E. 2002. "An Unprofitable Masculinity." In *Money, Labour and Land: Approaches to the Economies of Ancient Greece*, edited by Paul Cartledge, Edward E. Cohen, and Lin Foxhall, 100–12. London: Routledge.

Cooper, John M. 2000. "Two Theories of Justice." *Proceedings and Addresses of the American Philosophical Association* 72 (2): 5–27.

Devereux, Daniel T. 1979. "Socrates' First City in the *Republic*." *Apeiron: A Journal for Ancient Philosophy and Science* 13 (1): 36–40.

Dorter, Kenneth. 2006. *The Transformation of Plato's "Republic."* Lanham, MD: Lexington Books.

Ekelund, Robert B., and Robert F. Hébert. 2007. *A History of Economic Theory and Method*. Fifth edition. Long Grove, IL: Waveland Press.

Finley, M. I. 1970. "Aristotle and Economic Analysis." *Past and Present* 47: 3–25.

———. (1973) 1999. *The Ancient Economy*. Berkeley: University of California Press.

Foley, Vernard. 1974. "The Division of Labour in Plato and Smith." *History of Political Economy* 6 (2): 220–42.

———. 1975. "Smith and the Greeks: A Reply to Professor McNulty's Comments." *History of Political Economy* 7 (3): 379–89.

Gadamer, Hans-Georg. (1934) 1980. "Plato and the Poets." Translated by P. Christopher Smith. In *Dialogue and Dialectic: Eight Hermeneutical Studies on Plato*, 39–72. New Haven, CT: Yale University Press.

Gordon, Barry J. 1961. "Aristotle, Schumpeter, and the Metallist Tradition." *The Quarterly Journal of Economics* 75 (4): 608–14.

———. 1975. *Economic Analysis before Adam Smith: Hesiod to Lessius*. London: Macmillan.

Greco, Anna. 2009. "On the Economy of Specialization and Division of Labour in Plato's *Republic*." *Polis* 26 (1): 52–72.

Harris, Edward M. 2002. 'Workshop, Marketplace and Household: The Nature of Technical Specialization in Classical Athens and its Influence on Economy and Society." In *Money, Labour and Land Approaches to the Economies of Ancient Greece, edited by Paul Cartledge, Edward E. Cohen, and Lin Foxhall, 67–99. London: Routledge.*

Hayek, F. A. 1992 (1988). *The Fatal Conceit: The Errors of Socialism*. London: Routledge.

Höffe, Otfried. 1997. "Zur Analogie von Individuum und Polis (Buch II 367e–374d)." In *Platon: Politeia*. Berlin: Akademie Verlag GmbH.

Janke, Caroline. 1999. *Schiller und Plato: vom Staate der Vernunft und dem Scheine der Kunst; Untersuchungen zur politico-ästhetischen Antinomie.* Amsterdam: Rodopi.

Jonas, Mark E., Yoshiaki M. Nakazawa, and James Braun. 2012. "Appetite, Reason, and Education in Socrates' 'City of Pigs.'" *Phronesis* 57 (4): 332–57.

Lowry, S. Todd. 1979. "Recent Literature on Ancient Greek Economic Thought." *Journal of Economic Literature* 17: 65–86.

———. 1987. "The Greek Heritage in Economic Thought." In *Pre-Classical Economic Thought: From the Greeks to the Scottish Enlightenment*, edited by Todd S. Lowry, 7–30. Boston: Kluwer Academic Publishers.

Mankiw, N. Gregory. 2012. *Principles of Economics.* Sixth edition. Mason, OH: South-Western Cengage Learning.

McKeen, Catherine. 2004. "Swillsburg City Limits (The 'City of Pigs': *Republic* 370c–372d)." *Polis: The Journal for the Society of Ancient Political Thought* 21 (1–2): 71–92.

McNulty, Paul J. 1975. "A Note on the Division of Labor in Plato and Smith." 7 (3): 372–78.

Medema, Steven G., and Warren J. Samuels, eds. 2013. *The History of Economic Thought: A Reader.* London: Routledge.

Mises, Ludwig von. 2007 (1949). *Human Action: A Treatise on Economics*, vol. 1. Edited by Bettina Bien Greaves. Indianapolis: Liberty Fund.

———. 2007 (1949). *Human Action: A Treatise on Economics*, vol. 2. Edited by Bettina Bien Greaves. Indianapolis: Liberty Fund.

Monroe, A. E. 2001 (1923). *Monetary Theory Before Adam Smith.* Kitchener, Ontario: Batoche Books.

Plato. 2003. *Platonis Rem Publicam.* Edited by S. R. Slings. Oxford: Oxford University Press.

Popper, K. R. 1947 (1945). *The Open Society and Its Enemies: The Spell of Plato*, vol. 1. London: George Routledge and Sons.

Pseudo-Aristotle. 1920. "Oeconomica." In *The Works of Aristotle*, edited by E. S. Forster. Oxford: Oxford University Press.

Pseudo-Plato. 1997. "Eryxias." Translated by Mark Joyal. In *Plato: Complete Works*, edited by John M. Cooper and D. S. Hutchinson. Indianapolis: Hackett Publishing Company.

Raiklin, Ernest, and Bulent Uyar. 1996. "On the Relativity of the Concepts of Needs, Wants, Scarcity and Opportunity Cost." *International Journal of Social Economics* 23 (7): 49–56.

Reeve, C. D. C. 1988. *Philosopher-Kings: The Argument of Plato's Republic.* Princeton, NJ: Princeton University Press.

Robbins, Lionel. 2000 (1998). *A History of Economic Thought: The LSE Lectures.* Princeton: Princeton University Press.

———. 1932. *An Essay on the Nature and Significance of Economic Science.* London: Macmillan.

Rosen, Stanley. 2005. *Plato's Republic: A Study.* New Haven, CT: Yale University Press.

Samuelson, Paul A. and William D. Nordhaus. 2001. *Economics*, 17th ed. New York: Irwin/McGraw-Hill.

Schofield, Malcolm. 1999. "Plato on the Economy." In *Saving the City: Philosopher-Kings and Other Classical Paradigms*, 69–81. New York: Routledge.

———. 2006. *Plato: Political Philosophy*. Oxford: Oxford University Press.

Schumpeter, Joseph A. 1959. *History of Economic Analysis*. New York: Oxford University Press.

Selgin, George. 2003. "Adaptive Learning and the Transition to Fiat Money." *The Economics Journal* 113 (484): 147–65.

Smith, Adam. (1776) 1904. *An Inquiry into the Nature and Causes of the Wealth of Nations*, vol. 1. London: Methuen.

Strauss, Leo. (1964) 1978. *The City and Man*. Chicago: University of Chicago Press.

Taylor, O. H. (1991) 1997. "Schumpeter's History of Economic Analysis." In *Joseph A. Schumpeter: Critical Assessments*, edited by John Cunningham Wood, 45–60. London: Routledge.

Tinsley, Patrick C. 2011. "Plato and the Spell of the State." *Libertarian Papers* 3: 1–52.

Varian, Hal R. 2010. *Intermediate Microeconomics: A Modern Approach*. Eighth edition. New York: W. W. Norton and Company.

Wallach, John R. 2001. *The Platonic Political Art: A Study of Critical Reason and Democracy*. University Park: Pennsylvania State University Press.

Weber, Max. (1921–1922) 1978. *Economy and Society: An Outline of Interpretive Sociology*. Edited by Guenther Roth and Claus Wittich, and translated by Ephraim Fischoff, Hans Gerth, A. M. Henderson, Ferdinand Kolegar, C. Wright Mills, Talcott Parsons, Max Rheinstein, Guenther Roth, Edward Schils, and Claus Wittich. Berkeley: University of California Press.

Weinstein, Joshua I. 2009. "The Market in Plato's *Republic*." *Classical Philology* 104 (4): 439–58.

Wilamowitz-Moellendorff, Ulrich von. 1919–1920. *Platon: Beilagen und Textkritik*, vol. 2. Berlin: Weidmannsche Buchhandlung.

Wolin, Sheldon S. 1960. *Politics and Vision: Continuity and Innovation in Western Political Thought*. Boston: Little, Brown and Company.

Zuckert, Catherine H. 2009. *Plato's Philosophers: The Coherence of the Dialogues*. Chicago: University of Chicago Press.

*Chapter 2*

# Beyond the Efficiency of the Market

## *Adam Smith on Sympathy and the Poor Law*

### Brianne Wolf[1]

There is an ongoing debate about the morality of the market system. This debate often takes the form of two arguments, that the market improves the situation of the least well-off and is morally beneficial, or that it encourages moral depravity and potentially worsens the situation of the least advantaged. One scholar has characterized this dual-nature of the market as "The Problems and Promise of Commercial Society" (Rasmussen 2008). On the one hand, we are familiar with the promise of commerce, and the argument that the market is effective in alleviating poverty and spreading wealth by allowing people to coordinate diverse interests. Adam Smith points to these positive capacities of the market in *Wealth of Nations* (WN), arguing that commercial society generally improves the situation for the poorest, making them as "rich as an African King" (WN I.i.11).[2] Economists have referred to improvements in standards of living as an outcome of the market process (e.g., Kirzner 1992). Economists have also referenced the market order to describe both the laws and social structure that make market coordination and the improvement of material conditions possible, and the several orders that can result from such coordination (Hayek [1976] 1978). They have described the market order as a "spontaneous order" that emerges from the coordination of diverse ends, arguing that it is neither an order that persists or is always visible nor one that seeks a specific end.[3] The rules that govern the market order, such as private property, rule of law, and freedom of contract create a space where individuals can pursue their unique ends while also connecting with one another. The market process also fosters economic growth by facilitating the coordination of these ends within the market order.

Further, some argue that the market not only facilitates material growth, but also encourages moral behavior by teaching virtues (e.g., McCloskey 2006), or even transforms actors into more moral human beings (Storr, forthcoming).

In this way, the market allows for more than simply a kind of negative liberty by preventing individuals from interfering with one another. It also does more than coordinate individuals to achieve material ends. The market has the potential to teach us how to be decent human beings or at the very least to treat others with respect so that we are better able to satisfy our interests.

However, we are also familiar with the tragedy of the market. The market can have morally problematic consequences, such as encouraging us to value material gains above human relationships.[4] In this description of the market, sometimes attributed to Adam Smith's "invisible hand" metaphor, the market encourages people to be greedy.[5] Actors in the market are not virtuous, and in fact, their very moral depravity is what spurs the market process on. As Mandeville ([1732] 1924) explains, "The Root of Evil, Avarice, That damn'd ill-natur'd baneful Vice, Was Slave to Prodigality, That noble Sin; whilst Luxury Employ'd a Million of the Poor, And odious Pride a Million more. . . . That strange ridic'lous Vice, was made The very Wheel that turn'd the Trade." While Smith vehemently disagrees with Mandeville's position on the role of selfishness in *Theory of Moral Sentiments* (TMS), he acknowledges the market's potential to be morally problematic.[6] He illustrates, for example, how the poor man's son seeks commercial pursuits to obtain the many material pleasures that the rich have; however, he finds at the end of his life that they have not made him feel happy or fulfilled. Indeed, while Smith says the paths to virtue and wealth are the same for most people because succeeding in the market depends on gaining the social esteem of one's peers, the pursuit of wealth can cause depravity in the most well-off members of society (TMS I.iii.3.5). It can also promote the substitution of wealth for virtue in the moral judgments of everyone. In these ways, the market has the potential to be both ameliorative and destructive for political and social life.

Economists have pointed to the ways that the market, by encouraging greed and selfishness, expands economic inequality (e.g., Piketty 2014). Political scientists (Gilens 2012; Hacker and Pierson 2011; Bartels 2008) also point out increasing inequality and argue that it leads to inequalities in political power. In these ways, the market fosters moral depravity and makes the material situation of the least advantaged worse.

Both of these views of the market have often been attributed to Smith's work, but another way of considering the moral effects of the market in his theory is to consider how policies that impede the market affect individuals. Smith is very concerned throughout *Wealth of Nations* with the ways in which the market can improve the situation of the least advantaged. He often discusses the market in terms of the "natural liberty of the market," which allows individuals to improve their situation. Because of this emphasis on the importance of the liberty of the market for improving the general economic situation of nations and the material condition of the least well-off, Smith also pays attention to policies and practices that impede this liberty. Among them is his famous discussion of the problems with monopoly and joint-stock companies.

A less famous example of a policy that impedes the market is his discussion of the Elizabethan poor law.[7] The poor law was established in the early seventeenth century when Elizabeth I revised and enforced The Act for Poor Relief of 1597. The original, or "old," poor law required each parish to deliver aid to the most deserving in their jurisdiction. Yet each parish's ability to administer aid adequately to their own varied. Further, the responsibility of the local parish for their own poor increased with the passing of the 1662 Settlement Act. This new component of the poor law reduced labor mobility because neighboring parishes would not take on new poor to their relief rolls. With the aid of a commission that included the economist Nassau Senior, the poor law was amended in 1834 to be less costly and to reach only those truly in need.[8]

In his discussion of the poor law, Smith argues that the new act is economically problematic because it prevents workers from following the market for their labor and prevents the market from fulfilling one of its central tenets, to improve the situation of the least well-off. However, Smith also argues against the law on seemingly moral terms. Why does Smith discuss the moral effects of the law rather than simply dismissing it on economic grounds? It is this puzzle that this chapter aims to address. I argue that by reading *Theory of Moral Sentiments* in light of this argument in *Wealth of Nations*, we see that in the case of the Settlement Act, economic liberty is also tied to healthy moral judgment and sympathetic relationships. I argue that what is unique about the poor law example in Smith's work, as opposed to the character of the poor man's son, for instance, is that what is problematic for the liberty of the market is similarly problematic for the liberty of individuals and their potential for forming relationships with one another. That is, what is problematic for economic liberty is also problematic for the formation of the moral ties that Smith thinks are so crucial to our happiness.[9] Smith often argues that the paths to virtue and wealth are the same, and this example shows why the market can help individuals relate to one another better than certain regulations of the market by law. The poor law example shows how interference in the market can actually foster some of the market's morally problematic potential. By further encouraging people to see the poor as objects of derision, the poor law not only prevents the circulation of free labor, it also harms their potential to be seen as people worthy of the sympathy of their peers.

I propose that to understand Smith's arguments about the moral aspects of the law, namely its negative effect on sympathetic relationships, we need to consider his discussion of the poor law in *Wealth of Nations* in light of his arguments in *Theory of Moral Sentiments*. Since the dismissal of "das Adam Smith Problem," scholars have increasingly been reading Smith's economic and moral works together (e.g., Storr, forthcoming; Herzog 2016; Rasmussen 2008). Scholars have also been making this argument for the unity of the two works on rhetorical grounds, by demonstrating that WN is a rhetorical exercise in which Smith makes the case for many concepts in TMS (e.g., Pitts, 2017; Fleischacker 2004, 209).[10]

To show how the poor law actually worsens the situation of the poor by preventing them from being sympathized with by their peers, I establish the connection between Smith's economic and moral arguments in the example of the poor law. I argue that there are two key aspects of the law that harm the moral situation of the poor. First, I argue that the poor law problematically establishes a position of arbitrary power for its overseers relative to the rest of society. Second, I argue that the law positions the poor as objects to be administered rather than individuals with moral worth.

My argument will proceed in three parts. In the first section, I present Smith's discussion of the poor law in WN. Then, I focus on the economic consequences of the law, particularly its effects on the labor market. In the second section, I turn to Smith's comments about the moral dimension of the poor law. I focus on the key problem that the poor law introduces into the market: the administration of the poor by overseers. I then demonstrate why this aspect of the law is problematic by applying the problem with the extent of sympathy that Smith outlines in TMS to the structure of the poor law as Smith analyzes it in WN, focusing on the issue of distance between people of different social rank. I build Smith's case for why it is difficult, but not impossible, to sympathize outside of our social circle. Whereas we might expect the market to expand our circles of sympathy, as I presented above, the poor law, by administering the poor, reduces this possibility for them. I show how this limitation of the extent of sympathy that the poor law propagates is problematic not just for the liberty of the poor, but also for all citizens. In the concluding section, I turn back to Smith's arguments about the economic problems of the poor law for limiting material well-being and tie this to his concerns about the effects of the law on moral well-being. I conclude with a discussion of what Smith's critique of the poor law on moral and material terms teaches us about the market process and market order. I argue that interfering with the market process makes it more likely that we enhance its negative potential for fostering selfishness to the detriment of Smithean sympathy.

## THE POOR LAW AND THE LABOR MARKET

Smith's discussion of the poor law initially appears to be only an economic one, as he refers to the law as part of a discussion in chapter 10 of Book I of *Wealth of Nations* about the advantages and disadvantages of employments of labor and stock. These advantages and disadvantages tend toward equality, in his language, if there is "perfect liberty." However, Smith recognizes that there is not perfect liberty in the market for labor and he has two sections to explain why. The first section argues that there are inequalities that arise from the nature of the employments, such as their difficulty, how much training and education is required to practice them, and how much trust is required of the employee. In the second section, on the other hand, he argues that there are some policies of Europe that occasion inequalities in the advantages and disadvantages of different employments of labor and stock and in doing so, impede the liberty of the market: "But the policy of Europe, by not leaving things at perfect liberty, occasions other inequalities of much greater importance" (WN I.x.c.1). There are three types of such policies: (1) policies that unnaturally restrain competition in some employments, (2) policies that unnaturally increase competition in employments, and finally (3) those that obstruct the circulation of labor. The poor law falls into the third category and is the main subject of Smith's discussion in the third part. Other kinds of distortions of the labor market discussed in the section come as the result of the laws that protect corporations and monopolies. Smith's discussion of the poor law focuses on England and the ways in which the government's attempts to provide relief are failing precisely because the requirements of the poor law impede the liberty of laborers by preventing them from finding work.

As is typical in Smith's accounts of various events in WN, he first provides his own history of the poor law. My purpose in reproducing Smith's account here is not to suggest that it is historically authoritative. Unlike most historians, Smith does not seem to be concerned about how efficient the law was as far as administering aid to the most deserving. My argument does not turn on whether or not Smith's account is perfectly accurate. I aim to illuminate how Smith's analysis of the law shows that when the labor market is restricted, there are both economic and moral consequences for the poor and their fellow countrymen.[11] Moreover, Smith's history is fairly consistent with historical and modern accounts, as he details the problems with the old poor law and the steps taken to remedy its problems, focusing especially on the Settlement Act. However, there are a few exceptions; Sir George Nichols's classic (1856) history seeks to remedy previous accounts, including the account of Dr. Burns that Smith used, by providing a comprehensive overview of the law instead of arguing for changes to be made. The economic historian, Mark Blaug (1963), like many modern historians, focuses on the poor law as the precursor to the modern welfare state. He argues against Smith's ideas here, saying that while most historians have focused on the issues of maladministration and inefficiency, the poor law was actually solving the legitimate problem of "structural unemployment in the countryside."[12]

Smith's discussion of the law focuses on how it was administered. But like other historians, he shows how the poor law was revised over time to strengthen its administration to ensure that only the truly deserving would receive relief. He tells the reader that the poor law was established to replace the charity that had been previously administered by local monasteries before they were destroyed. It was passed by Queen Elizabeth I in 1597 in an attempt to continue this tradition by ensuring "that every parish should be bound to provide for its own poor; and that overseers of the poor should be annually appointed, who, with the churchwardens, should raise by a parish rate, competent sums for this purpose" (WN I.x.c.46). However, Smith is less concerned about the efficiency of administration than the limitations the law put on the circulation of labor. From the beginning of his description, we see that the two components of the law with which Smith is most concerned are that local parishes need to provide for their own poor, and that there are overseers responsible for raising funds to pay for relief.

Because of his concern with how the administration of the law affected the liberty of the laborers, he details how the law was revised several times to improve its efficiency. First, it was revised by Charles II, who required

> that forty days undisturbed residence should gain any person a settlement in any parish; but that within that time it should be lawful for two justices of the peace, upon complaint made by the churchwardens or overseers of the poor, to remove any new inhabitant to the parish where he was last legally settled; unless he either rented a tenement of ten pounds a year, or could give such security for the discharge of the parish where he was then living, as those justices should judge sufficient. (WN I.x.c.47)

This provision of the poor law was known as the Settlement Act. Here again, Smith emphasizes the important role of the overseers and wardens, who could determine if a poor person deserved to be in the parish. In fact, there were eventually revisions to this Act because of the corruption of the parish officers who were responsible for determining settlement. James II and William III, therefore, required laborers to give notice to the parish in which they were settling, and eventually added that this notice could only be given in church on Sunday to ensure that it would be heard by the whole parish. In a later development of the Settlement Act that was supposed to restore the free circulation of labor, William III and later Queen Anne declared that the parish where the laborer had resided was to provide them a certificate to allow them to work in a new parish, and if they should need relief, it would be the responsibility of their original parish to provide it.

Yet, Smith is not convinced that these new provisions, passed over time, successfully restored the free circulation of labor; he argues instead that these revisions merely encouraged the granting parish not to give certificates at all, and when they did, the receiving parish to be strict in its requirement of certificates (WN I.x.c.56). The Settlement Act and its revisions did not improve the functioning of the market.[13] It only made the situation for the poor laborers trying to find work more difficult.

## Economic Consequences for the Labor Market

There are several issues at stake in Smith's discussion of how the poor law impedes perfect and natural liberty, but the first and most obvious are the economic consequences of wages of labor. The poor law distorts the market for labor in two ways. The first is that it does not allow workers to follow the market for labor. Smith describes the importance of the workers being able to freely seek out labor: "Every man's interest would prompt him to seek the advantageous, and to shun the disadvantageous employment" (WN I.x.a.1). Laborers naturally follow the market for labor according to the best employment because it is their interest to do so. In this way, self-interest serves to regulate this and other parts of the market.

Smith outlines the many ways that limitations on the free circulation of labor affect the market. The wages of labor and the price of goods are set in part because of the market for labor. Goods are priced according to the labor it takes to produce them. If workers are not allowed to follow the market for labor, this distorts the prices of both employment and of goods. Indeed, it was Smith who established the labor theory of value where the cost of a good is determined by either the "toil and trouble of acquiring it" or "the toil and trouble which it can save to himself" from having to acquire it (WN I.V.2). Similarly, the wages of labor are also tied to the profits and stock of any company: "The rise and fall in the profits of stock depend upon the same causes with the rise and fall in the wages of labour, the increasing or declining state of the wealth of the society; but those causes affect the one and the other very differently" (WN I.ix.1). In an earlier part of WN, Smith also notes how the price of labor is connected with many other economic concerns, but particularly the overall national wealth: "The liberal reward of labour, therefore, as it is the necessary effect, so it is the natural symptom of increasing national wealth. The scanty maintenance of the labouring poor, on the other hand, is the natural symptom that things are at a stand, and their starving condition that they are going fast backwards" (WN I.viii.27). How the nation's poor are paid—that is, their "liberal reward of labour," indicates the economic health of the nation. If these wages are distorted, it affects many other components in the market process.

Second, the poor law also distorts the market for labor by causing drastically different prices for labor in neighboring parishes. Laborers are not always able to relocate to follow the highest wages, and therefore distortions in price harm the development of industry. The labor market depends on signals from the supply and demand of laborers. "It is in this manner that the demand for men, like that for any other commodity, necessarily regulates the production of men" (WN I.viii.40). For Smith, the price of labor determines not just how much stock the company will produce, or the nation's wealth, but also how much labor there will be in the future. On the demand side, he says that laboring families determine how many children to have based on the "liberal reward of labor" (WN I.viii.42). Further, because it either encourages or discourages child-bearing, the wages of labor are also tied to "the encouragement of industry" (WN I.viii.43). For Smith, more children equals more potential for industry to grow, as there will be laborers to support its growth. Industry can only grow if there is a large enough supply of new workers. He argues that the price of labor should only be influenced by two things: demand and the cost of the living of the workers so that they can be paid enough to raise a family (WN I.viii.15). In these ways, we can see that there are several aspects of the market that are affected by the accuracy of the price of labor. The poor law distorts many of these signals by impeding the ability of workers to travel between parishes to find work, demand for labor, and the information they have about what the best jobs are, given different prices for labor between parishes.

## MORAL CONSEQUENCES OF THE POOR LAW

Though Smith's first concern with the poor law is economic—the distortion of the labor market—he spends a good deal more time in this section discussing moral effects of the law. He points out how the law affects the public perception of the poor laborers, which is tied to their ability to find work under the poor law. He also focuses on the justice of the law, namely whether or not workers who have families and especially need work or relief will be able to get it, and how the law affects the liberty of workers.

Smith characterizes the main problem with the law as the oversight of the parish wardens over the settlement of the poor laborers. They represent how the poor law, by administering poor people, teaches others to treat them as objects to be relocated, rather than as moral beings deserving of sympathy and respect. Smith explains again and again how workers were removed "at the caprice of any churchwarden or overseer" (WN I.x.c.54). In his eyes, these overseers were corrupt and did not make judgments according to principles of propriety.[14] The Settlement Act was ineffective in its goal to promote free circulation of labor because laborers depended on the objectivity of the overseers. In what follows, I explain how what looks like an economic problem only, preventing laborers from following the market for labor, was actually a moral problem. By treating the poor as objects to be administered, the poor law placed overseers in a position of authority over the poor where the conditions of the law made it difficult for them to overcome social distance and sympathize with the poor. Though Smith discusses solutions to the problem of the extent of sympathy, such as the development of the impartial spectator and general rules of morality, the specific provisions of the Settlement Act that required poor laborers to be judged via a certificate that overseers would review prevented these solutions from being effective.

In *Theory of Moral Sentiments*, Smith explains why the objectivity of overseers was unlikely because of the gap between rich and poor in sympathetic relationships. As part of his explanation of sympathy, Smith presents the difficulty of sympathizing beyond one's social group, sometimes called the extent of sympathy problem. Sympathy is defined as "fellow-feeling with any passion whatever" (TMS I.i.1.5). It requires that we imagine the emotions of another person and try to experience them ourselves because we can never directly experience the emotions of another person. However, sympathizing then becomes difficult if we cannot imagine the emotions of another as they would experience them. He argues that though all people naturally sympathize with others, it is more difficult to sympathize with those outside of our immediate physical or social context (Forman-Barzilai 2005). In other words, it is difficult to sympathize with those who are unfamiliar to us, because we cannot imagine the emotions of this "other" or enter into their situation (Otteson 2002). Smith says, for example, "men, though naturally sympathetic, feel so little for another, with whom they have no particular connexion, in comparison of what they feel for themselves; the misery of one, who is merely their fellow-creature, is of so little importance to them in comparison even of a small conveniency of their own" (TMS II.ii.3.4). Though Smith asserts that sympathy for others is natural, he recognizes that it is difficult for us to think outside of ourselves and our immediate situation. This is precisely why in order to develop the impartial spectator and be able to judge ourselves, we must also gain distance from ourselves to be able to judge as an external person would judge us. Smith presents the same idea earlier in TMS. He argues that even if we succeed in imagining the situation of another, our own feelings prevent us from sympathizing with them completely. He puts it:

> Mankind, though naturally sympathetic, never conceive, for what has befallen another, that degree of passion which naturally animates the person principally concerned. That imaginary change of situation, upon which their sympathy is founded, is but momentary. The thought of their own safety, the thought that they themselves are not really the sufferers, continually intrudes itself upon them; and though it does not hinder them from conceiving a passion somewhat analogous to what is felt by the sufferer, hinders them from conceiving any thing that approaches to the same degree of violence. (TMS I.i.4.7)

We can experience the emotions of another person, but never as fully as they experience them because the emotions are not ours. Therefore, though sympathy is a natural predisposition, it is also naturally limited by our own self-interest. And yet, "sympathy, however, cannot in any sense be regarded as a selfish principle" (TMS VII.iii.1.4). Self-interest for Smith does not mean selfish, but rather that we are "confined to ourselves" (Griswold 1999, 78). We will likely never achieve perfect unison with another person's emotions, but we achieve correspondence "and this is all that is wanted or required" (TMS I.i.4.7). We always desire to sympathize with others and to be an object of the sympathy, even with those who are distant from us, but we are also limited by our experiences and surroundings.

It is also difficult for us to sympathize with those outside of our social rank, even if they share a physical environment with us (Hanley 2008, 48). Smith builds the case for this argument throughout TMS. First, we all desire to be the object of another person's sympathy. Their fellow-feeling with our emotions "enlivens our joy" and "alleviates our grief" (TMS I.i.2.2). We desire to be the object of another's approbation. However, this desire for relief means we are more likely to sympathize with joy rather than sorrow. We would rather take home to ourselves happy emotions rather than sad ones. Smith theorizes about this saying, "Nature, it seems, when she loaded us with our own sorrows, thought that they were enough, and therefore did not command us to take any further share in those of others, than what was necessary to prompt us to relieve them" (TMS I.iii.1.12). This proclivity extends to people whose condition is not pleasant for us to imagine or enter into, especially if we are unsure if we can provide relief. He offers several reasons for this and ties this tendency to sympathize with joy rather than sorrow to why we are predisposed to look down upon the poor:

> It is because mankind are disposed to sympathize more entirely with our joy than with our sorrow, that we make parade of our riches, and conceal our poverty. Nothing is so mortifying as to be obliged to expose our distress to the view of the public, and to feel, that though our situation is open to the eyes of all mankind, no mortal conceives for us the half of what we suffer. Nay, it is chiefly from this regard to the sentiments of mankind that we pursue riches and avoid poverty. (TMS I.iii.2.1, 50)

We do sympathize with "great sorrows" but not everyday ones, because it is easier and feels better to sympathize with small joys (TMS I.ii.5.1). Because we are more inclined to sympathize with joy, and because it is difficult to sympathize outside of our social group, we are predisposed not to sympathize with the poor.

Our desire for approbation and our proclivity to sympathize with joy rather than sorrow causes us to praise the rich and look down upon, or worse, ignore the poor. He describes how harmful this is for the person denied the relief of the sympathy of his peers:

> The poor man, on the contrary, is ashamed of his poverty. He feels that it either places him out of sight of mankind, or, that if they take any notice of him, they have, however, scarce any fellow-feeling with the misery and distress which he suffers. He is mortified upon both accounts; for though to be overlooked, and to be disapproved of, are things entirely different, yet as obscurity covers us from the daylight of honour and approbation, to feel that we are taken no notice of, necessarily damps the most agreeable hope, and disappoints the most ardent desire of human nature. (TMS I.iii.2.1)

We view the poor as others who are unworthy of our sympathy, and we avoid them so we do not have to experience the unpleasant realities of their lives. In another example, when discussing why religion should not be funded by the state but instead should raise its own funds, Smith explains the appeal of religious sects for the poor. These sects give the poor the recognition they do not receive in the large, industrial city. Whereas the rich man is always respected,

> A man of low condition, on the contrary, is far from being a distinguished member of any great society. While he remains in a country village his conduct may be attended to, and he may be obliged to attend to it himself. In this situation, and in this situation only, he may have what is called a character to lose. But as soon as he comes into a great city, he is sunk in obscurity and darkness. His conduct is observed and attended to by nobody, and he is therefore very likely to neglect it himself, and to abandon himself to every sort of low profligacy and vice. (WN V.i.g.11)

The poor man is not given the approbation—or disapprobation—of his peers. His peers do not notice him at all. This is problematic for his sense of self, but also for his development of moral standards, especially of the impartial spectator. We develop our ability to judge our own behavior and that of others through our many, repeated sympathetic interactions with others in society.

The difficulty of sympathizing with others from a different social rank also causes us to try to make ourselves seem wealthy so we will garner the attention and sympathy of others. Smith notes that we are often the object of another's attention when we adorn ourselves with nice things. We therefore desire to be wealthy because we know this attracts the attention of our peers: "From whence, then, arises that emulation which runs through all the different ranks of men, and what are the advantages which we propose by that great purpose of human life which we call bettering our condition? To be observed, to be attended to, to be taken notice of with sympathy, complacency, and approbation, are all the advantages which

*Brianne Wolf*

we can propose to derive from it" (TMS I.iii.2.1). Conversely, we want to avoid poverty, because this makes it less likely that we will be able to gain the approbation of our peers. In these ways, when making moral judgments about our peers we substitute wealth, or the appearance of wealth, for virtue in our judgment of their character and moral worth as people deserving of our fellow-feeling.

Smith offers two solutions to the problem of the extent of sympathy in *Theory of Moral Sentiments*: (1) moral education through the development of the impartial spectator and (2) general rules of morality.[15] The impartial spectator is a perspective one can adopt to judge one's behavior as an objective observer would view it, or to view other's behavior in the same way. "It is he who, whenever we are about to act so as to affect the happiness of others, calls to us, with a voice capable of astonishing the most presumptuous of our passions, that we are but one of the multitude, in no respect better than any other in it; and that when we prefer ourselves so shamefully and so blindly to others, we become the proper objects of resentment" (TMS III.3.4). The impartial spectator is developed through repeated sympathetic interactions with others. Because it necessarily involves being objective or "impartial" with regard to our own behavior, it is difficult to adopt the perspective of this man within the breast, as Smith refers to him; however, this perspective can be developed and exercised with practice. Smith explains the exercise of the impartial spectator as self-command.

Similarly, general rules of morality are formed based on what human beings would decide if they were being their best selves and exercising self-command in various particular situations. Smith explains, "The general rule . . . is formed, by finding from experience, that all the actions of a certain kind, or circumstanced in a certain manner, are approved or disapproved of" (TMS III.4.8). General rules exist as "standards of judgment" to be referred to in moments of human weakness, when we would tend to be overly partial to ourselves, or when we cannot judge impartially because of the influence of our passions (TMS III.4.11). They are established on a society-wide basis to help guide human behavior toward standards of justice.

Though Smith offers these two solutions to the problem of what he calls "self-deceit" or our tendency to prefer ourselves to others, these solutions are ineffective in the case of the poor law.[16] The rule being applied in the case of the poor law reinforces our tendency toward self-deceit; that is, it plays upon our difficulty with sympathizing outside of our social rank and our predisposition to value wealth and deride poverty. The law does not encourage the overseers or, as I will explain in the next section, the people of England to overcome themselves, but appeals to their base inclinations that the poor should be treated as objects.

Smith explains how the problem of the extent of sympathy with respect to social rank plays out in the administration of the overseers. He explains that the main issue lies in how the legitimacy of the settlement of laborers is established—through the judgment of the overseers. As Smith explains in TMS, those of higher social rank, such as the overseers, are predisposed to ignore or look down upon the poor: "The mere want of fortune, mere poverty, excites little compassion. Its complaints are too apt to be the objects rather of contempt than of fellow-feeling. We despise a beggar; and, though his importunities may extort an alms from us, he is scarce ever the object of any serious commiseration" (TMS III.3.18). The overseers are unlikely to approach their interactions with the laboring poor as opportunities for sympathetic interaction. Further, it is unlikely that they will approach the poor with a favorable perspective. There was a similar assumption of guilt and depravity in the laboring poor on the part of lawmakers who assumed that the poor would try to take advantage of the system to get on the relief rolls of another parish. Indeed, Smith quotes Dr. Burns's history of the poor law where he notes that all amendments to the law were to prevent poor people from "clandestinely" establishing residence in a parish (WN I.x.c.50).

Further, our propensity to substitute wealth for virtue when making moral judgments is an important part of Smith's story of the failure of the poor law. The overseers are again and again put in charge of determining the legitimacy of incoming laborers to a new parish, and yet Smith notes how often they were corrupt: "Some frauds, it is said, were committed in consequence of this statute; parish officers sometimes bribing their own poor to go clandestinely to another parish, and by keeping themselves concealed for forty days to gain a settlement there, to the discharge of that to which they properly belonged" (WN I.x.c.48). Recall that the overseers were also responsible for raising the funds that would pay for the relief of the poor. They wanted to avoid being responsible for more poor than was necessary, even if this prevented men who wanted work from finding a job. Smith's argument in TMS that our propensity to substitute wealth and rank for virtue often allows us to overlook corruption in the wealthy is particularly relevant here:

> We desire both to be respectable and to be respected. We dread both to be contemptible and to be contemned. But, upon coming into the world, we soon find that wisdom and virtue are by no means the sole objects of respect; nor vice and folly, of contempt. We frequently see the respectful attentions of the world more strongly directed towards the rich and the great, than towards the wise and the virtuous. We see frequently the vices and follies of the powerful much less despised than the poverty and weakness of the innocent. (TMS I.iii.3.2)

Smith notes that we tend to use wealth as a measure for virtue when determining what behavior and which people deserve our approbation. This tendency causes us to approve of the rich and look down on the poor. Even worse than substituting wealth for virtue, we use their wealth to excuse the vices of the rich:

> To superficial minds, the vices of the great seem at all times agreeable. They connect them, not only with the splendor of fortune, but with many superior virtues, which they ascribe to their superiors; with the spirit of freedom and independency, with frankness, generosity, humanity, and politeness. The virtues of the inferior ranks of people, on the contrary, their parsimonious frugality, their painful industry, and rigid adherence to rules, seem to them mean and disagreeable. They connect them, both with the meanness of the station to which those qualities commonly belong, and with many great vices, which, they suppose, usually accompany them; such as an abject, cowardly, ill-natured, lying, pilfering disposition. (TMS V.2.3)

Because we want to be like the rich and rise to their rank, assuming that we will be happier and more comfortable if we have the "superfluities" (TMS I.iii.2.1) and "trinkets" like ear pickers and nail clippers (TMS IV.1.8) the rich have, we excuse the means that it took for them to get there. We excuse the bad behavior of the rich even though the standards of justice are "accurate in the highest degree, and admit of no exceptions or modifications" (TMS III.6.10). According to Smith, there was widespread corruption in the practices of the officers who were to administer the terms of the law: "But parish officers, it seems, were not always more honest with regard to their own, than they had been with regard to other parishes, and sometimes connived at such intrusions, receiving the notice, and taking no proper steps in consequence of it" (WN I.x.c.49). And yet, with each new revision to the Settlement Act, the overseers were given more power, in the form of certificates, to determine if a poor laborer would be allowed to move parishes.

## Social Rank, the Corruption of Our Moral Judgment, and the Effect on Liberty

As we can see through the case of the poor law, our ability to fairly judge the behavior of others and therefore determine who should be objects of our sympathy is often corrupted by our propensity to substitute wealth for virtue and by the distance between peoples of different social status. As Smith puts it, "This disposition to admire, and almost to worship, the rich and powerful, and to despise, or, at least, to neglect persons of poor and mean condition, though necessary both to establish and to maintain the distinction of ranks and the order of society, is, at the same time, the great and most universal cause of the corruption of our moral sentiments" (TMS I.iii.3.1). The poor law played upon this propensity and corrupted the moral judgment of those involved. The terms of the Settlement Act put laborers in the position of being scrutinized and looked down upon by the overseers. This tendency of not seeing the poor as people worthy of sympathy or worthy of trust that they would do their work without taking advantage of the relief rolls was very widespread. Smith reflects, "There is scarce a poor man in England of forty years of age, I will venture to say, who has not in some part of his life felt himself most cruelly oppressed by this ill-contrived law of settlements" (WN I.x.c.59).

Understanding the ways Smith suggests that distance in sympathetic relationships can be overcome is important, and yet they demonstrate why his discussion of the poor law is even more crucial—because the law inhibits these solutions and preys upon the natural propensities that corrupt our moral judgment. Because the law puts the laborers in a subordinate position to the overseers and the rest of society, everyone is encouraged not to experience the poor as sympathetic beings, but instead to treat them as objects to be administered. Therefore it was very difficult for those who most needed work to find it. Smith argues that the unequal price of labor between parishes makes it so that those who have the potential to be bigger burdens on parish relief rolls are less likely to be given a certificate to work in another parish: "A single man, indeed, who is healthy and industrious, may sometimes reside by sufferance without one; but a man with a wife and family who should attempt to do so, would in most parishes be sure of being removed, and if the single man should afterwards marry, he would generally be removed likewise" (WN I.x.c.58). Ironically, those with families and children who would be the biggest burden on a relief roll are the ones least likely to be given a chance to find work. Their social rank precludes any potential for them to be seen as people worthy of sympathy. Additionally, Smith notes that because the certificates do not tell anything more than the origin of the laborer and perhaps also his family situation (i.e., the amount of relief the parish would be responsible for should he need it), they are not a good representation of character. The laborer's certificate, by indicating their potential burden in numeric terms only precludes any opportunity for those administering them to sympathize with them. Yet the overseers used these certificates as though they did determine the character of the worker, merely because they indicated his social rank. Smith describes the problem saying, "Though a certificate carries along with it no testimonial of good behaviour, and certifies nothing but that the person belongs to the parish to which he really does belong, it is altogether discretionary in the parish officers either to grant or to refuse it" (WN I.x.c.57). Because of its requirement of establishing residency and obtaining a certificate from one's previous parish, the poor law promoted the judgment of poor laborers as social deviants, as objects, rather than people deserving of sympathy.

The sympathetic distance between rich and poor is also reflected in the vast difference in wages between physical distances. Smith describes the gap created between different parishes and unequal wages of labor in terms of distance: "Yet we [Scotland] never meet with those sudden and unaccountable differences in the wages of neighbouring places which we sometimes find in

England, where it is often more difficult for a poor man to pass the artificial boundary of a parish, than an arm of the sea or a ridge of high mountains, natural boundaries which sometimes separate very distinctly different rates of wages in other countries" (WN I.x.c.58). Just as it was difficult for poor men to pass the physical boundary between parishes as though there were physical impediments, it is also difficult for them to surpass the sympathetic boundary between them and men of higher rank. The way Smith describes this boundary is striking. The distance between parishes and between the poor laborers and everyone else is as tangible, in Smith's account, as physical boundaries like water or a mountain.

As we have seen, for Smith, the poor law violated more than economic liberty. It also violated natural liberty and justice. The distance between rich and poor prevented overseers from sympathizing with the laborers they were responsible for judging and administering. Worse than this, their own rank and their propensity to look down upon the poor caused the overseers to judge them as moral miscreants whose only value was their social rank, rather than as people worthy of sympathy. The parish officers prevented workers from finding jobs and establishing residence in their parishes because they assumed they would become a burden to them. Smith argues, "To remove a man who has committed no misdemeanour from the parish where he chuses to reside, is an evident violation of natural liberty and justice" (WN I.x.c.59). As he points out here, the poor law distorted more than the liberty of the market. He clearly states that the consequences of the law had moral effects for the natural liberty of the workers and for standards of justice more broadly defined.

Smith also laments that the masses cannot see the impropriety and injustice of the law. They cannot see how it affects not only the workers' liberty and well-being, but theirs as well. First, Smith reflects on the negotiations of wages between masters and workmen and how this affects both the economy and moral relationships between rich and poor (WN I.x.c.60-63). He recalls an earlier discussion about the organization of workers as opposed to the organization of masters. "Whenever the legislature attempts to regulate the differences between masters and their workmen, its counsellors are always the masters" (WN I.x.c.61). The imposition of the legislature into issues of wage labor rarely favors the workers, Smith tells us. When the legislature tries to regulate the wages of labor, they favor the masters, partly because of their ability to sympathize with those who are in the same social situation as they are, and for the other reasons Smith gives for why the poor are often not considered as objects of sympathy. Here again is another argument for the ability of the market to improve the condition of the least well-off. Smith notes a similar problem with negotiations over the wages of labor between masters and workers. He argues that while people typically think of workers organizing to raise their wages, masters also collude to lower the wages of labor, often with the help of the civil magistrate (WN I.viii.14).

Smith also worries about the common citizens of England who are negatively affected by the way the poor law frames the poor among them, their fellows: "The common people of England, however, so jealous of their liberty, but like the common people of most other countries never rightly understanding wherein it consists, have now for more than a century together suffered themselves to be exposed to this oppression without a remedy" (WN I.x.c.59). Again, it is not only the overseers who cannot view the poor as people worthy of sympathy, the masses cannot and do not either; however, Smith notes that they should, because their liberty is also affected by the economic and sympathetic distortions the law causes. Though we have a "sacred regard to general rules" and therefore the natural standards of justice are strong within us and are supposed to prevent us from making judgments according to custom and fashion, as Smith demonstrates in this example, sometimes our sentiments, and even our moral standards, can be corrupted (TMS III.5.2). Because of the structure of the law, even the general citizens of England fell prey to self-deceit, being more concerned about "the thought of their own safety, the thought that they themselves are not really the sufferers" than realizing how they were being deprived of their liberty because of the harm done to the economy and their relationship with their fellow citizens (TMS I.1.4.7).

## THE MORAL AND MATERIAL CONSEQUENCES OF THE POOR LAW: ON THE MARKET ORDER AND MARKET PROCESS

In this chapter, I have shown through the example of the poor law that Smith both argues for the potential moral benefits of commercial society and cautions against its potential moral harms. By reading his account of the poor law in WN together with his theory of sympathy in TMS, I have shown that Smith argues against the poor law on both economic and moral grounds. The poor law is economically problematic because it prevents labor mobility and thus a free market. Smith focuses on how the requirement of a certificate of settlement to live in a particular parish prevents the poor from freely following the market for labor between parishes. Parishes are reluctant to take on new workers, as each parish is responsible for the care of their poor. This causes several problems for the market process, among them the difference in the price of labor between neighboring parishes. The poor law is morally problematic because it plays upon our propensity to approve of the rich and ignore the poor as people worthy of our sympathy. The rules of the Settlement Act that required the poor to carry certificates from their parish to move between parishes reduced them to their social rank. Therefore, the overseers in charge of judging these poor laborers treated them not as other people deserving of sympathy, but as objects to be administered that they often deemed harmful to society. The problem of the extent of sympathy in this case also encouraged the rest of society to overlook the corruption of the wardens and to take their moral judgments of the poor as true because of their high social rank. These two problems with the poor law demonstrate how the distortion of the market by one rule actually furthered the morally problematic nature of the market and prevented the market from improving the situation of the least well-off.

Smith's comments about this law are also important for understanding the market process and market order. Hayek ([1976] 1978) argued that the market order does not seek a particular end, but is characterized by the science of catallaxy, in which people coordinate their ends under a set of rules (107–9). Smith's argument about the poor law shows how one particular rule distorted the process and made the conditions of the market less fair, namely because it prevented laborers from following the market for labor, especially men with families who arguably needed work the most. This is turn caused parishes to have even more laborers on their relief rolls, and it artificially raised wages in certain parishes and depressed wages in others.

Further, the poor law also prevented individuals from seeking information from the market. Kirzner talks about the market as a process characterized by ignorance and discovery (1992, 44), where people are constantly engaging in information seeking. However, this information can be misleading if the process has been interfered with by a centralized administration. He puts it: "Not only is it the case, as traditional economics has demonstrated since Adam Smith, that market efficiency can prevail in spite of the absence of centralized direction. It turns out, as it happens, that the market process approach shows that such absence of centralized direction is in fact necessary, if the kind of co-ordination (we have seen to be achievable through the market process) is to be attained at all" (Kirzner 1992, 51). This is exactly what Smith explains has happened in the case of the poor law. The law caused vastly different prices for labor in neighboring parishes, which distorted people's information and therefore their ability to act as entrepreneurs who find opportunities in the market—namely through finding work. Like Smith, Kirzner links this disruption of the market process back to liberty: "Individual liberty is that ingredient in that definition upon which the success of the market process depends. Individual liberty is not a circumstance in spite of which markets work; it is the crucial circumstance which permits the market process to work" (Kirzner 1992, 53). In other words, people can coordinate their efforts if they are receiving the right information through the market process. The poor law expanded the propensity of individuals to treat one another as objects.

It is important to note that for both Hayek and Kirzner, the market order and market process require treating other people as equal if we are to coordinate our ends with them. That is, we do not view others as less than ourselves. Smith's work in WN, and as I have argued here, TMS, was also predicated on this idea of "analytical egalitarianism."[17] In his famous street porter and philosopher example, Smith shows that in terms of the market, we are all on equal footing. That is, for the purpose of analysis, Smith treats people as fundamentally equal. The market process shows us how we both need one another and can be a help to one another. Smith explains how the market shows us our mutual dependence:

> Is this improvement in the circumstances of the lower ranks of the people to be regarded as an advantage or as an inconvenience to the society? The answer seems at first sight abundantly plain. Servants, labourers and workmen of different kinds, make up the far greater part of every political society. But what improves the circumstances of the greater part can never be regarded as an inconveniency to the whole. No society can be flourishing and happy, of which the far greater part of the members are poor and miserable. It is but equity, besides, that they who feed, cloath and lodge the whole body of the people, should have such a share of the produce of their own labour as to be themselves tolerably well fed, cloathed and lodged. (WN I.viii.36)

The poor law encourages viewing the poor laborers as "other," as different and undeserving, but Smith argues that they are essential to the flourishing of society as a whole and therefore ought to be treated as equals. In this way, the market should extend our ability to sympathize with others.[18] However, as his arguments about the poor law demonstrate, interference in this process can play upon our proclivity not to see one another as equals and people deserving of fellow-feeling. The English masses were "jealous of their liberty" because they feared the laborers; therefore, they sought to secure their own interests by limiting the mobility of the laboring poor, rather than working with them through the market process. The distortion of the market caused by the law cultivated a morally undesirable outcome, viewing distant others as unequal.

Smith's goal was to allow the market to do its work of improving the situation for the least well-off, while mitigating its potential to prevent people from engaging in sympathetic relationships with one another. While Smith praised the division of labor for including more workers in the market, he also acknowledged that some laws would be necessary to uphold justice. The market order is governed by certain rules. For example, he acknowledged the government should provide the laboring poor with an education so that their ability to participate in sympathetic relationships with others would not be impeded. It is not a complex education that Smith calls for, but one that would be sufficient enough to improve faculties of judgment, so that the laborer could participate more robustly in his private life, namely "rational conversation," "sentiment," and judgments about the actions of his country (WN V.i.f.50).

In Smith's effort to show both the economic and moral dimensions of the problem of the poor law, he demonstrates how the market could work if people were given the liberty to pursue their ends. In the case of the poor law, laborers would have a better chance of finding work if they could follow the market for labor. Further, they could follow the circulation of labor with dignity and could interact with and be judged by their fellows as objects worthy of sympathy, rather than merely as objects.

## NOTES

1. The author is grateful to Richard Avramenko, Peter Boettke, Christopher Coyne, Michelle Schwarze, Virgil Storr, and the members of the Adam Smith Fellowship Research Sequence 2015–2016: Jerrod Anderson, Nick Cowen, Jason Douglas, Crystal Dozier, Frank Garmon, Bryan Leonard, Nick O'Neill, Audrey Redford, Nathan Sawatzky, Dan Shahar, and Samuel Zeitlin, for helpful feedback on earlier versions of this chapter. All remaining errors are my own.

2. All references are to Adam Smith, *An Inquiry into the Nature and Causes of the Wealth of Nations*, ed. R.H. Campbell, A. S. Skinner, and W. B. Todd, 2 vols. (Indianapolis: Liberty Fund, 1981 [1776]).

3. Smith scholars have recently been questioning the extent to which Smith advocates spontaneous order rather than disorder. (See, for example, Schwarze and Scott 2015).

4. Sandel (2012) makes a similar argument, saying that not everything should be "up for sale" or governed by market norms because market values can replace non-market values.

5. Wight (2005) explains that this view of the market as promoting "greed as good" is so prevalent that there is both a supply and demand argument for greed taken from Adam Smith's work.

6. See for example Smith's opening line "How selfish soever man may be supposed. . ." (TMS I.i.1.1); or Smith's comments near the end of TMS: "Dr. Mandeville . . . Man, he observes, is naturally much more interested in his own happiness than that of others, and it is impossible that in his heart he can ever really prefer their prosperity to his own" (TMS VII.ii.4.7). (Smith [1759] 1982).

7. Smith scholars have not often engaged Smith's discussion of this law. Samuel Fleischacker (2004, 205) mentions it as part of his defense of how revolutionary Smith's treatment of the poor was in WN, namely that Smith advocated for the state to redistribute aid. See also Fleischacker's *Third Concept of Liberty: Judgment and Freedom in Kant and Adam Smith* (1999, 167), though Fleischacker refutes this reading of the passage in his later book. (See also Rasmussen 2008, 106–7.)

8. For a historical account of the poor law see Boyer (2006), Beito (2000), Himmelfarb (1983), Slack (1990). Additionally, it is worth noting that Smith was not the only thinker in his time and beyond to have recognized problems with the law. Alexis de Tocqueville, for example, also wrote against the law for its harmful economic and moral effects in his *Memoir on Pauperism* (1835). David Hume ([1778] 1938, iv, 380) briefly mentions the poor law in Volume IV of *The History of England* saying, "In the fifth of this reign [Queen Elizabeth] was enacted the first law for the relief of the poor."

9. For an argument on how the market can provide happiness by helping to secure political liberty and security see Rasmussen (2006).

10. Fleischacker (2004, 209) writes, "WN's greatest triumph is a shift in our moral imaginations—it leads readers to imagine the poor person differently—and it was the central teaching of TMS that how we imagine other is what most profoundly shapes our characters and moral attitudes."

11. Similarly, McCloskey (1973) analyzes the ways the agricultural labor market was distorted by the law, arguing that the poor law functioned like an income subsidy. The editors of *Wealth of Nations* note that Smith likely overestimated the extent to which the poor law interfered with labor mobility. (See Smith [1776] 1981, 152n50.)

12. Walter I. Trattner (1994) provides an example of a modern historian citing the poor law as the beginning of the modern welfare state.

13. It is important to note that Smith did not argue for the repeal of the law, but only against the part of the law that limited both labor and sympathy, namely the Settlement Act. (See Himmelfarb 1983, 61). It is apparent in the rest of his work that he was very interested in improving the material condition of the least well-off (e.g., Herzog, 2016; Storr, forthcoming).

14. See Hill (2006) for more on the concept of corruption in Smith's work.

15. There could be a third solution to the problem of proximity in sympathy—the market. Paganelli (2010) explores this idea, arguing that the market provides the appropriate amount of distance for moral development.

16. See Fleischacker (2011) for an extended discussion of Smith's arguments about and solutions to self-deceit.

17. See Levy and Peart (2009) for more on analytical egalitarianism.

18. See Storr (forthcoming) for a recent analysis of this idea.

# REFERENCES

Bartels, Larry M. 2008. *Unequal Democracy: The Political Economy of the New Gilded Age*. Princeton, NJ: Princeton University Press.

Beito, David T. 2000. *From Mutual Aid to the Welfare State: Fraternal Societies and Social Services, 1890–1967*. Chapel Hill: University of North Carolina Press.

Blaug, Mark. 1963. "The Myth of the Old Poor Law and the Making of the New," *Journal of Economic History* 23 (2): 151–84.

Boyer, George. 2006. *An Economic History of the English Poor Law, 1750–1850*. New York: Cambridge University Press.

Fleischacker, Samuel. 2004. *On Adam Smith's Wealth of Nations: A Philosophical Companion*. Princeton, NJ: Princeton University Press.

———. 1999. *Third Concept of Liberty: Judgment and Freedom in Kant and Adam Smith*. Princeton, NJ: Princeton University Press.

———. 2011. "True to Ourselves? Adam Smith on Self-Deceit." *Adam Smith Review* 6: 75–92.

Forman-Barzilai, Fonna. 2005. "Sympathy in Space(S): Adam Smith on Proximity." *Political Theory* 33 (2): 189–217.

Gilens, Martin. 2012. *Affluence and Influence: Economic Inequality and Political Power in America*. Princeton, NJ: Princeton University Press.

Griswold, Charles L. 1999. *Adam Smith and the Virtues of Enlightenment*. Cambridge: Cambridge University Press.

Hacker, Jacob S., and Paul Pierson. 2011. *Winner-Take-All Politics: How Washington Made the Rich Richer, and Turned Its Back on the Middle Class*. New York: Simon & Schuster.

Hanley, Ryan Patrick. 2008. "Commerce and Corruption: Rousseau's Diagnosis and Adam Smith's Cure." *European Journal of Political Theory* 7 (2): 137–58.

Hayek, F. A. (1976) 1978. "The Market Order or Catallaxy." Chap. 10 in *Law, Legislation and Liberty*. Chicago: University of Chicago Press.

Herzog, Lisa. 2016. "The Normative Stakes of Economic Growth; or, Why Adam Smith Does Not Rely on 'Trickle Down.'" *Journal of Politics* 78 (1): 50–61.

Hill, Lisa. 2006. "Adam Smith and the Theme of Corruption." *Review of Politics* 68 (4): 636–62.

Himmelfarb, Gertrude. 1983. *The Idea of Poverty: England in the Early Industrial Age*. New York: Alfred A. Knopf.

Hume, David. (1778) 1938. *The History of England from the Invasion of Julius Caesar to the Revolution in 1688*. 6 vols. Indianapolis: Liberty Fund.

Kirzner, Israel. 1992. "The Meaning of Market Process." Chap. 2 in *The Meaning of the Market Process*. New York: Routledge.

Levy, David M., and Sandra Peart. 2009. *The Street Porter and the Philosopher: Conversations on Analytical Egalitarianism*. Ann Arbor: University of Michigan Press.

Mandeville, Bernard. (1732) 1924. *The Fable of the Bees; or, Private Vices, Publick Benefits*. Oxford: Clarendon Press.

McCloskey, Deirdre N. 1973. "New Perspectives on the Old Poor Law," *Explorations in Economic History* 10 (4): 419–36.

McCloskey, Deirdre N. 2006. *The Burgeois Virtues: Ethics for an Age of Commerce*. Chicago: University of Chicago Press.

Otteson, James R. 2002. *Adam Smith's Marketplace of Life*. Cambridge: Cambridge University Press.

Paganelli, Maria Pia. 2010. "The Moralizing Role of Distance in Adam Smith: *The Theory of Moral Sentiments* as Possible Praise of Commerce." *History of Political Economy* 42 (3): 425–41.

Piketty, Thomas. 2014. *Capital in the Twenty-First Century*. Cambridge: Harvard University Press.

Pitts, Jennifer. 2017. "Irony in Adam Smith's Critical Global History." *Political Theory* 45 (2): 141–63.

Rasmussen, Dennis C. 2006. "Does 'Bettering Our Condition' Really Make Us Better Off? Adam Smith on Progress and Happiness." *American Political Science Review* 100 (3): 309–18.

———. 2008. *The Problems and Promise of Commercial Society: Adam Smith's Response to Rousseau*. University Park: Pennsylvania State University Press.

Sandel, Michael J. 2012. *What Money Can't Buy: The Moral Limits of Markets*. New York: Farrar, Straus and Giroux.

Schwarze, Michelle, and John T. Scott. 2015. "Spontaneous Disorder in Adam Smith's Theory of Moral Sentiments: Resentment, Injustice, and the Appeal to Providence." *Journal of Politics* 77 (2): 463–76.

Slack, Paul. 1990. *The English Poor Law, 1531–1782*. Edited by Economic History Society. Cambridge: Cambridge University Press.

Smith, Adam. 1981 [1776]. *An Inquiry into the Nature and Causes of the Wealth of Nations*. Edited by R. H. Campbell, A. S. Skinner, and W. B. Todd. 2 vols. Indianapolis: Liberty Fund.

———. (1759) 1982. *The Theory of Moral Sentiments*. Edited by D. D. Raphael and A. L. Macfie. Indianapolis: Liberty Fund.

Storr, Virgil Henry. Forthcoming. "The Impartial Spectator and the Moral Teachings of Markets." In *Oxford Handbook of Freedom*, edited by D. Schmidtz. New York: Oxford University Press.

Trattner, Walter I. 1994. *From Poor Law to Welfare State: A History of Social Welfare in America*. Fifth edition. New York: Free Press.

Wight, Jonathan B. 2005. "Adam Smith and Greed," *Journal of Private Enterprise* 21 (1): 46–58.

*Chapter 3*

# Why Be Robust?

## *The Contribution of Market Process Theory to the Robust Political Economy Research Program*

### Nick Cowen

The purpose of this chapter is to show how the robust political economy (RPE) framework can provide a unique perspective to political theory. The premise of RPE is that institutions should be evaluated by comparing their capacities to solve knowledge and incentive problems. I argue that these problems are also important concerns for political theorists who would like their research to reflect realistic challenges to economic cooperation. This raises a question: Through what conceptual framework should different institutions be compared? My case is that a combined application of Austrian market process theory and public choice is the most promising way of comparing the robustness of institutions. This combination offers an enriched account of individual behavior in political settings compared to traditional public choice analysis and neoclassical economic approaches to institutional analysis.

The structure of this chapter is as follows. I begin with a vignette of an experience playing a prisoners' dilemma game in a behavioral economics laboratory that illustrates some limits of formal rational choice analysis. I link this description to Vincent Ostrom's critical appraisal of the public choice research program, where he proposed absorbing Austrian market process insights into the analysis of individual behavior in collective decision settings. I then describe my approach to RPE as such a combination, its characteristic features, and its underlying assumptions.

My approach highlights the epistemic properties of market institutions as opposed to their more commonly recognized role in aligning individual incentives with socially beneficial outcomes. In order to do this, I make use of Kirzner's (1987, 46; 2000, 264) two levels of spontaneous order analysis, codified by Boettke (2014) as the market process and the market order. This approach has parallels with Buchanan's distinction between constitutional and post-constitutional arenas of political exchange (Boettke 2014, 243; Buchanan and Tullock 1999) but recognizes in greater depth the epistemic barriers to constitutional formation (Pennington 2015).

This division between the market process and the market order allows us to differentiate accounts of agents coordinating within a given institutional framework of private property and voluntary exchange, and the much more challenging collective task agents face when establishing that protective framework in the absence of an informative price mechanism. This explains how RPE can extend neoclassical accounts of the performance, development, and failure of political institutions. I argue that this epistemic account offers a wider role for normative ideas, including ideas in political theory, as mechanisms for understanding each other's behavior and coordinating modes of social cooperation, than other more incentive-led or materialist accounts of institutions. I show what this perspective can contribute to Rawls's contractarian theory of justice and to realism in political theory.

## THE LIMITS OF A NEOCLASSICAL FRAMEWORK

Some years ago, I took a methodology course in rational choice theory. As part of our first class, we were taken to a new, gleaming behavioral economics laboratory to play a repeated prisoners' dilemma game. The system randomly paired anonymous members of the class to play against each other. We were told the objective of the game was to maximize our individual scores. Thinking that there were clear gains to make from cooperation and plenty of opportunities to punish a defector over the course of repeated interactions, I attempted to cooperate on the first round. My partner defected. I defected a couple of times subsequently to show I was not a sucker. Then I tried cooperating once more. My partner defected every single time in the repeated series.

At the end of the game, we were de-anonymized and it turned out, unsurprisingly, that I had the lowest score in the class. My partner had the second lowest. I asked her why she engaged in an evidently suboptimal strategy. She explained: "I didn't think we were playing to get the most points. I was just trying to beat you!"

Game theoretic models like the prisoners' dilemma have proved to be compelling and productive analytical tools in social science, clarifying the core of many challenges to collective action. The prisoners' dilemma illustrates how given certain situations, or rules of the game, self-interested agents will be stymied from reaching optimal or mutually beneficial outcomes. But my experience illustrates a general finding that there is often something more complex going on even in relatively simple social interactions.

The laboratory situation replicated the formal prisoners' dilemma model as closely as possible with explicit rules, quantified "objective" (though admittedly, in this case, low-value) payoffs, and a situation designed to isolate players as if they were prisoners in different cells. Yet even in these carefully controlled circumstances, it turns out that the situation is subject to multiple interpretations and understandings. Whatever the textual explanation accompanying the game, the score on the screen could mean something different to the various players. The payoffs for the representative agents in the game were not the same as the payoffs in the minds of the human players. In a sense, my partner and I were unwittingly playing different games (although I lost within either rules of the game!).

When we engage with the social world, it is not only the case that our interests may not align with other people's, rather it's a question of who gets a seat on the bus or the last chocolate torte at the buffet. We are also uncertain as to what people's interests and motivations are. Social interaction is open ended. We do not know all the possible moves in the game, and we do not know much about the preference set of everyone else who is playing. Indeed, neither they nor we know what a "complete" set of preferences and payoffs would look like, even of our own (Shackle 1970, 100). We can map out a few options and likely outcomes through reflection and experience, but even then we may face outcomes we do not anticipate. As Boettke (2014, 236) explains: "We strive not only to pursue our ends with a judicious selection of the means, but also to discover what ends that we hope to pursue."

In addition, the rules of the game themselves are not, in the final analysis, merely exogenous impositions on us as agents. They are constituted intersubjectively by the practices, beliefs, and values of the actors who are also participants in the social game (Grube and Storr 2015; Boettke and Storr 2002). The social world thus presents inherent uncertainty and change that cannot be captured in a formal model that assumes fixed rules of the game and the given knowledge of the players.

This account illustrates some limits to a neoclassical economic framework that assumes given preferences and utility maximizing agents who act independently with complete information (Weintraub 1993). I now turn briefly to why these limits are relevant for behavior in political settings in particular.

## Ostrom's Challenge to Public Choice

What is left unexplained by the formal rational choice approach? In "Epistemic Choice and Public Choice," Ostrom (1993) considered how these sorts of limits to modeling human behavior within given rules, actions, and beliefs impact on the economic analysis of politics. He assessed the prospects of the public choice research program as he then saw it. On his account, public choice made substantial contributions to understanding collective choice through the application of neoclassical economic analysis to nonmarket situations (cf. Ostrom and Ostrom 1971, 205). It showed that a simple account of empirical or theoretical "market failures" was insufficient to show that a government alternative was more efficient or inevitably preferable to voluntary exchange. In order to know whether government or market institutions are superior for a particular case requires a more systematic comparison of institutions where behavioral assumptions can be clarified.

At the same time, public choice throws up some problems of its own, notably a conceptual ambiguity with regard to rationality. Are all human decisions rational by definition or do rational actors possess some empirically falsifiable characteristics, such as a tendency to selfishness (Kogelmann 2015)? How can actors commit to, or carry out, actions that, on most plausible definitions, diverge significantly from their self-interest, such as self-sacrifice (Sen 1977)?

This sort of behavior is more relevant in collective-decision settings, where publicly shared values are at stake. Such situations stretch the assumptions of rational action as applied classically to market exchange. One result of this is that it is has proved relatively easy for skeptics of public choice methodology to dismiss its insights as an irrelevant, abstract, and implausibly cynical way of modeling political actors (Dunleavy 2002).

Ostrom notes that these limits to public choice are known and acknowledged among its founding theorists. Buchanan and Vanberg (1991), for example, expound on the non-economizing aspects of individual production and exchange behavior. When discussing an idealized constitutional framework, Buchanan (2001, 184) presumes actors have social values and motivations that extend far beyond any narrow selfish conception of individual welfare. Nevertheless, thinking around these issues has taken place on what Ostrom calls the "periphery" of the public choice research program because it lies outside the relative comfort of thin formal modeling and statistical empirical testing that make up a great deal of public choice research, as well as the dominant quantitative approaches of contemporary political science.

In response to these sorts of challenges, Ostrom asks theorists to consider more thoroughly the assumptions underlying the logic of public choice, a program he calls "epistemic choice." He suggests that the capacity for individuals to engage in collective choice depends on their ability to generate and share information about themselves, and subsequently frame and influence each other's individual desires and capacities. He calls for an exploration of how human beings are capable of transforming their understanding of the world such that their observable "interests" that guide action can be transformed as well, noting the significance of "the Austrian emphasis upon the information-generating aspects of free trade in the presence of stable monetized exchange relationships" (V. Ostrom 1993, 169) for this endeavor. RPE is one answer to this challenge.

## WHAT IS ROBUST POLITICAL ECONOMY?

RPE is a framework of analysis inspired by the broad research program of "mainline" economics (Boettke 2012). It has been used to make a specific defense of classical liberal approaches to public policy (Pennington 2011). The core presumption of RPE is that, in order to be commendable, institutions aiming at human welfare should be *robust* to realistic challenges that are significant features of human political and social life.

Proponents characterize robustness as institutions capable of dealing with "hard" cases rather than merely "easy" cases in public policy (Boettke and Leeson 2004, 100). This means evaluating institutions on the basis of a range of possible conditions rather than the ideal conditions to which they are perfectly suited. They impute the two core realistic problems facing a political community to be those of knowledge and incentives (Pennington 2011; Leeson and Subrick 2006). Thus, robust institutions are those able to induce successful social cooperation even when participants lack important relevant information and have divergent individual interests of their own. In this sense, robustness is a "stress test" for institutions and theories. By focusing on these problems, RPE avoids political romanticism (Buchanan 1999, 45; Levy 2002) and utilizes instead the "worst-case scenario" theorizing that is embedded in much traditional liberal political thought (Farrant and Crampton 2008).

Communities have ameliorated these challenges through the use of social institutions—that is, formal and informal rules and norms that guide individual conduct (Pennington 2011, 192). For proponents of robustness, these institutions are primarily private property and voluntary exchange within a framework of the rule of law. Such a regime establishes domains of exclusive, but alienable, control over resources. This allows individuals to engage in productive activity and exchange on the presumption that they will not be interfering with the similar activity of others in different domains and are, at the same time, themselves protected from predation and interference. This facilitates individually beneficial activity and social cooperation, generates and shares dispersed knowledge, and aligns individual incentives with activity that subjectively benefits all participants.

### Why Knowledge and Incentives?

Why does RPE identify the key social problems as knowledge and incentives? My contention is that these two problems emerge from three key compelling, though inevitably contested (Lukes 1968; Hodgson 2007), assumptions, or constraints on our form of explanation: (1) methodological individualism, (2) subjectivism, and (3) analytical egalitarianism.

By methodological individualism, I mean the assumption that social activity is constituted, in the final analysis though not necessarily at all points in an explanation, by embodied human beings, rather than aggregated structures. By subjectivism, I mean the notion that individuals act on the basis of their own separate beliefs, experiences, and values (Hayek 1937; 1943, 5) that at best can only ever be partially articulated and shared with other agents. Our methods of communicating our thoughts and feelings are not given, and even when present, imperfect. By analytical egalitarianism, I mean a presumption of rough equality of power or capacity between individuals. This excludes the examination of inherent individual characteristics as an explanation of different social outcomes.

The problems of knowledge and incentives are two sources of disorder, or lack of coordination, that emerge from these assumptions. That is, they are present when humans have the characteristics of embodied individuals with their own mental lives and rough equality of power between them. There is no special agent that can naturally overpower the others and dictate the outcomes of the interaction. The knowledge problem is the result of these individuals encountering and interpreting a dynamic natural and social world through their limited senses and cognitive capacities. They face radical uncertainty as to the opportunities and threats they face, and bounded rationality when processing relevant information to guide their actions. The incentive problem emerges as a result of individuals or groups encountering others with subjective interests and objectives that are unreconciled with their own.

Although knowledge and incentive problems are distinct, their influence on each other means that considering them together allows us to better understand the challenge of human sociability (cf. Gamble 1989, 1). The knowledge problem extends to ignorance of the intentions and interests of others so that individuals are uncertain, for example, as to what might constitute an effective incentive for other individuals or groups. At the same time, lack of knowledge heavily influences the incentives that individuals face. In some contexts, this generates narrow, defensive attitudes that prevent potentially productive co-operation.

## THE MARKET PROCESS AS A SOLUTION
## TO THE KNOWLEDGE PROBLEM

The knowledge problem, alongside incentives problems, is a barrier to social coordination that formal models cannot capture in its entirety. This is because such models assume a given range of choices and cannot include unknown choices within a set that have yet to be discovered. An institutional framework that enables the market process helps to ameliorate this problem.

How does the market process operate? In the first instance, markets allow actors to summarize some of the relevant characteristics of their inarticulate knowledge in a way that can usefully guide the choices of others throughout a community. An actor may need widgets as part of a production plan but lack the personal knowledge or skill to create them. Market prices inform the actor what the going rate for a widget is, which is a sufficient guide so far as their particular business plan is concerned. It means that dispersed knowledge that is relevant for evaluating a range of given choices become accessible to decision makers.

Moreover, prices also act as a signal to potential price makers, or entrepreneurs, showing them where demand for particular resources is currently outstripping supply (Kirzner 1997, 2013). They represent a signal of unmet needs that someone with relevant knowledge or expertise can use as a guide to where their efforts could be productively employed. These entrepreneurs are alert to how the given price data may fail to reflect other observations that they have based on their particular circumstances. In this sense, entrepreneurs act in disagreement with the given price, believing it to be erroneous from their subjective standpoint (Kirzner 1978, 11).

This aspect of the process is not one of narrow, rational economizing precisely because agents are not optimizing their choices within budgetary constraints (Kirzner 1996, 127). Instead, these agents engage in the creative and speculative activity of challenging publicized prices, winning profits should they be correct and experiencing loss should they turn out to be mistaken. It is this open-ended feature of the market process, impossible to conceptualize in a formal rational choice model, that allows for the discovery of previously unknown options in a given choice situation. It is a mechanism that does not merely discover what choice produces the best outcome within a given set, but also allows people to identify and explore "blank" or hidden areas in the choice set.

This market process understanding adds an epistemic emphasis to prevailing neoclassical economic accounts of the function of market institutions. The cornerstone of neoclassical economic theory is the notion of competitive equilibrium. On this account, institutions that support market activity work because they are technically efficient. Assuming rational agents and perfect information, markets allocate resources to their most valuable uses and encourage self-interested actors to accumulate capital without fear of expropriation (Alston, Eggertsson, and North 1996; North 1990). They remove "dollars from the sidewalk." Institutions that unnecessarily impede the price mechanism fail to address transaction costs, or enable predation to reduce long-run economic welfare (Olson 1996). For sure, economists in this tradition do not ascribe such simplistic notions to reality. They only suggest that the abstraction is sufficient to explain a great deal of the variation between regimes.

*Nick Cowen*

For the RPE account, this is lacking part of the answer because it fails to explain how individuals with bounded rationality and limited information could ever even approach, much less satisfy, the conditions required for this model to be relevant. The presumption that markets work only to coordinate given information suggests that they are apt to fail in cases where such information is absent, calling for a different explanation of what makes liberal markets historically workable. It would also mean that, in principle, any institutions similarly designed to follow price signals (such as market socialism) could serve in the place of liberal market institutions (Meade 1945). Yet, historical observation suggests that only regimes with substantial allowance for market activity within a system of private property have consistent welfare gains (Boettke 1993).

This is where the contribution of market process theory differs from neoclassical approaches. As Hayek (1945, 2014) and Kirzner (1996) describe, market institutions facilitate a process of social learning whereby agents discover more valuable uses of resources. In participating in this process, people seeking to satisfy their own ends come to contribute to the ends of their fellow participants. Although limited knowledge is the primary economic problem to be overcome on this account, incentives remain central. Without objective, stable, given information; incentives; and the subjective experience of gains and losses, essential feedback to individual decision makers will not be provided: "What renders the market process a systematic process of coordination is the circumstances that each gap in market coordination expresses itself as a pure profit opportunity" (Kirzner 1996, 12).

Critically, this establishes a realistic baseline for comparing institutional efficacy and viability. A model of markets based on perfect competition implies that any observed deviation from equilibrium, such as supra-normal profits, is a sign of a market failure, whether the result of a diseconomy or information asymmetry. On a market process account, optimality is not the relevant baseline for judgment. Instead, the question is whether the framework in place allows alert actors to discover inefficiencies and failings, and engage in an ongoing open-ended process of experimentation in an attempt to ameliorate them. In this sense, the market process bears some similarity to theories of democratic processes that, under certain conditions, possess similar opportunities for piecemeal experimentation and self-correction (J. Knight and Johnson 2007; Cf. Pennington 2003, 2010).

## The Market Order as a Perilous Precondition for Social Cooperation

A second limitation to simple rational choice analysis is that the rules of the social game are typically assumed as given and exogenous to the decisions of the participants. For example, players in the classic prisoners' dilemma situation do not have a role in establishing the rules and nor are they given an opportunity to revise the rules. In the real social world, the rules of an encounter or set of social circumstances are not given but constituted by the beliefs and practices of the participants (Trantidis 2016, 22). So rational choice analysis can show the significance of the rules of the game for determining outcomes but has less of an account of how agents determine the rules of the game. Yet the rules themselves are absolutely critical. Depending on the rules, the same actors could end up cooperating successfully as a community or falling into desperate conflict.

Buchanan and Tullock (1999) offer a quasi-normative solution within the public choice framework by distinguishing between constitutional and post-constitutional stages in the political process. They conceptualize agents as mutually agreeing on the rules of their interactions prior to playing, competing, and cooperating, self-interestedly within the rules. The weakness is that the constitutional stage in this framework is implausibly idealized. It involves far-sighted actors convening at a constitutional moment and coming to unanimous agreement (Meadowcroft 2014) on a shared institutional framework in a way that is completely unlike any real constitutional convention. For this reason, Buchanan (2000, 100) ultimately treats this scenario as a hypothetical contract that, in some sense, legitimizes a status quo that has some relatively stable rules of the game, regardless of the real origins of those institutions. The actual development of institutions remains somewhat mysterious.

How might agents go about the process of institutional development in a more realistic scenario? This is where the market process's second level of analysis, the market order, can supplement the public choice account. The same agents who participate in the market process engage in a process of political entrepreneurship, attempting to develop modes of cooperation that better protect their interests. Institutions of communication, coordination, and dispute resolution emerge through trial-and-error processes combining spontaneous experimentation and bargaining between groups in a way that parallels acting within a preexisting set of rules (Pennington 2015, 470). When sufficiently advanced and productive, these institutions can disseminate useful guidance and coordinating information that is beyond the direct comprehension of any single individual that participates in and benefits from them.

Unlike individual action within a preestablished framework of voluntary exchange, there is no expectation that institutional formation will work spontaneously in the direction of an efficient, or even generally socially beneficial, outcome. There is no preestablished prohibition on exploitation or predation, or their formalization in institutions such as slavery. Indeed, Kirzner (2000, 77) is suspicious of any attempts to apply economic analysis to the creation of private property institutions rather than exchange activity within them. Leeson and Boettke (2009) are more open to an account of market governance that is endogenous to entrepreneurial activity but acknowledge the contingency of convergence on institutions that facilitate, rather than impede, exchange. Entrepreneurial activity, the actor's pursuit of more effective ways of discovering and achieving their interests, is omnipresent. However, it is only within a given framework of market institutions that such pursuit leads systematically towards socially beneficial outcomes:

> In social evolution, without recourse to the mechanisms provided by property rights, freely adjusting prices, and the lure of profit and the discipline of loss, all we can say is that practices that evolve serve as focal points of action. (Boettke 2014, 241)

This still-open question regarding the differences and similarities between political and market entrepreneurship, these unguided, nonrational, evolutionary accounts contribute to a richer description of the emergence of institutions (Boettke and Storr 2002, 164) than neoclassical accounts. Within a neoclassical lens, elite or powerful actors establish institutions on the basis of their interests and capacities (North 1991, 104). This is classically modeled as Olson's (1993) account of the transition of roving bandits to stationary bandits to the despotism of the primitive state. This is an evolutionary account of institutions, but it is driven primarily by self-interested actors, especially those attempting to engage in more efficient forms of predation. So when, for example, Acemoglu, Johnson, and Robinson (2001) attempt to demonstrate that institutions are an important factor determining long-run economic progress, it is based on the presumption that individuals facing different incentives will settle on different institutional compromises, thus inducing exogenous variation.

A potential paradox of this neoclassical approach is that, insofar as institutions are tightly determined by the incentives and capacities of elites at critical points in time, they actually weaken the relevance of the "institutions matter" hypothesis (Przeworski 2004). The institutions become merely the mechanism through which powerful actors attempt to reap relative rewards, with some configurations of incentives and given resources contingently generating more attractive growth outcomes over the long run.

By contrast, a market process account suggests that institutions need not be, and indeed usually are not, the result of conscious design, nor strictly determined by the self-interest of actors. Institutions such as language, law, property, and money more often emerge through bottom-up practices and traditions that, in some cases, solve social problems for those participating in them (Pennington 2011, 42). This means that the range of people capable of participating in institutional innovation (the "policy makers") is larger than that of people with preexisting forms of political power. While innovators are likely to face conflict with those that subjectively benefit or approve of existing institutions, this conflict need not be intractable, as the disagreement may be the result of an epistemic deficit rather than genuinely divisive interests. Interestingly, in one of his lesser known essays, Olson (1989) recognizes the importance of ideas, as opposed to interests, but also acknowledges this point is somewhat at odds with the thrust of his general work.

## SO WHY BE ROBUST?

Why should we commend robustness? One justification is that we are looking for sound social scientific explanations of real-world outcomes. Levels of human welfare vary enormously across space and time. For a great deal of human history, severe poverty (McCloskey 2011) and violent conflict (Pinker 2012) were prevalent features of the human experience. This prompts the central question in political economy of how some regions and regimes underwent a change from a bad state of affairs to a comparatively remarkable degree of prosperity, or from what Adam Smith (1981, chap. 1) called a "rude state" to an "improved one"?

It is this broadly Hobbesian recognition that conflict and poverty are in some sense common or "natural" elements of the human experience that inspires part of the RPE stance. The RPE focus on worst-case scenarios is not necessarily a pessimistic undertaking as such but a mode of analysis for exploring possible causal explanations for transitions away from this natural condition. For most of history, and in many parts of the present world, this worst-case scenario is a realistic scenario. This means that we need an explanation for how people, similar in key respects to ourselves, who are ignorant of their environment, lacking scientific know-how, technology, physical resources, personal security, and assurance, are nevertheless in some circumstances able to improve their condition, typically over the course of many generations but sometimes much more rapidly. The best answer is robust institutions. By contrast, a theory that explains how people of goodwill and already in possession of essential knowledge for social cooperation is not as convincing an explanation of these real-world phenomena.

Cognizance of the possible depths of human experience also provides a normative justification for considering worst-case scenarios. It means critically evaluating potential changes in policy not just with a view to what they could achieve if they succeed, but also what the outcome would be if they failed. This precautionary principle is more attractive once we recognize that political institutions are the result of path-dependent, incremental evolutionary processes rather than the product of rational design alone. Policies that alter the incentive structures of actors, or deprive them of information that was previously known or even assumed, may mean that it is impossible to undo changes that turn out to produce poorer outcomes than anticipated. It is possible for "public capital" (Buchanan 2000, 163) to be destroyed and made unrecoverable.

Robustness also represents an attempt to integrate humility into scholarly research itself. It suggests we recognize that aspects of any model we are using to defend a causal narrative or justify a particular public policy could be wrong. While we cannot eliminate error from our analysis, we can approach problems in such a way that our answers remain relevant even if our model is substantially inaccurate or our measurements of its parameters mistaken in crucial respects. In this way, a robust research methodology has similar virtues to robust statistical analysis that sacrifices point precision for greater confidence in the general pattern of a result (Levy 2002). Robust results are those that remain trustworthy and valid even after accounting for the likely errors and biases that are generated by any inevitably imperfect research project. In this respect, robustness has parallels with the use of triangulation in research approaches, whereby findings are validated by using evidence from multiple perspectives and sources (Blau 2015).

## APPLIED TO RAWLS'S CONTRACTARIAN THEORY OF JUSTICE

My account suggests that institutions matter, but, in addition, *ideas* about institutions matter, because the contents of institutions are merely influenced, not structurally determined, by the power dynamics of political compromises. Better institutions are possible if they can be conceptualized: if they become "thinkable." My approach recognizes a space in which better ideas of the social world can lead to better collective outcomes because they can help people reformulate their own subjective interests. Scholarship in political theory can help us map out possible constitutional bargaining spaces and contribute to more desirable institutional arrangements by furnishing political actors, or anyone with some capacity to influence social processes, with the knowledge of possible alternative rules of the game.

Pennington (2011) applies the insights of robust political economy to several key issues in public policy, namely problems of market failure, environmental policy, the welfare state, and international development. His account includes analysis of some key issues in political theory, including distributive justice. His perspective is mainly critical. He points out how normative commitments to some institutions that aim to support distributive justice, deliberative democracy (2003), social capital, or multiculturalism are likely to fail the stress-tests of robustness at the point of implementation as public policies. This leaves his preferred alternative, classical liberalism, as the more commendable approach. I propose an extension to this approach to RPE. Robustness can be applied to political theories at a higher level of abstraction than the policy implications of the theories alone.

Applying this approach to Rawls's theory of justice can be particularly fruitful since even his idealized theory includes problems of knowledge (2005, 56–57) and self-interest (2001a, 175) as challenges that social institutions should overcome. Rawls's central philosophical aim is to establish what just social institutions would look like and be expected to achieve. He defines just institutions as those under which a community of free and equal citizens would agree to be governed and that would stably reproduce the conditions of their public acceptance over indefinite future generations (2001b, sec. 7).

As a mechanism for discovering what free and equal citizens would choose, Rawls proposes a hypothetical contract situation, the Original Position, whereby representative agents go behind a veil of ignorance that removes from them knowledge of their personal characteristics, social position, and conception of the good (2001b, sec. 6). However, they are aware of certain basic facts of social theory. In this condition, they engage in a bargaining process that selects the principles that should guide the establishment of social institutions. As such, both the means (a hypothetical social contract) and the ends (allowing free and equal citizens to engage in respectful and productive social cooperation) are similar to Buchanan's. The veil of ignorance in Rawls's theory plays a parallel role to a veil of uncertainty in Buchanan's constitutional choice situation (Buchanan 2001, 180).

Rawls (2001b, sec. 13) proposes that these representative agents would agree to two principles of justice. First, the Liberty Principle which guarantees as part of a basic constitutional framework a significant range of civil liberties (including freedom of speech, religion, association, political participation) equally to all. Second, the Difference Principle which requires all social positions to be available to all on the basis of fair equality of opportunity, and that any inequalities of social resources be arranged so as to benefit the least advantaged in society.

Critically, the application of Rawls's theory is restricted to reasonably ideal conditions where agents have a shared commitment to justice, have sufficient knowledge to judge the effectiveness of institutions, and where citizens can hold the political system to account. When it comes to less-than-ideal conditions, Rawls still believes that the ideal should represent a benchmark that is, in principle, achievable and against which real institutions should be judged.

By contrast, the sort of institutions that exhibit robustness when defending justice may be quite different from the kinds that reflect the principles of justice in an ideal setting. For Rawls, justice is best enshrined in the constitution of a centralized unitary democratic state with an independent judiciary to protect basic liberties and powerful branches of government that exert ultimate control over the economy. A robust perspective advises that lack of relevant knowledge and the presence of opportunistic political behavior could render such a scheme apt to fail. A more decentralized federal regime where powers are separated in such a way that citizens can hold institutions to account through exit powers may not permit the same fine-tuned distribution of rights and resources that justice commends in an ideal setting. However, it may be more likely to protect basic liberties in the less-than-ideal setting where political actors cannot be perfectly trusted.

This approach also offers a different perspective on the interests of the least advantaged. Rawls considers how different institutional choices would impact the least advantaged in various ideal scenarios. He concludes that only a liberal socialism or radically redistributive property-owning democracy could be just. He rules capitalism out as unjust because of its insensitivity to wealth inequality (Rawls 2001b, 136). A robust approach compares alternatives like socialism and capitalism in the non-ideal as well as the ideal setting. If the failures of socialism in non-ideal settings are much more substantial than the failures of capitalism, then it turns out that the worst conceivable social position is to be among the disadvantaged under a socialism that fails to reach its objectives. By contrast, being among the disadvantaged under an imperfect capitalism may turn out to be the far less risky option. Hence, using similar rationales of "maximin" (Rawls 2001b, sec. 28; cf. Buchanan and Faith 1980) and political stability that underpin Rawls's Difference Principle and justify socialism in the ideal setting could justify capitalism in the non-ideal setting, which is more relevant for establishing the relevant position of the least advantaged.

In making robustness a commendable criterion for institutions, I help clarify the normative case for constitutional principles (Rawls 2005, 161) and decentralization of power rather than following more narrowly expedient utilitarian rationales. The recognition of robustness as a commendable property of institutions can also aid in Rawls's (2001b, 3) philosophical task of reconciling individuals with the real political world that they encounter.

## APPLIED TO POLITICAL REALISM

Political realism is a loosely related group of approaches to normative political theory that has emerged out of dissatisfaction with the apparent irrelevance of political philosophy for evaluating real-world politics and orienting actors toward practical goals (Geuss 2008; Galston 2010; Williams 2008). A common feature of this literature is a rejection of a conception of political theory as a form of applied ethics. Within the framework of applied ethics, the purpose of political institutions is typically to establish justice. Institutions are, therefore, evaluated on their ability to allow individuals to discharge each other's moral duties as members of a community. Political realism, by contrast, suggests that there is a more basic shared interest in establishing a social order that is the primary function of political institutions. Realists wish to evaluate political decisions and regimes on the basis of this more fundamental concern (Jubb 2015).

Political realism thus has many of the same concerns of RPE. Unlike more idealistic approaches, realism recognizes violence and conflict as possible scenarios when institutions fail. The key question, therefore, is what additional contribution my approach to RPE can offer to existing forms of realist political theory.

The first is an additional justification for the realist focus on seeking a minimally legitimate regime rather than morally just institutions as such. An evolutionary understanding of the social order suggests that institutional development is fraught with difficulties because that development takes place outside a framework that copes with problems of dispersed knowledge and opportunistic actors. Any significant institutional shift will necessarily present agents with significant costs, as well as inherent risk and uncertainty. This suggests that rather than theorizing and affirming the perfect institutional outcome and rejecting all others, a realistic approach commends convergence around a focal point of minimally legitimate institutions that extend the basic benefits of peace and tranquility to those subject to them (Hardin 2003).

There is a more optimistic side to this evolutionary account. Once established, even minimal conditions that are far from ideal are nevertheless capable of generating incremental improvements in human welfare if they permit a market process to operate. Purposive actors in a civil society do not require the constant deliberate support and direction of political institutions in order to set about cooperating to improve their lives, and the lives of those around them. They merely require a framework that discourages predation and allows the sharing of dispersed knowledge. In this sense, conditions of peace, toleration, and the rule of law can lead over the long run to more substantive welfare improvements.

A second contribution of my approach to RPE is an observation about the nature of the problem that politics must solve. For a great many realists, it is the problem of moral disagreement among human beings. On the realist account, theories in the applied ethics tradition assume away this problem of disagreement by suggesting that, at least in principle, everyone would agree to the same set of moral principles (or a workable shared subset of principles for a community). In so doing, realists suggest that idealists lose sight of the coercive nature of real politics. In suitably ideal circumstances, where agents comply with both the letter and the spirit of a shared sense of justice, it can appear that there is hardly any distinctive role for political institutions at all, as opposed to voluntary governance. Realists, by contrast, suggest that institutions must be able to legitimize themselves in the absence of such agreement.

The deep subjectivist stance drawn from market process theory suggests a more basic problem of coordination: the primitive fact that people each have the same capacity and desire to lay their hands on objects and resources. In the absence of communication, there is no possibility of coordination, but nor is there any space for moral disagreement as such. In this sense, the emergent institution of language is the first mechanism of coordination.

Subsequently, communication mechanisms used to establish coordination, such as oaths, rituals, and shared moral norms, become sources of discursive disagreement. Individuals can come to blows not over resources themselves but over misunderstanding (or perhaps worse, correctly understanding) the beliefs, desires, and values of others once it is possible for them to be articulated. Silent actors "disagree" over what is mine and thine through attempting to follow their uncoordinated desires. Discursive actors, by contrast, can disagree over what *makes* mine and thine.

Looked at from this perspective, one might see moral disagreement not always as a problem in need of a solution, but rather as an outcome and contributor to successful coordination. The fact that people can successfully communicate disagreement demonstrates the existence of some shared institutions, at least a shared language of moral concepts. Discourse about morality and conduct may be a part of an institutional background that permits ongoing productive cooperation while highlighting areas of dispute.

There is a parallel here between the profit and loss signals of the market process and the protest and debate of political environments. In the ideal circumstances of perfect competition, profits and losses should not exist. They are a sign of error, ignorance, or miscalculation that, in principle, could be ameliorated through state intervention or redistribution. On a market process account, it is only through those signals that error and ignorance can be made known both to market and political actors. A regime that intervenes constantly and arbitrarily to fix market failures ends up depriving itself of the social knowledge necessary to identify them in the first place. Similarly, on many ideal accounts of politics, the presence of widespread disagreement is a sign of failure of a set of institutions to justify its rules to those bound by them. A more robust account suggests that voicing such disagreement, as well as allowing actors to pursue alternatives through exit rights, may be the only realistic way of discovering superior rules by which to live.

Finally, my account offers a methodological rejoinder to some realist theorizing by insisting on an explicitly comparative (Boettke, Coyne, and

Leeson 2013; Boettke et al. 2005) element to the examination of worst-case scenarios, and not simply a critique of existing regimes. To take one example of how this difference applies in practice, consider Geuss's explanation of how his realist approach was influenced by a

> growing conviction that the present political, social, and economic situation of our world is desperate. The combination of already intolerable overpopulation and effectively irreversible pollution and degradation of the environment which may have no "solution". . . minimally acceptable for the human species. . . . If complexly organized social life survives at all, political agencies will have the task of exercising much of the discipline needed to force people in the West to adopt drastic reductions in their absolute level of consumption. . . . A solution . . . will not lie in any scheme that permits the continuation of . . . the so-called "free market." (Geuss 2010, xii–xiii)

Geuss (2002, 2008) has a strong claim to dealing with worst-case scenarios and premises his work on a fierce rejection of romantic ideological illusions. Yet, as one can imagine, Geuss's proposals (such as they are) stand almost at a polar opposite of the liberal ideas that RPE commends. From Geuss's standpoint, one can imagine that the supposed robustness on offer from Pennington et al. at best relies on the naive belief in the ability of imperfect human beings to produce defensible outcomes in the absence of the continual deliberate exercise of political force. At worst, it is an ideologically motivated defense of unsustainable and unjustifiable market institutions.

Geuss is correct to identify ecological problems as a kind that are unlikely to be ameliorated alone through the undirected, spontaneous activity of the market process. Environmental problems are beset with epistemic and motivational challenges of a particular kind that makes generating knowledge of the relevant costs of individual decisions difficult. A great deal of environmental damage occurs through the unintentional, uncoordinated, and unobserved decisions of large numbers of people over long periods of time. These harms are, at least, resistant to the private-property solution of establishing exclusive domains of activity and control.

For these reasons, it is almost inevitable that the market process's incremental, marginal adjustments on the basis of local knowledge will fail to address adequately some environmental problems. This applies especially to global ecological problems such as climate change. A commendable public policy is informed by the systematic scientific knowledge of the likely long-run impact of human activity on the environment and not just the implicit knowledge embedded in market prices.

However, there are critical weaknesses to Geuss's approach as well. A simple counsel of despair does not have any practical implications for public policy and reflects an attitude more than a motivation to action. As

Knight (1939, 1) writes, "to call a situation hopeless is for practical purposes the same thing as calling it ideal." Insofar as political realism identifies bad features of political life that cannot possibly be overcome, it is rendered as irrelevant as its mirror image, ideal theories that describe perfect political conditions that could never be attained even in principle.

RPE also suggests that establishing that a particular regime has failed is insufficient to suggest an authoritarian alternative. In order to commend harsh disciplinary solutions that would intentionally dramatically reduce the material welfare of human beings subject to the new regime, we would need some account of how that solution would deal more adequately with the epistemic challenges of ecology than the imperfect results observed under liberalism. As Shahar (2015) argues, the poor record of authoritarian solutions to ecological problems suggests that liberal market solutions may turn out to be superior even if they remain far from ideal. The question prompted by the claim that our present situation is "desperate" is simply "compared to what?" An RPE approach is more rounded in considering the worst-case scenario of the proposed solution as well as the problem.

The notion of the market process as necessarily taking place within an institutional framework, the market order, allows us to avoid the simple binary of an unbounded "free market" versus centralized authoritarian political solutions to social problems. Individual freedom within a private-property framework is instead one point along a continuum of possible institutional frameworks that includes various forms of common ownership and forms of subsidiary governance and federalism before reaching unitary government. We can also distinguish between policies that attempt to command individual conduct directly and policy approaches that change the rules of the game—that is, the underlying order—in a way that allows agents to experiment and discover solutions for policy problems (E. Ostrom 1990).

My approach does not prescribe any particular set of rules as such, and is quite compatible with a variety of distributions of rights and powers over resources, some of which will be better at dealing with environmental problems than others. My argument is for the use of rules in general, rather than arbitrary discretion, without which actors will be exposed to predatory behavior and not be able to produce the knowledge necessary for even basic cooperation.

## CONCLUSION

This chapter has outlined the contribution that RPE can make to understanding realistic social problems that should concern political theory. It shows how the particular contribution of market process theory to the RPE framework helps to improve existing economic accounts of individual behavior in political settings. My approach to RPE can be seen as one response to the Ostromian challenge to produce a richer account of human interaction in exchange settings where assumptions of rational utility maximization do not satisfactorily explain agent motivation and behavior. The need to reconcile individual subjective interests and beliefs in the midst of widespread ignorance shows the challenge of facilitating social cooperation and contributes to our understanding of what constitutes "worst-case scenarios."

However, a market process account also offers cause for optimism. It suggests that humans acting within a satisfactory institutional framework are able to use their limited faculties to adapt, albeit imperfectly, to an ever-changing social world and cooperate in enormously inventive ways. A particular social situation is never perfect, but only rarely is it desperate. Social conflicts, or institutional failures, are not the result of intractable divergences of interest, but more often differences of opinion brought about by epistemic challenges that can, in principle, be resolved through peaceful means, including the persuasive application of better political theory.

## NOTE

For their feedback and support, I am enormously grateful to my fellow contributors to this volume from the Adam Smith Fellowship research colloquia; to Virgil Storr, Peter Boettke, and Chris Coyne; as well as Peter Lipsey and the tireless administrative team at Mercatus. I extend heartfelt thanks to my colleagues at the Department of Political Economy, King's College London, and especially Mark Pennington, Aris Trantidis, Emily Skarbek, and Matias Petersen for commenting on drafts of this paper.

## REFERENCES

Acemoglu, Daron, Simon Johnson, and James A. Robinson. 2001. "The Colonial Origins of Comparative Development: An Empirical Investigation." *American Economic Review* 91 (5): 1369–401.

Alston, Lee J., Thrainn Eggertsson, and Douglass C. North, eds. 1996. *Empirical Studies in Institutional Change*. Political Economy of Institutions and Decisions. Cambridge: Cambridge University Press.

Blau, Adrian. 2015. "History of Political Thought as Detective-Work." *History of European Ideas* 41 (8): 1178–94. doi:10.1080/01916599.2015.1082768.

Boettke, Peter J. 1993. *Why Perestroika Failed: The Politics and Economics of Socialist Transformation*. London: Routledge.

———. 2012. *Living Economics: Yesterday, Today, and Tomorrow*. Oakland, CA: Independent Institute.

———. 2014. "Entrepreneurship, and the Entrepreneurial Market Process: Israel M. Kirzner and the Two Levels of Analysis in Spontaneous Order Studies." *Review of Austrian Economics* 27 (3): 233–47. doi:10.1007/s11138-014-0252-1.

Boettke, Peter J., Christopher J. Coyne, and Peter T. Leeson. 2013. "Comparative Historical Political Economy." *Journal of Institutional Economics* 9 (3): 285–301. doi:10.1017/S1744137413000088.

Boettke, Peter J., Christopher J. Coyne, Peter T. Leeson, and Frederic Sautet. 2005. "The New Comparative Political Economy." *Review of Austrian Economics* 18 (3–4): 281–304.

Boettke, Peter J., and Peter T. Leeson. 2004. "Liberalism, Socialism, and Robust Political Economy." *Journal of Markets and Morality* 7 (1): 99–111.

Boettke, Peter J., and Virgil Henry Storr. 2002. "Post-Classical Political Economy: Polity, Society and Economy in Weber, Mises and Hayek." *American Journal of Economics and Sociology* 61 (1): 161–91.

Buchanan, James M. 1999. "Natural and Artifactual Man." In *The Logical Foundations of Constitutional Liberty*, 246–59. The Collected Works of James M. Buchanan, vol. 1. Indianapolis: Liberty Fund.

———. 2000. *The Limits of Liberty: Between Anarchy and Leviathan*. The Collected Works of James M. Buchanan, vol. 7. Indianapolis: Liberty Fund.

———. 2001. "Criteria for a Free Society." In *Federalism, Liberty, and the Law*, 173–84. The Collected Works of James M. Buchanan, vol. 18. Indianapolis: Liberty Fund.

Buchanan, James M., and Roger L. Faith. 1980. "Subjective Elements in Rawlsian Contractual Agreement on Distributional Rules." *Economic Inquiry* 18 (1): 23–38. doi:10.1111/j.1465-7295.1980.tb00557.x.

Buchanan, James M., and Gordon Tullock. 1999. *The Calculus of Consent: Logical Foundations of Constitutional Democracy*. The Collected Works of James M. Buchanan, vol. 3. Indianapolis: Liberty Fund.

Buchanan, James M., and Viktor J. Vanberg. 1991. "The Market as a Creative Process." *Economics and Philosophy* 7 (2): 167–86. doi:10.1017/S0266267100001383.

Dunleavy, Patrick. 2002. *Democracy, Bureaucracy and Public Choice: Economic Explanations in Political Science*. London: Prentice Hall.

Farrant, Andrew, and Eric Crampton. 2008. "Robust Analytical Egalitarianism: Worst-Case Political Economy and the Socialist Calculation Debate." In *The Street Porter and the Philosopher: Conversations on Analytical Egalitarianism*, edited by Sandra Peart and David M. Levy, 108–32. Ann Arbor: University of Michigan Press.

Galston, W. A. 2010. "Realism in Political Theory." *European Journal of Political Theory* 9 (4): 385–411. doi:10.1177/1474885110374001.

Gamble, Andrew. 1989. "Ideas and Interests in British Economic Policy." In *Ideas, Interests and Consequences* (Liberty Fund Symposium), edited by Andrew Gamble, 1–21. IEA Readings 30. London: IEA.

Geuss, Raymond. 2002. "Liberalism and Its Discontents." *Political Theory* 30 (3): 320–38. doi:10.1177/0090591702030003003.

————. 2008. *Philosophy and Real Politics*. Princeton, NJ: Princeton University Press.

————. 2010. *Politics and the Imagination*. Princeton, NJ: Princeton University Press.

Grube, Laura E., and Virgil Henry Storr. 2015. "The Role of Culture in Economic Action." In *New Thinking in Austrian Political Economy*, edited by Christopher J. Coyne and Virgil Henry Storr, 19, 21–46. Bingley, UK: Emerald Group Publishing. http://www.emeraldinsight.com/doi/10.1108/S1529-213420150000019002.

Hardin, Russell. 2003. *Liberalism, Constitutionalism, and Democracy*. Oxford: Oxford University Press.

Hayek, Friedrich A. von. 1937. "Economics and Knowledge." *Economica* 4 (13): 33–54. doi:10.2307/2548786.

————. 1943. "The Facts of the Social Sciences." *Ethics* 54 (1): 1–13.

————. 1945. "The Use of Knowledge in Society." *American Economic Review* 35 (4): 519–30.

————. 2014. "Competition as a Discovery Procedure." In *The Market and Other Orders*, edited by Bruce Caldwell, 304–13. Chicago: University of Chicago Press.

Hodgson, Geoffrey M. 2007. "Meanings of Methodological Individualism." *Journal of Economic Methodology* 14 (2): 211–26. doi:10.1080/13501780701394094.

Jubb, Robert. 2015. "The Real Value of Equality." *Journal of Politics* 77 (3): 679–91. doi:10.1086/681262.

Kirzner, Israel M. 1978. "Entrepreneurship, Entitlement, and Economic Justice." *Eastern Economic Journal* 4 (1): 9–25.

————. 1987. "Spontaneous Order and the Case for the Free Market Society." In *Ideas on Liberty: Essays in Honor of Paul L. Poirot*, 45–50. Irvington-on-Hudson, NY: Foundation for Economic Education. https://mises.org/library/ideas-liberty-essays-honor-paul-l-poirot.

————. 1996. *The Meaning of Market Process: Essays in the Development of Modern Austrian Economics*. Foundations of the Market Economy Series. London: Routledge.

————. 1997. "Entrepreneurial Discovery and the Competitive Market Process: An Austrian Approach." *Journal of Economic Literature* 35 (1): 60–85.

————. 2000. *The Driving Force of the Market: Essays in Austrian Economics*. Foundations of the Market Economy. London: Routledge.

————. 2013. *Competition and Entrepreneurship*. Edited by Peter J. Boettke and Frédéric E. Sautet. The Collected Works of Israel M. Kirzner. Indianapolis: Liberty Fund.

Knight, F. H. 1939. "Ethics and Economic Reform: I. The Ethics of Liberalism." *Economica* 6 (21): 1–29. doi:10.2307/2549075.

Knight, Jack, and James Johnson. 2007. "The Priority of Democracy: A Pragmatist Approach to Political-Economic Institutions and the Burden of Justification." *American Political Science Review* 101 (1): 47–61. doi:10.1017/S0003055407070062.

Kogelmann, Brian. 2015. "Modeling the Individual for Constitutional Choice." *Constitutional Political Economy* 26 (4): 455–74. doi:10.1007/s10602-015-9197-z.

Leeson, Peter T., and Peter J. Boettke. 2009. "Two-Tiered Entrepreneurship and Economic Development." *International Review of Law and Economics* 29 (3): 252–59. doi:10.1016/j.irle.2009.02.005.

Leeson, Peter T., and J. Robert Subrick. 2006. "Robust Political Economy." *Review of Austrian Economics* 19 (2–3): 107–11. doi:10.1007/s11138-006-7342-7.

Levy, David M. 2002. "Robust Institutions." *Review of Austrian Economics* 15 (2–3): 131–42.

Lukes, Steven. 1968. "Methodological Individualism Reconsidered." *British Journal of Sociology* 19 (2): 119. doi:10.2307/588689.

McCloskey, Deirdre N. 2011. *Bourgeois Dignity: Why Economics Can't Explain the Modern World.* Chicago: University of Chicago Press.

Meade, James Edward. 1945. "Mr. Lerner on 'The Economics of Control.'" *Economic Journal* 55 (217): 47–69. doi:10.2307/2225882.

Meadowcroft, John. 2014. "Exchange, Unanimity and Consent: A Defence of the Public Choice Account of Power." *Public Choice* 158 (1–2): 85–100. doi:10.1007/s11127-012-9925-0.

North, Douglass C. 1990. *Institutions, Institutional Change, and Economic Performance.* The Political Economy of Institutions and Decisions. Cambridge: Cambridge University Press.

———. 1991. "Institutions." *Journal of Economic Perspectives* 5 (1): 97–112.

Olson, Mancur. 1989. "How Ideas Affect Societies." In *Ideas, Interests and Consequences* (Liberty Fund Symposium), edited by Andrew Gamble, 23–51. IEA Readings 30. London: IEA.

———. 1993. "Dictatorship, Democracy, and Development." *American Political Science Review* 87 (3): 567–76. doi:10.2307/2938736.

———. 1996. "Distinguished Lecture on Economics in Government: Big Bills Left on the Sidewalk: Why Some Nations Are Rich, and Others Poor." *Journal of Economic Perspectives* 10 (2): 3–24.

Ostrom, Elinor. 1990. *Governing the Commons: The Evolution of Institutions for Collective Action.* The Political Economy of Institutions and Decisions. Cambridge: Cambridge University Press.

Ostrom, Vincent. 1993. "Epistemic Choice and Public Choice." In *The Next Twenty-Five Years of Public Choice*, 163–76. New York: Springer. http://link.springer.com/chapter/10.1007/978-94-017-3402-8_17.

Ostrom, Vincent, and Elinor Ostrom. 1971. "Public Choice: A Different Approach to the Study of Public Administration." *Public Administration Review* 31 (2): 203–16. doi:10.2307/974676.

Pennington, Mark. 2003. "Hayekian Political Economy and the Limits of Deliberative Democracy." *Political Studies* 51 (4): 722–39.

———. 2010. "Democracy and the Deliberative Conceit." *Critical Review* 22 (2–3): 159–84. doi:10.1080/08913811.2010.508632.

———. 2011. *Robust Political Economy: Classical Liberalism and the Future of Public Policy.* New Thinking in Political Economy. Cheltenham, UK: Edward Elgar.

———. 2015. "Constitutional Political Economy and Austrian Economics." In *The Oxford Handbook of Austrian Economics*, edited by Christopher J.

Coyne and Peter J. Boettke. Oxford: Oxford University Press. http://www.oxfordhandbooks.com/view/10.1093/oxfordhb/9780199811762.001.0001/oxfordhb-9780199811762-e-20.

Pinker, Steven. 2012. *The Better Angels of Our Nature: A History of Violence and Humanity.* London: Penguin.

Przeworski, Adam. 2004. "Institutions Matter?" *Government and Opposition* 39 (4): 527–40.

Rawls, John. 2001a. "Justice as Fairness." In *Collected Papers*, 47–72. Cambridge, MA: Harvard University Press.

———. 2001b. *Justice as Fairness: A Restatement.* Cambridge, MA: Harvard University Press.

———. 2005. *Political Liberalism.* Expanded ed. Columbia Classics in Philosophy. New York: Columbia University Press.

Sen, Amartya K. 1977. "Rational Fools: A Critique of the Behavioral Foundations of Economic Theory." *Philosophy & Public Affairs* 6 (4): 317–44.

Shackle, G. L. S. 1970. *Expectation, Enterprise and Profit: The Theory of the Firm.* Studies in Economics 1. London: Allen & Unwin.

Shahar, Dan Coby. 2015. "Rejecting Eco-Authoritarianism, Again." *Environmental Values* 24 (3): 345–66. doi:10.3197/096327114X13947900181996.

Smith, Adam. 1981. *An Inquiry into the Nature and Causes of the Wealth of Nations.* The Glasgow Edition of the Works and Correspondence of Adam Smith 2. Indianapolis: Liberty Classics.

Trantidis, Aris. 2016. *Clientelism and Economic Policy: Greece and the Crisis.* Routledge Advances in European Politics 126. Abingdon, UK: Routledge.

Weintraub, E. Roy. 1993. "Neoclassical Economics." Edited by David Henderson. In *The Concise Encyclopedia of Economics*. Library of Economics and Liberty. http://www.econlib.org.

Williams, Bernard Arthur Owen. 2008. *In the Beginning Was the Deed: Realism and Moralism in Political Argument.* Edited by Geoffrey Hawthorn. Princeton, NJ: Princeton University Press.

*Chapter 4*

# Hayek's Legacy for Environmental Political Economy

## Dan C. Shahar

In recent decades, writers in the classical liberal tradition have sought to show how their frameworks can address concerns about the natural environment. To this end they have often invoked the ideas of F. A. Hayek, a giant of liberal theorizing, in the course of arguing that a greener future can be forged through economic liberty, private property, and capitalistic markets (Anderson and Leal 2015; Cordato 1997; Pennington 2005). Yet Hayek's power to vindicate such "free-market environmentalist" perspectives has been controversial. According to some commentators, Hayek's analyses reflect a failure to appreciate the true gravity of environmental issues. "Had he understood the potential scale of contemporary problems such as climate change and biodiversity loss," writes one critic, "Hayek might have recognized that a larger degree of regulation is required to address them" (Greenwood 2007, 82). Others have gone further, arguing that Hayekians should support aggressive environmental protections on the same grounds that they defend liberty, property, and markets in economic arenas (DiZerega 1992, 1996a, 1996b; Gamble 2006; O'Neill 2012).

Much of the controversy over Hayek's legacy for environmental political economy results from the fact that different writers have interpreted him in very different ways. This in turn can be traced to the fact that, despite regular invocation of Hayek as an inspiration or foil, no one has yet provided a systematic and charitable investigation of his views as they pertain to environmental issues. This paper aims to remedy this deficiency by developing and unifying three environmentally relevant themes in Hayek's corpus.

According to one narrative in Hayek's writings, the challenges presented by natural resource systems are essentially the same as those concerning other forms of economic capital. Like other capital assets, natural resources can be degraded or destroyed through use, especially without investments to sustain them. This presents a problem for societies, but not a special one: economies are constantly overcoming this kind of challenge through the market coordination of economic activities. To address the challenges posed by ecological degradation, then, this first Hayekian theme points to the facilitation of market processes as a straightforward and attractive solution.

A second, contrasting thread in Hayek's work emphasizes the distinctive problems posed by "neighborhood effects" in many environmental contexts. According to Hayek, one key precondition for the functionality of markets is a tight connection between individuals' incentives and the interests of others. Environmental problems can emerge when these connections are weak or absent, and strengthening them can sometimes be a difficult task. Hence Hayek suggests that political intervention may sometimes be appropriate in order to prevent undesirable outcomes from emerging.

A third narrative drawn from Hayek's work suggests that the most serious ecological problems reflect a failure by societies to protect the complex, self-organizing systems on which they rely. From a Hayekian perspective, the functionality of such systems can be worthy of preservation as a matter of principle, even when doing so might seem inconvenient in the moment. Insofar as human activities threaten critical ecological systems, then, this third Hayekian narrative might yield a case for aggressive environmental reforms.

Applying Hayek's political economy to contemporary environmental issues means coming to terms with all of these ideas. In the first three sections below, I elaborate each of these themes in turn. In the fourth section, I synthesize them into one coherent view. Contrary to the characterizations of free-market environmentalists, the resulting paradigm makes significant room for political interventions to address environmental problems. But a Hayekian approach to environmental policy making also demands that interventions respect certain constraints to preserve the functionality of economic markets. Ultimately, I argue that it is this guidance on the proper character of environmental policies that represents Hayek's most significant contribution to environmental debates.

## CALLING ON MARKETS

Let us begin with a theme that formed the core of Hayek's own thinking about the environment. According to this first narrative, the problems presented by humanity's relationship with the natural world instantiate more general challenges concerning the production and use of economic capital. As we will see, applying this narrative to environmental problems yields important difficulties that will occupy us in the sections to come. For now, however, it will be helpful to present this first Hayekian theme uncritically, reserving needed caveats and qualifications for later.

## Natural Resources and the Structure of Capital

Hayek's discussion of environmental issues begins in *The Pure Theory of Capital*. Here he observes that societies prosper by employing productive assets that can be deteriorated or used up (1941, 72–76). This generates what he calls the "peculiar problem" of capital: how "a stock of *non-permanent* resources enables us to maintain production *permanently* at a higher level than would be possible without them" (74). On Hayek's understanding, society's "non-permanent" capital includes tools and facilities created to assist production as well as human capacities cultivated for the same end. But it also includes "the greater part of the natural resources. Some . . . such as the fertility of the soil, can only be expected to endure permanently if we take care to preserve them. Others, such as mineral deposits, are inevitably exhausted by their use and cannot possibly tender the same services forever" (72).

Hayek observes that natural resources are not unique in their vulnerability to being destroyed. In fact, it is a feature of all capital assets that they can be exhausted or degraded through use (1941, 75–77). Given this, Hayek insists that natural resource issues should be analyzed in terms of the more general problem of maintaining and reproducing capital to permanently elevate prosperity (102). In *The Constitution of Liberty*, he reemphasizes this point against what he sees as an "unreasoned prejudice" for maintaining natural resources in their existing forms (1960, 322–23):

> [I]f we want to maintain or increase our income, we must be able to replace each resource that is being used up with a new one that will make at least an equal contribution to future income. This does not mean, however, that it should be preserved in kind or replaced by another of the same kind, or even that the total stock of natural resources should be kept intact. From a social as well as from an individual point of view, any natural resource represents just one item of our total endowment of exhaustible resources, and our problem is not to preserve this stock in any particular form, but always to maintain it in a form that will make the most desirable contribution to total income. (323)

Driven by this assessment, Hayek concludes that "all resource conservation constitutes investment and should be judged by precisely the same criteria as all other investment" (323).

## Solving the Problem of Capital

In Hayek's view, the solution to the "peculiar problem" of capital involves using existing resources to invest in future capital. This can be done by maintaining existing assets or by producing new ones. As Hayek sees it, what matters most is not that particular assets be preserved, but rather that society consistently secures an adequate overall capital portfolio.

Hayek ultimately claims that the best way to accomplish this task is to allow markets to coordinate capital production and utilization. Yet to understand the significance of this position, we must appreciate why he considers the problem of economic coordination so vexing in the first place. According to Hayek, the most important obstacle to prosperity in complex modern societies is that the information needed for successful economic organization can never be acquired by any one mind (1945, 519). Public officials hoping to plan an economy might possess considerable scientific expertise, but they are irretrievably lacking in "knowledge of the particular circumstances of time and place" (521)—facts about momentary conditions, changing desires, and productive means available for use. This sort of knowledge is critical for economic organization, but it is also dispersed throughout society and cannot be aggregated in a centralized form (521–24).

Hayek contends that the only way to make an economy responsive to time-and-place information is to decentralize economic decisions to the private individuals who possess this information (1945, 524–25). Yet this suggestion raises puzzles of its own: Given that individuals must remain ignorant of the great majority of what others know, how can they be any more sensitive to this information than central planners could be? And given that individuals' priorities may not align directly with the broader public good, how can they be motivated to promote it?

Hayek finds answers to these questions in the operations of the price system. When individuals transact, they help to establish general exchange rates between goods in a common metric of dollar prices (1945, 525). These prices, and especially their fluctuations, communicate important information about economic circumstances, desires, and available resources in a form that individuals can readily understand. Moreover, prices drive people to act on this information for the sake of protecting their financial interests (526). By relying on prices to coordinate economic decisions in a decentralized way, market economies can thus solve society's fundamental economic problems in a way that no central planner could. Hayek therefore writes:

> It is through the mutually adjusted efforts of many people that more knowledge is utilized than any one individual possesses or than it is possible to synthesize intellectually; and it is through such utilization of dispersed knowledge that achievements are made possible greater than any single mind can foresee. (1960, 28)[1]

This general perspective helps to explain why Hayek sees the decentralization of decision making in a market economy as the most effective way to solve the problem of capital, and hence of environmental capital as well. By responding to price signals, economic actors are led to utilize their resources with sensitivity to broader societal needs, and a system of free enterprise so organized can achieve better coordination than could ever be realized through central planning. Hayek admits that decentralization puts decisions into the hands of individuals who lack bureaucrats' scientific expertise, especially in the environmental domain. But he insists that this disadvantage is over-balanced by the fact that, alongside scientific expertise, "There will always exist . . . an even greater store of knowledge of special circumstances that ought to be taken into account in decisions about specific resources which only the individual owners will possess and which can never be concentrated within a single authority" (1960, 321). Moreover, "while it is possible to communicate to the owners of particular resources the more general considerations that they ought to take into account, it is not possible for authority to learn all the different facts known to the individuals" (321).

## Preconditions for Well-Functioning Markets

In order for markets to effectively coordinate economic activities, individuals must be embedded in a political environment that facilitates good economic decision making. Hayek identifies several factors as important for market functionality, all of which are relevant to environmental issues. Some of these factors follow from what we have just been saying: if markets are to operate effectively, then the authority to make most economic decisions must be decentralized to individuals and not centralized in a single political authority.[2] Moreover, the prices of goods and services in the marketplace must be allowed to fluctuate in response to underlying economic circumstances.[3]

Another precondition for markets' functionality is related to these. If individuals are to draw on each other's knowledge as well as their own, then they need to be free to make their own decisions and not be subordinated to others' plans. When societies compel their citizens to follow external commands, individuals are left with "no chance to use their own knowledge or follow their own predilections. The action performed according to such commands serves exclusively the purposes of him who has issued it" (1960, 132). By depriving individuals of the opportunity to make their own decisions, coercion "prevents a person from using his mental powers to the full and consequently from making the greatest contribution he is capable of to the community" (118).

Although Hayek advocates broad latitude for individual decision making, he does not take this stance to license every activity that people might want to undertake. On the contrary, he notes that even the protection of personal liberty requires some limitations on what people may do (1960, 19–20;

122). In order to minimize the negative effects of needed coercive measures, Hayek insists that when individuals' choices must be constrained, this should be done exclusively in accordance with known general rules. Coercion so limited would be rendered innocuous because the rules themselves would provide each individual with "part of the data which, together with his knowledge of the particular circumstances of time and place, he can use as the basis for his decisions" (133).

Hayek believes that decentralized decision making, a working price system, and a robust scheme of individual autonomy are necessary to achieve prosperity. But these conditions alone do not suffice for a well-functioning market economy. For if individuals lack the resources or motivation to act on their knowledge in beneficial ways, then granting them liberty to respond to prices might prove unhelpful.

Part of the solution to this problem can be found in the rules defining institutions of property. Property rights play a crucial role in empowering individuals to act on their knowledge for, as Hayek writes, "We are rarely in a position to carry out a coherent plan of action unless we are certain of our exclusive control of some material objects; and where we do not control them, it is necessary that we know who does if we are to collaborate with others" (1960, 123). Hayek also sees property rights as providing citizens with an important source of discipline. Even though these rights give people authority to use resources as they please, they also ensure that individuals bear the costs of poor decisions. Hayek views this as especially important when discussing natural resources, since so many historical examples of ecological degradation align with the absence of property rights:

> [T]he most important instance . . . —the depletion of forests—was largely due to the fact that they did *not* become private property but were retained as public land and given over to private exploitation on terms which gave the exploiters no incentive for conservation. (1960, 318–19)

This enthusiasm for the disciplining power of property rights is illustrative of a broader concern. Hayek believes that if individuals are to be empowered to make their own decisions in the marketplace, then they must also benefit and suffer depending on their success in responding to market demands:

> In a free society we are remunerated not for our skill but for using it rightly; and this must be so as long as we are free to choose our particular occupation and are not to be directed to it. True, it is almost never possible to determine what part of a successful career has been due to superior knowledge, ability, or effort and what part to fortunate accidents; but this in no way detracts from the importance of making it worthwhile for everybody to make the right choice. (1960, 72)[4]

Hayek's concern with incentives goes beyond ensuring that individuals' well-being is tied to their economic contributions. Particularly important is the idea that individuals must not be able to achieve success at each other's expense. Not only is such predation objectionable in itself, but it also severs the connection between individuals' incentives and others' interests that drives the efficacy of the market process. Hayek contends that societies must utilize their coercive powers to prevent citizens from coercing one another (1960, 122–23), as well as to combat other forms of predation, such as fraud (126). In the context of natural resource issues, Hayek also emphasizes "the neighborhood effects and . . . the more far-reaching consequences which the use of a particular piece of land may have for the rest of the community" (316). Here he argues that governments have an important function to perform in "the gradual improvement of the legal institutions which make the market function more effectively and induce the individual to take fuller account of the effects of his actions" (315).

In Hayek's view, well-functioning markets will be built around decentralized decision making, unimpeded price systems, economic liberty, robust property institutions, and individual accountability. When these factors are absent or deficient, long-term prosperity might depend on remedying the relevant shortcomings. This could require action by government officials, who could help by defining and enforcing property rights (and sometimes by simply removing bad policies). But Hayek also emphasizes the power of evolutionary social processes to produce conditions in which markets can flourish, especially through the development of common law standards and cultural innovations (1973; 1976, 26).[5]

## Avoiding Utopianism

Our discussion thus far has suggested that the best way to utilize society's natural resources is to empower individuals to make decentralized decisions about their own assets in the context of a well-functioning market order. Yet it is important to clarify what is meant by the claim that such a solution would be "best." For one thing, Hayek surely cannot mean that such a scheme would deploy natural resources in ways that all citizens would regard as ideally desirable. Nor can he believe that no one would make mistakes and squander particular resources. In fact, Hayek's expectation of failure lies at the foundation of his insistence that individuals should bear the costs as well as the benefits of their choices: "The order of the Great Society does rest and must rest on constant undesigned frustrations of some efforts—efforts which ought not have been made but in free men can be discouraged only by failure" (1976, 2–3).

Hayek also cannot be interpreted as supposing that leaving natural resource decisions to private individuals would enable societies to foresee exactly how their future capital needs would be met. Indeed, he explicitly claims:

> In a sense . . . most consumption of irreplaceable resources rests on an act of faith. We are generally confident that, by the time the resource is exhausted, something new will have been discovered which will either satisfy the same need or at least compensate us for what we no longer have, so that we are, on the whole, as well off as before. We are constantly using up resources on the basis of the mere probability that our knowledge of available resources will increase indefinitely. (1960, 319)

In saying that the decentralized development of natural resources is best, then, Hayek is making a claim about the best response to circumstances in which impotence and ignorance can never be completely overcome. In his view, there is no way for societies to act with perfect efficacy and perfect foresight: all available options require us to cope with the limits of human abilities and understandings. It is with this in mind that Hayek characterizes reliance on markets as the best of our options. Allowing market actors to use assets in line with their private understandings is the only way for societies to reap the benefits of knowledge not available to centralized minds. But this does not guarantee perfection: rather, it simply represents the best of a range of imperfect alternatives.[6]

Hayek makes this point most forcefully through the observation that heeding the past warnings of "expert" conservationists would have likely blocked the prosperity of his own time:

> Industrial development would have been greatly retarded if sixty or eighty years ago the warning of the conservationists about the threatening exhaustion of the supply of coal had been heeded; and the internal combustion engine would never have revolutionized transport if its use had been limited to the then known supplies of oil (during the first few decades of the era of the automobile and the airplane the known resources of oil at the current rate of use would have been exhausted in ten years). Though it is important that on all these matters the opinion of the experts about the physical facts should be heard, the result in most instances would have been very detrimental if they had had the power to enforce their views on policy. (320)

Looking forward to the future, Hayek claims as a general phenomenon that our stock of productive assets "does increase in part because we are using up what is available at such a fast rate. Indeed, if we are to make full use of available resources, we must act on the assumption that it will continue to increase, even if some of our particular expectations are bound to be disappointed" (319–20).

Hayek's core position on natural resource issues can thus be seen as a kind of pragmatic anti-utopianism. In actual practice, the best way for societies to respond to natural resource challenges is to create a political environment in which markets can solve them on our behalf. Admittedly, the "solutions" produced through such an approach do not guarantee against every disappointment or hardship. But the key point is that there is no way to completely eliminate disappointment and hardship in the domain of political economy, and attempts to do so by truncating markets will typically only make things worse.

## NEIGHBORHOOD EFFECTS AND COLLECTIVE GOODS

The preceding exposition has laid out an uncritical Hayekian case for solving environmental problems through market processes. In the eyes of some of his recent exponents, this analysis largely exhausts Hayek's contribution to environmental political economy. As Roy Cordato puts the point:

> Hayek's guidelines point toward a true free-market approach to environmental issues. We must establish rules of conduct that clearly define people's rights, their "protected domain." The primary goal of all public policy, including environmental policy, should be the enforcement of rights once they are clearly defined. (1997, 385)

Comments like these help to illustrate Hayek's influence as an inspiration for free-market environmentalism. Yet, as I will show in this section, Hayek himself made important qualifications to the claim that environmental problems should be left to the market. These arguments open the door for a very different interpretation of Hayek's legacy than free-market environmentalists have emphasized—one that makes considerable room for political interventions to address environmental issues.

### Neighborhood Effects

In Hayek's writings, the phenomenon of "neighborhood effects" provides a key source of reservations in applying the foregoing analysis to the environmental domain (1960, 316 and 319; 1981, 43–46).[7] We have already seen that Hayek's expectations of market functionality are tied to the idea that individuals must bear the consequences of their actions. Yet in environmental contexts, the conditions for such accountability are sometimes absent. Individuals can sometimes benefit from imposing burdens on others or face personal losses as a result of publicly beneficial actions. In cases like these, market incentives can fail to drive individuals to act with sensitivity to broader economic needs (1981, 43).

In the previous section, we briefly discussed the possibility of resolving such problems through the extension of property rights and legal institutions. Yet Hayek does not expect that such resolutions will always be available. One reason is that certain resource systems have features that make it difficult to incorporate them into effective patterns of property ownership. "Fugitive resources," which cannot be assigned to particular individuals prior to consumptive appropriation, provide an illustrative example. When it comes to resources like fish, water, and oil, Hayek writes, "no individual exploiter will have an interest in conserving, since what he does not take will be taken by others" (1960, 319). He notes that in some cases it will be possible to improve market functionality by redrawing property boundaries so that "the units of property are of such size that at least all the more important effects of any one owner's actions are reflected in the value of his own property" (319). But when this cannot be done to a sufficient degree, he concedes, "we must resort to alternative forms of regulation" (319).

Similar problems arise in the context of air and water pollution. Here, too, Hayek suspects that property rights will not always suffice to yield favorable outcomes, as "calculation by the individuals which takes into account only the effects upon their protected domain will not secure that balancing of costs and benefits which will in general be achieved where . . . the owner alone will experience the effects" (1981, 43). In such cases Hayek again allows that public intervention may be warranted, though he insists that replacing market coordination with political direction is in many respects an "*inferior* method" of providing citizens what they desire (46).

A different kind of issue emerges when individuals stand to *benefit* their neighbors through actions that would produce little gain for themselves. Hayek observes that "it is either technically impossible, or would be prohibitively costly, to confine certain services to particular persons, so that these services can be provided only for all (or at least will be provided more cheaply and effectively if they are provided for all)" (1981, 44). He continues:

> In many instances the rendering of such services could bring no gain to those who do so, and they will therefore not be provided by the market. These are the collective or public goods proper, for the provision of which it will be necessary to devise some method other than that of sale to the individual user. (44)

Hayek does not immediately conclude from the existence of public goods that governmental involvement is warranted. For he observes that in many historical contexts citizens have managed to organize themselves to provide these goods on their own (1960, 109 and 324; 1981, 50). But he nevertheless acknowledges that in large communities where the benefits from public goods would be broadly dispersed, the most practicable way to secure these goods will often be for each citizen "to agree to be compelled, provided this compulsion is also applied to others" (1981, 44). In the category of collective goods that might call for public assistance Hayek includes the provision of environmental amenities, recreation opportunities, natural parks, and nature reservations, as well as the preservation of natural beauty, historic sites, and places of scientific interest (1960, 324).[8]

## A Question of Consistency

The foregoing comments suggest that in the face of significant environmental problems, a Hayekian approach might be compatible with a very active government. This observation gives bite to Dan Greenwood's objection to proponents of free-market environmentalism (FME) who downplay the proper role of political action:

> [W]here environmental problems involve costs and negative impacts across a large, even global scale, as is the case with climate change, the role of states and international governance in establishing an overarching framework for market mechanisms would need to be more substantial than FME theorists acknowledge. (2015, 427)

Far from grounding a radically market-oriented approach to environmental political economy, Hayek's theory might seem to license aggressive schemes of environmental regulation.

At this point we must therefore ask how Hayek's endorsement of potentially significant regulation can be reconciled with the emphases on robust individual liberty and unfettered markets that we saw in the previous section. To see the answer, we must remind ourselves exactly what Hayek considers problematic about government intervention in the first place. As we saw in the previous section, Hayek's primary interest is to bar governments from interfering in economic activities in ways that would prevent individuals from using their personal knowledge to the benefit of their communities. Political activities might run afoul of this concern by centralizing economic discretion, fixing market prices, subjecting citizens to extensive or arbitrary coercion, undermining property rights, and decoupling individuals' incentives from the interests of their neighbors. By the same token, however, interventions could avoid Hayek's misgivings by maintaining economic decentralization, allowing prices to float freely, preserving broad individual liberty limited only by known general rules, honoring private property rights, and maintaining close connections between individuals' incentives and the broader good.

Respecting such constraints on public policy making would leave open a considerable variety of options for governments to promote public environmental objectives. For example, administrators might seek to mitigate pollution by prohibiting the emission of certain harmful chemicals. Or they might charge set fees for the privilege to emit, reducing overall levels of pollution without banning emissions outright. Such policies would limit the kinds of activities that individuals could undertake without being coerced, but so long as these limits were enforced through known general rules, they would create no special problems from a Hayekian point of view. As Hayek explains, "a free system does not exclude on principle all those general regulations of economic activity which can be laid down in the form of general rules specifying conditions which everybody who engages in a certain activity must satisfy" (1960, 197).

Hayek also emphasizes that governments can achieve many goals by organizing themselves like private firms (1973, 48). For example, a public nature preserve could be created on land purchased on the open market through voluntary transactions. Officials could then operate the preserve using government-owned resources, avoiding interference with others' rights in the process. In doing these things, the government's role in the economy would be analogous to that played by any other economic actor, and hence it would be unproblematic from the standpoint of market functionality. The main difference would be the government's ability to fund these activities through its power to coercively tax its citizens. Yet Hayek insists that so long as this coercion were employed in line with known general rules, there would again be no special problems from the standpoint of his theory (1960, 126).

Hayek's comments about political interventions into environmental affairs thus reflect no deep tension in his view. So long as proposed interventions did not threaten the basic preconditions of market functionality, they could be affirmed on a Hayekian perspective without inconsistency. This helps to make sense of Hayek's repeated endorsements of such interventions,[9] which might otherwise be mysterious.

Yet by the same token, we can also see that in order to merit Hayek's endorsement, policies would need to take particular forms. If government proposals threatened the foundations of the market process, then Hayek's position would offer principled grounds for rejecting them (1960, 194–95). It is the preservation of markets that therefore represents Hayek's primary criterion for assessing the admissibility of policy proposals. He writes:

> [I]t is the character rather than the volume of government activity that is important. A functioning market economy presupposes certain activities on the part of the state; there are some other activities by which its functioning will be assisted; and it can tolerate many more, provided that they are of the kind which are compatible with a functioning market. (194)

## Matters of Expediency

Although Hayek offers no *principled* objection to many government interventions, we must take care not to interpret him as offering blanket endorsement for them. On the contrary, Hayek's main intention is to draw a bright distinction between policies that are merely inexpedient or imprudent and those whose characteristics would be corrosive to the market's functionality. He writes:

> [T]here are good reasons why all government concern with economic matters is suspect and why, in particular, there is a strong presumption against government's actively participating in economic efforts. But these arguments are quite different from the general argument for economic freedom. They rest on the fact that the great majority of governmental measures which have been advocated in this field are, in fact, inexpedient, either because they will fail or because their costs will outweigh the advantages. . . . The habitual appeal to the principle of non-interference in the fight against all ill-considered or harmful measures has had the effect of blurring the fundamental distinction between the kinds of measures which are and those which are not compatible with a free system. (1960, 194)

By suggesting that certain interventions may sometimes be appropriate, then, Hayek is not suggesting that they should be undertaken without scrutiny. Rather, he is saying that these interventions should be evaluated on their respective merits and not rejected out of hand.

This attitude carries straightforwardly into the environmental domain. Although Hayek grants that certain kinds of interventions may be warranted in response to "neighborhood effects," he is careful to emphasize that particular proposals should be carefully evaluated to ensure their practical value. This caveat is especially important given what Hayek sees as a propensity of environmental policy analysts to exaggerate their abilities to forecast and improve the future (1974). Political actions to promote environmental values should proceed only "so long as the community approves this, in full awareness of the cost, and realizes that this is one aim competing with others and not a unique objective overriding all other needs" (1960, 324).

If free-market environmentalists wish to dispute the arguments raised by critics like Greenwood, then these are the grounds on which they must do so. In the face of serious environmentally mediated externalities, it will not do to say that political interventions are ruled out in principle by Hayek's theory. So long as such interventions are designed to preserve the market's functioning—an important caveat, to be sure—their acceptability must be assessed in terms of their relative expediency, and not rejected out of general hostility to political action.

## Inexpediency Guaranteed?

In a cynical twist on what I have just said, several free-market environmentalist writers have sought to deploy Hayekian insights to show that political responses to externalities are virtually guaranteed to be inexpedient (Carden 2013; Cordato 1997; McGee and Block 1994). The general thrust of these arguments has been that because government officials possess severely limited economic knowledge as a matter of course, it would be virtually impossible for them to design public policies that improved on the outcomes generated by markets.

Squarely in the sights of these arguments have been "market-based" policy instruments such as pollution taxes and permit trading schemes. These policies seek to redirect market processes toward more favorable outcomes by manipulating individuals' incentives. Taxes directly increase the costs of engaging in environmentally harmful behaviors, while permit trading schemes force individuals to obtain costly permits (or forego profits from selling permits to others) in order to pollute. In both cases, individuals are left with broad latitude to decide whether and how to engage in polluting activities, but the costs and benefits of their options are altered so as to incentivize more environmentally friendly choices.

Free-market environmentalist critics claim that these policies are rooted in misguided ideas about the epistemic powers of regulators. Pollution taxes must be set at particular rates and permit-trading schemes must release particular numbers of permits. Yet as we have seen, much of the information relevant to making these determinations is dispersed throughout the general population. Although pollution taxes should be set to reflect the "external harms" associated with particular increments of pollution (and although permit availability should reflect an optimal balance between the costs and benefits of particular levels of pollution), the knowledge needed to align tax rates with "external harms" (and permit totals with optimal cost-benefit balances) is never made available to central minds. The epistemic conditions required for effective market-based policies are therefore claimed to be unrealizable in practice.

Edwin Dolan has rightly observed that these arguments fail by making the perfect the enemy of the good. They imply that as long as political interventions cannot produce ideal results, then they must be rejected as inexpedient (2014, 211–13). As we saw in the previous section, Hayek's entire position in the domain of environmental political economy is built around the view that our enduring limitations may make imperfect alternatives our best options in practice. Just as Hayek rejects the claim that the argument for competitive markets depends on their perfection (1981, 65–67), so too must he reject the claim that political interventions can only be justified when they are perfect. Insofar as proposed policies conform to the basic principles of a well-functioning market society, the more sensible view from a Hayekian perspective would be the one expressed by John Dales, the pioneer of market-based environmental policy: "Even if social problems are logically insoluble, something is always being done about them, and the practical question is always whether we can do something *better* about them than we are now doing" (1968, 40).[10]

Of course, it is critically important not to lose sight of the fact that the answer to Dales's question will often be no. By investigating the expediency of potential environmental policy interventions, we should expect to find good reason to reject many proposals. Government agents really do face serious limitations in their abilities to improve the conditions we face, and political actors are all too often inclined to push for interventions that would make things worse. The key point is simply that skepticism about the merits of environmental policies should not blind us to the need to actually evaluate them.

## DEFERRING TO COMPLEXITY

Our discussion thus far has captured the core elements of Hayek's own views on environmental political economy. However, Gus DiZerega (1992; 1996a; 1996b), Andrew Gamble (2006, 129–30), and John O'Neill (2012) have emphasized a further theme in Hayek's work that also bears on environmental issues. According to these commentators, the ideas motivating Hayek's allegiance to economic markets also apply to natural ecosystems, with DiZerega in particular drawing the inference that consistent Hayekians should be principled environmentalists as well. Although Hayek never developed such a position himself, exploring this point will help to round out our investigation of how Hayekian political economy can be applied in environmental debates.

### The Significance of Complex Systems

Let us begin by recalling why Hayek advocates reliance on markets to coordinate economic affairs. As we saw above, economic prosperity relies on effectively using a massive amount of information, and yet this information is irretrievably dispersed. The only way for societies to become sensitive to all of this information is to decentralize decision making to individuals embedded in a market economy. Market activities give rise to prices, and the price system guides individuals to act with sensitivity to others' circumstances. Markets thereby cause favorable patterns of economic activity to "emerge" even when such outcomes could never have been produced by a central designer.

In Hayek's view, our reliance on markets is illustrative of a broader issue. Many worldly phenomena are too complex to be produced through deliberate construction, but they can emerge "spontaneously" when conditions are right. Perhaps the most straightforward examples come from chemistry:

> We can never produce a crystal or a complex organic compound by placing the individual atoms in such a position that they will form the lattice of a crystal or the system based on benzol rings which make up an organic compound. But we can create the conditions in which they will arrange themselves in such a manner. (Hayek 1973, 39–40)

Hayek sees market economies as similar in that they could never be arranged through conscious planning. If they are to exist at all, they must be permitted to "grow" on their own (36–38). Hayek finds other analogous cases throughout society, rejecting as fundamentally misguided the view that "Morals, religion and law, language and writing, money and the market were . . . deliberately constructed by someone" (10). He prefers instead to explain these phenomena by appeal to unguided processes of social evolution (17–19).

Hayek claims that our reliance on self-organizing complex systems both extends and limits our abilities to realize our goals. These systems empower us by facilitating outcomes we could never produce through deliberate planning. But they also limit us in that we typically cannot control them in their finer details (41–42). Indeed, Hayek writes, "There will be many aspects . . . over which we will possess no control at all, or which at least we shall not be able to alter without interfering with—and to that extent impeding—the forces producing the spontaneous order" (42).

Hayek's concerns about interfering with complex systems are well illustrated by the policy positions discussed in the previous sections. But they become most emphatic when he lays out the case for maintaining broad latitude for individual liberty in society. Since liberty is essential to the functioning of market processes, Hayek argues that its preservation is critical if societies are to continue to prosper. Yet he recognizes that the consequences of undermining liberty will often be unclear in individual cases, since our understandings of social and economic systems are insufficient to enable accurate, detailed predictions. Hence he writes:

> [W]hen we decide each issue solely on what appear to be its individual merits, we always over-estimate the advantages of central direction. Our choice will regularly appear to be one between a certain known and tangible gain and the mere probability of the prevention of some unknown beneficial action by unknown persons. If the choice between freedom and coercion is thus treated as a matter of expediency, freedom is bound to be sacrificed in almost every instance. (57)

It is for this reason that Hayek contends that "A successful defence of freedom must . . . be dogmatic and make no concessions to expediency, even where it is not possible to show that, besides the known beneficial effects, some particular harmful result would also follow from its infringement" (61). Maintaining social and economic functionality requires a principled devotion to liberty, not because we will always be able to understand the specific benefits of acting on such principles, but because robust individual liberty is necessary for the operations of the complex systems on which we rely.

## Complexity in Nature

DiZerega, Gamble, and O'Neill seek to extend Hayek's theory by observing that his arguments concerning complex systems are general in form and not limited to the particular systems he happens to discuss. Where there are complex, self-organizing systems on which humanity relies; where we cannot completely control these systems but may still undermine them through our actions; and where we cannot accurately foresee the full consequences of interfering with these systems, Hayek's account would seem to recommend principled deference to the mechanisms underlying their functionality. This conclusion should hold for any system with the characteristics just enumerated. At the level of theory, there is nothing about market economies that makes them uniquely worthy of respect.

DiZerega, Gamble, and O'Neill contend that the ecological domain contains complex, self-organizing systems on which people rely—systems that we cannot completely control but that can be undermined through our actions, and that are insufficiently understood to enable accurate assessments of the costs and benefits of interference. Hence they argue that Hayek's arguments should extend to these systems as well. As DiZerega has stated, consistency requires Hayekians to affirm the need to protect natural ecosystems in the same principled manner—and for essentially the same reasons—that governs their advocacy for markets (1992, 357; 1996a, 10–11; 1996b, 730–31). O'Neill likewise remarks that the complacent attitude that Hayek seemingly exhibits toward environmental issues represents a "failure to apply his own strictures about ignorance and complexity to human abilities to know and control complex open systems in the natural world" (2012, 1081).

## Principled Hayekian Environmentalism

Suppose that we grant for the sake of argument that DiZerega, Gamble, and O'Neill are correct about the need to protect ecological systems as a matter of principle. What would this mean in practice? Let us begin by saying something about what it would *not* mean. According to DiZerega, a proper commitment to protecting the natural environment would compel us to fundamentally rethink individuals' rights to degrade natural resources under their control. As he sees it, "there should be no right to indulge in extractive use of a sustainable resource in ways that impair its indefinite renewal" (1996a, 11). Instead, societies should adopt principles whereby "In using an ecosystem for resource extraction, actions such as polluting ground water, destroying soil fertility, and eliminating ecosystems such as salmon rivers and old growth forests would be inadmissible" (1996b, 731). In DiZerega's view, people should ensure that every resource system they utilize "not be left worse off, in the sense that its basic role within the environment should not be seriously compromised" (1992, 356). And this should be done "regardless of how inconvenient we find the changes it will require in current logging, fishing, and agricultural practices" (358).

If humanity relied for its prosperity on the functioning of every natural ecosystem, then DiZerega's suggestions might be warranted. For even if it looked like some environmental protections would sacrifice significant benefits for the sake of avoiding merely possible harm to key systems, a principled devotion to environmental protection might demand such sacrifices. However, in truth our future prospects are not nearly so fragile. Humanity may rely on the protection of "the natural order as a whole," as DiZerega puts it (1996a, 4), but this does not mean that prosperity depends on the preservation of specific ecosystems like individual forests, fisheries, and croplands.

Here Hayek's analogy to manufactured capital is illuminating. Societies must have an adequate portfolio of productive capital in order to prosper, but this does not mean that they depend on the preservation of any particular capital assets. The mark of a successful economy is not the ability to preserve all of its initial capital endowments. Rather, it is the ability to deal effectively with the deterioration and loss of assets over time. In the same way, dependence on ecological systems does not mean that every natural resource should be preserved intact.[11] Instead, it implies the more overarching commitment recognized by Gamble: "to prevent the fatal undermining of the ecosphere on which all human activity ultimately depends" (2006, 130).

Threats to this order would look more like catastrophic global climate change than like the destruction of a particular forest or river. And these threats could be resisted as a matter of principle without opposing all insults to the smaller-scale ecosystems involved in everyday economic affairs. If Hayekians were serious about preserving the complex systems on which humanity relies, then a principled stance of this kind would seem straightforwardly attractive.

What measures could a Hayekian recommend to address threats to "the natural order as a whole"? In previous sections, we have seen Hayek advocate responses to environmental problems that would work by strengthening market institutions or remedying their gaps through political interventions. To this point, the rationales behind these suggestions have revolved around making markets more effective on their own terms—that is, by making economic activities more sensitive to the knowledge and desires of citizens. But if we grant that crucial ecological systems should be protected as a matter of principle, then similar actions might also be undertaken in order to sensitize individuals to the need to preserve overarching ecological systems as well.

Extending Hayek's theory to demand protection for ecosystems on which we rely would not have to change much about the kinds of policy prescriptions that could be reconciled with his account. But it would have significant consequences for the circumstances under which particular proposals could be embraced. Earlier it was said that proposed interventions would need to be shown expedient before their adoption could be recommended. But if critical natural systems were to be protected as a matter of principle, then this criterion would need to be relaxed. More appropriately, proposals would need to be assessed on the basis of whether they really would protect systems on which humanity relies, as well as whether they represented the most efficient and effective means available for delivering such protections.

In line with our previous discussion, a crucial desideratum for environmental policies would continue to be the preservation of the functionality of the market process. For it should not be forgotten that markets are essential to societies' abilities to prosper, and to the coordination of natural resource use more specifically. Insofar as critical ecological systems could be protected while also maintaining economic decentralization, allowing prices to fluctuate, protecting individual liberty within the bounds of known general rules, honoring property rights, and preserving individual accountability, then this is plainly what a Hayekian approach would recommend.

Of course, there are interesting questions to be asked about what a Hayekian should say in cases where critical ecological systems *cannot* be protected without undermining the market order. But given the wide range of options for advancing ecological goals without eroding markets, Hayekians should be highly skeptical of allegations that such choices must be made. In practice, it seems likely that such dilemmas will be exceedingly rare. Hence, as a general matter, Hayekian environmentalism can safely define itself by its refusal to sacrifice economic functionality in the name of environmental protection, even though in certain exceptional cases this position might need to be qualified.

## BRINGING IT ALL TOGETHER

We are now finally in a position to try to synthesize the implications of Hayek's paradigm for environmental political economy. As we have seen, the core of Hayek's theory is the idea that natural resources form just one part of society's capital portfolio, and that for the most part the use of these resources is best governed by decentralized market decision making. However, Hayek sees the existence of "neighborhood effects" as providing openings for the government to helpfully intervene into environmental affairs, taking expedient measures to restrict "external" harms and to facilitate the provision of valuable "public goods." To the extent that humanity's prosperity depends on self-organizing complex systems in nature, a Hayekian paradigm could also conceivably recommend a range of principled measures aimed at maintaining the functionality of these systems over time.

These conclusions cast doubt on the straightforward link that has often been drawn between Hayek's political economy and contemporary articulations of "free-market environmentalism." Hayek would surely agree with free-market environmentalists that political interventions should be carefully scrutinized and that many environmental problems should be addressed by leaning on markets. But he would reject the view that political action should be deprecated as a matter of principle in the environmental domain. From the perspective of Hayekian political economy, it is the character of interventions that determines whether they can cohere with a well-functioning market order. When policies are designed in appropriate ways, they become eligible for consideration on their respective merits.

Hayek's guidance on the character of proposed interventions represents his real contribution to environmental policy debates. Well-functioning societies rely on decentralization of economic decision making, price systems free from political manipulation, broad latitude for individual choice, robust institutions of private property, and alignments between individuals' interests and the consequences of their actions. Environmental policies that undermine these conditions—for example, by fixing prices or centralizing natural resource management under bureaucratic control—warrant resistance as a matter of principle, even when we may not be able to foresee the specific bad consequences of adopting them. For environmentalists who would seek to make their proposals compatible with market functionality, these constraints set significant limits on the kinds of policies that can properly be pursued. But they also offer a template for formulating policies to achieve their goals without running afoul of market principles. Hayekian political economy can thus point the way toward an approach to environmental policy that takes both markets and environmental problems seriously.

## NOTES

1. For another expression of this idea, see Hayek 1973, 14.

2. This concern with avoiding the centralization of economic decision making is behind Hayek's most pointed criticisms of the conservation movement of his time. As Hayek explains, "Few arguments have been used so widely and effectively to persuade the public of the 'wastefulness of competition' and the desirability of a central direction of important economic activities as the alleged squandering of natural resources by private enterprise" (1960, 319). In Hayek's view, the drive to economic centralization motivated by these perspectives is precisely the wrong response to the emergence of environmental challenges.

3. It is on these grounds that Hayek condemns real-world interventions into global agricultural markets that manipulate prices for political purposes. These manipulations prevent individuals from gaining the information and incentives that would lead them to use their resources in socially beneficial ways (1960, 310–12).

4. This point helps to explain why Hayek is so vocal in resisting widespread subsidies for agricultural lifestyles, which he considers so obviously harmful that "almost everywhere the more thoughtful specialists no longer ask what would be a rational policy to pursue but only which of the courses that seem politically feasible would do the least harm" (1960, 313).

5. For elaboration of this last point, see Hasnas (2009).

6. This point bears importantly on John O'Neill's concern that market actors in Hayek's scheme must overcome excessive epistemic obstacles in order to determine what courses of action are truly best (2012, 1084–86). If Hayek were employing a high bar for evaluating the quality of economic decisions, then O'Neill's point would be merited. But insofar as Hayek is only saying that decentralized decision making will tend to yield *better* outcomes than available alternatives, there is no reason to think that the epistemic quality of each individual's decisions would need to be very high in order to vindicate the view.

7. It is worth noting that the presence of neighborhood effects is not the only reason that Hayek expects it to be profitable for governments to intervene in environmental affairs. To cite just one example, Hayek notes that bureaucrats will often command superior scientific expertise to that of private citizens, and that at certain stages of economic development it will be difficult for natural resource users to gain access to similar expertise in the marketplace. Hayek accordingly suggests that bureaucrats may provide a valuable service by providing resource users with technical information about how best to utilize the assets under their control (1960, 315).

8. Here my assessment directly contradicts Robert Bradley Jr.'s characterization of Hayek as believing that "Market failure as a rationale for government intervention was effectively rebutted" (2007, 75).

9. To cite one especially emphatic example relating to the provision of public goods, Hayek writes in *Law, Legislation, and Liberty*: "[W]e find it unquestionable that in an advanced society government ought to use its power of raising funds by taxation to provide a number of services which for various reasons cannot be provided, or cannot be provided adequately, by the market. Indeed, it could be maintained that, even if there were no other need for coercion, because everybody voluntarily obeyed the traditional rules of just conduct, there would still exist an overwhelming case for

giving the territorial authorities power to make the inhabitants contribute to a common fund from which such services could be financed" (1981, 41).

10. One important distinction to be drawn in this context is between policies that seek to achieve ideal states of affairs and those that seek to improve upon the status quo by remedying specific problems. In practice, environmental policies are often proposed on the grounds that public officials can remedy "market failures" and realize "efficient" outcomes through intervention. All too often this results in government agents operating under the pretense that they know more than they do and are more in control than they really are (Hayek 1974). Worthwhile interventions will typically aim at more humble objectives, seeking to ameliorate society's most egregious problems through measures that are straightforwardly worth the costs.

11. This point echoes Hayek's insistence that communities may sometimes be best served by allowing some of their resource systems to deteriorate: "As in certain circumstances it will be desirable to build up the fertility of a piece of land by artificially enriching it . . . so in certain other circumstances it will be desirable to allow the fertility to decline. . . . In some instances this may even mean that it is uneconomical to aim at permanent cultivation and that, after the accumulated natural fertility has been exhausted, the land ought to be abandoned, because in the geographical or climatic conditions it cannot with advantage be permanently cultivated" (1960, 322).

# REFERENCES

Anderson, Terry L., and Donald Leal. 2015. *Free Market Environmentalism for the Next Generation*. New York: Palgrave.

Bradley, Robert L. 2007. "Resourceship: An Austrian Theory of Mineral Resources." *Review of Austrian* Economics 20: 63–90.

Carden, Art. 2013. "Economic Calculation in the Environmentalist Commonwealth." *Quarterly Journal of Austrian Economics* 16: 3–16.

Cordato, Roy E. 1997. "Market-Based Environmentalism and the Free Market: They're Not the Same." *Independent Review* 1: 371–86.

Dales, John. 1968. *Pollution, Property and Prices: An Essay in Policy-Making and Economics*. Toronto: University of Toronto Press.

DiZerega, Gus. 1992. "Social Ecology, Deep Ecology, and Liberalism." *Critical Review* 6: 305–70.

———. 1996a. "Towards an Ecocentric Political Economy." *Trumpeter* 13.

———. 1996b. "Deep Ecology and Liberalism: The Greener Implications of Evolutionary Liberal Theory." *Review of Politics* 58: 699–734.

Dolan, Edwin. 2014. "The Austrian Paradigm in Environmental Economics: Theory and Practice." *Quarterly Journal of Austrian Economics* 17: 197–217.

Gamble, Andrew. 2006. "Hayek on Knowledge, Economics, and Society." In *The Cambridge Companion to Hayek*, edited by Edward Feser, 111–31. New York: Cambridge University Press.

Greenwood, Dan. 2007. "The Halfway House: Democracy, Complexity, and the Limits to Markets in Green Political Economy." *Environmental Politics* 16: 73–91.

————. 2015. "In Search of Green Political Economy: Steering Markets, Innovation, and the Zero Carbon Homes Agenda in England." *Environmental Politics* 24: 423–41.

Hasnas, John. 2009. "Two Theories of Environmental Regulation." *Social Philosophy & Policy* 26: 95–129.

Hayek, F. A. 1941. *The Pure Theory of Capital*. Indianapolis: Liberty Fund.

————. 1945. "The Use of Knowledge in Society." *American Economic Review* 35: 519–30.

————. 1960. *The Constitution of Liberty*. New York: Routledge.

————. 1973. *Law, Legislation, and Liberty, vol. I: Rules and Order*. Chicago: University of Chicago Press.

————. 1974. "The Pretence of Knowledge." Available online at http://www.nobelprize.org/nobel_prizes/economic-sciences/laureates/1974/hayek-lecture.html.

————. 1976. *Law, Legislation, and Liberty, vol. II: The Mirage of Social Justice*. Chicago: University of Chicago Press.

————. 1981. *Law, Legislation, and Liberty, vol. III: The Political Order of a Free People*. Chicago: University of Chicago Press.

McGee, Robert W., and Walter E. Block. 1994. "Pollution Trading Permits as a Form of Market Socialism and the Search for a Real Market Solution to Environmental Pollution." *Fordham Environmental Law Journal* 6: 51–77.

O'Neill, John. 2012. "Austrian Economics and the Limits of Markets." *Cambridge Journal of Economics* 36: 1073–90.

Pennington, Mark. 2005. "Liberty, Markets, and Environmental Values: A Hayekian Defense of Free-Market Environmentalism." *Independent Review* 10: 39–57.

*Part II*

# INTERDISCIPLINARY APPLICATIONS OF MARKET PROCESS THEORY

## Chapter 5

# The Origins of Entrepreneurship and the Market Process

## An Archaeological Assessment of Competitive Feasting, Trade, and Social Cooperation

### Crystal A. Dozier

The market system is traditionally characterized as a complex mechanism through which goods and services are distributed according to the laws of supply and demand. The mechanics of this system are crucial to understanding the complex world in which we live today; no place on earth remains untouched by the globalizing forces of the market system. The market is not simply the rush of numbers across the news ticker; there are foundational cultural practices and beliefs that allow for market exchanges to occur and that dictate the nature of those exchanges (Lavoie and Chamlee-Wright 2000; Chamlee-Wright 1997; Storr 2010, 2013). While the modern market system of exchange—goods and labor for pieces of paper or numbers on a computer screen—seems second nature to those within this complex maelstrom, humanity has only fairly recently adopted this system of exchange.

Various researchers have explored reasons why Western capitalistic systems have historically dominated (e.g., Diamond 1999; McCloskey 2010b; A. Smith 1982); the origins of complex trading and the accompanying incentive systems, however, predate written history. Several phenomena are often cited as contributing factors within the development of market systems; I discuss three of these phenomena here: property, specialization, and long-distance trade. These three hallmarks of the market order are not inherent to the human condition. Only in the last ten thousand years is there evidence for sedentism and territoriality (property), the creation of specialized occupations (specialization), and trade across natural, large geographical areas (long-distance trade). The sociocultural circumstances under which private property, division of labor, and long-distance trade emerges, however, seem to have been catalyzed by competitive feasting. Although sociocultural circumstances are similar in the development of these important economic traits, there is diversity in the geographic and temporal situations in the development of complex foraging traditions (Arnold et al. 2015) and thereby the origins of the market process.

Competitive feasting, as will be expounded in the following pages, requires competing individuals to host increasingly excessive events (Hayden 2014b). The host of the feast provides material goods, such as special foods or symbolic totems, to their guests, and in turn, gains great social status. These feasts provide a mechanism through which different groups of people get together for long-distance trade, plan marital/political unions, and allow for intensification in division of labor, as new specialized goods and services are desired. Competitive feasting allows for individuals to gain social (and biological) influence while enhancing the experience of the group at large. These aggrandizers utilize entrepreneurial awareness to create avenues for sociocultural and economic complexity.

I argue, as archaeologists have done before, that increasing population pressure during stable climatic periods results in intensified action across the landscape (e.g., Binford 1968, 2001). Social coordination is required in order to maintain peaceful relationships in increasingly populated areas (Richerson and Boyd 1995). In these situations, where population pressure is mounting, putting diverse and competing groups of people in contact with one another, a similar phenomenon, competitive feasting, is observed.

To illustrate this mechanism at work, I present three archaeological examples of competitive feasting. I chose my three examples (Neolithic Anatolia, Bronze Age European Celts, and Late Prehistoric Texas) to represent three different continents at three different periods of time. All three examples are preceded by a period of low population densities of hunter-fisher-gatherers; with climatic stability and increasing population densities, all three examples show archaeological evidence of competitive feasting. Evidence for competitive feasting is correlated with the first evidence in each respective region for territoriality, creation of specialized labor, and long-distance trade. These three expressions of increasing sociocultural complexity arose prior to and independently of the adoption of agriculture (c.f. Arnold et al. 2015), and in the Texas example, farming was not practiced in the region until European colonization.

In the following pages, I present archaeological evidence to support the interpretation of competitive feasting regimes as catalysts in the development of pillars of the market order. In order to do so, I highlight the theoretical, ethnographic, and archaeological evidence that informs on the mechanisms of competitive feasting, as well as the sociocultural and material repercussions of feasting regimes. I analyze how this theoretical framework differs from other conceptualizations of the market order. In conclusion, I find that competitive feasting mechanisms are consistent with neo-evolutionary understandings of social entrepreneurship and human hypersociality. Feasting studies reaffirm the importance of cultural systems as predicating economic action.

But in order to do so, I must start at the beginning of human orders.

## BEFORE MARKET ORDERS

The first *Homo sapiens* lived in Africa over 190,000 years before present (BP), according to the fossil record (Trinkaus 2005; Cann and Wilson 2003). The archaeological record indicates that humans spread across the globe conquering new and extreme environments in small mobile groups that hunted, fished, and gathered wild plants. The Pleistocene, the geological epoch of this period—often referred to as the Ice Age—was much cooler and wetter than today but also experienced more dramatic shifts in worldwide temperature (Farrand 1990). The archaeological record shows no strong evidence for sedentism, division of labor, or long-distance trade in the Pleistocene, and in some places no evidence for such shows up until much later.

A notion of individual ownership of items seems to be innate to the human condition; even the most ancient burials contain goods that are presumed to be owned by the deceased. But for the purposes here, property should be conceived of as ownership or authority over a particular landscape. Remains of dwellings are rarely found from the Pleistocene. An extraordinary shelter at the site of Mal'ta in Siberia from thirty thousand years ago indicates that Ice Age peoples sometimes used mammoth bones to fasten their shelters, presumably with leather coverings, in the frigid tundra (Klein 1971; Vasil'ev 1993). Most shelters would likely have been made from organic material (wood, reed, grass, leather) that have not survived. The food and trash remains (middens) from this period indicate that camp sites were not occupied year-round (Feder 2014, 170–83). There are very few cemeteries from this period (Feder 2014, 180; Wengrow and Graeber 2015)—cemeteries require that families/groups return to a special place for burial. As such, cemeteries are usually interpreted as a sign of sedentism/territorialism because they are a marked place on the landscape that a particular group has claimed for their ancestors (Kelly 1992). The archaeological record therefore shows little to no evidence for sedentism/territorialism, and therefore conceptions of property ownership, for the majority of human history.

In these migrating family groups, there is little evidence for specialized labor. While there are slight variations in stone tool manufacture and use between groups, the basic tool kit remains the same. Both men and women are found with stone tools and there are no significant differences in health between the sexes observed skeletally (Holt and Formicola 2008). Burials themselves generally contain grave goods that are presumed to be tools of the deceased, but there is no elaboration of tombs and only rarely special treatment made to individuals, though exceptions exist (e.g., Pettitt and Bader 2000). While objects of art have been found in the Pleistocene (e.g., "Venus" figurines [Dixson and Dixson 2011; Soffer, Adovasio, and Hyland 2000]), there is not enough evidence to suggest that an individual in the group would have been primarily occupied by anything other than resource/food acquisition.

Resource acquisition in the Pleistocene was from the local environment. The remains of stone tools, the most common archaeological evidence, are almost exclusively from local sources (Feder 2014, 177). Food items are also exclusively from the local environment; there is very little evidence of food storage (Ingold 1983; Whelan et al. 2013), with no ceramics and no evidence for domesticated plants until ten thousand years ago, at the earliest. There is little evidence for sustained, regular long-distance trade in the Ice Age.

These Pleistocene patterns remained fairly unchanged in many areas of the world until the advent of colonialism. Very few long-distance foraging societies remain today (Kelly 1995). Ethnographic studies of foraging peoples, however, can provide limited analogy into the sociopolitical structures that archaeologists would expect to see in the Pleistocene (Binford 1967, 2001). In these societies, individual bands are led by elders who gain their status through their knowledge and works for the group. These leaders, however, do not experience a significant improvement in their condition relative to the groups. Within mobile hunting-fishing-gathering societies, boasting or showboating is heavily discouraged or even tabooed (Lee 1969; Henrich et al. 2001). This does not mean that inherent inequalities are completely absent from egalitarian foraging groups (Speth 1990).

Around ten thousand years ago, the patterns from the Pleistocene suddenly changed in what archaeologists call the Neolithic revolution. As will be expounded on below, the advent of the Holocene, our current geological epoch, brought warmer and more stable climates worldwide. Population densities started to rise in fertile river valleys, and new archaeological traditions indicate increased social complexity. The patterns seen in the Neolithic revolution are not observed at the same chronological point worldwide; rather, transitions into more complex political and economic situations seem to be predicated by individual situations of population pressure, landscape productivity, and climatic stability. Multiple subsistence strategies are observed in this transition from mobile egalitarianism to inherited leadership positions; while agricultural regimes regularly receive more attention as a stark contrast to prior lifeways, archaeological consensus is now coalescing around the phenomenon of complex hunting-fishing-gathering lifeways as predicating the hierarchical, sedentary, complex societies that now dominate the globe

(Arnold et al. 2015). Before illustrating three archaeological examples of transitions in complexity, I first describe the theoretical underpinnings to feasting regimes.

## FEASTING REGIMES: ALERT ENTREPRENEURS AND PRO-SOCIAL BEHAVIOR

Feasting phenomena have been the object of anthropological study for over a hundred years (Hayden and Villeneuve 2011). Feasts, celebrations that feature conspicuous consumption of food and goods, occur worldwide and often leave archaeologically visible remains (Hayden 2014b; Dietler and Hayden 2010). Hayden (2014b, 10) recognizes several kinds of feasts: alliance and cooperation, economic (for gain), and diacritical (for status display).

Competitive feasting is of primary interest here; it describes the ethnographically and archaeologically observed phenomenon of feasts held within an extended community that intensify through time. The classic ethnographic example of feasting of this type is recorded along the Pacific Coast of North America (J. Arnold 2001). Hayden (2014b) highlights the importance of the hosts in propagating competitive feasts; he uses the term "aggrandizers" to describe individuals who have the social awareness and sophistication to organize large consumption events. Aggrandizers utilize their social network to amass goods that they allocate to their guests. In turn, aggrandizers are respected for their generosity and the grandness of the feasts they are able to host. Hayden's notion of aggrandizers equates well to Kirzners's (2013) notion of entrepreneurs.

Kirzner describes the entrepreneur as alert to opportunities to improve their own situation, while serving the needs of others. Entrepreneurs recognize new opportunities to serve others (customers) with goods or services such that entrepreneurs profit. In this perspective, entrepreneurs play a crucial role in pro-social distribution of goods. As long as exchanges are voluntary, both the entrepreneur and the customer are satisfied with the transaction. The competitive nature of feasts of interest here encourages hosts/entrepreneurs to obtain luxury goods and foods (van der Veen 2003) that are increasingly gratuitous, in terms of volume, quality, or exotic origin (Hayden 2014b). Thereby, competitive feasting actually distributes goods in a way that motivates greater trade within (or outside) a region.

The opportunities that entrepreneurs notice are shaped by contextual constraints, such as technology, institutions, and cultural expectations. Entrepreneurs in different settings, therefore, recognize and pursue different opportunities. As already mentioned, there are often complex sharing rules that apply to small bands of foragers (Kelly 1995); low population densities mean that contractual group obligations ensure group survival during times of stress. The cultural taboos around the kind of self-aggrandizement seen in feasting societies, therefore, limit the entrepreneurial recognition for some societies. From the archaeological record, those kinds of cultural institutions are impossible to recognize, as they leave no trace in the material record. Conversely, the recognition of feasting types of economic activity in the archaeological record must reflect crucial changes in that society's social structure and cultural institutions.

Hayden's aggrandizers are Kirzner's entrepreneurs, who are alert to opportunities to appease others' desires at a gain for themselves by hosting ever more elaborate feasts. By emphasizing the role of the entrepreneur (the host, or aggrandizer) as the driving mechanism for the advancement of market processes, the evidence presented here closely aligns with prior work that emphasizes the interpersonal relationships that foster cooperation in human groups (Boettke 2004; Boettke and Coyne 2005; Granovetter 1973; Kimbrough, Smith, and Wilson 2010; Kirzner 2013; Leeson 2006; Storr 2008, 2010, 2013).

Hayden acknowledges the contradictory nature of competitive feasting—the pattern of amassing goods just to give the majority away seems counterintuitive. Feast hosts reap actualized benefits from their hosting activities; archaeological evidence indicates differences in the quality of diet between members of feasting societies, whereas hosts enjoy a higher quality diet (e.g., Coupland 2006; Martindale 2006; Samuels 2006). Ethnographic evidence from Papua New Guinea indicates that hosts enjoy a slightly higher quality of goods in general (Sahlins 1963). While harder to quantify, hosts also enjoy reproductive advantages, likely both in number of children and in choices of mates (Hayden 2014b, 17). In other terms, feasting activities are expressions of conspicuous consumption, which communicates the affluence of the host and affords the host with social prestige, which translates into material advancement. The relationship between feasting and wealth accumulation warrants further study; the literature is divided as to whether the relationship between the two is linear (feasting leads to wealth), coevolutionary (they bolster each other), or unrelated (wealth accumulation purely result of productivity).

In conclusion, host aggrandizers/entrepreneurs advance their own prerogatives while providing goods and services to their communities. Beyond the community, competitive feasting allows for peaceful interaction between groups. These feasting traditions helped motivate innovations in trade connections, trade goods, and specialized technologies, as will be highlighted following a few archaeological examples of feasting.

## ARCHAEOLOGICAL CASE STUDIES

### Ancient Anatolia

Anatolia (now the modern state of Turkey) has an incredibly rich archaeological past and was witness to the first agricultural (Neolithic) revolution around ten thousand years ago, referred to as the Pre-Pottery Neolithic. Anatolia mirrors the transitions seen across the Levant during this period, as traditional hunter-gatherer societies start accumulating in greater numbers and start building architecture using stone. These hunter-gatherer societies relied on wild foods: wild goats and gazelle, wild cereals, fruits, and tubers (Dietrich et al. 2012, 690). Pottery post-dates these societies. Archaeologists know relatively less from this period; hunting and domestic camps seem transitory and as such leave less impact on the landscape—there are no cemeteries, just occasional burials.

Beginning around nine thousand years ago, however, various changes in the archaeological record indicate that fundamental aspects of social life were changing in Anatolia and across greater Southwest Asia. Research at the sites of Çatalhöyük (Atalay and Hastorf 2006; Bogaard et al. 2009; Carter et al. 2006; Hodder and Cessford 2004) and Göbekli Tepe (Dietrich et al. 2012) have revolutionized archaeologists' understanding of the origins of complex societies.

Göbekli Tepe is a ritual tell (mound) site dated between nine thousand and twelve thousand years ago (Schmidt 2000). The site is considered the world's first temple, with exquisitely carved anthropomorphic features. Similarly, Çatalhöyük is a tell site dated between nine thousand and seven thousand seven hundred years BP, which held between three thousand five hundred and eight thousand people (Hodder 2007, 2014). The site is one of the first urban settlements worldwide. Both of these sites have given insights into the expanding economic network of the Neolithic through the expansion of feasting regimes.

Çatalhöyük and Göbekli Tepe have left considerable records of the feasting activities that occurred at these sites through the preservation of extensive middens (trash pits or deposits). These deposits indicate that even before the domestication of grains or animals humans were gathering in fairly large numbers to consume large amounts of specialized foods (Atalay and Hastorf 2006; Bogaard et al. 2009; Dietrich et al. 2012). Evidence for food preparation at Çatalhöyük occurred within individual residences (Atalay and Hastorf 2006), though extensive middens throughout the site, as well as installations of animal bones, indicate that public feasting was an integral part of the social life of these people (Bogaard et al. 2009). Stable isotope analyses of human burials indicate that cattle was unlikely to have been the majority source of protein for individuals (Richards et al. 2003), yet the preponderance of bovine bones at the site indicate their prolonged use and social importance (Russell and Martin 2007). Individual rooms at Çatalhöyük, likely from slightly later periods, have built-in cubbies for food storage in some of the earliest examples of private storage of goods (Bogaard et al. 2009); most hunter-gatherers do not store food for an extended period of time, nor do they keep food in one place. Bogaard et al. (2009, 663) estimate that storage capacity in buildings indicates modest surpluses of 50–100 percent of the estimated requirement; this level of food storage is extremely rare for foraging societies (Testart et al. 1982; Ingold 1983). As a ritual site, Göbekli Tepe has evidence for the production of relatively large amounts of beer, in support of the interpretation of feasting events that were occurring all over Anatolia in the pre-pottery Neolithic (Dietrich et al. 2012). The difference in storage and consumption patterns can be interpreted to be one of the first indications of inequality (Wright 2014).

Feasting and permanent architecture emerge in Anatolia prior to the domestication of pack/food animals and plants. It is evident that these feasts would have attracted visitors from the wider interaction sphere. Although the vast majority of goods (textiles, wooden objects, perishable foods) decay, recent lithic sourcing studies of obsidian, an extremely valuable type of volcanic rock that can produce incredibly sharp stone tools, have shown that obsidian from Anatolia made its way down into the southern Levant during this period, before the use of any pack animals (Carter et al. 2006)! This traded obsidian is not treated the same as locally available lithic raw material; most of the obsidian evidence comes from high-prestige burials, indicating they were of particular importance.

## The Celts

Hunting-gathering-fishing communities in northern and western Europe during the Bronze Age and into the Roman Period are often referred to as the Gauls (especially within France) or generally as Celts (Dietler 1994, 585–86). Celtic peoples are well known through the archaeological record as well as through the recordings of the Roman Empire, which fought against various groups along its northern border for centuries. The term today is sometimes used to describe peoples who carry on a Gaelic linguistic tradition, although the link between archaeological Celts and linguistic Gaelic speakers is tenuous. Modern neo-paganists, especially within the British Isles, have also taken up the term in resistance to dominant sociopolitical regimes and to claim heritage over Celtic archaeological sites (Dietler 1994).

Some archaeological Celtic groups were acculturated into Roman society through the colonization of southern Gaul and the British Isles, while other groups, especially Germanic peoples, actively resisted Roman intrusion. Celtic societies utilized feasting regimes to regulate power and trade (Dietler and Hayden 2010). In the Bronze Age, prior to the growth of the Roman Empire, the first public works are associated with feasting events. The well-known site of Stonehenge has a lesser-known midden surrounding the stones, which were dragged several hundred miles from their quarry (Thorpe et al. 1991). The Celtic peoples who built Stonehenge were semi-sedentary hunter-gatherers that occasionally husbanded pigs, yet the extensive midden indicates that large consumption activities occurred at the site on a regular basis. The site, which has several earthworks, also has a large cemetery—one of the first in the region—which shows stratification in the distribution of grave goods (Pearson et al. 2009). The grave goods also indicate that trade extended perhaps onto the mainland of Europe. At the site of Llanmaes in South Wales, hundreds of pig right forelimbs in an early Iron Age midden indicate that feasting activities were highly organized events that could motivate the labor of presumably as many households (Madgwick and Mulville 2015).

Roman interactions with Celtic peoples allow for an ethno-historical perspective on competitive feasting regimes (Dietler 1990; Dietler and Hayden 2010). The Romans characterized the Celts in much the same way as European colonists stereotyped the indigenous peoples of the Americas: barbarians. While Romans certainly enjoyed feasting in their own way, Roman colonists were able to create inroads with Celtic peoples by understanding Celtic competitive feasting regimes (Woolf 2000; Dietler 1990). Participation in elite Celtic feasting practices gave Roman officials peaceful access to the full suite of Celtic trade goods, even in a political economy without a formalized marketplace culture (Woolf 2000).

## Toyah Phase

North America has been home to a diversity of indigenous cultures. While the ethnographic record informs much about the cultures present during European colonizations, the archaeological record is the primary source of information about more ancient cultures. Between seven hundred and three hundred years ago (1300–1700 CE), a new archaeological phenomenon tradition in central Texas is recognized; this phenomenon is characterized by the proliferation of bone-tempered pottery, beveled stone knives, and bison hunting (Collins 2004). While the archaeological record cannot speak to what these peoples would have called themselves, archaeologists recognize this new social field under the name Toyah (Arnn 2012).

Toyah is the first archaeological tradition in central Texas to take on a ceramic tradition, even though neighboring groups to the east (Caddoan) and west (Puebloan) had utilized ceramics for thousands of years. While stone arrowhead points of a certain style called Perdez are widely distributed throughout Texas, many Toyah sites contain a variety of point styles and pottery from surrounding cultural areas (Kibler 2012). While archaeologists should not strictly assume that differing point or pottery styles represent different ethnic peoples, some of the pottery styles are found primarily within different archaeological contexts. Rockport pottery, for example, is primarily found on the Gulf Coast of Texas and is associated with the historic Karankawa, who were limited to coastal sites (Ricklis 2010). Puebloan pottery from New Mexico has also been found with Toyah sites (Kibler 2012).

In addition to goods from multiple archaeological traditions, Toyah sites also contain evidence of processing of large quantities of food. Toyah was initially associated with bison hunting, though more recent studies have indicated that a wider subsistence base that included deer, rabbit, and small game was common (Black 1986). Plant food was an important part of the diet as well; agave and root foods were commonly cooked through earth ovens. Earth ovens use heated rocks as an energy source within a pit; food is wrapped in leaves or cloth and buried over the rocks for three to thirty-six hours. The moisture content of the leaves and packing materials ensure that the food never burns, but steams over a long period of time while conserving fuel (Black and Thoms 2014; Thoms 1993). Earth oven quantity and size increased in the Toyah period, indicating that population size and densities increased (Thoms 2008, 2009; Kenmotsu and Arnn 2012). Some of these cooking features are incredibly large, indicating that large amounts of food were being cooked at one time. The evidence for large-scale cooking, as well as trade, is indicative of feasting activities.

Unfortunately, site formation processes (how long sites have been open to the elements) are not well defined for many Toyah sites; most sites have been recovered from cultural resource management surveys that have limited resources. Because Toyah is a relatively recent archaeological tradition, many sites have not been buried very deeply and may have been plowed over. Unfortunately, that does not allow for very precise sequencing of how long sites were occupied. As such, most archaeologists presume that Toyah sites were only occupied seasonally (Black 1986; Johnson 1994; Arnn 2012; Kenmotsu and Arnn 2012).

As is evidenced above, the Toyah phase represents a time of population density increase. This increase in Texas indigenous populations follows the de-population of the large Puebloan sites in New Mexico; cities such as Paquime were abandoned around 1300 CE after a period of extreme droughts in the 1230s–1250s and an increase in violence (Benson et al. 2007; Foster 2012). It has been suggested, as I agree, that many large Toyah sites represent multicultural gatherings in which luxury and utilitarian goods could be traded. These feasts arose with increased population pressure; presumably similar trading parties were observed in the historical period, where hundreds, if not thousands, of indigenous peoples of disparate origin met for important discussions concerning alliances (for war and for marriage), trade, politics, and food (see Foster 2008). Historical records of these feasts make it clear that while native groups did not necessarily stay in a single location for the entirety of a year, there were well understood geographical boundaries (territorialism) and rules for the exchange of goods (property) (Krieger 2002; F. T. Smith 2005).

## UNINTENDED CONSEQUENCES OF FEASTING

Feasting is the first archaeologically observable mechanism of long-distance trade and inter-group social cooperation. Beyond the three case studies investigated here, feasting has been implicated in the archaeological record as a positive motivator for complexity in the Levant (Hayden, Canuel, and Shanse 2013), early dynastic China (Underhill 2002), northern Europe (B. Arnold 1999; Zori et al. 2013; Guerra-Doce 2015), the Hopewell complex in the Midwest of the United States (Pauketat et al. 2002), and along the Pacific coast (Arnold et al. 2015). The ubiquity of feasting societies as antecedent to more complex civilizations speaks to the evolutionary benefits of the system (Boyd and Richerson 1996). As feast hosts (Kirzner's entrepreneurs, Hayden's aggrandizers) met the desires of their guests (customers, peers), the unintended consequences of institutional and technological development also followed. Feasting mechanisms provided the motivation for the development of crucial concepts of the market system, namely in the establishment of dedicated geographical boundaries and claims to land and material goods (private property [Demsetz 1967]) as well as in the development of specialized trade and services (specialization).

I have already explored some of the ways that the concept of private property manifests: from the establishment of community cemeteries and permanent settlement to more complex land tenure systems. The association between feasting events and the emergence of geographical notions of ownership is important as land ownership and tenure are crucial for understanding market processes.

A more subtle consequence of feasting mechanisms is the development of new and important technological innovations (Hayden 1998). As explored above, entrepreneurs utilized feasting mechanisms through the distribution of special goods; these goods in turn become elaborated as feast hosts looked to impress their guests even more. Specialized food is a centralized aspect of feasting activities, and here the archaeological evidence is overwhelming; feasting activities intensified cooking technologies that are correlated with the development of pottery and the domestication of cereals (Hayden 1998, 2003, 2009 2014a).

In all three examples presented here, the independent development of indigenous pottery production arises with evidence of feasting. While the first occupations of Çatalhöyük in Anatolia do not contain pottery, the technology is widely adopted following its prominence. Similarly, some of the first evidence of local pottery production, Beaker Ware, for the Celts is found in association with burials with evidence of feasting (Guerra-Doce 2006, 2015; Rojo-Guerra et al. 2006). Toyah pottery is even more striking, as neighboring groups, such as the Caddo or the Puebloans, produced pottery for more than a thousand years before groups in central Texas adopted the technology. The development of pottery technologies is one of the first indications of craft specialization and the beginnings of a division of labor. Complete specialization, where individuals take on one industry for the majority of their time, occurs first within sedentary groups under hierarchical, city-state level societies (Feder 2014, 344). Nonetheless, division of labor allows for crucial specialization in markets and propels the development of complex economic production, the importance of which has been known since before the time of Adam Smith.

In coordination with the development of specialized labor, important technological advancements accompanied feasting societies across the globe. The domestication of cereal grains (such as wheat, corn, and rice) precipitated agriculture and revolutionized food production worldwide. Cereal grains were domesticated from wild tropical grasses; the domestication process increased yields, size of the grains, as well as ease of harvest and processing (Zeder et al. 2006). Mounting archaeological and genetic data indicate that humans utilized wild forms of these grains without changing general hunter-gatherer-fisher lifeways. In cases where agriculture was adopted, there seems to be a several-hundred-years gap between the utilization of cereals (such as wheat [Blockley and Pinhasi 2011], corn [Bryant 2007], and rice [Zhu et al. 2007]) and their use as agricultural staples. These grains would have taken much energy to process and were often utilized as specialty foods within feasting contexts (e.g., Jennings 2004; Guerra-Doce 2015). Wheat, for example, has been found in several wild forms at archaeological sites in the Levant from the Natufian, around twelve thousand years ago; these grains would have tough outer coats (glumes), which make it harder to process, and weak stems that hold the grain to the stalk (rachis) that make the grains difficult to harvest (Feder 2014, 287). Following the feasting regimes in the Pre-Pottery Neolithic, grains with softer glumes and weak rachis were increasingly selected, as were varieties with increasing numbers of seeds; this selection process altered the genetic structure and phenotype of wheat to what it is today. Early wheat has been seen in many early tell sites, with the possibility that the grain was being processed to produce beer (Atalay and Hastorf 2006; Katz and Voigt 1986; Crewe and Hill 2012; Guerra-Doce 2015; Hayden, Canuel, and Shanse 2013; Maeir and Garfinkel 1992; Sallaberger 2015).

The evidence for maize domestication follows a similar narrative. Maize is an extremely altered form of the tropical grass teosinte (*Zea mays spp.*); teosinte has extremely small grains that are covered in a hard glume. The earliest evidence for teosinte exploitation is not for the grain, but rather for the sweet sap in the stalk. This sap can be enjoyed simply by chewing the stalk, but also through fermenting the sap into a weak wine. The transformation from a hard shell to soft grain is a single-point mutation; human exploitation of the plant cannot then be explained through use of the plant as a grain from its origins. Following increasing use of maize in the Mexican lowlands, which has primarily been identified through microfossils of the stalk (Piperno and Pearsall 1993, 1998), maize developed and became the staple crop for much of the New World. Chicha, corn beer, was an important part of feasting events under the Olmec, Maya, Aztec, and Inca and likely has held importance as a specialty food for much longer into the prehistory of the region (Bray 2009; Bruman 2000; Goodman-Elgar 2009; Jennings 2004; Weismantel 2009).

It has been well argued that exploitation of cereal grains for feasting events, as described here, strengthened the relationship between humans and these carbohydrates, which led to their unintended domestication (Hayden 2009, 2014a; Smalley and Blake 2003). Feasting regimes often emphasize the use of alcoholic beverages from cereal grains (B. Arnold 1999; Bray 2003, 2009; Dietler 1990; Dietrich et al. 2012; Joffe 1998; Guerra-Doce 2015; Weismantel 2009; Hayden 2009; Zori et al. 2013); the archaeological evidence is mounting, but the association between brewing for feasting and domestication is increasingly convincing (Braidwood et al. 1953; Hayden 2003). The onset of the Holocene, the current geologic epoch, brought drier, warmer temperatures that undoubtedly improved conditions for cultivating tropic grasses (Blockley and Pinhasi 2011; Flannery 1973). Domesticated grains became the staple crop in agricultural revolutions worldwide, of which the impact cannot be understated.

As discussed here, as a result of feasting mechanisms, the archaeological evidence points to developments in technologies essential to the development of agriculture as well as the emergence of land ownership regimes. These innovations are foundations under which market systems operate.

## DISCUSSION

Many theorists have tried to understand the origins of the market; these theories have often arisen in economic thought and are quite varying, due to the fact that no one facet of what is considered a market—or a market system—is agreed upon, as with the confusion over the concept of "emergence" (Beaulier and Prychitko 2006). In the economic development narrative, however, there is no mention of feasting paradigms. Rather, these paradigms argue normatively, after Adam Smith, that agriculture led to surplus and the creation of wealth, which led to trade, private property, and the market system. Also, economic treatises of feasting mechanisms have recently argued that feasting is insurance against theft. These two narratives, as I will address below, fail the anthropological and archaeological evidence for the emergence/maintenance of regular long-distance trade.

Economic textbooks often mythicize a period of bartering as the mode of pre-currency exchange (Graeber 2014), as popularized by Adam Smith (1982). Smith's emphasis on the natural division of labor surmises an individualized surplus (i.e., a baker has extra bread, the shoemaker has extra shoes), which is then bartered to meet the needs of the individuals. With the expansion of markets, he argues, metal currency comes to replace bartering as a more effective mechanism for trade. Graeber (2014) traced this idea to the 1500s through the lectures of an Italian banker, Bernardo Davanzati (Waswo 1996). In the modern era, emphasis has been placed on agriculture as this mythical origin to surplus, which catapults the division of labor (see Arnold et al. 2015 for discussion).

Anthropological work, however, has long denied the reality of such an institutional system of pre-currency bartering (Mauss 1969) as well as the necessity for agriculture to create surplus (Arnold et al. 2015). As Humphrey (1985, 48) emphasizes, "No example of a barter economy, pure and simple, has ever been described, let alone the emergence from it of money; all available ethnography suggests that there never has been such a thing." Rather, bartering arises out of complex situations in which other forms of exchange predominate (Chapman 1980), such as when currency systems are considered unreliable (Humphrey 1985). Chagnon (1968, 100) states that, for the Yanomanö, "a prerequisite to stable alliance is repetitive visiting and feasting, and the trading mechanism serves to bring about these visits," though the trading aspects are downplayed in the social and political theatre of the feast. Feasting is the explicitly understood reason for inter-group peaceful celebration; like the Kula Ring phenomenon (Malinowski 1922), the bartering and trades are (necessary) by-products of feasting societies.

The archaeological record also negates this narrative of surplus leading to bartering leading to extensive trade and currency. Little evidence for the division of labor exists for the majority of prehistory, and when specialized labor (such as pottery production or spiritual practice) does arise, it's within the framework of feasting exchange systems, which predate agricultural regimes. If the individualized or communal accumulation of surplus was required for the development of long-distance trade and markets, archaeologists should find storage features that predate or co-currently arise with evidence of trade. This is not so. Toyah feasts, for example, show that incredible amounts of food were cooked at feasting events, but the ceramics are seldom larger than individual bowls. The storage pits that contain Toyah remains are no larger than the non-feasting peoples' of the Archaic before them. Bartering likely also occurred within these prehistoric societies, as Chapman (1980) argues, precisely because another form of exchange (feasting) predominated and facilitated the peaceful interaction of different groups. This regularized opportunity for bartering helped solidify relationships as formalized trading institutions. In other terms, the institution of feasting lowers the transaction cost (Heady 2005, 264–65) for economic and social exchange by providing a rationale for the peaceful gathering of disparate groups.

Beyond narratives of economic development that neglect feasting activities, some economic treatises of feasting have characterized the tradition as a rational expression of adherence to property rights (Johnsen 1986; Leeson 2014). In this narrative, the costly action of feasting destroys high-valued goods as a signal of wealth, as well as redistributes wealth as social insurance. These narratives, however, are limited to situations with permanent, settled peoples with preexisting property conceptions and geographically constrained subsistence patterns (i.e., agriculture or anadromous fish). Potlatching in the Pacific Northwest of North America, perhaps the most intensely studied form of feasting, was variable across time and space. To this point, I have avoided the term because I believe, and as Hayden (2014b) makes the distinction, that potlatching is a different mechanism than the competitive feasting discussed here. While potlatching is a form of competitive feast, with the conspicuous consumption and drive for increasing elaboration, the destructive aspect is not seen in the archaeological record. In fact, the destructive aspect of at least Kwakiutl potlatching seems to have been driven to elaboration with European settlement (Johnsen 1986, 47)—a disruption in the social structure of native peoples. Therefore, these narratives are fairly constrained to particular circumstances in which property rights have already been established, and there is some form of social or economic pressure against the system. The *longue durée* perspective here focuses on the first forms of feasts, where property rights are only territorial rather than institutionalized and formal. Potlatching, Kula Ring, and human sacrifice forms of feasting are fascinating, unique forms of feasts, but due to their situation within complex, sedentary groups, they may well represent those attachments to existing property rights rather than fit within the narrative for the origin of markets.

To take the heart of the argument of the association of conspicuous destruction and feasting, conspicuous destruction is undeniably a signal of wealth, but whether it actually suppresses plunder and theft is unclear in these archaeological contexts. As stated above, these early feasting societies did not have large storage of resources, no long-term storage of surplus (cf. Ingold 1983; Testart et al. 1982). Plundering other groups is relatively rare in hunter-gatherer and non-state societies (Kelly 1995; Leeson 2006)—only under extreme environmental distress or sudden influx of population is systematic violence recorded. And in those times of environmental distress or population pressure, feasting is not practiced (Hayden 2014b).

As indicated above, other paradigms that try to understand the emergence of market properties do not satisfactorily fit the historical and archaeological evidence. The narrative presented here, however, does not mean to imply that feasting was the only mechanism that peoples across time and space have adopted to cope with increasing population density. All of the examples presented here that implemented feasting mechanisms arose from hunting-gathering-fishing subsistence patterns during periods of relative climate stability and ecological abundance. To contrast feasting, there is archaeological evidence that conflict arises in periods of stable or increasing population density with unstable climates, particularly among agriculturalists (Benson et al. 2007; Foster 2012). The erupting violence in the Casas Grandes region of the American Southwest (Benson et al. 2007) as well as growing militarization in the Levant in the Bronze Age (Drews 1995) speak to how agriculturally dependent societies descend into warfare following ecological uncertainties and amid population growth.

## CONCLUSION

The origins of market systems lie in the deep human past. The examples presented here showcase how individual motivation of status helped drive innovations in conceptions of property as well as technological innovation. The development of feasting mechanisms did not occur at the same chronological point, but rather, this similar framework emerged worldwide in different, disparate societies following increasing population density. As a pro-social, non-violent mechanism, feasting provides an apparatus for cooperation between independent groups of people. Human pro-sociality between non-kin groups (Tomasello 1999; Tomasello and Vaish 2013) is incredibly important for building complex societies, both in prehistory and today.

In discussions of feasting mechanisms, the hosts of the feast, which Hayden (2014b) refers to as *aggrandizers*, can be equivocated with classical liberal understandings of entrepreneurs (Boettke 2004; Kirzner 2013; Storr 2013,

2008). As Hayden (2014b, 17) posits, "Aggrandizers are probably responsible for many of the fundamental transformations of culture that archaeology has been able to chronicle over the last 40,000 years." These entrepreneurs recognize a space for both personal and social advancement. As such, the archaeological evidence indicates that social aspects of the market (Storr 2013, 2010, 2008) were critical to its advancement.

McCloskey (2010a) argues that the cultural shift in associating dignity and respect for the accumulation of material goods and services precipitated the expansion of European capitalism. Her argument champions cultural motives for the acceleration of market processes; in many ways, the argument presented here does the same. Rather than a materialistic urge to collect goods and services, market processes are enhanced by cultural milieu that allows individual dignity and respect in the collection, management, and intensification of such resources. A neo-evolutionary view of human action asserts that all people are motivated by a wish to reproduce, whether that be a biological or psychological influence (Richerson and Boyd 2005). Systems in which group fitness is enhanced through individual motivation lead to group expansion, either in the birth rate or in the conversion (willing or otherwise) of others to that system. While this particular perspective, grounded in methodological individualism (Boettke and Coyne 2005; von Mises 2005), is not a new concept, archaeology can provide substantial material evidence to elucidate mechanisms of the market order.

# REFERENCES

Arnn, John W. III. 2012. "Defining Hunter-Gatherer Sociocultural Identity and Interaction at a Regional Scale: The Toyah/Tejas Social Field." In *The Toyah Phase of Central Texas: Late Prehistoric Economic and Social Processes*, edited by Nancy A. Kenmotsu and Douglas K. Boyd, 44–75. Anthropology Series 16. College Station: Texas A&M University Press.

Arnold, Bettina. 1999. "'Drinking the Feast': Alcohol and the Legitimation of Power in Celtic Europe." *Cambridge Archaeological Journal* 9 (1): 71–93. doi:10.1017/S0959774300015213.

Arnold, Jeanne E., S. Sunell, K. J. Bishop, B. T. Nigra, T. Jones, and J. Bongers. 2015. "Entrenched Disbelief: Complex Hunter-Gatherers and the Case for Inclusive Cultural Evolutionary Thinking." *Journal of Archaeological Method and Theory* 23 (2): 448–99. doi:10.1007/s10816-015-9246-y.

Arnold, Jeanne E. 2001. *The Origins of a Pacific Coast Chiefdom: The Chumash of the Channel Islands*. Salt Lake City: University of Utah Press.

Atalay, Sonya, and Christine A. Hastorf. 2006. "Food, Meals, and Daily Activities: Food Habitus at Neolithic Çatalhöyük." *American Antiquity* 71 (2): 283–319. doi:10.2307/40035906.

Beaulier, Scott A., and David L. Prychitko. 2006. "Disagreement over the Emergence of Private Property Rights: Alternative Meanings, Alternative Explanations." *Review of Austrian Economics* 19 (1): 47–68.
Benson, Larry V., Michael S. Berry, Edward A. Jolie, Jerry D. Spangler, David W. Stahle, and Eugene M. Hattori. 2007. "Possible Impacts of Early-11th-, Middle-12th-, and Late-13th-Century Droughts on Western Native Americans and the Mississippian Cahokians." *Quaternary Science Reviews* 26 (3–4): 336–50. doi:10.1016/j.quascirev.2006.08.001.
Binford, Lewis R. 1967. "Smudge Pits and Hide Smoking: The Use of Analogy in Archaeological Reasoning." *American Antiquity* 32 (1): 1–12. doi:10.2307/278774.
———. 1968. "Post-Pleistocene Adaptations." In *New Perspectives in Archeology*, edited by L. R. Binford and S. R. Binford, 213–42. Chicago: Aldine.
———. 2001. *Constructing Frames of Reference: An Analytical Method for Archaeological Theory Building Using Ethnographic and Environmental Data Sets.* Berkeley: University of California Press.
Black, Stephen L. 1986. "The Clemente and Herminia Hinojosa Site, 41JW8: A Toyah Horizon Campsite in Southern Teas." 18. Special Report. San Antonio: University of Texas Center for Archaeological Research.
Black, Stephen L., and Alston V. Thoms. 2014. "Hunter-Gatherer Earth Ovens in the Archaeological Record: Fundamental Concepts." *American Antiquity* 79 (2): 204–26.
Blockley, S. P. E., and R. Pinhasi. 2011. "A Revised Chronology for the Adoption of Agriculture in the Southern Levant and the Role of Lateglacial Climatic Change." *Quaternary Science Reviews* 30 (1–2): 98–108. doi:10.1016/j.quascirev.2010.09.021.
Boettke, Peter. 2004. "Morality as Cooperation." In *Morality of Markets*, edited by P. J. Shah, 43–50. New Delhi: Academic Foundation.
Boettke, Peter J., and Christopher J. Coyne. 2005. "Methodological Individualism, Spontaneous Order and the Research Program of the Workshop in Political Theory and Policy Analysis." *Journal of Economic Behavior & Organization* 57 (2): 145–58.
Bogaard, Amy, Michael Charles, Katheryn C. Twiss, Andrew Fairbairn, Nurcan Yalman, Dragana Filipoviç, G. Arzu Demirergi, Füsun Ertuğ, Nerissa Russell, and Jennifer Henecke. 2009. "Private Pantries and Celebrated Surplus: Storing and Sharing Food at Neolithic Çatalhöyük, Central Anatolia." *Antiquity* 83 (321): 649–68.
Boyd, Robert, and Peter J. Richerson. 1996. "Why Culture Is Common, but Cultural Evolution Is Rare." *Proceedings of British Academy* 88: 77–94.
Braidwood, Robert J., Jonathan D. Sauer, Hans Helbaek, Paul C. Mangelsdorf, Hugh C. Cutler, Carleton S. Coon, Ralph Linton, Julian Steward, and A. Leo Oppenheim. 1953. "Symposium: Did Man Once Live by Beer Alone?" *American Anthropologist* 55 (4): 515–26.
Bray, Tamara L. 2003. *The Archaeology and Politics of Food and Feasting in Early States and Empires.* New York: Springer.

————. 2009. "The Role of Chicha in Inca State Expansion: A Distributional Study of Inca Aribalos." In *Drink, Power, and Society in the Andes*, edited by Justin Jennings and Brenda J. Bowser, 108–32. Gainesville: University Press of Florida.

Bruman, H. J. 2000. *Alcohol in Ancient Mexico*. Salt Lake City: University of Utah Press.

Bryant, Vaughn M. 2007. "Microscopic Evidence for the Domestication and Spread of Maize." *Proceedings of the National Academy of Sciences* 104 (50): 19659–60. doi:10.1073/pnas.0710327105.

Cann, Rebecca L., and Allan C. Wilson. 2003. "The Recent African Genesis of Humans." *Scientific American* 13: 54–61.

Carter, Tristan, Gérard Poupeau, Céline Bressy, and Nicholas J. G. Pearce. 2006. "A New Programme of Obsidian Characterization at Çatalhöyük, Turkey." *Journal of Archaeological Science* 33 (7): 893–909. doi:10.1016/j.jas.2005.10.023.

Chagnon, Napoleon. 1968. *Yanomanö: The Fierce People*. New York: Holt, Rinehart and Winston.

Chamlee-Wright, Emily. 1997. *The Cultural Foundations of Economic Development: Urban Female Entrepreneurship in Ghana*. London: Routledge.

Chapman, Anne. 1980. "Barter as a Universal Mode of Exchange." *L'Homme* 20 (3): 33–83.

Collins, Michael B. 2004. "Archeology in Central Texas." In *The Prehistory of Texas*, edited by T. K. Pertulla, 101–26. College Station: Texas A&M University Press.

Coupland, Gary. 2006. "A Chief's House Speaks: Communicating Power on the Northern Northwest Coast." In *Household Archaeology on the Northwest Coast*, edited by E. Sobel, A. Gahr, and K. Ames, 80–96. Ann Arbor, MI: International Monographs in Prehistory.

Crewe, Lindy, and Ian Hill. 2012. "Finding Beer in the Archaeological Record: A Case Study from Kissonerga-Skalia on Bronze Age Cyprus." *Levant* 44 (2): 205–37. doi:10.1179/0075891412Z.0000000009.

Demsetz, Harold. 1967. "Toward a Theory of Property Rights." *The American Economic Review* 57 (2): 347–59.

Diamond, Jared. 1999. *Guns, Germs, and Steel: The Fates of Human Societies*. New York: W. W. Norton & Company.

Dietler, Michael. 1990. "Driven by Drink: The Role of Drinking in the Political Economy and the Case of Early Iron Age France." *Journal of Anthropological Archaeology* 9 (4): 352–406. doi:10.1016/0278-4165(90)90011-2.

————. 1994. "'Our Ancestors the Gauls': Archaeology, Ethnic Nationalism, and the Manipulation of Celtic Identity in Modern Europe." *American Anthropologist* 96 (3): 584–605.

Dietler, Michael, and Brian Hayden. 2010. *Feasts: Archaeological and Ethnographic Perspectives on Food, Politics, and Power*. Tuscaloosa: University of Alabama Press.

Dietrich, Oliver, Manfred Heun, Jens Notroff, Klaus Schmidt, and Martin Zarnkow. 2012. "The Role of Cult and Feasting in the Emergence of Neolithic Communities. New Evidence from Göbekli Tepe, South-Eastern Turkey." *Antiquity* 86 (333): 674–95.

Dixson, Alan F., and Barnaby J. Dixson. 2011. "Venus Figurines of the European Paleolithic: Symbols of Fertility or Attractiveness?" *Journal of Anthropology* 2011: 1–11.

Drews, Robert. 1995. *The End of the Bronze Age: Changes in Warfare and the Catastrophe ca. 1200 BC*. Princeton, NJ: Princeton University Press.

Farrand, William. 1990. "Origins of Quaternary-Pleistocene-Holocene Stratigraphic Terminology." In *Establishment of a Geologic Framework for Paleoanthropology*, edited by L. F. Laporte, 15–21. Geological Society of America Special Paper 242. Boulder, CO: Geological Society of America.

Feder, Kenneth L. 2014. *The Past in Perspective: An Introduction to Human Prehistory*. Sixth edition. New York: Oxford University Press.

Flannery, Kent V. 1973. "The Origins of Agriculture." *Annual Review of Anthropology* 2: 271–310. doi:10.2307/2949273.

Foster, William C. 2008. *Historic Native Peoples of Texas: 1528–1722*. Austin: University of Texas Press.

Foster, William C. 2012. *Climate and Culture Change in North America AD 900–1600*. Austin: University of Texas Press. http://www.jstor.org/stable/10.7560/737419.

Goodman-Elgar, Melissa. 2009. "Places to Partake: Chicha in the Andean Landscape." In *Drink, Power, and Society in the Andes*, edited by Justin Jennings and Brenda J. Bowser, 49–107. Gainesville: University Press of Florida.

Graeber, David. 2014. *Debt: The First 5,000 Years*. Updated and expanded edition. Brooklyn, NY: Melville House.

Granovetter, Mark S. 1973. "The Strength of Weak Ties." *American Journal of Sociology* 78 (6): 1360–80.

Guerra-Doce, Elisa. 2006. "Exploring the Significance of Beaker Pottery through Residue Analyses." *Oxford Journal of Archaeology* 25 (3): 247–59. doi:10.1111/j.1468-0092.2006.00260.x.

———. 2015. "The Origins of Inebriation: Archaeological Evidence of the Consumption of Fermented Beverages and Drugs in Prehistoric Eurasia." *Journal of Archaeological Method and Theory* 22 (3): 751–82. doi:10.1007/s10816-014-9205-z.

Hayden, Brian. 1998. "Practical and Prestige Technologies: The Evolution of Material Systems." *Journal of Archaeological Method and Theory* 5 (1): 1–55. doi:10.1007/BF02428415.

———. 2003. "Were Luxury Foods the First Domesticates? Ethnoarchaeological Perspectives from Southeast Asia." *World Archaeology* 34 (3): 458–69. doi:10.1080/0043824021000026459a.

———. 2009. "The Proof Is in the Pudding." *Current Anthropology* 50 (5): 597–601.

———. 2014a. "Competitive Feasting before Cultivation?" *Current Anthropology* 55 (2): 230–31.

———. 2014b. *The Power of Feasts*. Cambridge: Cambridge University Press.

Hayden, Brian, Neil Canuel, and Jennifer Shanse. 2013. "What Was Brewing in the Natufian? An Archaeological Assessment of Brewing Technology in the Epipaleolithic." *Journal of Archaeological Method & Theory* 20 (1): 102–50.

Hayden, Brian, and Suzanne Villeneuve. 2011. "A Century of Feasting Studies." *Annual Review of Anthropology* 40 (1): 433–49. doi:10.1146/annurev-anthro-081309-145740.

Heady, Patrick. 2005. "Barter." In *Handbook of Economic Anthropology*, edited by James Carrier, 262–74. Cheltenham, UK: Edward Elgar.

Henrich, Joseph, Robert Boyd, Samuel Bowles, Colin Camerer, Ernst Fehr, Herbert Gintis, and Richard McElreath. 2001. "In Search of Homo Economicus: Behavioral Experiments in 15 Small-Scale Societies." *American Economic Review* 91 (2): 73–78.

Hodder, Ian, ed. 2007. *Excavating Çatalhöyük: South, North and KOPAL Area Reports from the 1995–99 Seasons*. Cambridge: McDonald Institute for Archaeological Research.

————, ed. 2014. *Çatalhöyük Excavations: The 2000–2008 Seasons*. Çatalhöyük Research Project Series 7. Los Angeles: Cotsen Institute of Archaeology at UCLA.

Hodder, Ian, and Craig Cessford. 2004. "Daily Practice and Social Memory at Çatalhöyük." *American Antiquity* 69 (1): 17–40. doi:10.2307/4128346.

Holt, Brigitte M., and Vincenzo Formicola. 2008. "Hunters of the Ice Age: The Biology of Upper Paleolithic People." *American Journal of Physical Anthropology* 137 (S47): 70–99. doi:10.1002/ajpa.20950.

Humphrey, Caroline. 1985. "Barter and Economic Disintegration." *Man* 20 (1): 48–72. doi:10.2307/2802221.

Ingold, Tim. 1983. "The Significance of Storage in Hunting Societies." *Man* 18 (3): 553–71. doi:10.2307/2801597.

Jennings, Justin. 2004. "La Chichera y El Patrón: Chicha and the Energetics of Feasting in the Prehistoric Andes." *Archeological Papers of the American Anthropological Association* 14 (1): 241–59.

Joffe, Alexander H. 1998. "Alcohol and Social Complexity in Ancient Western Asia." *Current Anthropology* 39 (3): 297–322. doi:10.1086/204736.

Johnsen, D. Bruce. 1986. "The Formation and Protection of Property Rights among the Southern Kwakiutl Indians." *Journal of Legal Studies* 15 (1): 41–67.

Johnson, LeRoy. 1994. *The Life and Times of Toyah-Culture Folk: The Buckhollow Encampment Site 41KM16 Kimble County, Texas*. Office of the State Archeologist Report 38. Austin: Texas Department of Transportation and Texas Historical Commission.

Katz, Solomon H., and Mary M. Voigt. 1986. "Bread and Beer: The Early Use of Cereals in the Human Diet." *Expedition: The Magazine of the University of Pennsylvania* 28 (2): 23–34.

Kelly, Robert L. 1992. "Mobility/Sedentism: Concepts, Archaeological Measures, and Effects." *Annual Review of Anthropology* 21: 43–66.

————. 1995. *The Foraging Spectrum: Diversity in Hunter-Gatherer Lifeways*. Washington, DC: Smithsonian Institution Press.

Kenmotsu, Nancy A., and John W. Arnn III. 2012. "The Toyah Phase and the Ethnohistorical Record: A Case for Population Aggregation." In *The Toyah Phase of Central Texas: Late Prehistoric Economic and Social Processes*, edited by Nancy A. Kenmotsu and Douglas K. Boyd, 19–43. Anthropology Series 16. College Station: Texas A&M University Press.

Kibler, Karl W. 2012. "The Role of Exotic Materials in Toyah Assemblages in a Late Prehistoric Economic and Social System." In *The Toyah Phase of Central Texas: Late Prehistoric Economic and Social Processes*, edited by Nancy A. Kenmotsu and Douglas K. Boyd, 76–89. Anthropology Series 16. College Station: Texas A&M University Press.

Kimbrough, Erik O., Vernon L. Smith, and Bart J. Wilson. 2010. "Exchange, Theft, and the Social Formation of Property." *Journal of Economic Behavior & Organization* 74 (3): 206–29.

Kirzner, I. 2013. "Competition and Entrepreneurship." In *The Collected Works of Israel M. Kirzner*, edited by Peter Boettke and Frederic Sautet, 24–69. Indianapolis: Liberty Fund, Inc.

Klein, Richard G. 1971. "The Pleistocene Prehistory of Siberia." *Quaternary Research* 1 (2): 133–61.

Krieger, Alex Dony. 2002. *We Came Naked and Barefoot: The Journey of Cabeza de Vaca across North America*. Edited by Margery H. Krieger. Texas Archaeology and Ethnohistory Series. Austin: University of Texas Press.

Lavoie, Don, and Emily Chamlee-Wright. 2000. *Culture and Enterprise: The Development, Representation and Morality of Business*. Routledge Studies in the Modern World Economy 26. London and New York: Routledge.

Lee, Richard B. 1969. "Eating Christmas in the Kalahari." *Natural History* 78 (14): 60–64.

Leeson, Peter T. 2006. "Cooperation and Conflict." *American Journal of Economics and Sociology* 65 (4): 891–907. doi:10.1111/j.1536-7150.2006.00480.x.

———. 2014. "Human Sacrifice." *Review of Behavioral Economics* 1 (1–2): 137–65. doi:10.1561/105.00000007.

Madgwick, Richard, and Jacqui Mulville. 2015. "Feasting on Fore-Limbs: Conspicuous Consumption and Identity in Later Prehistoric Britain." *Antiquity* 89 (345): 629–44.

Maeir, Aren M., and Yosef Garfinkel. 1992. "Bone and Metal Straw-Tip Beer-Strainers from the Ancient Near East." *Levant* 24 (1): 218–23. doi:10.1179/007589192790220793.

Malinowski, Bronislaw. 1922. *Argonauts of the Western Pacific*. London: George Routledge & Sons.

Martindale, A. 2006. "Tsimshian Houses and Households through the Contact Period." In *Household Archaeology on the Northwest Coast*, edited by E. Sobel, A. Gahr, and K. Ames, 140–58. Ann Arbor, MI: International Monographs in Prehistory.

Mauss, Marcel. 1969. *The Gift: Forms and Functions of Exchange in Archaic Societies*. Translated by Ian Cunnison. London: Cohen & West.

McCloskey, Deirdre N. 2010a. *Bourgeois Dignity: Why Economics Can't Explain the Modern World*. Chicago: University of Chicago Press.

———. 2010b. *The Bourgeois Virtues: Ethics for an Age of Commerce*. Chicago: University of Chicago Press.

Pauketat, Timothy R., Lucretia S. Kelly, Gayle J. Fritz, Neal H. Lopinot, Scott Elias, and Eve Hargrave. 2002. "The Residues of Feasting and Public Ritual at Early Cahokia." *American Antiquity* 67 (2): 257–79. doi:10.2307/2694566.

Pearson, Mike P., Andrew Chamberlain, Mandy Jay, Peter Marshall, Joshua Pollard, Colin Richards, Julian Thomas, Chris Tilley, and Kate Welham. 2009. "Who Was Buried at Stonehenge?" *Antiquity* 83 (319): 23–39.

Pettitt, Paul B., and Nicolai O. Bader. 2000. "Direct AMS Radiocarbon Dates for the Sungir Mid Upper Palaeolithic Burials." *Antiquity* 74 (284): 269–70.

Piperno, Dolores R., and Deborah M. Pearsall. 1993. "Phytoliths in the Reproductive Structures of Maize and Teosinte: Implications for the Study of Maize Evolution." *Journal of Archaeological Science* 20 (3): 337–62. doi:10.1006/jasc.1993.1021.

———. 1998. *Origins of Agriculture in the Lowland Neotropics*. Cambridge: Academic Press.

Richards, M. P., J. A. Pearson, T. I. Molleson, N. Russell, and L. Martin. 2003. "Stable Isotope Evidence of Diet at Neolithic Çatalhöyük, Turkey." *Journal of Archaeological Science* 30 (1): 67–76. doi:10.1006/jasc.2001.0825.

Richerson, Peter J., and Robert Boyd. 2005. *Not by Genes Alone: How Culture Transformed Human Evolution*. Chicago: University of Chicago Press.

Ricklis, Robert A. 2010. *The Karankawa Indians of Texas: An Ecological Study of Cultural Tradition and Change*. Austin: University of Texas Press.

Rojo-Guerra, Manuel Ángel, Rafael Garrido-Pena, Íñigo García-Martínez-de-Lagrán, Jordi Juan-Treserras, and Juan Carlos Matamala. 2006. "Beer and Bell Beakers: Drinking Rituals in Copper Age Inner Iberia." *Proceedings of the Prehistoric Society* 72: 243–65. Cambridge: Cambridge University Press.

Russell, N., and L. Martin. 2007. "The Çatalhöyük Mammal Remains." In *Excavating Çatalhöyük: South, North and KOPAL Area Reports from the 1995–1999 Seasons*, edited by Ian Hodder, 33–98. McDonald Institute for Archaeological Research.

Sahlins, Marshall D. 1963. "Poor Man, Rich Man, Big-Man, Chief: Political Types in Melanesia and Polynesia." *Comparative Studies in Society and History* 5 (3): 285–303.

Sallaberger, Walter. 2015. "Beer Brewing in EBA Mesopotami." In *Exploring the Production and Consumption of Fermented Beverages and Food in Pre- and Protohistoric Communities*. Glasgow, UK: European Association of Archaeologists.

Samuels, S. 2006. "Households at Ozette." In *Household Archaeology on the Northwest Coast*, edited by E. Sobel, A. Gahr, and K. Ames, 200–32. Ann Arbor, MI: International Monographs in Prehistory.

Schmidt, Klaus. 2000. "Göbekli Tepe, Southeastern Turkey: A Preliminary Report on the 1995–1999 Excavations." *Paléorient* 26 (1): 45–54.

Smalley, John, and Michael Blake. 2003. "Sweet Beginnings." *Current Anthropology* 44 (5): 675–703.

Smith, Adam. 1982. *An Inquiry into the Nature and Causes of the Wealth of Nations*. Edited by R. H. Campbell and A. S. Skinner. 2 vols. The Glasgow Edition of the Works and Correspondence of Adam Smith, II. Indianapolis: Liberty Fund.

Smith, F. Todd. 2005. *From Dominance to Disappearance: The Indians of Texas and the Near Southwest, 1786–1859*. Lincoln: University of Nebraska Press.

Soffer, O., J. M. Adovasio, and D. C. Hyland. 2000. "The 'Venus' Figurines." *Current Anthropology* 41 (4): 511–37. doi:10.1086/317381.

Speth, John D. 1990. "Seasonality, Resource Stress, and Food Sharing in So-Called 'Egalitarian' Foraging Societies." *Journal of Anthropological Archaeology* 9 (2): 148–88. doi:10.1016/0278-4165(90)90002-U.

Storr, Virgil Henry. 2008. "The Market as a Social Space: On the Meaningful Extra-Economic Conversations That Can Occur in Markets." *Review of Austrian Economics* 21 (2–3): 135–50.

———. 2010. "The Social Construction of the Market." *Society* 47 (3): 200–206.

———. 2013. *Understanding the Culture of Markets*. Routledge Foundations of the Market Economy 31. London: Routledge.

Testart, Alain, Richard G. Forbis, Brian Hayden, Tim Ingold, Stephen M. Perlman, David L. Pokotylo, Peter Rowley-Conwy, and David E. Stuart. 1982. "The Significance of Food Storage among Hunter-Gatherers: Residence Patterns, Population Densities, and Social Inequalities [and Comments and Reply]." *Current Anthropology* 23 (5): 523–37.

Thoms, Alston V. "Knocking Sense from Old Rocks: Typologies and the Narrow Perspective of the Angostura Point Type." *Lithic Technology* 18 (1/2): 16–27. doi:10.2307/23272860.

———. 2008. "Ancient Savannah Roots of the Carbohydrate Revolution in South-Central North America." *Plains Anthropologist* 53 (205): 121–36. doi:10.2307/25670980.

———. 2009. "Rocks of Ages: Propagation of Hot-Rock Cookery in Western North America." *Journal of Archaeological Science* 36 (3): 573–91. doi:10.1016/j.jas.2008.11.016.

Thorpe, Richard S., Olwen Williams-Thorpe, D. Graham Jenkins, and J. S. Watson. 1991. "The Geological Sources and Transport of the Bluestones of Stonehenge, Wiltshire, UK." *Proceedings of the Prehistoric Society* 57 (2):103–57. Cambridge: Cambridge University Press.

Tomasello, Michael. 1999. "The Human Adaptation for Culture." *Annual Review of Anthropology* 28: 509–29.

Tomasello, Michael, and Amrisha Vaish. 2013. "Origins of Human Cooperation and Morality." *Annual Review of Psychology* 64 (1): 231–55. doi:10.1146/annurev-psych-113011-143812.

Trinkaus, Erik. 2005. "Early Modern Humans." *Annual Review of Anthropology* 34: 207–30.

Underhill, Anne P. 2002. *Craft Production and Social Change in Northern China*. Fundamental Issues in Archaeology. New York: Springer. http://link.springer.com/book/10.1007%2F978-1-4615-0641-6.

van der Veen, Marijke. 2003. "When Is Food a Luxury?" *World Archaeology* 34 (3): 405–27. doi:10.1080/0043824021000026422.

Vasil'ev, Sergei A. 1993. "The Upper Palaeolithic of Northern Asia." *Current Anthropology* 34 (1): 82–92.

Von Mises, Ludwig. 2005. "Human Action." *Compel* 30.

Waswo, Richard. 1996. "Shakespeare and the Formation of the Modern Economy." *Surfaces* 6 (217): 32.

Weismantel, Mary J. 2009. "Have a Drink: Chicha, Performance, and Politics." In *Drink, Power, and Society in the Andes*, edited by Justin Jennings and Brenda J. Bowser, 257–78. Gainesville: University Press of Florida.

Wengrow, David, and David Graeber. 2015. "Farewell to the 'Childhood of Man': Ritual, Seasonality, and the Origins of Inequality." *Journal of the Royal Anthropological Institute* 21 (3): 597–619. doi:10.1111/1467-9655.12247.

Whelan, Carly S., Adrian R. Whitaker, Jeffrey S. Rosenthal, and Eric Wohlgemuth. 2013. "Hunter-Gatherer Storage, Settlement, and the Opportunity Costs of Women's Foraging." *American Antiquity* 78 (4): 662–78.

Woolf, Greg. 2000. *Becoming Roman: The Origins of Provincial Civilization in Gaul.* Cambridge, UK: Cambridge University Press.

Wright, Katherine I. (Karen). 2014. "Domestication and Inequality? Households, Corporate Groups and Food Processing Tools at Neolithic Çatalhöyük." *Journal of Anthropological Archaeology* 33: 1–33. doi:10.1016/j.jaa.2013.09.007.

Zeder, Melinda A., Eve Emshwiller, Bruce D. Smith, and Daniel G. Bradley. 2006. "Documenting Domestication: The Intersection of Genetics and Archaeology." *Trends in Genetics* 22 (3): 139–55. doi:10.1016/j.tig.2006.01.007.

Zhu, Qihui, Xiaoming Zheng, Jingchu Luo, Brandon S. Gaut, and Song Ge. 2007. "Multilocus Analysis of Nucleotide Variation of Oryza Sativa and Its Wild Relatives: Severe Bottleneck during Domestication of Rice." *Molecular Biology and Evolution* 24 (3): 875–88. doi:10.1093/molbev/msm005.

Zori, D., J. Byock, E. Erlendsson, S. Martin, T. Wake, and K. J. Edwards. 2013. "Feasting in Viking Age Iceland: Sustaining a Chiefly Political Economy in a Marginal Environment." *Antiquity* 87 (335): 150–65.

*Chapter 6*

# The Political Economy

## The Invocation of Liberal Economics by the Catholic Press in the French Right-to-Work Debates of 1848

### Nicholas O'Neill

As 1848 dawned on France, despair and disillusionment permeated the nation. For generations the Parisian working class had confronted stagnant subsistence wages, deadly urban overcrowding, and a precarious dependence on wage labor as industrial capitalism reshaped the economy around market-oriented transactions (Lévy-Leboyer and Bourguignon 1990, 20; Marchand 1993, 27–35). Then, in 1845 and again in 1846, poor harvests across the continent led to a sharp rise in grain prices that further decimated the working-class family's already meager level of subsistence (Sperber 2005, 23–25, 109–12).[1] As credit froze and consumer demand for non-agricultural goods plummeted, a financial and commercial crisis shocked the economy into recession at the end of 1847 and ignited a manufacturing crisis that culminated in the unemployment and further immiseration of the urban working class. In Paris, whose market-oriented economy was hit particularly hard, general unemployment topped 54 percent and in some trades reached over 90 percent (Traugott 1985, 5–12). In response to these economic conditions and a growing lack of confidence in the laissez-faire policies of the July Monarchy, on February 22, 1848, demonstrators from all classes of society turned out in the streets to protest the state suppression of reform banquets. After just three days of mass unrest, the reign of Louis Philippe collapsed with but a whimper and opened the door for the coming of the Second French Republic.

While citizens of all political and religious backgrounds joined hands under the restored tricolor banner of French republicanism, it quickly became apparent that their understandings of the republic differed (Price 1972, 95–98). As Samuel Hayat (2014) has argued, the first three months of the Second Republic—what he has labeled the "February Republic" between the revolution in February and the commencement of the Constitutional Assembly in May—marked an uncertain period. Power itself was divided between the Provisional Government dedicated to stabilizing the nation and preparing elections; the Luxembourg Commission, focused solely on organizing labor; and the National Guard, which served as the guarantor of order. More importantly, each of these institutions was also supported by different sources of legitimation: on the one hand, the will of the people understood as the manifestation of popular opinion in elections with universal male suffrage; on the other hand, the will of the people understood as the true interest of the most marginalized members of society. Was this to be a republic that represented its citizens in the abstract or that represented its citizens directly? Was the voice of the people to echo in the ballot box or roar from atop the barricades? Would the Second Republic be a moderate republic or a democratic and social republic?

To answer these questions, political actors appealed to the authority of the revolutionary principles of liberty, equality, and fraternity. As Hayat (2014, 21–24) has emphasized, however, these principles formed a common discourse for both the moderate and radical republicans of 1848. Each side justified its own position by invoking the republic against its "double." There was not one understanding of the Second Republic in 1848, but two. Those on the left and those on the right each claimed that their vision for France represented the real, authentic, or true republic; and that of their political opponents represented a double, mirrored, or false republic.

Given the presence of competing claims of legitimacy invoking the same rhetoric within a polarized political discourse, this paper argues that political actors debating policy actions in 1848 were forced to justify their claims by appealing to two external sources of authority: moral economy and political economy. Michel Foucault (2008, 33–35) has theorized that those attempting to define the limits and path of the State rely on what he termed "sites of veridiction." For Foucault, a site of veridiction serves as "a site of verification-falsification for governmental practice" that establishes an overarching "regime of truth" within which truths or truth-telling can be established. This regime of truth serves not as "a law of truth, [but] the set of rules enabling one to establish which statements in a given discourse can be described as true or false." Such sites of veridiction and regimes of truth offer an external vantage point from which to evaluate the actions of the state in relation to established criteria of justice.

For the political actors of 1848, the disagreements over the spirit of the republic that played out in policy debates, being expressed in the same language, had to reference competing sites of veridiction as external sources of authority and legitimation to prove that their understanding of the republic was the true, the authentic one, and that of their political opponents was the false, the double one. In addressing the problem of unemployment and the distribution of wealth, radicals relied on a moral economy that justified state intervention in the economy while liberals and conservatives invoked a political economy that urged state inaction in favor of an order determined by market processes.

This chapter examines the invocation of liberal political economy within the French Catholic press of 1848. First, it describes the moral economy advocated by social Catholic journalists who relied on Christian moral teachings as the site of veridiction from which to advocate interventionist policies for a more just distribution of wealth and the elimination of unemployment. Second, it outlines three core elements underpinning liberal political economy as a regime of truth in the mid-nineteenth century and two resulting laissez-faire policy implications. Finally, it explains why conservative Catholics abandoned their criticism of political economy based on moral economic grounds during the violent unrest of 1848 when they discovered that liberal political economy offered an effective rhetorical weapon for the preservation of the existing social and economic order. This chapter contributes to conversations about the morality of the market order by problematizing its adoption as a site of veridiction and thus highlighting the impact of political discourse and power relations on ideology.

## SOCIAL CATHOLICISM AND MORAL ECONOMY

French citizens from across economic, political, and religious backgrounds heralded the birth of the Second Republic and its efforts to shelter the unemployed masses from the dislocations they believed stemmed from an unalloyed and unrestrained capitalist economy. In the early weeks of the revolution, prompted by the mass protests of armed and agitated workers, the Provisional Government established the duty of the State to guarantee the right to work and created the Luxembourg Commission to advise the nation how it could most effectively solve the social problems caused by industrialization. Foremost among the resulting policies were the establishment of National Workshops that provided work to the unemployed and labor legislation that shortened the workday while maintaining existing wage rates.[2] In announcing each action, officials invoked the republican principle of fraternity and justified their decisions by appealing to a moral economic regime of truth that obligated the State to intervene in the nation's economic life as necessary to guarantee the right to work.[3]

Moral economy entails a moral justification for action based on traditional notions of rights within the marketplace, one that is expressed deliberately to provoke state intervention in the market and formulated in opposition to laissez-faire political economy (E. P. Thompson 1971; 1991, 337–38; Reddy 1984, 331–34).[4] Underpinning the moral economy, therefore, must lie a site of veridiction capable of determining true versus false: established moral precepts. Given the weight of tradition in shaping moral economy and the omnipresence of Christianity in French social thought during the early nineteenth century, it is natural that champions of working-class rights would invoke Christian morality to buttress the claims they made upon the State.

Among those political actors who most heartily welcomed such measures as the National Workshops and industrial legislation, religion frequently furnished the moral basis for their claims to justice. For the artisans at the vanguard of working-class politics, religion offered a set of traditions, organizations, and a vocabulary that could be wielded in support of worker associations such as trade corporations, *compagnonnages*, and mutual aid societies (Sewell 1980, 33–52, 165). Beyond a radical discourse, Christianity provided these workers with a moral authority, a timeless determinant of right and wrong on which to found their calls for justice (Prothero 1997, 248–72). Workers and their allies subsequently harnessed this moral authority to justify challenges to any human authority, appealing to a popular religiosity founded on the spiritual authority of Jesus the humble commoner, Jesus the first socialist (Berenson 1984, 36–73). By invoking the image of Jesus as a radical worker, early nineteenth-century socialists promised to return humanity to true Christianity and to realize heaven on Earth (Pilbeam 2000, 39–53).[5]

Many Catholics expressed concerns about the impact of capitalism on the poor in similar ways. The French Catholic Church in the mid-nineteenth century was far from a monolithic and centralized institution (Cox 1968; Fitzpatrick 1983; Gough 1986). Despite the Church's emphasis on the training and authority of the elite clergy, the Catholic community was actually a broad and lively hive of discussion in which the laity could voice their political opinions as Catholics through several newspapers that spanned the ideological spectrum (Harrison 2014, 1–27; Dougherty 1998; Moody 1972).

One of the most influential branches of French Catholicism in the decades leading up to 1848 was social Catholicism. Social Catholics were motivated primarily by a concern for the structural causes of poverty existing under industrial society. At the heart of their critique lay the problem of pauperism. Poverty as an individual condition, they argued, was a timeless fact of life and could even serve a positive function in the social order. Pauperism as a social condition, by contrast, was a product only of industrial society, was inimical to the social order, and required social solutions (Procacci 1993, 207–13). According to social Catholics, industrialization had torn the nation's social fabric and thus necessitated the intervention of the faithful between capitalist and worker. Working through organizations such as Church charity, the Society of Saint Vincent de Paul, and worker associations, they provided direct spiritual and moral comfort to the poor. At the same time, they intervened in policy discussions in order to protect the family unit from the ravages of the market (Lynch 1988, 43–64). As Jacqueline Lalouette (2002) has suggested, such interventions represented three basic Catholic approaches to poverty: philanthropy, centered around paternalistic relations of giving and dependence; charity, with its emphasis on a mix of interpersonal giving, organizational response, and state intervention; and solidarity, based on community association, especially among workers and peasants.[6]

By identifying the unrestrained capitalist economy as the source of present ills, social Catholics directly confronted the prophets of that system, the political economists. In doing so they were able to draw on a long tradition of Catholic thought about economic exchange cast in moralistic terms that held up the ideal of the market as a site of justice (Muller 2002, 6–19). Leading theoreticians of social Catholicism sought to harness the methods and insights of political economy toward moral ends (Almodovar and Teixeira 2012).

Perhaps the earliest and most influential of these theorists was Alban de Villeneuve-Bargemont. In his seminal 1834 text, *Économie politique chrétienne*, Villeneuve-Bargemont acknowledged that the rise of an industrial society founded upon the teachings of the political economists had brought with it fantastic promises of wealth, but "for the time being, gave neither work, nor bread."[7] He supported many of the teachings of political economists like Adam Smith and Jean-Baptiste Say, but believed their science was "based on an insatiable selfishness and on a deep misunderstanding of human nature," that these political economists suffered from a "heartlessness, [an] absence of humanity and charity, and finally, [a] selfish materialism" in their endless exhortations to "*laissez faire and laissez passer*."[8] According to Villeneuve-Bargemont, the root problem was that the political economists focused solely on the production of wealth and ignored entirely its distribution.[9] The solution, he said, was to submit the valuable teachings of political economy to Christian morality, to harness this engine of wealth creation for the benefit of the entire population, especially the working class.[10]

As A. M. C. Waterman (1991, 11–14) has described, the Christian political economy of Villeneuve-Bargemont represented the subjugation of political economy to Christian morality; the political economy of Catholics before 1848 used political economic methodology to analyze the market process, but upheld the supremacy of Catholic morality in designing the resulting order. In this sense, social Catholicism during the July Monarchy was dominated by a moral economy.

The working-class, socialist, and Christian contributors to *L'Atelier* were dedicated to the reorganization of labor around lines of cooperation and association and founded on Christian morality (Duroselle 1951, 114–20). While acknowledging that the National Workshops and industrial regulations were imperfect and temporary stopgaps, contributors to this paper nonetheless

confidently stated: "Work is a duty. The State is charged to take the necessary steps to bring about the accomplishment of this duty."[11] The journal
repeatedly justified its policy position—that in the face of mass unemployment the State had an obligation to provide work—by appealing to the traditional sources of French revolutionary legitimacy—liberty, equality, and
fraternity.[12] The authors of *L'Atelier* believed that their appeal to republican
principles legitimized their demands and that they were upholding the true
meaning of these terms in contrast to the false meaning expressed by their
political opponents.[13]

*L'Atelier*'s political opponents were the "professors of optimism," their
biased and error-prone "colleagues in political economy."[14] The understanding of liberty, equality, and fraternity invoked by political economists, *L'Atelier* argued, turned these words "in the hands of the wealthy
class [into] an instrument of oppression, and for the poor class a cause
of poverty."[15] The positive elements of the principles of liberty, equality,
and fraternity, in other words, did not inhere automatically in these words,
but stemmed only from the morality that underlay their use. The authors
argued that in order to avoid limitless exploitation it was necessary to balance all three republican principles against each other, to temper the pitfalls
of each with the strengths of the others: "We know too well, by long and
painful experience, that liberty without regulation quickly generates anarchy and tyranny, we know too well the industrial history of the last thirty
years to not repel with all of our strength these advocates of unlimited
competition."[16]

The contributors to *L'Atelier* justified their policies calling for the state
provision of labor by invoking the republican principles of liberty, equality,
and fraternity and stressed that the understanding of these terms promoted
by political economists led to disastrous results. The true spirit underlying
the beneficial application of these principles was to be found in the teachings of Christianity. "The State," they asserted, "has a sacred duty to provide
work to those who lack it, and sufficiently paid work."[17] They claimed that
the sole solution to the problems of industrial society lay "[in] the instinct of
an honest heart, [in] the sole inspiration of charity and good sense, [in] the
application of true Christian sentiment."[18] They argued that the solution to the
problems of industrial society actually lay in socialism founded on Christian
morality.[19]

Those calling for state intervention in the economy during 1848 thus
invoked a moral economic regime of truth to advance their political goals.
As social Catholics discovered, a moral economy expressed in republican
language, contrasted directly with liberal political economy, and founded
on the authority of Christian ethics provided an effective tool for garnering
working-class support.

## POLITICAL ECONOMY AS PRESERVATIONAL REGIME OF TRUTH

By 1848, political economy formed a coherent ideology founded on the veri-diction of the market process as an external check on the sovereignty of the State. Supported by legions of savants, the *Journal des économistes*, and an active press, political economists provided a consistent source of opposition to state intervention in the economy that found specific expression against the National Workshops and industrial regulation (Bouchet 2006). In doing so, they invoked a particular regime of truth founded on the outcome of market processes to promote their laissez-faire policies.

The aims of the early political economists were neither more nor less moral than those embracing a traditional moral economy of exchange (E. P. Thompson 1991, 265–93). Indeed, political economists arguing in 1848 against right-to-work laws emphasized that their animating desire was pre-cisely to improve the condition of the working class.[20] For the chair of politi-cal economy at the Collège de France, Michel Chevalier, "Political economy thus presupposes the simultaneous existence of competition and of Christian sentiment."[21] For Frédéric Bastiat, paragon of liberal economic thought, what distinguished political economy was not the morality of the ends it sought, but the temporality it used in considering the "ulterior and final effects" rather than "the immediate consequences."[22] What had changed with the emergence of political economy was the mediation of moral ends through the functioning of a market process that aggregated the self-interests of rational individual actors, and that operated in accordance with discoverable natural law, the scientific understanding of which would reveal the harmonious consequences of unimpeded human action (Staum 1998).

Within the political economic regime of truth, the economy existed as a natural and immutable system. According to Jean-Baptiste Say, acolyte of Adam Smith and perhaps the most influential French political economist of the nineteenth century, "Wealth is independent of the nature of govern-ment. The exact forms of public administration only indirectly, accidentally, influence the formation of wealth, which is almost entirely the work of indi-viduals."[23] Say believed that political economy was a science, a method that "has always come to place itself between man and truth."[24] For subsequent practitioners such as Bastiat, the economy represented an eternal truth ante-rior, exterior, and superior to the State that manifested itself in such "divine institutions" as property rights.[25] The task of the political economist was to scientifically reveal these *"general laws"* of nature in order to bring the laws of the State into accordance with them and thus harmonize society.[26] For lead-ing economist Joseph Garnier, political economy provided the only source of guidance capable of ensuring that the State was operating "in accordance with the nature of things."[27] Thus, political economy depended on the ideation of a natural order outside the realm of the State before the State could be brought into accordance with its laws: "political economy regulates interests, the same [way] that politics regulates the state of persons: this one governs, that one administers."[28]

In order for market processes to reveal a spontaneous natural law, however, they had to operate through individual human actors pursuing limited interests. Acknowledging that people acting in the real world responded to a wide range of motivations, Chevalier maintained that individual self-interest played a central and necessary role in motivating human action by making the individual act socially.[29] Bastiat echoed this point in insisting that people acted primarily out of "personal interest," but that in doing so the "individual becomes social."[30] Thus, the role of the State in reference to the natural law of the market was to protect the profits of individuals so that their pursuit would catalyze economic growth.[31]

Rather than the unrestrained self-interest of individual actors leading to chaos in the marketplace, political economists argued that the self-interest of individual actors would balance each other and generate the greater good for all of society. In fact, political economy founded its implicit claim to morality on the outcome of an invisible hand: "Economists believe in the natural harmony, or rather the necessary and progressive harmonization of interests."[32] For example, the attempt of manufacturers to maximize profits would create a harmonizing balance between the returns to capital and labor while lowering prices, thereby raising the standard of living for all.[33] The natural laws underpinning the political economic understanding of the world thus emerged from the decisions of individuals taken in response to their environments and led to the benefit of society as a whole by harnessing individual interests towards the social good (Hirschman 1977).

At this point, however, political economists reached a Panglossian conundrum. Their acceptance of the invisible hand as the aggregating foundation of the market order entailed the negation of political economy's capacity to evaluate the order resulting from the market process. If the self-interested actions of individuals culminating in observable trends and following natural laws were taken to lead to the harmonization of social exchange, then the artificial interference of the State into market processes could only destabilize the market order.[34] Although political economy in mid-nineteenth-century France entailed a broad range of subtle and nuanced opinions, when confronted with the radical socialist threat in the spring of 1848, the leading advocates of this science fell back on a reductive and dogmatic opposition to any and all state intervention in the economy. According to the political economists of 1848, the truths revealed by the science of political economy could "all be summarized in these words alone: *laissez faire, laissez passer*; simple words, sublime words."[35] When confronted with widespread poverty and unemployment resulting from market fluctuations, as was the case in 1848, such an argument amounted to the claim that all was for the best in the best of all possible worlds. By defending the market order against the intrusions of the State in 1848, political economists became champions of the status quo as it existed and thus, given the predominance of a capitalist system, promoters of an essentially preservational ideology.[36]

To support their interdiction of state intervention, these political economists warned against the threat of a slippery slope. They believed that "the division of property, in whatever way it happens, is the present ruin of society."[37] For Bastiat, even public discussion of state intervention in the market would undermine the confidence of capital owners in their property rights, "and that is enough for uncertainty, the greatest scourge of labor."[38] Any violation of property rights by the State would be tantamount to full communism: "a drop of water is as much water as the entire Ocean."[39] Political economy in 1848 represented at once an internally coherent, consistent, and totalizing ideology and a regime of truth that could be invoked in policy debates to justify noninterventionist policies and state inaction in the face of persistent unemployment. Thus, political economy supplied a direct counter to the moral economy invoked by socialists (Walton 1988).

## POLITICAL ECONOMY TURNED AGAINST MORAL ECONOMY

The chief dilemma facing French Catholicism in the mid-nineteenth century was how to retain and renew the guiding principles of the faith in an increasingly secular and positivist world, how to mediate between conservatism and liberalism while offering a compelling alternative vision of the nation united in the Church (Reardon 1975, vii–viii). While many young Catholics saw in political liberalism a path to modernize Catholicism by specifying the relation between Church and State, they were highly suspicious of an economic liberalism that lacked the guiding force of Christian morality (Harrison 2014, 103–48; Faccarello and Steiner 2008). Many of these liberal Catholics turned toward Ultramontanism—the privileging of papal authority over that of the Gallican Church—as a protest movement against the conservatism of the latter. But for Louis Veuillot, Ultramontanism offered a deeply conservative rejection of liberal politics and economics alike, a position he proclaimed as editor of the leading voice of conservative Catholicism, the newspaper *L'Univers* (Gough 1986, 60–102).

Unlike in the revolutions of 1789 and 1830, in 1848 even the Catholic Church joined in the ebullient welcoming of the republic (David 1992,

222–26). With the sudden victory of revolution in February 1848, *L'Univers* proclaimed the arrival of a period of Christian fraternity to be a divine judgment and called on its readers to care for the poor: "God speaks through the voice of events. The Revolution of 1848 is a notification from Providence. . . . The first man who called another man: *My brother*, was a Christian. It is a Christian also who first brought himself to voluntary poverty . . . in order to give his possessions to the poor."[40] Letters flooded into the newspaper's office and onto its pages from clergy around the nation, with the Archbishop of Lyon calling on all Catholics to "pursue with zeal . . . your holy mission, care for the poor, contribute to all the measures that can improve the lot of the workers. Hopefully," he added, "we will at last show a sincere and effective interest in the working class."[41] Meanwhile, the Bishop of Marseilles called on the faithful to honor the dead of the February revolution by contributing "your charity for the poor and unemployed worker."[42] These Catholics rallied to support a revolution that was social as well as political, that saw its duty as the amelioration of the conditions of the working class cast into poverty by the economic crisis. Even Pope Pius IX signed his name to a fundraising drive to provide charity for the unemployed French worker.[43]

Despite its initial enthusiasm for the February Revolution and calls for support on behalf of the French unemployed, *L'Univers* offered a paternalist and preservational philanthropy in its prescriptions to remedy social ills (Duroselle 1951, 474–75). The authors of *L'Univers* feared that working-class and especially socialist demands for state intervention in the economy were republican in name only and, in fact, an existential threat to the four social foundations of property, family, religion, and order as well as to the three republican principles of liberty, equality, and fraternity.[44] To defend the republic against the threat of socialism, contributors to *L'Univers* could not rely on the same source of truth as the social Catholics promoting moral economic solutions to the present malaise. If moral economy relied on an idea of established or traditional morality to determine the justice of state action or inaction, it would be difficult to convincingly counter with the binary opposition of another category of ethical analysis. This was especially true when both competing moral economies drew from the same religious source of moral principles. But moral economy also existed in dialectical antithesis with political economy, where the opposition lay in the reliance on either the market order or moral precepts as the determinant of what constituted just economic conditions.

For moderate republicans, state interventionism in 1848 far overstepped the bounds of responsible governance. The National Workshops quickly became a catchall for unemployed men and women throughout France, who flocked to the city to enroll in the program; within months, the National Workshops had swelled to support nearly one hundred twenty thousand workers. Given the lack of shovel-ready projects, however, the National Workshops were never able to provide work for more than fourteen thousand people on any given day, and even these positions generally required only unskilled manual labor and paid a correspondingly low wage (McKay 1933, 22–33). Nonetheless, the overall costs of the program spiraled out of control and placed a heavy burden on the young republic struggling to honor the debts of the previous regime. By the time of national elections in April, the French propertied classes and peasantry had come to resent bankrolling what increasingly appeared to be an institution of Parisian indolence. The result was a resounding victory for moderate republicans and conservative monarchists, and their freshly elected representatives arrived in Paris determined to shutter the failed experiment in public works (Price 1972, 120–21).

This determination solidified into a conservative reaction hostile to any state intervention in the labor market that May as workers in Rouen, Limoges, and Paris rose up against rumored threats to the National Workshops and had to be put down with force (McKay 1933, 80–104; Merriman 1978, 1–24).[45] The Constitutional Assembly's clumsy, overeager, and sudden decision to disband the National Workshops in mid-June prompted one of the bloodiest revolutionary uprisings in French history, the June Days, as fifty thousand Parisian workers confronted the forces of order arrayed under the command of General Eugène Cavaignac. By the time the battle was over, thousands of workers and soldiers lay dead, and thousands more were in prison.[46] To many French citizens and especially to their elected representatives, these events proved that there was an inexorable line leading from the right to work and the National Workshops to socialism and the death of the Republic (Démier 2002).

In the summer of 1848, *L'Univers* attempted to counter social Catholics' religious justifications for state intervention by supplying its own religious justifications for state abstention. As the newspaper explained to suffering workers, "To live poor in precarious work, that is nothing. That is how most of humanity has always lived and will always live. God made this law, without which society would be impossible; man can therefore suffer."[47] The Bishop of Langres emphasized the need for workers "above all to live according to God; however, in order to stay within God's established order, we must know how to respect the inequality found in the goods and pleasures of this world."[48] Appealing to immutable and divine morality to justify continued widespread poverty could hardly be expected to convince the working class to embrace this preservational moral economy.

In place of a Christian moral economy, therefore, in the spring of 1848 Veuillot steered *L'Univers* away from social Catholicism and toward a Christian political economy in which God acted through the natural laws of economics (Duroselle 1951, 422, 480). Socialists, he argued, had promised "the kingdom of God on earth," but could never truly "understand God's law" the way political economists could.[49] Contributors to *L'Univers* insisted that the State could not intervene in market outcomes because these outcomes came as the result of market forces over which the State had no direct control.[50] Efforts undertaken by the Provisional Government to shorten work hours while retaining wages thus "suppose a profound ignorance of the laws of production" and instead demonstrated the impossibility of socialism.[51]

In the pages of *L'Univers*, these divine natural laws of economics stemmed from the self-interested actions of individual actors. "From the economic point of view," the paper argued, "labor is human will applied to production. If it [labor] is the essence of free will, how can it be hoped that labor would one day submit itself to a fixed and immutable rule?" Within a free society, therefore, competition and dislocations were inevitable: "Competition is war, and in all war there are dead and wounded; we cannot change human nature. This is the price of civilization."[52] Thus, individual self-interest was ultimately the source of all wealth and operated as a natural law. Republishing in several installments a letter from Abbé Calinon, a French missionary serving on the South Pacific island of Tonga-Tabou, the newspaper argued that communism there had led directly to extreme poverty, indolence, and starvation because it had violated the conditions necessary for individual self-interest to motivate labor and thus unleash prosperity.[53]

Within a laissez-faire economy, however, the pursuit of self-interest would lead to the harmonization of competing interests and the benefit of society as a whole, provided the social order remained intact. "If competition has done bad, it has also done good," because it was competition driven by the profit motive that led to mechanization, readily available consumer goods, and a higher standard of living for everyone in society. And even if the hard work of the capitalist entrepreneur resulted in an unequal repartition of wealth "Man should be content," *L'Univers* concluded, "he will be a well-fed beast of burden."[54] Worker and employer, each in pursuing his own self-interest, entered into a social relationship whose consequences appeared as the result of natural laws impervious to the will of the State yet forming a fragile balance. "We must not forget that the conditions of labor that weigh on the worker also weigh on the manufacturer." To the authors of *L'Univers*, this was the essence of political economy.[55] Their understanding of the invisible hand as the harmonization of self-interested actors served to justify or excuse inequalities within the existing social order because the division of labor meant that the division of wealth occurred as the result of natural laws according to the abilities and motivation of the separate actors. Each party was equal in that the same laws of the market applied to both and apportioned the proceeds accordingly.[56]

The employment of the logic of political economy by *L'Univers* fulfilled dual political purposes in the preservation of the status quo. First, it naturalized and thus justified the existing social order as the inevitable result of impersonal and eternal laws established by God. Second, it proceeded from this position to argue against socialism by declaring the impossibility of state intervention to change the status quo. In both senses, conservative Catholics invoked political economy as a regime of truth to declare that the status quo represented the best possible condition. "The State, in any case," the paper declared, "should not enter private industry."[57] The only course of action open to the State to repair the faltering economy was to announce a rigid policy of nonintervention in order to "engender the security and the confidence that are the bases of public credit" and thus allow production to return "to the private workshops, which are the true national workshops."[58]

We see in this logic the dual process by which the market order established itself as the source of truth only to negate the outcomes of the market process. *L'Univers* argued that through a policy of reassurance, the State could allow the economy to heal itself as workers and capitalists attempting to maximize their own wages and profits were able "to determine themselves the quality, the quantity, and the price of their products. . . . So unemployment would be if not impossible, at least exceedingly rare."[59] *L'Univers*, having embraced political economy as a weapon against socialism and founded its political position on the market order as site of veridiction, now turned away from the very truths of the market evident in declining wages, rising unemployment, and epidemic bankruptcies. It could dismiss these very real sufferings "because it is not in the nature of human institutions to be perfect; but these moments [of economic crisis] are of short duration, and the malaise only ever reaches a small part of the population."[60]

The journalists contributing to *L'Univers* resorted to hyperbole and summoned up the specter of a slippery slope leading directly from state interventionism to social and economic collapse. Creating public works projects, they argued, would "paralyze all industry" and make all workers into slaves of the State.[61] A progressive income tax, meanwhile, would disincentivize business, eradicate luxury spending, and thus lead to mass unemployment culminating in communism.[62] Finally, they appealed to the wisdom of the political economists, those who "reason armed with facts, with figures, adorned and almost armored with good sense," to demonstrate "the rapid consequences that lead infallibly from the right to work to the organization of labor, from the organization of labor to communism, from communism to barbarism."[63]

The political role played by political economic reasoning manifested itself clearly in an article appearing in *L'Univers* on April 29, 1848. The authors dismissed the moral economic justification of the right to work, which they called absurd and impossible, by shifting the source of truth from Christian morality to the market order. The logic underlying their argument was that "labor is the application of will to production," or the pursuit of self-interest. In order to maximize productivity, therefore, it would be necessary to recognize the contributions of the "capitalist" class with a new slogan: "What is the producer? Nothing! What should he be? Everything!"[64] This emphasis on the contributions of profit-driven entrepreneurs reflected the belief that the aggregated actions of individuals create a natural law external to the control of the State: "A decree will not change the quantity of wheat, of wine, etc. that France produces. [The State] can create for production and liberty the best conditions for existence and development and thus prepare the moral and material improvement of the people. . . . The improvement of our kind depends on us and not on the government." Therefore, any state intervention in the economy could only disrupt it and worsen unemployment because the status quo was already the optimal possible outcome. Finally, the article concluded with the warning that granting the right to work would "lead logically to universal ruin by communism" and the death by starvation of all of France.[65] The very next day, *L'Atelier* published a response calling "the Christian political economy of *L'Univers*" decidedly unchristian. This article argued that *L'Univers* had been driven by a middle-class fear of social revolution and of a slippery slope from the right to work straight to communism, to abandon its religious roots in favor of "a doctrine so odiously selfish," that is to say political economy.[66]

Thus, in its struggle against socialism, *L'Univers* had fully shifted from a moral economy founded on the legitimation of Christian ethics to a political economy founded on the authority of the market order that transcended into a preservation of the status quo.

## CONCLUSION: MORAL ECONOMY TURNED AGAINST POLITICAL ECONOMY

By the fall of 1848, the imminent threat of socialism had been driven back and the capitalist order faithfully preserved. The conservative contributors to *L'Univers* had clearly never fully embraced the social revolution and had instead from early on found in liberal political economy a useful weapon against it. But they also occasionally revealed an underlying distrust of the bourgeoisie, whom they suspected of trying to sabotage the Revolution of 1848 in favor of a return to 1789.[67] They warned their Spanish compatriots, who were likewise undergoing industrialization, that "the economic science was created in the last century, in the interest of the bourgeois class," in order to justify enriching itself at the expense of the rest of the nation.[68] But it was only with the successful retirement of the socialist threat late in 1848 that these authors could safely turn against the ideology of political economy. They now declared it to contradict the law of God. They portrayed usury, for example, as a creation of "English political economy," a heresy conjured up by Protestant theologians that formed the basis of the dismal science. They claimed that capitalist society had resulted in conditions that were "bad, unjust, anti-social and anti-Christian." Contributors to *L'Univers* argued that the natural laws of the economy they themselves had embraced just months before did "not rule truly Christian societies, where the worker is regarded as a man, as a brother, as the image of God and the representative of Jesus Christ."[69] Similarly, they dismissed the political economists' utilitarian arguments for allowing work on Sunday because, whether profitable or not, it violated the divine law of the Sabbath.[70]

In an especially damning condemnation, the authors of *L'Univers* accused political economists of idolatry: having "cut religious faith away from their society in order to see in man only an accumulated capital. . . . They have substituted for the yoke of the Gospel that of political economy; they begin to feel that they have not won in the exchange. Laissez faire and laissez passer," they asserted, "that is quite easy for the economists," who act without mercy and reduce the wages of life to a commodity whose price is to be determined by the market.[71] They even went so far as to claim that political economy had been created specifically to undermine the Church.[72] Contributors to *L'Univers* increasingly called for the creation of a "social economy" that would bring the scientific methods of political economy under the guidance of Christian teachings in order to finally shepherd the nation toward an equitable prosperity.

In mid-nineteenth-century France, political actors from across the ideological spectrum were deeply concerned about the morality of the market order gradually reshaping every layer of social life. They drew on competing methods of analysis and evaluation in order to legitimize their policy proposals. While some thus emphasized the importance of ethical conscious will on the part of economic actors, others focused on the unwilled outcomes of self-interested actors. While both could thus claim to be interested in attaining a more moral economic, social, and political order, they used drastically different sites of veridiction in order to judge policies. This offered each group a distinct external regime of truth they could invoke to justify their political positions: a moral economy in favor of state intervention, and a political economy in favor of state abstention.

As the example of the conservative Catholic newspaper *L'Univers* demonstrates, these competing sites of veridiction could be invoked as political rhetorics toward specific ends. Confronted by the threat of radical socialist mobilization, the contributors to this newspaper grasped for a legitimizing ideology they could wield in defense of the established order. Liberal political economy existed in dialectical antithesis to the Christian moral economy invoked by many of these socialists; political economy could claim to be a universal, scientific, and disinterested source of truth; political economy suffered from a Panglossian conundrum in which its adherents could declare that all was already for the best in the best of all possible worlds and that, despite whatever ills the working class were facing, any efforts at amelioration would only make conditions worse. Liberal political economy thus offered the conservative Catholic press an effective discursive weapon against the democratic and social understanding of the republic. Once that threat had passed, this discourse could just as easily be dropped in favor of one more expedient to the political exigencies of the moment. In assessing the historical invocation and embrace of different regimes of truth, therefore, it is necessary to examine their logic and appeal in light of the social and political context.

## NOTES

1. As Roger Price (1972, 5–30) has highlighted, the transition into industrial capitalism was still incomplete in this period and largely confined to a few industrial cities, with most workers still employed in small-scale workshops. However, major cities like Paris were sufficiently industrialized for the economic crisis to cause severe dislocations.

2. *Le Moniteur universel: Journal officiel de la République française* (Paris) March 7, 1848; *Moniteur universel*, February 29, 1848; *Moniteur universel*, March 5, 1848.

3. *Moniteur universel*, May 3, 1848.

4. See Miller (1999) for a demonstration of the tension between the moral economy of the crowd and bread riots in response to the increasing liberalization of the French economy in the eighteenth and nineteenth centuries.

5. F. Berthault-Gras, *Identité des morales chrétienne et phalanstérienne et emploi que les hommes intelligents peuvent donner à ces morales pour réaliser très prochainement l'heureuse destinée de l'humanité, ou le règne de Dieu sur terre* (Châlon-sur-Saône, France: Chez Fouque, 1843); Henri de Saint-Simon, *Nouveau christianisme, dialogues entre un conservateur et un novateur* (Paris: Bossange père, 1825).

6. Lalouette highlights that one of the only state labor policies agreed upon by all of these groups was the use of the Algerian colony as an escape valve for surplus labor. See Andrews (2011) and Heffernan (1989).

7. Alban de Villeneuve-Bargemont, *Économie politique chrétienne, ou recherches sur la nature et les causes du paupérisme, en France et en Europe, et sur les moyens de le soulager et de le prévenir* (Paris: Paulin, 1834) 1:7. All translations are those of the present author. Unless otherwise noted, all italics are those of the original author.

8. Ibid., 1:22, 46, 64.

9. Ibid., 1:82. This distinction between political economy as a science of wealth production and Christian morality as guide of wealth distribution was a common theme within early nineteenth-century French social Catholicism (Duroselle 1951, 52, 70).

10. Alban de Villeneuve-Bargemont, *Économie politique chrétienne*, 26.

11. "Le Droit au travail," *Atelier*, July 10, 1848, 193.

12. "Ateliers Nationaux," *Atelier*, June 11, 1848, 173.

13. "Manifestation populaire du 17 mars," *Atelier*, March 19, 1848, 92.

14. "M Thiers et l'Association ouvrière," *Atelier*, October 7, 1848, 222–24.

15. "Organisation du travail: La réforme industrielle selon le chef d'une filature," *Atelier*, February 5, 1848, 70.

16. "Du décret sur la limitation des heures de travail," *Atelier*, October 7, 1848, 226.

17. "À nos lectures ordinaires et extraordinaires," *Atelier*, April 12, 1848, 115–16.

18. "Les apprentis et les ouvriers sous la direction de Mastaï (Pie IX)," *Atelier*, February 1848, 78.

19. "Qu'est-ce que le socialisme?" *Atelier*, August 7, 1848, 197–98.

20. Michel Chevalier, "Question des travailleurs: L'Amélioration du sort des ouvriers—l'organisation du travail," *Revue des deux mondes* 21 (Paris: Imp de Gerdès, 1848), 1058–59.

21. Michel Chevalier, "La liberté du travail: Discours d'ouverture du cours d'économie politique du Collège de France," *Journal des économistes: Revue mensuelle d'économie politique et des questions agricoles, manufaturières et commerciales* 19 (Paris: Chez Guillaumin et cie, 1848), 132.

22. Frédéric Bastiat, *Propriété et loi: Justice et fraternité* (Paris: Imp de Guillaumin et cie, 1848), 70–1.

23. Jean-Baptiste Say, *Traité d'économie politique, ou simple exposition de la manière dont se forment, se distribuent, et se consomment les richesses* (Paris: Imp de Crapelet, 1803), ii.

24. Ibid., iv.

25. Bastiat, *Propriété et loi*, 2–4.

26. Frédéric Bastiat, "Organisation naturelle, Organisation artificielle," *Journal des économistes* 19 (1848): 113–26.

27. Joseph Garnier, *Sur l'association, l'économie politique et la misère: Position du problème de la misère, ou considérations sur les moyens généraux d'élever les classes pauvres à une maeilleure condition matérielle et morale* (Paris: Guillaumin et cie, 1846), 38.

28. Chevalier, "Liberté du travail," 128.

29. Chevalier, "Question des travailleurs," 1072.

30. Bastiat, "Organisation naturelle," 118.

31. Bastiat, *Propriété et loi*, 21.

32. Bastiat, *Propriété et loi*, 67.

33. Joseph Garnier, "Étude sur la répartition de la richesse," *Journal des économistes* 19 (1848) 143–64.

34. Michel Chevalier, "Loi immuable de l'offre et de la demande," *Journal des économistes* 19 (1848): 1061–82.

35. Charles Coquelin, "L'Organisation du travail: La liberté," *Journal des économistes* 20 (1848) 14.

36. Historians writing on the rise of political economy in early nineteenth-century Britain have referred to this preservational spirit as a "conservative" movement that emerged in response to Jacobin threats against property rights and gave an intellectual framework to both political and religious conservatism (Polanyi 1957; Rothschild 1992; Waterman 1991). In using the term "preservational," however, I emphasize that in 1848 France, political economy did not necessarily align with conservative politics or religion—which sought to return the nation to a pre-capitalist organization of the economy and society—but instead highlighted the extent to which, given the dominance of a capitalist mode of production and exchange, this ideology was able to preserve the existing economic and social status quo against radical threats.

37. Achille De Colmont, "De l'amélioration de la situation sociale des ouvriers," *Journal des économistes* 20 (1848): 196.

38. Bastiat, *Propriété et loi*, 53–54.

39. Ibid., 26.

40. *L'Univers* (Paris), February 27, 1848, 1.

41. *Univers*, March 4, 1848, 1.

42. *Univers.*, March 11, 1848, 1.

43. *Univers*, March 5, 1848, 3.

44. *Univers*, March 19, 1848, 1; *Univers*, March 26, 1848, 1–2.

45. See Christofferson (1980) for an exploration of the practice and reception of National Workshops outside of Paris.

46. Mark Traugott (1985) has shown that the overwhelming majority of workers, even those employed in the National Workshops, either refused to join the June uprising or actively fought against it. Roger Gould (1995, 32–64), meanwhile, has countered that while not all workers fought in the streets of Paris, those who fought did so as workers. For a summary of this debate, see Traugott 2002. This chapter is not primarily concerned with the self-identification of the insurgents, but rather with the popular representations of them that subsequently influenced political discourse and labor policy. For a depiction of Cavaignac's repression, see de Luna (1969, 128–73).

47. *Univers*, July 7, 1848, 1.

48. L'Evêque de Langres, "Sur le communisme," *Univers*, August 6, 1848, 2.

49. *Univers*, May 28, 1848, 1.

50. *Univers*, March 10, 1848, 2.

51. *Univers*, April 1, 1848, 1.

52. *Univers*, April 6, 1848, 1.

53. Abbé Calinon, "Le Communisme mis en pratique," *Univers*, 10, 11, 14 July, 1848, 1–2.

54. *Univers*, April 9, 1848, 1.

55. *Univers*, April 1, 1848, 1. It is important to note that a key rhetorical difference between moderate republicans and democratic and social republicans in 1848 centered on the role of women. Women played an important role in the family economy and

participated in National Workshops and working-class parades as women workers (De Groat 1997). Some socialists advocated for the extension of voting rights to women, while others like Proudhon embraced misogynist positions that kept women in the home (Pilbeam 2000, 75–106). Throughout the 1840s, the impact of liberal economics on working-class women and the family's cost of living formed a common topic of discussion for social Catholics such as the contributors to *L'Atelier* (V. Thompson, 2000, 52–85). However, conservatives like Veuillot seem to have assumed that all workers were male and lampooned their socialist opponents, including Proudhon, for threatening the social order by uprooting traditional gender roles. This furnished the polarized reasoning that allowed them to claim the mantle of defenders of the family. See Fortescue (1997) for the role of women in Christian charity organizations.

56. *Univers*, July 15, 1848, 1.
57. *Univers*, April 7, 1848, 1.
58. *Univers*, March 29, 1848, 1; *Univers*, July 4, 1848, 1.
59. *Univers*, June 1, 1848, 1.
60. *Univers*, May 3, 1848, 2.
61. *Univers*, March 29, 1848, 1–2.
62. *Univers*, April 19, 1848, 1.
63. *Univers*, September 14, 1848, 1.
64. A play on the famous first words of the Abbé Sièyes's revolutionary 1789 pamphlet, *Qu'est-ce que le Tiers État?*
65. *Univers*, April 29, 1848, 1–2.
66. "Le droit au travail," *Atelier*, April 30, 1848.
67. *Univers*, April 18, 1848, 1.
68. *Univers*, June 5, 1848, 1.
69. *Univers*, September 4, 1848, 2.
70. *Univers*, September 5, 1848, 1–2.
71. *Univers*, September 9, 1848, 1.
72. *Univers*, October 27, 1848, 1–2.

# REFERENCES

Almodovar, António, and Pedro Teixeira. 2012. "French Catholic Political Economy in the 1830s." *European Journal of the History of Economic Thought* 19 (1): 197–225.
Andrews, Naomi J. 2011. "'The Universal Alliance of all Peoples': Romantic Socialists, the Human Family, and the Defense of Empire during the July Monarchy, 1830–1848." *French Historical Studies* 34 (3): 473–502.
Berenson, Edward. 1984. *Populist Religion and Left-Wing Politics in France, 1830–1852*. Princeton, NJ: Princeton University Press.
Bouchet, Thomas. 2006. "Droit au travail sous le 'Masque des Mots.'" *French Historical Studies*, 29 (4): 595–619.
Christofferson, Thomas R. 1980. "The French National Workshops of 1848: The View from the Provinces." *French Historical Studies* 11 (4): 505–20.
Cox, Marvin R. 1968. "The Liberal Legitimists and the Party of Order under the Second French Republic." *French Historical Studies* 5 (4): 446–64.

David, Marcel. 1992. *Le printemps de la fraternité: Genèse et vicissitudes, 1830–1851*. Paris: Aubier.

De Groat, Judith A. 1997. "The Public Nature of Women's Work: Definitions and Debates during the Revolution of 1848." *French Historical Studies* 20 (1) 31–47.

De Luna, Frederick. 1969. *The French Republic under Cavaignac, 1848*. Princeton, NJ: Princeton University Press.

Démier, François. 2002. "Droit au travail et organisation du travail en 1848." In *1848: Actes du colloque international du cent cinquantenaire tenu à l'Assemblée nationale à Paris, les 23–25 février 1998*. Edited by Jean-Luc. Paris: Créaphis.

Dougherty, M. Patricia. 1998. "The French Catholic Press and the July Revolution." *French History* 12 (4): 403–28.

Duroselle, Jean-Baptiste. 1951. *Les débuts du catholicisme social en France (1822–1870)*. Paris: Presses Universitaires de France.

Faccarello, Gilbert and Philippe Steiner. 2008. "Religion and Political Economy in Early-Nineteenth-Century France." *History of Political Economy* 40 (supplement) 26–61.

Fitzpatrick, Brian. 1983. *Catholic Royalism in the Department of the Gard, 1814–1852*. New York: Cambridge University Press.

Fortescue, William. 1997. "The Role of Women and Charity in the French Revolution of 1848: The Case of Marianne de Lamartine." *French History* 11 (1): 54–78.

Foucault, Michel. 2008. *The Birth of Biopolitics: Lectures at the Collège de France, 1978–1979*. Edited by Michel Senellart. Translated by Graham Burchell. New York: Palgrave Macmillan.

Gough, Austin. 1986. *Paris and Rome: The Gallican Church and the Ultramontane Campaign, 1848–1853*. New York: Oxford University Press.

Gould, Roger V. 1995. *Insurgent Identities: Class, Community, and Protest in Paris from 1848 to the Commune*. Chicago: University of Chicago Press.

Harrison, Carol E. 2014. *Romantic Catholics: France's Postrevolutionary Generation in Search of a Modern Faith*. Ithaca, NY: Cornell University Press.

Hayat, Samuel. 2014. *Quand la République était révolutionnaire: Citoyenneté et représentation en 1848*. Paris: Éditions de Seuil.

Heffernan, Michael J. 1989. "The Parisian Poor and the Colonization of Algeria during the Second Republic." *French History* 3 (4): 377–403.

Hirschman, Albert O. 1977. *The Passions and the Interests: Political Arguments for Capitalism before Its Triumph*. Princeton, NJ: Princeton University Press.

Lalouette, Jacqueline. 2002. "Charité, philanthropie et solidarité en France vers 1848: Pour une histoire des mots et des doctrines." In *1848: Actes du colloque international du cent cinquantenaire tenu à l'Assemblée nationale à Paris, les 23–25 février 1998*. Edited by Jean-Luc Mayaud. Paris: Créaphis.

Lévy-Leboyer, Maurice, and François Bourguignon. 1990. *The French Economy in the Nineteenth Century: An Essay in Econometric Analysis*. Translated by Jesse Bryant and Virginie Pérotin. New York: Cambridge University Press.

Lynch, Katherine A. 1988. *Family, Class, and Ideology in Early Industrial France: Social Policy and the Working-Class Family, 1825–1848*. Madison: University of Wisconsin Press.

Marchand, Bernard. 1993. *Paris, histoire d'une ville (XIXe–XXe siècle).* Paris: Éditions du Seuil, 1993.

McKay, Donald Cope. 1933. *The National Workshops: A Study in the French Revolution of 1848.* Cambridge, MA: Harvard University Press.

Merriman, John. 1978. *The Agony of the Republic: The Repression of the Left in Revolutionary France, 1848–1851.* New Haven, CT: Yale University Press.

Miller, Judith A. 1999. *Mastering the Market: The State and the Grain Trade in Northern France, 1700–1860.* New York: Cambridge University Press.

Moody, Joseph N. 1972. "The French Catholic Press in the Education Conflict of the 1840's." *French Historical Studies* 7 (3) 394–415.

Muller, Jerry Z. 2002. *The Mind and the Market: Capitalism in Modern European Thought.* New York: Alfred A. Knopf.

Pilbeam, Pamela. 2000. *French Socialists before Marx: Workers, Women and the Social Question in France.* Montreal: McGill-Queen's University Press.

Polanyi, Karl. 1957. *The Great Transformation: The Political and Economic Origins of Our Time.* Boston: Beacon Press.

Price, Roger. 1972. *The French Second Republic: A Social History.* Ithaca, NY: Cornell University Press.

Procacci, Giovanna. 1993. *Gouverner la misère: La question sociale en France, 1789–1848.* Paris: Éditions de Seuil.

Prothero, Iorwerth. 1997. *Radical Artisans in England and France, 1830–1870.* New York: Cambridge University Press.

Reardon, Bernard. 1975. *Liberalism and Tradition: Aspects of Catholic Thought in Nineteenth-Century France.* New York: Cambridge University Press.

Reddy, William M. 1984. *The Rise of Market Culture: The Textile Trade and French Society, 1750–1900.* New York: Cambridge University Press.

Rothschild, Emma. 1992. "Adam Smith and Conservative Economics." *Economic History Review* 45 (1): 74–96.

Sewell, William H. Jr. 1980. *Work and Revolution in France: The Language of Labor from the Old Regime to 1848.* New York: Cambridge University Press.

Sperber, Jonathan. 2005. *The European Revolutions, 1848–1851.* Second edition. Cambridge: Cambridge University Press.

Staum, Martin S. 1998. "French Lecturers in Political Economy, 1815–1848: Varieties of Liberalism." *History of Political Economy* 30 (1): 95–120.

Thompson, E. P. 1971. "The Moral Economy of the English Crowd in the Eighteenth Century," *Past & Present* 50: 76–136.

———. 1991. *Customs in Common: Studies in Traditional Popular Culture.* New York: W. W. Norton.

Thompson, Victoria E. 2000. *The Virtuous Marketplace: Women and Men, Money and Politics in Paris, 1830–1870.* Baltimore: Johns Hopkins University Press.

Traugott, Mark. 1985. *Armies of the Poor: Determinants of Working-Class Participation in the Parisian Insurrection of June 1848.* Princeton, NJ: Princeton University Press.

———. 2002. "Les ateliers nationaux en 1848." In *1848: Actes du colloque international du cent cinquantenaire tenu à l'Assemblée nationale à Paris, les 23–25 février 1998.* Edited by Jean-Luc Mayaud. Paris: Éditions Créaphis.

*Nicholas O'Neill*

Walton, Whitney. 1988. "Political Economists and Specialized Industrialization during the French Second Republic, 1848–1852." *French History* 3 (3) 293–311.
Waterman, AMC. 1991. *Revolution, Economics, and Religion: Christian Political Economy, 1798–1833*. New York: Cambridge University Press.

*Chapter 7*

# How the West Was Watered

*Private Property and Collective Action*

Bryan Leonard

A fundamental problem of society is the coordination of numerous individuals who all have diverse, possibly competing plans and diffuse knowledge. The importance of resolving competing plans in a mutually beneficial way is especially apparent in natural resource settings, where failure to coordinate can lead to resource depletion, resulting in welfare losses that persist far into the future. The problem of natural resource management has traditionally been confronted with either "top-down" or "bottom-up" institutions to coordinate individual actions. Top-down institutions prescribe particular outcomes or impose restrictions on individual behavior with the goal of preventing socially costly behavior. Bottom-up institutions tend to be more open-ended and focus on defining basic rules of the game to promote socially beneficial behavior.

Political institutions in particular rely on regulation and/or state ownership of natural resources. In essence, these institutional responses to environmental challenges make the state the residual claimant to natural resources and environmental amenity values, and the state then dictates the terms of resource use or protection. In these settings decisions about the optimal use of a natural resource or optimal level of environmental quality are made through the political process. Political decision making is subject to the information problems emphasized by Hayek (1945) as well as strategic behavioral issues raised by Buchanan and Tullock (1962).

Alternatively, bottom-up solutions for resolving collective action problems include two broad categories of institutions: informal cultural institutions where norms guide behavior and market-based institutions built around formal property rights. The power of informal institutions for resolving collective action problems has been emphasized by Elinor Ostrom and others, who have demonstrated the success of these institutions across a variety of contexts (Ostrom 1990, 2007, 2009, 2011; Ostrom and Gardner 1993; Janssen and Anderies 2011; Janssen and Rollins 2012; York and Schoon 2011). This chapter focuses on how formal property rights can also serve as the basis for coordination and explores the conditions under which property rights are a more effective solution to collective action problems than either political or informal institutions.

Property rights emerge as particular sets of rules to economize on the transactions costs of resource use and coordination—the specific structure of a new property rights regime is determined by the underlying institutional environment, resource characteristics, and user groups.[1] But while the factors that shape the formation of legal property rights are historically contingent, property rights regimes are incredibly persistent and rarely change except during revolution or war. This chapter explores the development of the prior appropriation doctrine—a novel first-possession system of allocating water in the American West—to shed light on the factors that determine how property rights emerge and persist.

## WATER IN THE WEST

Western water rights have long been of interest to economists—at least since Catherine Coman's article, "Some Unsettled Problems of Irrigation" appeared in the first issue of the *American Economic Review* in 1911—and the pattern of historical diversions incorporated in western surface water rights continues to dominate today. Studying the emergence of the prior appropriation doctrine can help us understand how property rights work to coordinate individuals for overcoming significant collective action problems and the advantages of property rights relative to political or informal institutions.

Property rights to surface water are formally administered under the prior appropriation doctrine in eighteen western US states and at least three Canadian provinces. Prior appropriation emerged voluntarily as an institutional innovation, replacing the riparian doctrine within twenty years across an immense area of over one million one hundred ninety-seven thousand square miles, suggesting large economic advantages. Water rights were not quantified under the incumbent riparian doctrine, which allowed "reasonable use" of surface water by owners of river-adjacent land. Digging a ditch and diverting a given quantity of water provided the basis for a prior appropriation claim—no riparian land ownership was necessary. The prior appropriation doctrine assigns priority to water rights based on when they were originally established—first in time, first in right—so that in times of drought users with high priority receive their full allocation before more junior users have the right to divert any water.

Water's unique characteristics induce particularly challenging social choice problems for developing, using, and conserving water resources. The essential nature of water gives rise to a myriad of uses that are both consumptive and non-consumptive. Water is an input for production of everything from agricultural to industrial products, but it is also an essential final good necessary for life. The suitability of water for different uses depends on both the quality and quantity of water available. The transmission of water is fraught with complications including evaporation, seepage, gravity flow, and minimum-flow constraints. Finally, the distribution of water resources across western landscapes in rivers and streams creates classic upstream/downstream externalities and common-pool resource management problems.

## WATER AS A COLLECTIVE ACTION PROBLEM

One of the chief economic problems facing water users in the arid western United States was the development of irrigation infrastructure (Leonard and Libecap, 2016). States west of the 100th meridian have much lower stream density and receive far less precipitation than the eastern United States. This was compounded by the fact that lands adjacent to many streams in the West are quite rugged and not suitable for farming. In order for water to be productive it had to be conveyed from where it was available in rivers and streams to where it was economically useful in distant lands.[2]

As noted by social scientists across a variety of disciplines, establishing large-scale irrigation works is a classic collective action problem (Coman 1911; Worster 1985; Ostrom 2011; Hanemann 2014). Irrigation systems required large, upfront investments but generated uncertain benefits for frontier migrants who were unfamiliar with farming techniques in the arid West. These high fixed costs were compounded by limited credit markets, creating the need for coordinated investment in diversion infrastructure. Because existing canals could be extended at a much lower cost once established, there was an incentive for individuals to free-ride and not contribute to outlays for the main ditches that spawned subsequent lateral ditches. This free-rider problem was exacerbated by the threat of upstream diversions that could reduce available flows after costly investment had already taken place.

Figure 7.1—taken from an 1874 edition of *Harper's Weekly* dedicated to examining "The Colorado System of Irrigation"—provides a visual depiction of these coordination problems. The rugged terrain along the streams prevents either urban or agricultural development directly adjacent to available water resources, requiring the construction of the main ditch—a major capital investment—to bring water to the town and to productive land for irrigation. Once this investment is undertaken, the marginal cost of expanding either

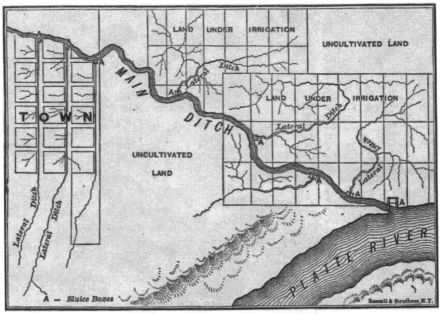

THE COLORADO SYSTEM OF IRRIGATION.

**Figure 7.1    Irrigation Infrastructure and the Free-Rider Problem.** *Source*: Harper's Weekly, June 20, 1874, p. 514.

urban development or adding lateral ditches is low and does not require coordination, creating an incentive for users to free-ride during the initial construction phase.[3] Finally, all of the water routed through the main ditch enters from a specific point on the river (in this case the Platte), and so could easily be captured upstream by a competing settlement or even individual. This threat of entry reduces investment incentives even further.

## THE LACK OF A LEVIATHAN

Although economists and political scientists are accustomed to prescribing government provision as the textbook solution for public good problems and the other "market failures" identified above, the most prolific scholarship exploring the role of the state in developing irrigation is due to historians Karl Wittfogel and Donald Worster. Early in his career Wittfogel studied the development of what he called "hydraulic societies" in China, where regimes with centralized political power constructed and maintained irrigation works (Wittfogel 1975). Initially, Wittfogel saw the concentration of political power around the provision of these basic public goods as inevitable, arguing that the state was necessary for such a grand undertaking.

Though Wittfogel later abandoned the claim that a centralized state was the necessary purveyor of irrigation works after emigrating to the United States and observing the property rights system there (the subject of this chapter), this did not stop Donald Worster from taking up the "hydraulic society" thesis and applying it to problems of twentieth-century irrigation in the United States (Worster 1985).[4]

Economists and historians alike are fond of depicting the state as the natural purveyor of public goods, but the realities of the western frontier in the latter half of the nineteenth century precluded such a textbook solution to the problem of irrigation development. As a practical matter, the federal government's ability to exert de facto control over most of the western United States was extremely limited. At the same time, the population of western territories was spread unevenly across the landscape and constantly in flux as the area was settled. Just as migrants lacked experience with large-scale farming, government at all levels was wanting in expertise for understanding how irrigation works should be organized, financed, and developed. Together, these factors amounted to a lack of state capacity for the provision of local public goods.

As Allen (1991) points out, the low density of US Army troops and outposts on the western frontier partially explains the pattern of land claiming enshrined in the Homestead Act and related laws. By allocating property rights to land via first possession, the federal government lowered enforcement costs relative to auctions—an alternative property rights allocation mechanism preferred by many economic theorists. Whereas auctioning land claims necessitated de facto control of all plots up for sale, allocation via first possession only required the government to enforce property rights for land that was actually claimed. Nor was land the only resource that was allocated in this way; rights to timber, minerals, and water were allocated in a similar fashion (Gates and Swenson 1968).

In addition to lowering overall enforcement costs by reducing the size of the federal estate that had to be monitored, first possession gave incentives for search by individual claimants. Promoting search by claimants helped reveal which locations and resources were worth defining rights to, ensuring that enforcement costs were allocated efficiently (Allen 1991; Leonard and Libecap 2016). Economists studying the relationship between property rights and innovation have long appreciated the role that first possession plays as a reward for costly yet socially valuable research activities. One reason this mechanism works so well is that the state lacks the knowledge *ex ante* to predict which areas of research will be profitable, precluding a more precise, direct form of research funding. In the same way, the federal government situated in Washington, D.C., lacked functional knowledge of the western frontier. Despite commissioning numerous reports and surveys, the efficient scope, scale, and location of irrigation was not well understood by political decision makers (Ostrom 2011).

Enforcement and information issues aside, the vastness of the US West and fluctuating nature of the region's population would have made systematic taxation initially difficult. State and territorial governments had uncertain boundaries that developed in response to the emergence of settlements in particular areas. Provision of public goods requires taxation, which in turn requires vested authority for collecting taxes and enforcing penalties for failure of payment. With the population and state boundaries themselves in flux, the logistics of tax collection presented a first-order challenge for public finance. As Tyler (1992) notes, organizing local taxing authorities was necessary for irrigation development even after the Federal Bureau of Reclamation became active in the early twentieth century.[5]

From a purely theoretical perspective, the efficient provision of a public-good-like infrastructure requires precise knowledge of the costs of providing the good and the marginal social benefit of additional amounts of the good to a variety of users. From a practical perspective, the provision of a public good requires the ability to finance construction via taxation. This, in turn, requires the ability to identify beneficiaries and hold them accountable for the benefits they receive. Irrigation development during westward expansion in nineteenth-century America lacked both the theoretical and the practical requirements for government provision of a public good. So, despite being identified by economists and historians alike as a classic job for the state, the development of irrigation works in the West would be addressed via alternate institutions.

## DEVELOPING THE COMMONS?

Ostrom (2011) recognizes that the traditionally proposed government solution to collective action problems associated with agriculture was not available in the US West before going on to argue that local social institutions and norms provide a viable alternative. Indeed, irrigation societies from across the globe often serve as case studies for scholars who study the role of informal norms in governing the use of common-pool resources. Citing examples ranging from Mormon settlers to Hispanic *acequias* in the American Southwest and elsewhere, Ostrom emphasizes the importance of local knowledge and trust for developing irrigation infrastructure in the western United States.

Ostrom (2011) applies the social-ecological systems approach developed by Ostrom (2007, 2009) to reinterpret the case studies of successes and failures of irrigation projects across the west from Coman (1911). Ostrom recognizes, as does Coman, that the resource problem facing claimants across different settlements on the western frontier were broadly similar, suggesting that different institutional arrangements are responsible for the variation in outcomes. Ostrom compares outcomes under the Desert Land Act of 1877, the California Wright Act, the Carey Act of 1894, and the Reclamation Act of 1902 and concludes that simple dichotomies between private vs. public provision of irrigation works were inadequate for explaining which acts were broadly successful and which were not.

For Ostrom (2011), the defining characteristic for predicting the success of an institutional response to the problem of western irrigation was its ability to capitalize on local knowledge and trust. Coman's (1911) analysis is replete with examples of failures, but two key successes are Mormon settlements of Utah and a Bureau of Reclamation project in Minidoka, Idaho. Ostrom contrasts these successes to the broad failures of the Desert Land Act and the California Wright Act and concludes that the former created incentives for individuals to seek out and apply knowledge that was crucial for successful irrigation works. Because of the risk associated with such large investments under uncertain conditions, trust between agents was crucial for promoting investment. What is less clear from Ostrom's analysis is what particular features of the different laws helped to develop this trust or how other institutions might supply it where absent. Indeed, the closing words of her article call for future research in this vein. What, then, are the limits of informal institutions for providing trust?

Hanemann (2014) provides a critical reading of Ostrom (2011) that elucidates the microeconomic structure of the coordination problem facing agents on the frontier. In particular, Hanemann stresses that the fundamental problem facing potential irrigators was access to capital:

> Compared to dryland farming, a distinctive feature of irrigation using surface water in the West was its capital intensity. This in the physical nature of the system . . . it was necessary to be able to install the complete system, from reservoir to farmers' fields, before a single drop of water could be delivered to users. Almost the entire cost of irrigation supply in the West was capital costs. There were relatively few operating costs—water distribution was either gravity flow or pumped using hydropower. It was necessary therefore to find a source of financing up front, well before there was a revenue stream. (Hanemann 2014, 15)

While Ostrom's focus is on knowledge and trust, Hanemann's is directed at finance.[6] The two are not so different.

Access to finance becomes a knowledge problem and a trust problem in settings where well-functioning markets are absent because without prices, creditors lack efficient signals to direct them as to the best use of their funds. There is a first-order knowledge problem associated with what types of projects might be profitable and where (indeed, both Ostrom (2011) and Hanemann (2014) emphasize migrants' relative ignorance of irrigated agriculture), but there was also the crucial question of who could be trusted. Indeed, Hanemann's own analysis emphasizes the collective nature of irrigation works due to the interconnectivity of irrigation systems. Interpreted in this way, Ostrom and Hanemann are asking similar questions through different lenses. But while Ostrom is able to pick out several examples where social institutions were able to supply knowledge and trust, Hanemann notes these are the exception rather than the norm.

Hanemann (2014) provides further clarity by drawing a crucial distinction between the coordination problems associated with developing a physical system of irrigation and managing a system that has already been constructed. While Ostrom (2011) recognizes this distinction in passing, her analysis tends to conflate the two types of coordination problems. In particular, the social-ecological systems approach of Ostrom (2007, 2009) is often applied to existing irrigation societies to understand how individuals coordinate over the use of existing infrastructure. Once irrigation works exist, the problem of irrigation is essentially akin to a classic common-pool resource setting, which Ostrom analyzed extensively throughout her career. This leads Ostrom (2011) to under-appreciate the unique problems associated with investment in water resources on the western frontier.

Both Ostrom (2011) and Hanemann (2014) overlook the importance of the characteristics of irrigators themselves in shaping the emergence of institutions for water development in the West. Hanemann says little on the subject, while Ostrom emphasizes claimants' homogeneity with respect to their ignorance of how to successfully farm in an arid environment.[7] What Ostrom does not address is the large number of claimants in many Western settlements and the degree of cultural heterogeneity among those claimants. This oversight is critical because these characteristics are at odds with fundamental aspects of Ostrom's (1990) design principles for common-pool resource management.

According to Ostrom (1990) the composition of the users of a resource is a critical component for determining the viability of informal, norm-based solutions to collective action problems associated with common-pool resources. First, having relatively homogenous user groups facilitates cooperation. As Ostrom (1990) notes:

> In a setting in which few individuals share norms about the impropriety of breaking promises, refusing to do one's share, shirking, or taking other opportunistic actions, each appropriator must expect all other appropriators to act opportunistically whenever they have the chance. In such a setting it is difficult to develop stable, long-term commitments. Expensive monitoring and sanctioning mechanisms may be needed. Some long-term arrangements that once were productive are no longer feasible, given their costs of enforcement. In a setting in which there are strong norms against opportunistic behavior, each appropriator will be less wary about the dangers of opportunism. (Ostrom 1990, 36)

Second, successful collective action depends on there being a relatively small group of resource users. Ostrom (1990) identifies the large number of users involved as a factor contributing to the failure of at least five different case studies, for the simple reason that the coordination becomes difficult as groups grow large (Olson 1965; Buchanan and Tullock 1962).

The instances of successful irrigation development in the West identified by Ostrom (2011) and others were broadly consistent with Ostrom's general requirements for successful management of common-pool resources. As Hanemann (2014)—citing Benson (1982)—notes, "Their [Mormon] settlements were governed 'by a cohesive hierarchical assembly of individuals. The settlements were able to administer the development of cooperative water projects through the existing church organization. The cooperative attitude among the settlers facilitated the financing of the irrigation projects'" (Benson 1982, 379 cited by Hanemann 2014, 6). Similarly, the Hispanic *acequias* of the American Southwest that successfully developed irrigation systems did so when they were insulated from the threat of entry by new users (Smith 2016).

Instances of small, stable groups of homogeneous users were the exception rather than the norm in the West. This oversight is odd for Ostrom, but critical in setting apart her success stories as special cases. Indeed, the key successes analyzed by Ostrom and others are rare exceptions to the general rule that the West was a cultural melting pot for misfits from a litany of backgrounds (Hicks and Peña 2003). As Crifasi (2015) makes clear in the case of Colorado, emigrants to the West arrived from across the United States, Europe, and elsewhere.

The sheer number of incoming migrants created significant challenges above and beyond the heterogeneity problem for small-scale collective action solutions built around social norms. In contrast to the eastern United States where land claims were well-established and often dated back to the colonial area, land in the West was up for grabs and distributed to individual parties 160 to 320 acres at a time (Allen 1991; Hanemann 2014; Leonard and Libecap 2016). This created the potential for there to be hundreds of landowners along a given stream or river and precluded informal arrangements from serving as an effective basis for coordination (Leonard and Libecap 2016). Ostrom (1990), Olson (1965), Agrawal (2003), and others all stress the importance of clearly defined user groups built on mutual trust relationships, but these groups were not the dominant social arrangement during the settlement of the West.

The problem of many potential entrants was dynamic in nature during westward expansion because new migrants arrived in several subsequent waves of settlement (Leonard and Libecap 2016). This made the coordination problem even more difficult than the classic "large N" problem because the total number of potential users was not even known when the earliest settlers faced the economic problem of irrigation development. The problem of coordination among a large number of heterogeneous users is indeed quite simple compared to the problem of coordinating with an unknown number of *potential* users who may or may not arrive at some point in the future.

Ostrom (1990), Libecap (1994), Alston et al. (2012), Smith (2016), and others have previously appreciated the problem of potential entry in the context of common-pool resource problems. Allowing for the dynamic arrival of new users not only creates inter-temporal coordination problems, it also creates the risk that productive investments will attract entry by new users who will dissipate the value of those investments (Leonard and Libecap 2015). Put another way, early settlers in the West could not be guaranteed residual claimancy to their investments via informal institutions because those institutions lacked mechanisms for either excluding new users or incorporating their resource demands in a way that did not make incumbent users worse off.[8]

Even in settings where strong cultural norms did exist and held promise for barring newcomers from group membership, the physical nature of river systems allowed de facto entry via upstream claiming. In the absence of formal or de facto protections, the water associated with a given irrigation community can always be intercepted upstream, making real enforcement of group boundaries nearly impossible. This type of "leap-frogging" was a real phenomenon that occurred between individuals, companies, and whole communities competing for water in Colorado before the development of the prior appropriation doctrine (Crifasi 2015). The ability of any future claimant to essentially remove the key productive input for communal investments (water), coupled with uncertainty about the number, nature, and even timing of these future claimants undercut communities' ability to secure benefits for their members through informal cooperation except where social structures that could mediate entry already existed (as in Utah and the *acequias*).

## COLLECTIVE ACTION THROUGH CONTRACTING

It is useful to clearly restate the essential features of the economic problem facing potential irrigators in the arid West before exploring how formal property rights developed to solve that problem in a setting where political and informal institutions had largely failed to do so. The rugged, arid terrain of the West made upfront investment in irrigation infrastructure a prerequisite for agriculture. The capital intensity of this infrastructure, the large public benefits it ultimately provided, and the potential for free-riding made irrigation investment a classic collective-action problem. Information problems, a vast federal estate, and a large number of heterogeneous agents arriving over a wide time frame reduced the government's capacity to provide irrigation works initially and largely precluded the development of informal, community-based irrigation projects. Instead, individuals turned to property rights as a coordinating device.

In reflecting on Ostrom (2011), Hanemann (2014) emphasizes the role that property rights played in providing an alternative solution to this problem, detailing the importance of having legal property in providing access to credit. Leonard and Libecap (2016) also study the role of property rights in promoting investment, focusing on the role of first possession as reward for socially valuable search and investment (a similar argument has been made in the context of patents). Another critical benefit of prior appropriation not emphasized by Hanemann (2014) or Leonard and Libecap (2016) was that it transformed irrigation works from a non-excludable into an excludable club good, providing a foundation for the market-based development of water resources in the West.

The economic theory of club goods first developed by Buchanan (1965) provides a convenient analytic framework for understanding how property rights can serve as a basis for collective action to develop socially beneficial projects like infrastructure. Buchanan proposed club goods as a more flexible approach to categorizing collective action problems than the strict private vs. public good dichotomy popularized by Samuelson (1954). In the original taxonomy, public goods like national defense are non-rivalrous (everybody gets the same amount) and non-excludable, whereas private goods like shirts are rivalrous (a shirt can only be worn by one person at a time) and excludable (it easy to prevent the theft of shirts).

Buchanan's innovation was to recognize the existence of club goods such as swimming pools which are partially rivalrous and partially excludable. As Buchanan notes,

> The interesting cases are those goods and services, the consumption of which involves some "publicness," where the optimal sharing group is more than one person or family but smaller than an infinitely large number. The range of "publicness" is finite. The central question in the theory of clubs is that of determining the membership margin, so to speak, the size of the most desirable cost and consumption sharing arrangement. (Buchanan 1965, 1)

This framework is useful for analyzing irrigation works because, as noted, the optimal group size for an irrigation project was greater than one but nevertheless faced an upper boundary based on the profitability of ditch investment and the amount of land and water that could be put to productive use in a given area.

The key economic question in the theory of clubs is determining the optimal club size and associated delivery size for a particular good. Taking the amount of the good as fixed and assuming a particular distribution of the club good (such as equal sharing), the optimal club size is found by setting the marginal benefit of a new member (their contribution to the cost of production) equal to the marginal cost of that new member (the reduction in existing members' consumption). For a given production function, sharing rule, and good size, the optimal club size is uniquely determined. Under these conditions, we would expect private clubs to form and provide goods that are "public" among their members but are not enjoyed by nonmembers. Classic examples include homeowner's associations, private swimming pools, and (of course) irrigation companies.

Even under the restrictive conditions outlined above, provision of club goods requires the ability to exclude nonmembers. Indeed, Buchanan saw exclusion as essential:

> If individuals think that exclusion will not be fully possible, that they can expect to secure benefits as free riders without really becoming full-fledged contributing members of the club, they may be reluctant to enter voluntarily into cost-sharing arrangements. This suggests that one important means of reducing the costs of securing voluntary co-operative agreements is that of allowing for more flexible property arrangements and for introducing excluding devices. (Buchanan 1965, 14)

While Buchanan explicitly recognizes the fact that his analysis ignores the costs of excluding outsiders and securing internal agreement, both are fundamental to determining whether clubs are a viable mechanism for collective action. At the same time, Buchanan's emphasis on the importance of property as a means for exclusion points the way to a cost-minimizing mechanism for both exclusion and coordination.

The emergence of prior appropriation water rights illustrates how property rights can provide a key means of exclusion to facilitate the formation of economic clubs while also serving as a basis for internal agreement among club members. Prior appropriation water rights are historically unique in that they are explicitly quantified and assigned a priority based on when they were established (Leonard and Libecap 2016).[9] These two distinctive features of prior appropriation address the two critical needs associated with the formation of clubs—allocating rights via first possession solved a complicated exclusion problem, while quantifying water rights provided a heretofore unavailable means of contracting over claims to surface water.

The challenges for informal cooperation presented by the inter-temporal arrival of new claimants also posed a problem for the formation of economic clubs. Ultimately, exclusion is only economically meaningful if agents have the de facto ability to preclude others from the rents associated with a particular good or resource. The unquantified share-based riparian water rights dominant in the eastern United States did not provide claimants with de jure protections for their investments because any new arrival would be allowed "reasonable use" of the river (Leonard and Libecap 2016). With large numbers of potential entrants and a fluctuating distribution of land owner-ship, location-based enforcement costs were high because new claimants could intercept existing users' water before it ever reached them by locating upstream. This was exacerbated by the fact that land claims—the basis for a riparian water right—were also in flux as the West was settled. While preex-isting land holdings had been a low-cost margin along which to demarcate property to water in the eastern United States, this was not a viable option in the West.

Faced with high enforcement costs for unquantified, land-based water rights, claimants on the Western frontier turned to an alternative, lower-cost dimension along which to define claims: time. Demarcating rights to water based on the timing of the claim may have initially emerged simply due to convenience; rights to land, timber, and minerals were all officially allo-cated via first possession, and claimants began using the same mechanism to assert quantifiable rights to water (Umbeck 1977, 1981; Libecap 1978; Kanazawa 1996). These claims lacked formal legal status initially, but the system was adopted in a de facto way by users across a variety of different settings.

Whether or not it was adopted out of convenience, first possession turned out to be just the sort of "excluding device" needed to support the formation of clubs envisioned by Buchanan (1965). Fixing claims based on their initial timing formed a low-cost basis for exclusion because in most cases it was apparent which claims were established earlier or later than others. Moreover, new claimants at any given time did not have to worry about the threat of potential entry because they had prior access to the water. This made agents willing to invest in costly ditch construction and made them more willing to enter into contracts with one another (Leonard and Libecap 2016).

Fixing claims based on time also lowered coordination costs once subsequent claimants did arrive because they could take existing claims as given in their own decision of where and how much to invest. Though trans-actions costs were certainly not zero, first possession claims to water were a way of establishing an initial distribution of quantifiable property rights that could then serve as a basis for negotiation and exchange vis-à-vis Coase (1960). Positive transaction costs may have impaired an efficient outcome in the sense of the first-best, but the existence of some form of property rights facilitated agreements that would not have been possible otherwise.

Crifasi (2015) provides a litany of examples of coordination, investment, and contracting that occurred throughout the Colorado Front Range even before first-possession water rights had been legally recognized. Often, claimants who formed a ditch company would pool their individual claims into one large claim and then allocate water among themselves on a proportional basis. This reduced the cost of enforcing their collective claim relative to outsiders and secured their joint interest in the success of the project. Even though water rights were not formal legal property rights initially, claimants legally incorporated their ditches and issued shares (Crifasi 2015). This provided a mechanism for securing capital necessary for investment before water rights were legally recognized as collateral. As Hanemann (2014) makes clear, this was a dominant feature of the economic problem of irrigating, making the clubs that formed as ditch companies a novel solution.

Water clubs in the form of ditch companies carried with them other advantages in addition to access to capital. By formally incorporating, users were able to avoid post-contractual opportunism that often plagued informal agreements about water deliveries and rights-of-way for constructing ditches (Crifasi 2015). Incorporation created a "backdoor," so to speak, to formal legal recourse for claimants. While irrigators could not initially take legal action over their informal water claims, they could hold one another accountable for breach of contract associated with the internal rules and responsibilities of a ditch company (Hanemann 2014). Settlers' willingness to incorporate around first possession claims thus provided a mechanism for reducing the organizing costs that worried Buchanan (1965).

While de facto first-possession claims allowed for a remarkable degree of coordination, they were subject to at least a potential threat of encroachment by new claimants because they lacked formal legal protection. When encroachment did eventually come, it led competing individuals and ditch companies to "leap frog" one another by constructing new irrigation works further and further upstream. With lack of legal means to enforce their first possession claims, users resorted to a spatial competition over access to water. In one particular instance, a group of frustrated irrigators with junior, downstream claims led by Rubin Coffin destroyed the head gate of the Left Hand Ditch Company, which had previously diverted much of the available water along St. Vrain Creek near Boulder, Colorado (Crifasi 2015). The destruction of physical property gave the Left Hand Ditch Company a basis for legal action. As it worked its way up to the Colorado Supreme Court, the resulting court battle would become the test case for the legal status of first-possession claims to water.

The Colorado Supreme Court was clearly sensitive to the need for secure property rights to provide incentives to invest. As Chief Justice Samuel Elbert explained:

It has always been the policy of the national, as well as the territorial and state governments, to encourage the diversion and use of water in this country for agriculture; and vast expenditures of time and money have been made in reclaiming and fertilizing by irrigation portions of our unproductive territory. Houses have been built, and permanent improvements made; the soil has been cultivated, and thousands of acres have been rendered immensely valuable, with the understanding that appropriations of water would be protected. Deny the doctrine of priority of superiority of right by priority of appropriation, and a great part of the value of all this property is at once destroyed. (Rocky Mountain News, January 2, 1878, as quoted in Crifasi 2015, 175)

The court rejected riparian rights in favor of the more secure, excludable first-possession claims that emerged first as de facto rights and had gradually become generally acknowledged. By providing a clear, legal recognition of first possession, the case became the basis for the "Colorado Doctrine" of water rights that would later become known as prior appropriation across the West (Schorr 2005; Crifasi 2015).

The formal recognition of appropriative water rights unleashed the market process as a mechanism for discovering more efficient forms of organization for irrigation. Hanemann (2014) notes that the asset specificity associated with land and water use in the West created challenges for traditional market relationships identified by Williamson (1975, 1985). This was solved through "vertical integration combining both sides of the transaction within a single entity. In an irrigation context, this means that the water supplier and land-owner become the same entity" (Hanemann 2015, 15). Indeed, this was exactly the strategy adopted by the wave of ditch companies that formed in the wake of *Coffin v. Left Hand Ditch Company.*

Though contracts and investment had already begun on the basis of informal first possession claims, the formal recognition of appropriative water rights allowed the market process to develop more fully than was previously possible. Formal codification involved quantification and recording of claims via flow measurement devices at head gates located along each stream. Measuring and recording claims provided a more standard method of quantification and created a registry of claims by priority, lowering the costs of learning about prior claims and enforcing existing claims. State enforcement of appropriative claims also provided greater certainty for outside investors who were crucial sources of capital (Hanemann 2014) while allowing claimants themselves to devote less effort to enforcement and more to solving the important information problems associated with developing agriculture in an arid climate.

Entrepreneurs recognized profit opportunities from solving the information problem facing new migrants while also ameliorating the asset specificity problem. Once property rights to water were legally recognized, the market solution was straightforward:

The business model for corporate ditch building in Colorado was quite elegant in its simplicity. First, private investors, railroad companies, or other corporate developers would acquire a large block of undeveloped land. . . . Once the land passed to private hands, engineers developed plans and claimed the necessary water rights. They would then incorporate a ditch and sell enough shares to build the ditch while reserving sufficient stock to irrigate lands they owned. Elsewhere developers would sell the land and then rent the water to farmers. Using these tactics, irrigation companies profited by bringing new settlers to Colorado. (Crifasi 2015, 184)

While Hanemann (2014) emphasizes the widespread failure of many such ventures, much of the existing irrigation infrastructure servicing cities like Boulder was initially constructed by a private ditch company and later acquired by municipal authorities.

The development of irrigation companies as clubs that could price membership allowed the market process to shape the course of water development early on in the movement west. As noted by Lavoie (1986), the market process generates information through entrepreneurial discovery. This was true in two important ways in the irrigation context. First, led by the profit motive, irrigation companies on Colorado's Front Range developed new techniques for irrigating lands previously thought un-irrigable and dramatically expanded the very definition of irrigable land. Second, successes and failures of irrigation companies of varying sizes, locations, and organizational types laid the groundwork for the water management institutions that allowed western irrigation to flourish over the next century.

The earliest American settlers in the rugged west began by irrigating the easily-reached "bottom-lands" near streams, but these lands were relatively scarce and soon exhausted. With the ability to acquire land cheaply and sell at a premium once water was provided, engineers had a strong incentive to find ways to irrigate the wide, flat bluffs that often lay above streams. Faced with large potential gains and a burgeoning market for joint land and water claims, entrepreneurs discovered that lands above the stream channel could be irrigated if the initial diversion was constructed farther upstream and made to slowly work its way above the bluffs. As soon as the earliest of these endeavors was successful, large-scale irrigation companies copied the technique and the land that could be brought under irrigation expanded dramatically not just in Colorado but across the rugged terrain of the West (Crifasi 2015).

Property rights to water also facilitated market-driven evolution of institutions for water management. The problems of club formation raised by Buchanan (1965) become more complex if the production function is not known, the amount of the club good is endogenous, or the shares enjoyed by club members are not equal. These were precisely the conditions in the

West. It was not obvious ex ante where or how irrigation works should be constructed. Nor was the efficient scale of irrigation development known. Finally, the inter-temporal nature of arrival coupled with heterogeneity in land endowments and crop choice meant that equal sharing was not a foregone conclusion. Put this way, the problem of irrigation development is determining the optimal number of users of a given irrigation works, the size of the irrigation works, and coordinating deliveries for each of the users.

While early ditch companies and cooperative arrangements had begun groping toward a solution to this economic problem, the growth of a broader market for bundled land and water rights was fundamental to the continued evolution of irrigation institutions. These institutions developed spontaneously through the market process à la Hayek (1964, 167) and were later emulated by local governments that formed irrigation districts. The joint necessity for both land and water in producing agricultural output meant that institutions for managing water use had to match to spatial extent of the associated land use. Ditch companies had initially formed around capital-intensive investment and focused more narrowly on water but later gave way to irrigation companies that bundled land and water claims and developed rules for the use of water on all relevant land.

As Hanemann (2014) and others are quick to point out, many irrigation companies ultimately failed. It is a mistake to characterize these failures as a failure of prior appropriation itself. On the contrary, the ability to price water rights based on priority, coupled with observation of the actual deliveries of water over time, led to rights that were not profitable to be retired. Leonard and Libecap (2016) document a bias in the timing of water claims that led claimants to over-claim water along a given stream because more claims are generally established during periods of unusually high flows, resulting in "calls" on water during more average years.[10] In other words, the failure of ditch companies that claimed more water than was actually available is a form of market correction, not a systemic failure of markets.

Even in settings where ditch and irrigation companies eventually faded away, their initial formation and activities laid the groundwork for contemporary water users. Early ditch companies were responsible for developing infrastructure that is still in use today because many of these initial projects became the basis for municipal water supplies and were ultimately purchased by local governments (Crifasi 2015). As noted earlier, the large number of entrants and the information problems they faced precluded either governments or informal communal arrangements from constructing these irrigation works themselves. Moreover, early entrepreneurial efforts to bundle land and water claims led to the development of mutual irrigation companies, an early form of the irrigation districts that dominate the West today (Hanemann 2014).

## CONCLUSION

First-possession rights to water emerged first as de facto claims because they made exclusion possible in a setting where agents arrived at different points in time and where land ownership—the traditional margin of demarcation for water rights—was in flux. The formal legal recognition of appropriative water rights made exclusion possible and not only caused clubs to form, but allowed a market to form and clubs to compete, generating information to help determine the efficient scope and size of irrigation works and governance. Competition among clubs for access to more and better lands led to innovation that dramatically expanded irrigation in the West, ultimately contributing as much 30 percent of some states' gross income by 1930 (Leonard and Libecap 2016).

First-possession property rights to water served as a basis for collective action in a setting where state provision of public goods and local informal arrangements built on cultural norms were equally infeasible. Ultimately though, private ditch construction and irrigation companies gave way to the Federal Bureau of Reclamation and formal irrigation districts with taxing authority. While exploring the evolution of irrigation in the West subsequent to its initial development is beyond the scope of this chapter, the transition from private to public provision and governance of water raises important questions about the scalability of property rights solutions to collective action problems and the role of the market process in shaping institutional evolution.

As the settlement of the West progressed, populations centers developed, uncertainties about the climate diminished, and government at the local, state, and federal level become more established. These developments may have reduced the comparative advantage of property rights in facilitating collective action relative to the period analyzed in this chapter (though perhaps not the absolute advantage). Burgeoning populations and the growth of nonagricultural uses of water, including hydroelectric power generation and municipal water supply, would have reduced the viability of a contractual solution to the externalities identified early in this chapter.[11] Finally, agricultural groups that initially formed as contractual arrangements constituted organized special interests that turned to the political process as a means to generate rents at the expense of a broader tax base (Rucker and Fishback 1983), hastening the transition from private to public provision of water works.

Water allocation in the West looks nothing like what might be described as the first best. Still, the thousands of heterogeneous migrants from a litany of backgrounds with crude technology were able to voluntarily form groups around de facto and then de jure property rights. These groups subsequently contracted, invested, and innovated in a way that brought millions of dry, difficult-to-reach acres under irrigation and generated billions of dollars' worth of agricultural output in the middle of what had been called "The Great American Desert."[12] The marvel of the marketplace lies in the fact that property rights formed the most effective basis for collective action under precisely the conditions where markets are traditionally said to fail.

## NOTES

1. There is a large literature in economics that examines how property rights influence long-term investment, market development and trade, economic growth, and use or misuse of natural resources (Acemoglu, Johnson, and Robinson 2001, 2005; Mehlum, Moene, and Torvik 2006; Besley 1995; Jacoby, Li, and Rozelle 2002; Grief, Milgrom, and Weingast 1994; Dixit 2009; Libecap and Wiggins 1985; Costello, Gaines, and Lynham 2008). Far less attention has been devoted to how property rights form and evolve. Demsetz (1967), Barzel (1997), and Anderson and Hill (1975) emphasize that property rights emerge when the marginal benefit of creating, defining, and enforcing those rights exceed the marginal costs of doing so, but the factors that determine the structure of emergent property rights are not well understood.

2. While the focus of this chapter is the development of water resources for agriculture, water also had to be moved in order to be useful in hydraulic mining. See Kanazawa (1996, 2015).

3. Although, as noted by Hanemann (2014), there are network externalities present in the subsequent expansion of existing canals.

4. Worster (1985) reviews Wittfogel's early theory about hydraulic societies in China and seeks to apply it to the development of water resources in the western United States. Though he acknowledges the role of prior appropriation and the development of water rights in nineteenth-century Colorado in passing, Worster's primary focus is the role of the Bureau of Reclamation, the state of California, and various local agencies in the development of water in California throughout the twentieth century. It is undeniable that local, state, and federal agencies shaped the development of the West through the political process in the twentieth century, but to focus on the twentieth century is to miss the beginning of the story and misunderstand the importance of property rights in shaping the initial settlement of the western United States.

5. Although the federal government bore the brunt of the up-front capital costs associated with these large-scale projects, their financing required the formation of local bodies with the authority to tax users in order to service the ensuing debt.

6. Indeed, Hanemann (2014) goes on to describe different mechanisms for financing irrigation works, detailing the merits and drawbacks of each.

7. Leonard and Libecap (2016) also stress homogeneity along this dimension in the development of their formal model of water use.

8. Again, the Mormon experience is a notable exception because the relatively formal institutional structures of the church did in fact provide mechanisms for assimilating new community members without allowing them to dissipate rents that had been generated prior to their arrival.

9. This is in sharp contrast to riparian water rights which dominate in the eastern United States. Riparian rights allow "reasonable use" of surface water to any river-adjacent landowner and are typically not quantified. Rose (1990) notes that this was due in part to the fact that most water uses in the eastern United States were non-consumptive (e.g., mostly waterwheels for mills initially).

10. This is the term for when junior rights holders are required to cut back their consumption in order to satisfy the rights of more senior claimants.

11. Even Coase (1960) recognized that the viability of bargaining solutions falls and the number of affected parties increases.

12. See Morris (1926).

# REFERENCES

Acemoglu, Daron, Simon Johnson, and James Robinson. 2001. "The Colonial Origins of Comparative Development: An Empirical Investigation." *American Economic Review* 91 (5): 1369–1401.

———. 2005. "The Rise of Europe: Atlantic Trade, Institutional Change, and Economic Growth." *American Economic Review* 95 (3): 546–79.

Agrawal, Arun. 2003. "Sustainable Governance of Common-pool Resources: Context, Methods, and Politics." *Annual Review of Anthropology* 32 (1): 243–62.

Allen, Douglas W. 1991. "Homesteading and Property Rights; or, How the West Was Really Won." *Journal of Law and Economics*. 34 (1991): 1–23.

Alston, Lee J., Edwyna Harris, and Bernardo Mueller. 2012. "The Development of Property Rights on Frontiers: Endowments, Norms, and Politics." *Journal of Economic History* 72 (3): 741–70.

Anderson, Terry L., and Peter J. Hill. 1975. "The Evolution of Property Rights: A Study of the American West." *Journal of Law & Economics* 18 (1): 163–79.

Barzel, Yoram. 1997. *Economic Analysis of Property Rights*. Cambridge: Cambridge University Press, 1997.

Benson, Lenni Beth. 1982. "Desert Survival: The Evolving Western Irrigation District." *Arizona State Law Journal* 377–417.

Besley, Timothy. 1995. "Property Rights and Investment Incentives: Theory and Evidence from Ghana." *Journal of Political Economy* 103 (5): 903–37.

Buchanan, James M. 1965. "An Economic Theory of Clubs." *Economica* 32 (125): 1–14.

Buchanan, James M., and Gordon Tullock. 1962. *The Calculus of Consent*. Ann Arbor: University of Michigan Press.

Coase, Ronald. 1960. "The Problem of Social Cost." *Journal of Law and Economics* 3: 1–44.

Coman, Katharine. 1911. "Some Unsettled Problems of Irrigation." *American Economic Review* 1 (1): 1–19.

Costello, Christopher, Steven D. Gaines, and John Lynham. 2008. "Can Catch Shares Prevent Fisheries Collapse?" *Science* 321 (5896): 1678–81.

Crifasi, Robert R. 2015. *A Land Made from Water*. Boulder: University Press of Colorado.

Demsetz, Harold. 1967. "Toward a Theory of Property Rights." *American Economic Review* 57(2): 347–59.

Dixit, Avinash. 2009. "Governance Institutions and Economic Activity." *American Economic Review* 99 (1): 3–24.

Gates, Paul Wallace, and Robert W. Swenson. 1968. *History of Public Land Law Development.* Washington, DC: Public Land Law Review Commission.

Greif, Avner, Paul Milgrom, and Barry R. Weingast. 1994. "Coordination, Commitment, and Enforcement: The Case of the Merchant Guild." *Journal of Political Economy* 102 (4): 745–76.

Hanemann, Michael. 2014. "Property Rights and Sustainable Irrigation: A Developed World Perspective." *Agricultural Water Management* 145 (2014): 5–22.

Hayek, Friedrich A. 1945. "The Use of Knowledge in Society." *American Economic Review* 35 (4): 519–30.

———. 1964. "The Theory of Complex Phenomena." In *The Critical Approaches to Science and Philosophy*, edited by Mario Bunge, 332–49. Piscataway, NJ: Transaction Publishers.

Hicks, Gregory Alan, and Devon G. Peña. 2003. "Community Acequias in Colorado's Rio Culebra Watershed: A Customary Commons in the Domain of Prior Appropriation." *University of Colorado Law Review* 74 (2): 387–486.

Jacoby, Hanan G., Guo Li, and Scott Rozelle. 2002. "Hazards of Expropriation: Tenure Insecurity and Investment in Rural China." *American Economic Review* 92 (5): 1420–47.

Janssen, Marco, and Nathan D. Rollins. 2012. "Evolution of Cooperation in Asymmetric Commons Dilemmas." *Journal of Economic Behavior and Organization* 81 (1): 220–29.

Janssen, Marco, and John M. Anderies. 2011. "Governing the Commons: Learning from Field and Laboratory Experiments." *Ecological Economics* 70 (9): 1569–70.

Kanazawa, Mark. 1996. "Possession Is Nine Points of the Law: The Political Economy of Early Public Land Disposal." *Explorations in Economic History* 33 (2): 227–49.

———. 2015. *Golden Rules: The Origins of California Water Law in the Gold Rush.* Chicago: University of Chicago Press.

Lavoie, D. 1986. "The Market as a Procedure for Discovery and Conveyance of Inarticulate Knowledge." *Comparative Economic Studies* 28 (1): 1–19.

Leonard, Bryan, and Gary D. Libecap. 2015. "Endogenous First-Possession Property Rights in Open-Access Resources." *Iowa Law Review.* 100 (2015): 2457–507.

———. 2016. "Economic Analysis of Property Rights: First Possession of Water in the American West." *NBER Working Paper No. 22185.*

Libecap, Gary D. 1978. "Economic Variables and the Development of the Law: The Case of Western Mineral Rights." *Journal of Economic History* 38 (2): 338–62.

———. 1994. "The Conditions for Successful Collective Action." *Journal of Theoretical Politics* 6 (4): 563–92.

Libecap, Gary D., and Steven N. Wiggins. 1985. "The Influence of Private Contractual Failure on Regulation: The Case of Oil Field Unitization." *Journal of Political Economy* 93 (4): 690–714.

Mehlum, Halvor, Karl Moene, and Ragnar Torvik. 2006. "Institutions and the Resource Curse." *Economic Journal* 116 (508): 1–20.

Morris, Ralph C. 1926. "The Notion of a Great American Desert East of the Rockies." *Mississippi Valley Historical Review* 13 (2): 190–200.

Olson, Mancur. 1965. *The Logic of Collective Action.* Cambridge: Harvard University Press.

Ostrom, Elinor. 2007. "A Diagnostic Approach for Going beyond Panaceas." *Proceedings of the National Academy of Sciences* 104 (39): 15181–15187.

———. 2009. "A General Framework for Analyzing Sustainability of Social-Ecological Systems." *Science* 325 (5939): 419–22.

———. 2011. "Reflections on 'Some Unsettled Problems of Irrigation.'" *American Economic Review* 101 (1): 49–63.

———. 1990. *Governing the Commons.* Cambridge: Cambridge University Press.

Ostrom, Elinor, and Roy Gardner. 1993. "Coping with Asymmetries in the Commons: Self-Governing Irrigation Systems Can Work." *Journal of Economic Perspectives* 7 (4): 93–112.

Rose, Carol M. 1990. "Energy and Efficiency in the Realignment of Common-Law Water Rights." *Journal of Legal Studies* 19 (2): 261–96.

Rucker, Randal R., and Price Fishback. 1983. "The Federal Reclamation Program: An Analysis of Rent-Seeking Behavior." In *Water Rights: Scarce Resource Allocation, Bureaucracy and the Environment*, edited by Terry Anderson, 45–81. Port Vila: Pacific Institute for Public Policy Research.

Samuelson, Paul A. 1954. "The Pure Theory of Public Expenditure." *Review of Economics and Statistics* 36 (4): 387–89.

Schorr, David. 2005. "Appropriation as Agrarianism: Distributive Justice in the Creation of Property Rights." *Ecology Law Quarterly* 32 (1): 3–71.

Smith, S. M. (2016). "Common Property Resources and New Entrants: Uncovering the Bias and Effects of New Users." *Journal of the Association of Environmental and Resource Economists* 3 (1): 1–36.

Tyler, Daniel. 1992. *The Last Water Hole in the West: The Colorado-Big Thompson Project and the Northern Colorado Water Conservancy District.* Boulder: University Press of Colorado.

Umbeck, John. 1977. "A Theory of Contract Choice and the California Gold Rush." *Journal of Law & Economics* 20 (2): 421–37.

———. 1981. "Might Makes Rights: A Theory of the Formation and Initial Distribution of Property Rights." *Economic Inquiry* 19 (1): 38–59.

Williamson, Oliver. 1975. *Markets and Hierarchies.* New York: Free Press.

———. 1985. *The Institutions of Capitalism.* New York: Free Press, 1985.

Wittfogel, Karl A. 1975. "The Theory of Oriental Society." In *Readings in Anthropology*, Vol. 2, edited by M. H. Fried, 94–113. New York: Crowell.

Worster, Donald. 1985. *Rivers of Empire: Water, Aridity, and the Growth of the American West.* Oxford: Oxford University Press.

York, Abigal and Michael Schoon. 2011. "Collective Action on the Western Range: Coping with External and Internal Threats." *International Journal of the Commons* 5 (2): 388–409.

*Chapter 8*

# Adam Smith's Principles of Taxation in the Early American Republic

Frank Garmon Jr.[1]

Compared to Smith's thoughts on trade, banking, and the market process, his views on taxation have been comparatively understudied. As Deborah Boucoyannis noted recently, "With only a few exceptions, Smith's system of taxation has not been assessed as a whole" (Boucoyannis 2013, 1058). This chapter examines the logic behind Adam Smith's principles of taxation and their application in the early American republic. It argues that early-American policy makers applied theories proposed by Smith and others because these fiscal strategies proved less distortional to the market process than other forms of taxation. Although it was Adam Smith who best distilled these maxims, the reasoning underpinning Smith's theories circulated widely among eighteenth-century political thinkers. While much of the literature has emphasized fiscal policy enacted by the new federal government, federal taxation existed concurrently with taxes collected by state governments. State governments levied the most visible and important taxes that taxpayers would have encountered in the early republic. Legislators in the early republic developed a unique system of taxation by centralizing the collection of indirect taxes in the form of the federal tariff, and simultaneously decentralizing direct taxes through federal apportionment and state tax collection. By studying state and federal taxes as part of a comprehensive system, this chapter examines how the founding generation both empowered and constrained the taxing powers of government.

The system of state and federal taxation that emerged out of the struggles under the Articles of Confederation shaped the development of early-American tax collection. Geoffrey Brennan and James Buchanan have demonstrated that tax systems take on semi-constitutional qualities by establishing the rules that guide individual and state actors. Tax systems establish a set of rights, a mechanism for enforcement, and a set of rules governing collective decisions. Consistent rules provide clear expectations for both taxpayers and public officials. Brennan and Buchanan argue that stable tax regimes amount to a form of social capital that is susceptible to destruction by altering the rules of the game (Brennan and Buchanan 2000). After an initial period of experimentation, tax collection in the early republic remained consistent for approximately fifty years, until several states began rewriting their state constitutions in the second quarter of the nineteenth century. The federal Constitution both empowered and constrained federal taxing authority by coupling unlimited indirect taxing powers with an imperfect system of direct taxation. State governments yielded their authority to levy taxes on imports under the Constitution in exchange for a preservation of their fiscal autonomy in the sphere of direct taxation. The combined federal and state system placed constitutional limits on taxation and divided taxing authority in a way that sought to minimize distortions in the market process (Hayek [1960] 2000; Buchanan 2000a, 2000b).

The framers of the Constitution hesitated to provide the federal government with unlimited taxing authority, believing instead that federalism would promote responsible government and that divided authority would prevent abuse. Political scientists studying fiscal federalism and economists following public choice theory have also stressed the importance of decentralized authority in a federal system. Fiscal federalists argue that when voters' preferences are geographically dispersed, local officials are best informed to make decisions on behalf of their constituents (Oates 1972). Public choice economists make a similar case for decentralization, arguing that decentralized government provides a check against wasteful expenditures by forcing self-interested state actors to compete for revenues (Brennan and Buchanan 1980). In the case of the early republic, decentralized tax collection reduced administration costs because state governments subcontracted the assessment and collection process to local officials at a fraction of the cost. Through applying the principles of Adam Smith and others, state governments implemented fiscal strategies that facilitated economic growth. The methods of tax collection formalized in the early republic allowed state governments to collect significant tax revenues while minimizing the burden of taxation on the average taxpayer. Although the early federal government would have appeared hidden from view to the average American, the combined state and federal system wielded significant taxing authority and fiscal capacity.

The first section of this chapter outlines Adam Smith's principles of taxation and investigates their relationship with other political theorists in the late eighteenth century. Although Smith provided the clearest explication of his tax theories, iterations of his proposals circulated widely in the half century following the publication of *Wealth of Nations*. The second half of the chapter examines Smith's reception in the early American republic. The founding generation read Smith avidly and incorporated elements of his maxims into their tax systems when they installed new tax administrations after the American Revolution. The combined system of federal and state taxation owes almost as much to Adam Smith's principles as it does to Alexander Hamilton, who read Smith closely and proposed a grand vision for concurrent tax powers. Hamilton articulated the benefits of Constitutional limitations on taxing authority in *The Federalist* Papers. The Constitution constrained the federal government's power to levy direct taxes but provided it with unlimited authority over indirect taxes. The combined federal and state system of taxation had the effect minimizing distortions in the market process by limiting the burden of taxation on average Americans. The chapter concludes by briefly exploring Smith's legacy in American tax policy.

## SMITH'S PRINCIPLES OF TAXATION

Adam Smith outlined four principles of taxation in the *Wealth of Nations* (Table 8.1), and devoted more than a hundred pages to the topic of taxation in explicating his theory of political economy. His first principle encapsulates two sometimes antagonistic propositions. First, Smith argued that the "subjects of every state ought to contribute towards the support of the government, as nearly as possible, in proportion to their respective abilities." Modern scholars have described this argument as the "ability to pay" rule, and interpreted the first half of this principle as Smith's defense of progressive taxation. Smith advocated for progressive taxation at several points in *The Wealth of Nations*, noting that it "is not very unreasonable that the rich should contribute to the publick expence, not only in proportion to their revenue, but something more than in that proportion" (Smith [1776] 1981, 2:825, 842). Jean-Baptist Say later drew the same conclusions from reading Smith, but adopted a bolder stance on progressive taxation. Say argued that "a tax merely proportionate to individual income would be far from equitable. . . . I have no hesitation in going further, and saying, that taxation can not be equitable, unless its ratio is progressive" (Say [1803] 1848, 455l; Sismondi [1815] 1966, 95).

Smith, however, clarified his position in the second half of his maxim by continuing, "That is, in proportion to the revenue which they respectively enjoy under the protection of the state" (Smith [1776] 1981, 2:825). Scholars have termed this second, somewhat conflicting, statement the "benefits theory," and understand it as Smith advocating for a system of taxation comprised of user fees based on the relative protections or services that citizens received from their governments.[2] A tax system built upon user fees would likely have a regressive character, which could appear to contradict

**Table 8.1  Adam Smith's Principles of Taxation**

| | |
|---|---|
| 1. Equity | "The subjects of every state ought to contribute towards the support of the government, as nearly as possible, in proportion to their respective abilities; that is, in proportion to the revenue which they respectively enjoy under the protection of the state." |
| 2. Transparency | "The tax which each individual is bound to pay ought to be certain, and not arbitrary." |
| 3. Convenience | "Every tax ought to be levied at the time, or in the manner, in which it is most likely to be convenient to the contributor to pay it." |
| 4. Efficiency | "Every tax ought to be so contrived as both to take out and to keep out of the pockets of the people as little as possible, over and above what it brings into the public treasury of the state." |

*Source*: Adam Smith, *An Inquiry into the Nature and Causes of the Wealth of Nations*, R. H. Campbell and A. S. Skinner eds., 2 vols. (1776; Oxford: Oxford University Press, 1976; rpt. Indianapolis: Liberty Fund, 1981), 2:825–26.

the first half of Smith's first principle. Although scholars have described the two propositions as incongruous, Smith did not find any inconsistency. Smith recognized that wealthy taxpayers derived greater benefits from the state than their poorer neighbors. Smith described the expenses of government as being like the expenses of "the joint tenants of a great estate, who are all obliged to contribute in proportion to their respective interests in the estate" (Smith [1776] 1981, 2:825). Just as a tenant occupying a larger share of an estate might pay a greater portion of the combined rent, Smith believed that wealthier taxpayers might contribute a greater share of their incomes toward the expenses of government. Smith also observed that wealthy taxpayers often found themselves better positioned to influence the rules of government, noting that it "is the industry which is carried on for the benefit of the rich and the powerful, this is principally encouraged by our mercantile system. That which is carried on for the benefit of the poor and the indigent, is too often, either neglected or oppressed" (Smith [1776] 1981, 2:644).

Smith's second maxim emphasized that the "tax which each individual is bound to pay ought to be certain, and not arbitrary." The amount to be paid, the forms of payment accepted, and the date of payment "ought all to be clear and plain to the contributor" (Smith [1776] 1981, 2:825–26). In making this argument, Smith followed David Hume, who had emphasized that "the most pernicious of all taxes are the arbitrary" (Hume [1742] 1955, 86). Smith expanded and elucidated his position; however, noting that the amount to be paid, the forms of payment accepted, and the date of payment "ought all to be clear and plain to the contributor." Uncertainty in tax collection promoted insolence and corruption among tax collectors, according to Smith, and exposed taxpayers to the possibility of extortion. Smith concluded that the "certainty of what each individual ought to pay is, in taxation, a matter of so great importance, that a very considerable degree of inequality, it appears,

I believe, from the experience of all nations, is not near so great an evil as a very small degree of uncertainty" (Smith [1776] 1981, 2:825–26).

In addition to transparency, other contemporary political economists argued that certainty and consistency in taxation provided a sort of equilibrium that minimized the burden of taxation by concealing taxes in everyday prices. Once market prices adjusted to reflect the cost of the tax, the duty remained hidden from the average taxpayer. New taxes, along with tax laws that changed frequently or abruptly, could be much more disruptive because they distorted market prices. Antoine Louis Claude Destutt de Tracy, whose treatise on political economy was translated by Thomas Jefferson, argued that the best taxes were "the most ancient, because they have entered into all prices and that all are regulated in consequence" (Tracy [1817] 2011, 241). Another political economist, Benjamin Constant, argued that "a new tax always causes a perturbation which spreads from taxed activities to untaxed ones. . . . Equilibrium is restored only slowly" (Constant [1815] 2003, 207). Smith and others believed that maintaining consistent and familiar tax collection practices would minimize taxpayer uncertainty and avoid disturbances in the market.

Thirdly, Smith noted that every tax "ought to be levied at the time, or in the manner, in which it is most likely to be convenient to the contributor to pay it." Smith reasoned that taxes could be collected with minimal inconvenience if legislators enacted taxes that coincided with harvests or when the taxpayer was "likely to have wherewithal to pay" (Smith [1776] 1981, 2:826). This principle bears a striking similarity to one proposed by Montesquieu, who wrote that the "laws must put a certain order in the manner of levying taxes so that the manner is not heavier than the burdens themselves" (Montesquieu [1748] 2005, 56). In the early nineteenth century Sismondi endorsed Smith's principle by drawing an analogy. Sismondi noted that a tax levied on capital rather than income was "as if tithes were levied on the seed, instead of being levied on the crop." Instead, Sismondi argued that "in gathering the product at the moment when nature grants it, we are sure exactly to meet the proprietor's convenience for paying it" (Sismondi [1815] 1966, 105, 97).

Smith clarified his position further by expounding a preference for indirect taxes on imported luxuries. Because market prices concealed the cost of the tariff and passed the tax on to the final consumer, Smith argued that duties on imported goods diffused the burden of taxation broadly in a manner that was most convenient for the average taxpayer. Smith reasoned that "he is at liberty too, either to buy, or not to buy as he pleases, it must be his own fault if he ever suffers any considerable inconveniency from such taxes" (Smith [1776] 1981, 2:826). Political theorists in the eighteenth and early nineteenth centuries believed that the incidence of taxation should be dispersed as broadly as possible across the base of eligible taxpayers, and many argued that indirect taxes on imports were the most convenient means of equitably distributing the tax burden. Benjamin Constant argued that indirect taxes spread the incidence of taxation evenly across a population just as "the weight of the air spread across the whole body of a man exceeds thirty thousand liters. He can take it without noticing, while a much lighter weight trained on a single part of the body would be unendurable" (Constant [1815] 2003, 211). In describing the ways in which legislatures could design taxes to minimize their burden, Smith followed David Hume and Montesquieu in arguing that taxes on consumption caused consumers to confound the tax with the market price.[3]

Finally, Smith argued that every tax "ought to be so contrived as both to take out and to keep out of the pockets of the people as little as possible, over and above what it brings into the public treasury of the state" (Smith [1776] 1981, 2:826). Montesquieu had expressed a similar sentiment, noting that one "must not take from the real needs of the people for the imaginary needs of the state" (Montesquieu [1748] 2005, 213). Smith identified four ways in which excessive taxes might have deleterious effects. High taxes might require additional revenue officers who could raise the cost of collecting the tax, and impose an additional burden on the population as a result. Immoderate taxes could also threaten to stifle industry, divert capital to the state treasury that could have been used to start a new business, or discourage taxpayers from adopting certain forms of employment. The punishments imposed on individuals who failed to make payment or attempted unsuccessfully to avoid paying their taxes provided a third method for enforcing an additional burden on the population. Smith argued that the penalties and forfeitures inflicted on these individuals had a tendency to ruin them and remove their labor and capital from the market. Lastly, Smith emphasized that unnecessary taxes posed a threat to taxpayers' liberties by subjecting them to repeated visits from revenue officers (Smith [1776] 1981, 2:826–27).

Many political economists from the period stressed the importance of protecting taxpayers' liberties. Montesquieu wrote that all "is lost when the lucrative profession of tax-collectors, by its wealth, comes to be an honored profession" (Montesquieu [1748] 2005, 227). Later authors echoed Smith's views. In restating Smith's maxims, Sismondi described Smith's fourth principle as one of liberty, noting that "finally, the citizen's liberty must be respected, that so he may not be exposed otherwise, than with extreme caution, to the inspection of revenue-officers, to the dependent, and all the vexatious measures too often conducted with the levying of taxes" (Sismondi [1815] 1966, 96). Benjamin Constant argued that the "nature and mode of collection should cause as little hardship as possible for the taxpayers, tending neither to harass nor corrupt them and not giving rise, by way of pointless expenditures, to further taxation" (Constant [1815] 2003, 207).

Jean-Baptist Say noted that "[e]xorbitant or inequitable taxation promotes fraud, falsehood, and perjury" (Say [1803] 1848, 459). By restraining the revenue demands of the state, Smith and other political theorists argued that taxpayers' liberties would be preserved.

Concern for the laboring poor figured prominently in Smith's theories of taxation and government. As John Tomasi has identified, Smith criticized mercantilism for favoring those individuals with access to political power, as these individuals could more easily craft legislation to their benefit (Tomasi 2012, 129–30). By restricting trade and limiting new entrants in the marketplace, mercantilist policies weighed heavily on the poorer classes. Smith argued that reducing restrictions on trade would benefit the poor by freeing them to pursue their best interests. As a result, Smith frequently considered the effects of various tax proposals on the poor when discussing the policies implications and relative merits. Smith realized that the laboring classes were unlikely to provide significant revenues to the state, and recognized that taxes paid by the poor raised the price of labor, which had distortional effects on prices and limited overall production and consumption. Because laborers could not bear any considerable portion of a tax levied on their wages, Smith argued that landlords and consumers ultimately paid, in the form of higher prices, any tax levied upon the poor. Other scholars have interpreted Smith's concern for the poor to support and argument for redistributive economic policies, and have made comparisons to John Rawls's position that inequality could only be justified if the least well-off benefit (Fleischacker 2004a, 39; 2004b). Concern for the poor also supports Smith's emphasis on sympathy and reciprocity developed in both the *Wealth of Nations* and in the *Theory of Moral Sentiments*.

## SMITH IN THE EARLY REPUBLIC

Americans in the early republic were more familiar with Adam Smith than previous generations of historians have acknowledged. Samuel Fleischacker notes that the "consensus among intellectual historians has been that Americans paid no special attention to *Wealth of Nations* in the founding period" (Fleischacker 2002, 899–900). Most intellectual historians have focused on the period leading up to the Constitution, and noted that references to Smith are scanty in the ratification debates. Surveys of early American libraries reveal that Smith's works were read more widely than the ratification debates suggest and that his works grew in popularity in the decades following their publication. David Lundberg and Henry May found that *Wealth of Nations* appeared in 28 percent of American libraries in the years 1776–1790, 42 percent of libraries sampled from 1791 to 1800, and 65 percent of libraries between 1801 and 1813 (Lundberg and May 1976, 288). Aside from a few religious tracts, Smith's *Wealth of Nations* appears to have been one of the most popular books in American libraries by the first decade of the nineteenth century.

Although the *Wealth of Nations* provided the clearest explication of Smith's maxims regarding taxation, iterations of these arguments could be found in many eighteenth- and early nineteenth-century treatises on political economy. State legislators would not have needed to consult Smith to have recognized which forms of taxation best satisfied the revenue needs of the state while minimizing distortions in the market. Americans benefited from being able to observe firsthand the multitude of tax reforms taking place in Europe.[4] New techniques in public finances spread quickly across countries and continents, and lawmakers readily discarded strategies that failed in favor of those that proved more reliable or efficient. In describing how quickly fiscal policy innovations had spread within Europe, Smith remarked that there "is no art which one government sooner learns of another than that of draining money from the pockets of the people" (Smith [1776] 1981, 2:861).

Popular histories written in the eighteenth century described the tax systems of ancient and early-modern governments in great detail.[5] For early American readers, understanding the seemingly trivial differences between various systems of taxation contributed to their knowledge of the fall of Rome and the development of early modern England and France. Like many of his contemporaries, Smith provided a historical overview of each form of taxation, using examples from history to demonstrate the advantages and shortcomings of each source of revenue. Other political theorists from the period used similar rhetorical techniques, but they often confined their examples to instances of taxes imposed in Europe or in ancient Rome. Smith exceeded previous discussions of taxation not only in his thorough treatment of the subject, but also in his range of examples. By including numerous references to taxation in the American colonies, Smith wrote a treatment of taxation that would have been more engaging for American readers.

Several of the most prominent members of the post-revolutionary generation revealed their familiarity with Smith's work. An early biography of Alexander Hamilton claimed that Hamilton wrote a detailed commentary on the *Wealth of Nations* while serving in the Confederation Congress in 1783 (Syrett 1966, 10:8). It is well known that Alexander Hamilton was influenced by Smith in developing his positions on political economy, but other leading members of the founding generation cited Smith approvingly. John Adams, James Madison, Thomas Jefferson, and James Monroe were all aware of Smith's work and in a few cases cited the *Wealth of Nations* directly. Jefferson praised Smith's treatise in a letter to Thomas Mann Randolph Jr., noting that in "political economy I think Smith's wealth of nations the best book extant. In the science of government Montesquieu's spirit of laws is generally recommended." In a later letter to John Norvell, Jefferson wrote that Smith's *Wealth of Nations* "is the best book to be read, unless Say's Political economy can be had." Beyond the founding elite, treatises on political economy were read more widely among early American statesmen. James Madison recorded a list of books purchased for the Confederation Congress in 1783. The list included both the first and second editions of Smith's *Wealth of Nations,* along with the collected works of Montesquieu and Hume's political essays.[6]

Although the theories developed by Smith and others circulated beyond the founding elite, their influence among state legislators is much more difficult to trace. It would be a tremendous undertaking to attempt to reconstruct the debates surrounding changes made to each state's tax laws over the course of four decades. State taxes in the early republic involved thousands of legislators and countless petitions from taxpayers and local officials seeking changes to the existing laws. State legislatures in the eighteenth century did not always keep detailed records of their debates, votes, or, in some cases, even the bills under consideration. Most legislatures recorded only summaries of the topics discussed and indicated whether or not the proposed bill had passed. These summaries occasionally provided the number of votes for and against the proposed legislation, but they rarely list the names of those voting or abstaining. Although policy makers and tax collectors left voluminous records and collections of personal papers, they rarely recorded their thoughts on taxation or identified the theories or theorists who had guided their decision making. It is not necessary to reconstruct the politics surrounding tax legislation to understand the guiding philosophies behind tax policy, however, as we can examine the extent to which the founding generation followed Smith's recommendations by examining the economic consequences of successful legislation.

Smith's principles of equity, transparency, convenience, and efficiency informed American policy makers' understanding of taxation in the early republic and were reflected in the state and federal systems of taxation. The period immediately following the American Revolution was one of bold experimentation as the state governments struggled to repay the immense debts incurred during the war. The absence of strong taxing authority under the Articles of Confederation left the burden of debt entirely on the newly formed state governments. Dealing with this burden proved particularly challenging in the decade following the Revolution, as consistent deflation magnified the states' obligations. Colonial officials had employed a strategy of raising taxes considerably for short periods of time after a war to avoid a standing public debt. Such policies had been employed successfully after the French and Indian War, when the colonists repaid their debts within a few years of the conclusion of hostilities. The debts incurred during the Revolutionary War exceeded that of any previous colonial conflict, however, and by some estimates amounted to more than twenty times the cost of the French and Indian War (Perkins 1994, 94). State governments also operated in a period of significant social unrest and taxpayer resistance that included the outbreak of Shays' Rebellion in Massachusetts and similar incidents in other states. The states pursued a variety of policy strategies to address their fiscal crises, with mixed results. One effect of this decade of experimentation was an expansion of state fiscal capacity. The crises of the Revolution pushed state policy makers to implement tax laws that could raise revenue but also minimize the burden on the average taxpayer.

As the states struggled to develop a functioning tax system, the fiscal crisis facing the Confederation Congress prompted calls for a Constitutional Convention. The delegates in Philadelphia proposed expanding federal taxing authority to move away from the haphazard collection system in place under the Articles of Confederation. Under the Articles of Confederation, the Confederation Congress could only levy a tax on imports with unanimous approval from the states, and could only enact direct taxes if those taxes were apportioned to the states based on each state's proportion of the total value of real estate in the United States. Because Rhode Island consistently resisted calls for a tax on imports, and because no state submitted a survey of its real estate to Congress, the opposition of only a few states scuttled plans that would have improved fiscal solvency. Congress had only the power to request "requisitions," tax quotas assigned to each state for the purposes of repaying loans contracted by the Continental Congress. No state came close to fulfilling its quota, and the Confederation Congress languished under the voluntary requisition system. In light of the nation's fiscal challenges, federalist delegates to the Constitutional Convention proposed a system of taxation that would prove remarkably resilient. Congress would have unlimited power to enact indirect taxes on imports, but its powers over direct taxation would be constrained. The Constitution required that direct taxes be apportioned based on population, and granted Congress the authority to conduct a census every ten years to provide a basis for that apportionment. State governments conceded their ability to enact their own tariffs, but maintained their system of direct property taxes. Granting Congress the power to collect its own revenues reduced the overall costs of collection and relieved the state governments of burdensome taxes, particularly after Hamilton's funding plan assumed and annuitized the state debts. Perhaps more importantly, the system of taxation that emerged out of the Constitution eased the tax burden for the average taxpayer. The tariff obviated the need for the requisition system, and state governments reduced property taxes substantially in the years following the ratification of the Constitution. The tariff provided the vast majority of federal tax revenues in the early republic, and between 1817 and 1861 the tariff was the only source of federal taxation. By establishing clear rules for tax collection, improving the efficiency of the collection system, and shifting the burden of taxation to voluntary consumption, the American system of taxation was consistent with Adam Smith's principles.

The advantages of the new tax system were not immediately apparent and many Americans challenged the wisdom of empowering federal tax collectors. In the debates over the ratification of the Constitution the anti-federalists raised a number of challenges to strengthening federal taxing authority. Anti-federalists argued that granting Congress expanded taxing powers would invite a host of abuses. The "necessary and proper" clause was a primary target of anti-federalist opposition. Robert Yates, writing as Brutus, argued that this clause would serve as a justification for a federal government whose "power, exercised without limitation, will introduce itself into every corner of the city, and country." Brutus emphasized that federal power would permeate every facet of American life, and that this power would even "wait upon the ladies at their toilet, and will not leave them in any of their domestic concerns" and that revenue collectors would "enter the house of every gentleman, watch over his cellar, wait upon his cook in the kitchen, follow the servants into the parlor, preside over the table, and note down all he eats and drinks; it will attend him to his bedchamber, and watch him while he sleeps." Brutus described the potential revenue demands of the new federal government as insatiable, adding that "[t]o all these classes of people, and in all these circumstances, in which it will attend them, the language in which it will address them, will be GIVE! GIVE!" (Borden 1965b, 88). Compared to the Articles of Confederation, the Constitution afforded Congress with broad taxing authority and few restrictions. The anti-federalists believed that, left unchecked, unrestrained taxing authority would lead to tyranny.

The attentiveness of the legislature presented another avenue for potential abuses according to anti-federalist writers. An anonymous Virginian writing as Cato Uticensis asked his fellow taxpayers if "it ever enter[ed] the mind of any one of you, that you could live to see the day, that any other government but the General Assembly of Virginia should have the power of *direct taxation* in this state?" (Borden 1965a, 80). Anti-federalists feared that legislators from other states would be unresponsive to the needs and concerns of taxpayers outside their constituencies. These authors worried also that Congress would levy taxes that would discriminate against particular trades, or introduce taxes that would place a disproportionate burden on some states in favor of others. Patrick Henry described the situation clearly in his arguments during the Virginia ratifying convention by emphasizing that it "has required the most constant vigilance of the legislature to keep them [the sheriffs] from totally ruining the people. . . . If sheriffs, thus immediately under the eye of our state legislature and judiciary, have dared to commit these outrages, what would they not have done if their masters had been at Philadelphia or New York?" Borden 1965c, 93). Fear of unsympathetic legislators enacting discriminatory taxes pervaded anti-federalist thought. Opposition to taxes imposed by an external power stemmed from the ideology of the American Revolution, and anti-federalist authors occasionally invoked comparisons with the British colonial system to bolster their arguments. As Cato Uticensis emphasized, "[Are] we not to expect that New England will send us revenue officers instead of opinions and apples?" (Borden, 1965a, 81).

Both anti-federalists and federalists greeted direct taxes with suspicion. The revolutionary generation drew a distinction between direct or internal taxes levied on land or capitation, and indirect taxes on imported commodities. Although many anti-federalists were willing to concede indirect taxing authority to the federal government, direct taxes proved a source of contention in the state ratifying conventions. As an alternative to direct taxing powers, the anti-federalists proposed adding an enforcement mechanism to the requisition system. If any state failed to remit their apportioned quota, Congress could use its own agents to collect the tax and increase the tariff on taxpayers in that state until the balance had been paid with interest. In granting Congress the power to levy direct taxes, the framers intentionally restricted Congressional power by requiring Congress to apportion direct taxes based on population. The framers did not intend to make the obstacle insurmountable, however, as the system of apportionment resembled previous limitations placed on the Confederation Congress under the Articles of Confederation.[7] The Articles required Congress to apportion direct taxes based on the value of each state's real estate in proportion to national wealth. The apportionment process also had historical antecedents in the system of taxation adopted in New England, where legislatures apportioned tax quotas to towns based on wealth or population and provided local officials with some flexibility in assessing and collecting the tax. The framers believed that apportionment would prevent Congress from levying a direct tax on forms of property that would discriminate against a particular trade, state, or region. By establishing a clear system for collecting a direct tax that could not be manipulated, Alexander Hamilton argued in Federalist 36 that apportionment "effectually shuts the door to partiality or oppression" (Hamilton 2008, 170).

Perhaps chief among the anti-federalists' complaints with respect to taxation was the fear of double taxation. The anti-federalists believed that providing strong taxing authority to Congress would undermine the states' ability to levy their own taxes, or worse, that federal revenue officers would duplicate the efforts of state tax collectors and effectively double the tax burden. In the Virginia ratifying convention, Patrick Henry contended that in "this scheme of energetic government, the people will find two sets of tax-gatherers—the state and the federal sheriffs. This it seems to me, will produce such dreadful oppression as the people cannot possibly bear. The federal sheriff may commit what oppression, make what distresses, he pleases, and ruin you with impunity; for how are you to tie his hands?" (Borden 1965c, 92). In every case, anti-federalists believed that strong federal taxing authority would lead to a concentration of federal power at the expense of state governments. As Brutus emphasized, "The command of the revenues of a state gives the command of every thing in it" (Borden 1965b, 84).

The anti-federalists resisted efforts to expand federal taxing authority because they believed ultimately that state governments were capable of handling the fiscal concerns of the new republic. Although every state failed to fulfill their requisitions to the Confederation Congress, and the immediate postwar years saw taxpayer revolt in the form of Shay's Rebellion, most states avoided widespread unrest by responding proactively to the needs of their constituents. Having witnessed the various tax relief measures introduced at the state level during the 1780s, the anti-federalists believed that state governments could be trusted to protect their interests. From the standpoint of the anti-federalists, the states had a long history of collecting colonial taxes, and had the infrastructure in place to collect significant revenues. While the Revolution had strained the limits of their taxing authority, the states had weathered the storm with their fiscal capacity intact. The anti-federalists could even point to a few successes under the Articles of Confederation. The Confederation Congress had recently negotiated a policy for organizing and settling western lands, and the states had agreed to cede the Northwest Territory to the new national government. The anti-federalists could not envision how a stronger national government might raise additional revenues without resorting to force, compelling delinquent taxpayers to make payment on their debts during periods of hard times. Federal taxes might be costly to administer, and additional taxes threatened to incite an already burdened populace.

In his defense of concurrent powers, Alexander Hamilton proposed a solution to placate anti-federalist fears of federal revenue collectors. Rather than the federal government subsuming state tax collection efforts, Alexander Hamilton argued in Federalist 36 that the federal government could rely on each state's fiscal infrastructure to collect federal revenues. Hamilton argued that "there is a simple point of view in which this matter may be placed, that must be altogether satisfactory. The national Legislature can make use of the *system of each State within that State*. The method of laying and collecting this species of taxes in each State, can, in all its parts, be adopted and employed by the Federal Government" (Hamilton 2008, 170). Hamilton envisioned using state tax collectors to collect federal direct taxes, believing that the direct taxes could be assessed and collected alongside state property taxes with little additional effort on the part of local officials. Although many

Federalists disparaged the states' unsuccessful attempts to meet their requisitions to the Confederation Congress during the 1780s in advocating for a stronger federal government, Hamilton believed that state governments were ultimately competent and could be relied upon to use their local knowledge to assess and collect federal direct taxes. Congress employed this method successfully in each of the four federal direct taxes levied in 1798, 1813, 1815, and 1861. The federal government supervised the collection of each tax by appointing federal commissioners to oversee the assessment process and ensure that the tax was applied equally between districts. Congress went further in 1813, 1815, and 1861 by incentivizing state governments to assume their portion of the tax burden, offering a 15 percent discount to states that agreed to collect the entirety of the tax themselves (Einhorn 2006).

The ratification of the Constitution provided tax relief for indebted tax payers by reducing the fiscal burdens facing state governments. The federal tariff provided Congress with an independent revenue source that eliminated the need to call upon the states for contributions. By assuming and annuitizing the Revolutionary War debts under Hamilton's assumption plan, Congress reduced its immediate revenue needs further and made steps toward fiscal solvency. With the pressure to produce revenues alleviated, many state governments elected to reduce taxes considerably in the years following 1787. For example, legislators in Virginia voted in October 1787 to repeal the poll tax on adult white males, along with taxes on cattle and slaves under the age of twelve. The poll tax and the tax on cattle would have been particularly welcomed by poorer taxpayers, as these taxes would have constituted the majority of their assessment. The legislature moved again, in December 1788, to reduce taxes for the following year by one-third but required that future payments be remitted in specie. In 1789, the General Assembly elected to reduce taxes further, this time slashing rates across the board by 25 percent.

Hamilton's belief that state governments could be relied upon to collect federal taxes remained persuasive as Congress made plans to levy the first direct tax. In 1796, Congress requested that the Secretary of the Treasury, Oliver Wolcott Jr., prepare a report on the practicality of levying and collecting the direct tax using the states' existing fiscal infrastructure. Wolcott extolled the benefits of employing state and local tax collectors, and emphasized that "the fiscal systems of the several States . . . have been long established; that, in general, they are well approved by the people; that habit has rendered an acquiescence under the rules they impose, familiar." State legislatures "possessed of a minute and particular knowledge of the circumstances and interests of the respective States" and Wolcott emphasized that "it may be conceded that, so far as the principles of the State systems can, with propriety, be adopted by Congress, the hazards of new experiments, and the delays incident to the organization of a new plan, will be avoided." Wolcott noted additionally that to

> establish officers in every district, possessed of skill competent to institute and maintain a check on the collectors, would be attended with enormous expense; to allow the people to elect assessors in the manner now practised, and, at the same time, to renounce the idea of local responsibility, would be manifestly unsafe. Under such a system, there could be no security that local partiality would not lead to the connivances for the suppression and concealment of property justly subject to taxation.

At the same time, Wolcott noted that the plan was "liable to great, if not insurmountable objections." The challenge of leveraging state tax administrations remained in the difficulty of standardizing tax collection efforts on a national scale. Wolcott noted that "the State systems are utterly discordant and irreconcilable, in their original principles" (Wolcott [1796] 1832, 1:436–38). Although the distinctive features of each state's tax administration prevented Congress from devising a national system based on existing state tax laws, Wolcott emphasized repeatedly that leveraging the states' fiscal capacity would provide the most efficient means of collecting a federal direct tax. The fact that Congress considered introducing a system of direct taxation that would have been entirely reliant on state property tax collectors, and that policy makers decided ultimately to enlist state and local officials in assessing and collecting the tax, suggests that the founding generation placed a high degree of trust in the reliability of state tax administrations.

The federalists developed an ingenious system of taxation that minimized distortions in the market process by outsourcing the collection of direct taxes to state governments and consolidating indirect taxes in the form of the tariff. A few hundred revenue officers in a handful of port cities succeeded in collecting the vast majority of federal revenues. Ratification of the Constitution brought tax relief to the state governments, who could reduce their property taxes now that the requisition system had been abandoned. The combined state and federal tax system allowed Americans to raise significant revenues from taxation without burdening the average taxpayer. Constraints on federal taxing authority guarded against oppressive taxes, and Congress resorted to direct taxes only four times to raise revenues in times of war. The system of taxation developed in the early republic followed Montesquieu's observation that governments "can levy heavier taxes in proportion to the liberty of the subjects" (Montesquieu [1748] 2005, 220). Decentralized taxing authority and constitutional limitations facilitated the market process by minimizing distortions in the early-American economy.

## SMITH'S LEGACY

Policy makers in the early republic generally followed the principles outlined by Adam Smith and adopted an effective system that succeeded in repaying the Revolutionary War debts. At the same time, Americans were not always consistent in applying Smith's principles, and the system of fiscal federalism introduced at the founding gradually broke down in the nineteenth century. Hamilton's funding plan called for a sinking fund that Smith explicitly rejected (Stabile 1998, 92). As the federal tariff emerged as the primary source of federal tax receipts, the very qualities that made the tariff so desirable also made it subject to abuse. Smith and Hume had argued that tariffs were invisible to the average taxpayer, as consumers conflated them with the cost of the imported good. Imperceptible taxes on luxuries quickly gave way to protectionism, logrolling, and vote trading in the nineteenth century as new theories of political economy emerged. As federal power expanded, the Congressional taxing authority outgrew its constitutional limitations. The Sixteenth Amendment to the Constitution expanded federal power to provide unlimited authority to raise taxes on income and state governments moved away from property taxes as their primary source of revenue. The federalist system of taxation developed in the early republic eroded gradually and paved the way for the modern administrative state.

## NOTES

1. The author would like to thank Peter J. Boettke, Christopher J. Coyne, Max Edelson, Virgil Henry Storr, the participants in the Transatlantic Seminar hosted jointly by the University of Virginia and the University of Edinburgh, and the participants in the Adam Smith colloquium hosted by the Mercatus Center at George Mason University for their comments and feedback on this and earlier versions of the chapter.

2. See Mehrotra (2013, 61–67) for a discussion of the "benefits theory" and its implications.

3. David Hume ([1742] 1955, 85) argued that the "best taxes are such as are levied upon consumptions, especially those of luxury; because such taxes are least felt by the people . . . being confounded with the natural the commodity, they are scarcely perceived by the consumers." Likewise, Montesquieu ([1748] 2005, 217–18) emphasized that "[d]uties on commodities are the ones least felt by the people . . . the buyer who ultimately pays it, confounds it with the price."

4. See Brewer (1989), Storrs (2009), Blaufarb (2012), and Kwass (2000) for eighteenth-century tax reforms in Europe. For Spanish and Portuguese reforms and their effect on their Latin American colonies, see Marichal (2006) and Elliot (2006).

5. Among the most popular histories in the early republic were David Hume's *History of England* (1754–1761), Edward Gibbon's *Decline and Fall of the Roman*

*Empire* (1776–1789), Adam Ferguson's *History of the Progress and Termination of the Roman Republic* (1783), and Voltaire's *Age of Louis XIV* (1751; translated 1752). Each of these works appeared in roughly a third of American libraries from the period, and all are littered with numerous mentions of taxation. Gibbon and Hume presented particularly sophisticated interpretations of historical tax policies, and both authors commented frequently on the aptness and effects of a range of fiscal reforms.

6. See Jefferson ([1790] 1961, 16:449); Jefferson (1807); Adams ([1783] 2008 14:435n3; Syrett (1963–1967, 7:236, 12:244); Jefferson ([1813] 2009, 6:583, 593); Madison ([1783] 1969–1975, 6:86, 9:84n).

7. Robin Einhorn (2006, 158) argues that apportionment was "intended to prevent the tax debates that would politicize slavery." Apportionment under the Articles of Confederation, according to Einhorn, represented an unworkable solution that ensured that no federal direct taxes could be collected. Because the Articles provided no process for compelling states to produce valuations of their taxable real estate, no state provided Congress with the necessary assessments and Congress could levy no direct taxes as a result.

## REFERENCES

Adams, John. (1783) 2008. John Adams to Edmund Jennings, 21 April 1783. In *Papers of John Adams*, edited by Gregg L. Lint, C. James Taylor, Hobson Woodward, Margaret A. Hogan, Mary T. Claffey, Sara B. Sikes, and Judith S. Graham, 14:421–23. Cambridge, MA: Harvard University Press.

Blaufarb, Rafe. 2012. *The Politics of Fiscal Privilege in Provence, 1530s–1830s.* Washington, DC: Catholic University of America Press.

Borden, Morton, ed. 1965a. "Antifederalist No. 30–31." In *The Antifederalist Papers*. East Lansing: Michigan State University Press.

———. 1965b. "Antifederalist No. 33." In *The Antifederalist Papers*. East Lansing: Michigan State University Press.

———. 1965c. "Antifederalist No. 34." In *The Antifederalist Papers*. East Lansing: Michigan State University Press.

Boucoyannis, Deborah. 2013. "The Equalizing Hand: Why Adam Smith Thought the Market Should Produce Wealth without Steep Inequality." *Perspectives on Politics* 11 (4): 1051–70.

Brennan, Geoffrey, and James M. Buchanan. 1980. *The Power to Tax: Analytical Foundations of a Fiscal Constitution.* Cambridge: Cambridge University Press.

Brennan, Geoffrey, and James Buchanan. 2000. "The Tax System as Social Overhead Capital: A Constitutional Perspective on Fiscal Norms." In *The Collected Works of James M. Buchanan*, 14:269–83. Indianapolis: Liberty Fund.

———. 2000. *The Reason of Rules: Constitutional Political Economy.* The Collected Works of James M. Buchanan. Indianapolis: Liberty Fund.

Brewer, John. 1989. *The Sinews of Power: War, Money and the English State, 1688–1783.* London: Unwin Hyman.

Buchanan, James M. 1967. *Public Finance in Democratic Process.* Chapel Hill: University of North Carolina Press.

———. 2000a. *Debt and Taxes.* The Collected Works of James M. Buchanan. Indianapolis: Liberty Fund.

———. 2000b. *The Limits of Liberty: Between Anarchy and Leviathan.* The Collected Works of James M. Buchanan. Indianapolis: Liberty Fund.

Constant, Benjamin. (1815) 2003. *Principles of Politics Applicable to All Governments.* Edited by Etienne Hofmann, translated by Dennis O'Keeffe. Indianapolis: Liberty Fund.

Einhorn, Robin. 2006. *American Taxation, American Slavery.* Chicago: University of Chicago Press.

Elliott, J. H. 2006. *Empires of the Atlantic World: Britain and Spain in America 1492–1830.* New Haven, CT: Yale University Press.

Fleischacker, Samuel. 2004. *A Short History of Distributive Justice.* Cambridge, MA: Harvard University Press.

———. 2002. "Adam Smith's Reception among the American Founders, 1776–1790." *William and Mary Quarterly* Third Series 59 (4): 897–924.

———. 2004. *On Adam Smith's Wealth of Nations: A Philosophical Companion.* Princeton, NJ: Princeton University Press.

Hamilton, Alexander. 2008. "Federalist 36." *The Federalist Papers,* edited by Lawrence Goldman. Oxford: Oxford University Press.

Hayek, F. A. (1960) 2011. *The Constitution of Liberty.* Definitive Edition. Edited by Ronald Hamowy. Chicago: University of Chicago Press.

Hume, David. (1742) 1955. "Of Taxes." In *David Hume: Writings on Economics.* Edited by Eugene Rotwein. Madison: University of Wisconsin Press.

Jefferson, Thomas. 1807. From Thomas Jefferson to John Norvell, 11 June 1807. Founders Online. National Historical Records and Publications Commission (unpublished early access edition). https://founders.archives.gov/documents/Jefferson/99-01-02-5737.

———. (1813) 2009. To John Wayles Eppes, 6 November 1813. In *The Papers of Thomas Jefferson,* Retirement Series, edited by Jefferson Looney, 6:583–93. Princeton, NJ: Princeton University Press.

———. (1790) 1961. To Thomas Mann Randolph Jr., 30 May 1790. In *The Papers of Thomas Jefferson,* edited by Julian P. Boyd, 16:449. Princeton, NJ: Princeton University Press.

Kwass, Michael. 2000. *Privilege and the Politics of Taxation in Eighteenth-Century France: Liberté, Egalité, Fiscalité.* Cambridge: Cambridge University Press.

Lundberg, David, and Henry F. May. 1976. "The Enlightened Reader in America." *American Quarterly* 28 (2): 262–93.

Marichal, Carlos. 2006. "Money, Taxes, and Finance." In *The Cambridge Economic History of Latin America,* edited by Victor Blumer-Thomas, John H. Coatsworth, and Roberto Cortés Conde, 1:427–36. Cambridge: Cambridge University Press.

Mehrotra, Ajay K. 2013. *Making the Modern American Fiscal State: Law, Politics, and the Rise of Progressive Taxation, 1877–1929.* Cambridge: Cambridge University Press.

Montesquieu. (1748) 2005. *The Spirit of the Laws.* Translated and edited by Anne M. Cohler, Basia C. Miller, and Harold S. Stone. Cambridge Texts in the History of Political Thought. Cambridge: Cambridge University Press.

Oates, Wallace. 1972. *Fiscal Federalism.* New York: Harcourt Brace Jovanovich.

Perkins, Edwin J. 1994. *American Public Finance and Financial Services 1700–1815.* Columbus: Ohio State University Press.

Madison, James. (1783) 1969–1975. "Report on Books for Congress." In *The Papers of James Madison,* edited by William T. Hutchinson, William M. E. Rachal, and Robert A. Rutland, 6:86, 9:84n. Chicago: University of Chicago Press.

Say, Jean-Baptist. (1803) 1848. *A Treatise on Political Economy; or, the Production, Distribution, and Consumption of Wealth.* Translated by C. R. Prinsep. New American Edition, edited by Clement C. Biddle. Philadelphia: Grigg, Elliot.

Sismondi, J. C. L. Simonde de. (1815) 1966. "Political Economy." Reprints of Economic Classics. New York: Augustus M. Kelley.

Smith, Adam. (1776) 1981. *An Inquiry into the Nature and Causes of the Wealth of Nations.* Edited by R. H. Campbell and A. S. Skinner. Indianapolis: Liberty Fund.

Stabile, Donald R. 1998. *The Origins of American Public Finance: Debates over Money, Debt, and Taxes in the Constitutional Era, 1776–1836.* Westport, CT: Greenwood Press.

Storrs, Christopher, ed. 2009. *The Fiscal-Military State in Eighteenth-Century Europe: Essays in Honour of P. G. M. Dickson.* Burlington, VT: Ashgate Publishing Company.

Syrett, Harold C, ed. 1961–1987. *The Papers of Alexander Hamilton.* 27 vols. New York: Columbia University Press.

Tomasi, John. 2012. *Free Market Fairness.* Princeton, NJ: Princeton University Press.

Tracy, Antoine Louis Claude Destutt de. (1817) 2011. *A Treatise on Political Economy.* Edited by Jeremy Jennings. Translated by Thomas Jefferson. Indianapolis: Liberty Fund.

Wolcott Jr., Oliver. (1796) 1832. "Direct Taxes." In *American State Papers: Documents, Legislative and Executive, of the Congress of the United States.* 3rd Series, *Finance.* Compiled by Walter Lowrie and Matthew St. Clair Clark, 1:414–65. Washington, DC: Gales and Seaton.

*Chapter 9*

# Narrating the Market Process

*How Stories Can Promote the
Economic Way of Thinking*

Jason Douglas

My first encounter with the idea of the market as a process also happened to be one of my first encounters with serious economic theory. Having read little beyond some Smith, Marx, and Mill as a kind of general, philosophical background, I somehow found myself in a lecture delivered by an economist named Israel Kirzner, whom I had never before heard of but whom I understood to be a figure of some consequence. I came away from the lecture impressed by the degree to which Kirzner's account of the economy seemed more like a description of how things worked in the actual marketplace than an attempt to gloss over variations and contingencies in pursuit of a tidy, theoretical model. Despite the fact that there was something compelling about a theory of the market that accounted for rather than assumed away the economy's inherent messiness, I couldn't, however, find a way to put all of the pieces together into a comprehensible whole. While the numerous elements—profit, opportunity, entrepreneurial function, alertness, consumer preference, ignorance, etc.—all seemed to make sense individually, it was difficult to come up with a simple and accessible way of describing the market process that reflected all of its essential features.

For a long time, I attributed my inability to construct for myself a satisfactory, comprehensive account of it all to deficiencies in my own knowledge, which was, no doubt, true to some extent. But as I read and reread more about market process theory, I noticed something peculiar about the overall shape of the discourse. Kirzner and virtually everyone else I read seemed to have only two ways of describing the market as a process; the market process is explained through price theory or through the history of economic thought. For example, in *The Meaning of Market Process* (Kirzner [1992] 1996), Kirzner produced an account of the market through its conceptual development, framed within the history of economic thought; and in *Market Theory and the Price*

*System* (Kirzner 1963), Kirzner delivered an account of the market through the technical framework of price theory. These are very fine and admirable books, but they also represent a certain kind of limitation in our options for accessing market process theory: you can study the market as a process through the specialized knowledge required for understanding the history of conceptual debates among economists that sometimes turn on very subtle distinctions, or you can study an economic theory of price in all its technical complexity. I'm sure there are important exceptions, but the point is, for the most part, market process theory is something written about by economists for other economists. We have a wealth of documentation on how economists understand or have come to understand the market as a process, but if it is such a basic and important part of understanding how the economy actually works, where is the account meant for everyone else? How can we explain the idea of the market as a process to those who aren't familiar with the difference between Marshallian equilibrium and Hayekian disequilibrium? Or those who don't see the conflict between neoclassical maximization and Misesian praxeology? How and to what degree has the idea of the market as a process been identified, recognized, and explained outside economics? Or, to put it yet another way, what does an account of the market process for the masses look like?

In this chapter I claim that stories and narrative can do essential work for communicating economic ideas to non-economists. Furthermore, I also claim that specific developments in the form of mid-twentieth century business novels align closely with the idea of the market as a process in particular. After outlining why disseminating disciplinary understanding beyond disciplinary boundaries is especially important for economics, I briefly sketch the essential features of existing approaches to similarly interdisciplinary projects. I will identify both the shared assumptions and the methodological deviations of my work from economic scholars who have drawn important insights from cultural studies and whom I draw upon in turn, such as Deirdre McCloskey ([1982] 1998), Peter Boettke (2005), Virgil Storr (Storr and Butkevich 2007), Tyler Cowen (1998, 2009), and Don Lavoie (Lavoie and Chamlee-Wright 2000). Having established the general features of my conceptual and methodological framework, I present a detailed analysis of the conceptual and formal parallels between Cameron Hawley's 1955 business novel, *Cash McCall* (Hawley 1955), and the theory of the market process as documented and developed by Israel Kirzner.

## WHY ECONOMIC UNDERSTANDING REQUIRES STORIES

I want to pose two parallel series of questions in order to demonstrate why it is important—perhaps even vital—that economists in particular should concern themselves with the problem of advancing public understanding of the economic way of thinking. I then want to briefly summarize some of the multidisciplinary collaborations that have been presented as a basis for applying or promoting the economic way of thinking beyond the boundaries of economics departments in order to demonstrate why, as I claim, stories and narrative are a necessary part of that effort.

What difference does it make whether or not there are people who specialize in the field of quantum physics? The fact that focused radiation therapy for cancer treatment has its roots in the subfield of accelerator physics and the fact that advanced medical imaging such as MRIs and CAT scans arise from the subfield of particle imaging at least suggest that specialized knowledge about quantum physics makes a big difference. In spite of such a significant and easily demonstrable impact on modern medicine, however, it's not at all clear that the answer remains the same with just a slight change in the question: What difference does it make whether or not the general public has specialized knowledge and understanding of quantum physics? Unlike the obvious impact of advances in medical technology, it's hard to image an increase in public knowledge of quantum mechanics delivering equally significant benefits either in magnitude or in kind. I don't think, however, that it in any way diminishes the importance of the discipline to say that increasing public knowledge in this field wouldn't make much of a difference because the benefits of quantum physics are available with only a relatively small number of specialists.

Can we, however, say the same thing for economics? What difference does it make whether or not there are people who specialize in the field of economics? What difference does it make whether or not the general public has specialized knowledge and understanding of how the economy works? What would we gain by a general increase in public understanding of economics? Are the benefits of economics fully realizable if disciplinary insights remain limited to a small number of specialists? I think it is fairly safe to say that an increase in the public's economic knowledge has the potential for a far greater impact than it does for a discipline whose application doesn't require the movement from specialized to general knowledge. In this sense, economics as a discipline should have a strong and robust interest in the means and methods of spreading the economic way of thinking. In fact, the importance of economics education is a point that Pete Boettke, among others, has made repeatedly, identifying, for example, both Henry Hazlitt's and Ludwig von Mises's insistence on the importance of the "project of economic literary" (Boettke 2005, 451).

The idea of advancing the economic way of thinking beyond its disciplinary boundaries is not a new idea and has been taken up in a variety of different approaches over the last forty years that seek to develop multidisciplinary collaborations between economics and various fields of studies in the social sciences and humanities. Despite the fact, however, that many of these efforts have produced important and interesting lines of inquiry, I argue that there have been relatively few discoveries that directly advance our ability to use the insights of other disciplines to advance economic understanding among non-economists. Furthermore, I argue that stories or narratives, as one of the most common formal structures of linguistic meaning at the pragmatic level, are an essential tool for communicating economic ideas. Because stories are essentially a method of sorting, filtering, arranging, and organizing events and information into a set of relationships leading to a particular outcome, but are also surprisingly resistant to definitive formal limits, they can serve a wider range of argumentative, expository, and analytical purposes than they are often given credit for. For reasons that will become apparent as I sketch a brief overview of some of the most significant efforts to establish an inter-disciplinary basis for broader economic understanding, I argue that stories are an essential tool of economic communication because they offer perhaps the most universal method of structuring information at the discourse level of meaning.

By far, the most common way for economists to describe the area of study they are reaching out to when they use extra-disciplinary economic understanding is the broad heading of culture. Culture is the vast domain of knowledge and practices that are governed and structured by convention and ritual, but don't reach the level of rigorously formalized knowledge. This creates one of two possible paths for thinking about the potential relationship between economics and cultural studies: the influence of culture on commercial life or culture as a kind of ethnographic data. In the case of examining the economy itself, studying culture has the potential to advance understanding because, as a set of beliefs and practices, culture influences behavior and preferences within the market. This is the approach taken by Don Lavoie and Emily Chamlee-Wright in *Culture and Enterprise*. They claim that "a better understanding of the economy and business life can result from taking seriously the role of culture in economic processes" (Lavoie and Chamlee-Wright 2000, 3). This is an approach shared by Tyler Cowen in his book, *In Praise of Commercial Culture* (Cowen 1998) and, with a slightly different emphasis, in the work of Albert O. Hirschman (Hirschman [1977] 2003) and Deirdre N. McCloskey (McCloskey [1982] 1998) who both claim that cultural values play a more profound, foundational role, not just influencing market behaviors, but as part of the market's institutional framework.

In the case of culture as a kind of ethnographic data, various cultural arti-facts can be read for how they reveal what people believe about the market. Stories, books, and movies become a record of how people think, feel, and perceive the economy. This is the approach that Virgil Henry Storr and

Bridget Butkevich employ in their effort to document the account of entre-preneurship held by various marginalized populations in "Subalternity and Entrepreneurship" (Storr and Butkevich 2007). This article is a good example of how stories can be used as a narrative record of economic ideas and beliefs. But it is also an important example because it demonstrates the importance of stories in another way. By identifying stories from marginalized popula-tions as cultural artifacts that express ideas outside the boundaries of formal institutions, it also demonstrates the way that stories can, more generally, be a vehicle for communicating knowledge across the systematic and formalized boundaries of disciplinary discourse.

This idea of reading cultural artifacts is the approach that also most closely aligns with disciplinary practices of cultural studies. It is also closely related to, but not synonymous with, other methods of connecting economics and cultural studies that draw more heavily on the discourse of language and literature, and which I draw from most heavily in constructing my own argument. Studying the formal structures and conventions of language isn't a way of discovering economic insights, but it is a way of understanding how economic insights are communicated. This is the kind of pioneering work that Deirdre McCloskey has done in the rhetoric of economics. When she argues that "science uses literary methods" (McCloskey [1985] 1998, 20), it does work toward demystifying some part of the claim to special-ized knowledge, but only in the sense that it seeks to return the specialist's means of persuasion to a more universal realm of human language. In this sense, advocating the use of stories and rhetoric isn't about stripping away ideas and insights; on the contrary, the idea is that by recognizing certain formalized structures of language, we can remove barriers to disseminating specialized knowledge. Asking economists to describe a particular account of the economy in a story rather than a mathematical model doesn't dimin-ish their claim to expert knowledge any more than using a term like "income inequality" conveys a special claim to expert knowledge by laymen. If ideas are rigorous, robust, and correct, their essential nature should survive the translation into the language of popular discourse.

The notion that ideas can persist across different modes of expression and, in fact, can better serve different communicative purposes when they are seen as encoded in rather than inherently part of a particular, specialized language is at the center of thinking about stories as a useful tool for spreading eco-nomic ideas. Thinking about the means of persuasion fairly quickly involves identifying both what you are trying to convince someone of and who this someone is that you are trying to convince. To put it another way, if you want to get your point across, a big part of the onus is on you to deliver your point in a way the audience will understand. Drawing on McCloskey's ideas of economic rhetoric and literature, Pete Boettke has argued that, it's not just that stories can be an effective "teaching tool in economics" (Boettke 2005, 445), but that "we cannot escape the narrative form of communicating" (Boettke 2005, 449). There is something about stories, as Boettke describes them, that is "enjoyable" (Boettke 2005, 445), that "excites the mind" and "sticks" (Boettke 2005, 446) with people. But there is also the potential for something more. Boettke points to McCloskey's use of an analogy that describes how "the economy itself is best seen as a conversation" (Boettke 2005, 450). Furthering the possibility of this deeper connection between the economy and language, Boettke claims that "the economy itself is an ever unfolding human drama" that "is necessarily revealed to us in narrative form" (Boettke 2005, 450). Putting it in terms of another linguistic analogy, whenever we take individual semantic units—dates, events, numbers, measures, words, and so on— and try to arrange them to convey meaning, we are narrating. Assembling individual units of any kind of communicative or representational system into something intended to convey meaning is functionally the same task as telling a story. That is why "we cannot escape the narrative form of communicating. Moreover, we shouldn't try to escape it" (Boettke 2005, 449–50).

Although I find these arguments compelling, I think they do run the risk of broadening their scope so much and moving to such a level of abstraction that they can undermine their own practical applicability. If we define everything as a story, if the characteristics of narrative are that universal, then what is the benefit of identifying anything as a story? I argue that to access the benefits of specialized knowledge in economics or in storytelling, we need to pull back a little and think more about particular variations of form within this potentially universalizing category of narrative. To that end, I suggest that in thinking about the dissemination of economic ideas through stories, we need a more specific set of economic ideas and a more specific idea of what we mean by a story. It is to that end that I am going to read *Cash McCall* in relation to a market process account of the economy. We can (and should) compare the economy to a conversation, but the analogy cuts both ways. The possibility that at least part of the *"unfolding human drama"* (Boettke 2005, 450, italics added) arises from ignorance, misinformation, and misunderstanding means that not all conversations are to be taken at face value; all stories aren't equally accurate representations of the economy. In fact, the idea of an economy that unfolds and reveals itself isn't that good a fit with many mainstream accounts. A market in a state of near-perfect competition that is constantly steering itself toward equilibrium doesn't sound like much of an unfolding drama. A mixed economy operating on Keynesian policies to steer the market away from volatility sounds like it is specifically meant to avoid dramatic revelations. The theory of the economy that sounds most like a system of unfolding revelations is the market as a process with its description of the drama arising from uncertainty, ignorance, and disequilibrium on the one hand, and the revelations provided by alertness, opportunity, discovery, and spontaneous coordination on the other. The economy sounds most like a narrative when narrative proceeds through a series of events that the reader necessarily experiences as a series of discoveries. Stories sound most like the economy when they are described as a series of events that present themselves as part of a process where each new event has the potential to both change the direction of the story and to revise the meaning of all the events that have come before. The market and narrative are most compatible when they are both described as a process. Market process theory sounds so much like the contingent, revisionary, and messy aspects of the market as a lived experience because it is a theory that repudiates the kinds of abstractions that gloss over the implications of uncertainty and dispersed knowledge. *Cash McCall* is a novel that, more than any other I have found, most closely describes the market as a process, in part because that is the account most closely resembling what Hawley believed, but also because it is an example of the procedural narrative that emerged in the mid-twentieth century as a story structured around a series of events as part of a particular kind of process rather than arranging the dramatically timed occurrence of symbolic events.

## CASH MCCALL: MARKET PROCESS NARRATIVE

Cameron Hawley's 1955 business novel, *Cash McCall*, is a story about price, narrating the process by which a particular company comes to be bought and sold. As such, it is a novel that presents an account of the economy that resembles market process theory more closely than any other I've found. The novel provides a viable and interesting, although not necessarily definitive, answer to the question of what an account of the market process for the non-economist looks like. Hawley was a successful businessman who retired in his early forties and, during the 1950s, turned his hand to writing novels. Living under the Keynesian policies that were enacted in the wake of the Great Depression, set as part of the war-time economy, and maintained into the 1960s, Hawley was in business and later writing during a time when there was significant economic growth and significant government intervention in the economy. Both of these conditions factor into his account of the nature of the problems that businessmen faced in trying to coordinate production. Hawley's narrative tries to make sense of a market where growth guarantees neither success nor failure and where commonly held beliefs in economic expertise alternately promise to alleviate uncertainty and threaten to undermine profitability.

From a formal perspective—that is, considering the story as an ordered sequence of events leading up to a particular outcome—*Cash McCall* tells the story of how a company is sold for $2 million one day and resold for $3 million the next. Structuring the story this way emphasizes the importance of the difference between the two sales prices. It is a formal structure that is highly compatible with the kinds of stories about unjust and unfair prices that make economists leery of stories as a potential method of communicating economics ideas. But one of the defining features of the novel's use of prices is that it evokes the narrative structure normally used to condemn market prices. The novel, however, refuses to allow that structure to follow through as a critique of the market, instead reversing the expectations associated with common business tropes in order to counter what he sees as a mistaken critique of market prices and a misunderstanding of uncertainty as a problem that can be solved by regulating prices. Hawley systematically structures the narrative to demonstrate that stories about unjust or unfair prices do not explain the actual conditions that lead to price differences. In other words, although Hawley structures the story around price difference, he thoroughly exorcises the notion that price difference as such presents any kind of problem.

The nature of an economic problem, as Hawley describes it, is that there is no rational, scientific method that will allow anyone to reliably determine with accuracy and precision how to effectively coordinate production to meet consumer demand under conditions of uncertainty and scarcity. In other words, ongoing but evolving demand in a nondeterministic system means that coordinating production is an endlessly recurring challenge and a defining characteristic of economic life rather than a problem that can, in any important sense, be definitively solved.

In contrast to the perpetual difficulty of coordination, the second problem that Hawley describes is a matter of what people believe about the economy rather than a feature of the economy itself. Among the challenges inherent to economic production are further complications introduced by the possibility that people can and in fact do misunderstand coordination, demand, scarcity, and, in particular, uncertainty. For Hawley, the fact that people can fail to recognize a certain degree of indeterminacy in coordinating economic activity has the potential to disrupt or restrict the ability to respond effectively to uncertainty. To put it another way, the fact that people think that economic problems are solvable makes them (ironically) less able to deal with economic uncertainty. Although mistaken beliefs serve mostly to exacerbate the same difficulties presented by the problem of coordination, they also present a problem that is solvable.

An essential part of Hawley's methodology is telling the story of how Suffolk Moulding comes to be sold by two different owners for two different prices. Suffolk Moulding is a medium-size manufacturing company owned and operated by Grant Austen in a fictional Pennsylvania town. Austen is an extremely dedicated man who totally immerses himself in his work until, increasingly frustrated by problems of staffing, long-term investment, client relations, and price negotiations, he finally receives news from his biggest client that makes him reconsider his position for the first time in his career. It is only when Austen is presented with the choice of borrowing heavily to make the capital upgrades required to manufacture his biggest customer's new product line or lose their business altogether that he even begins to entertain the idea of selling his company. Austen is faced with the choice of losing more than 50 percent of his revenue or taking on a heavy debt load.

Hawley very carefully describes the nature of the choice that Austen faces in order to both evoke and fundamentally transform a particular conflict common to popular business stories. This kind of financial situation is most often reproduced in stories as some form of systemic injustice that threatens to deprive a hardworking man of what he deserves. Despite Austen's understandable dismay at his situation, Hawley very deliberately stages it as more of a crossroads than a crisis. In contrast to most stories that present a moment of critical financial decision, the choice Austen faces isn't between keeping and losing his business in any immediate sense. He is informed by his consulting business advisor that the company has sufficient but not extravagant cash reserves, and he is assured by his banker that he has plenty of credit available on very favorable terms. No matter what he decides, Austen has resources that allow him time to pursue either option. The problem that Austen faces isn't that he's been forced into a no-win situation or that he has to pick from among bad options. What worries Austen most is that neither option offers him any guarantee of success. The problem that Austen really faces is that he has no way of evaluating which is the better option. It's entirely possible that his company can bear to manage the debt required for capital improvements. It's also entirely possible that the company can withstand a temporary period of declining revenue while finding new customers. Alternatively, it's possible that the company could fold under the pressure from either of these options. What makes this such a difficult situation is that it requires Austen to make choices about the use of productive resources even though he has no way of determining whether or not they will turn out to be effective. Suffolk's financial difficulties are fundamentally a problem of uncertainty. From the very beginning, Hawley repeatedly demonstrates that a defining characteristic of production is a certain degree of inherent uncertainty.

Although Hawley maintains throughout the novel that uncertainty is a defining aspect of economic activity that can never be eliminated, he presents Austen's desire to escape dealing with uncertainty as a way to introduce the possibility of separating the work of production from some other kind of work. After spending decades dedicated to his company, even to the point of almost totally ignoring his wife and virtually all other aspects of life, the fact that Austen suddenly decides that this situation warrants selling his company is part of how Hawley demonstrates that this problem is different in kind rather than just in magnitude from what Austen has faced before. Hawley describes the way that Austen tirelessly dealt with all the problems of machinery and materials that are part of manufacturing because he enjoyed the process and the challenge of making things. This latest crisis is, however, a question about the future value of products in the marketplace, only indirectly connected to the physical work of production. For Austen, this crisis pushes him to the limit of his willingness to do the work of accounting for uncertainty. Austen may not espouse a formal theory that differentiates the work of production from the work of dealing with uncertainty, but Hawley uses Austen's desire for purely productive work to raise the possibility of some kind of categorical distinction between the two kinds of work.

It is when Austen is trying to escape anything that isn't the work of production by selling his company that the novel introduces Cash McCall, an unknown character who is presented initially only as a potential buyer for Suffolk. For the most part, McCall remains an unseen character, known mainly by reputation throughout almost the entire first half of the novel, only appearing for a few brief meetings to find out about the sale of Suffolk and to accept Austen's full asking price of $2 million. If Austen represents the idea of work that is purely productive in the sense of the labor required to physically make things, then McCall represents the idea of work that is precisely not-productive in this physical sense. McCall, as a self-described "dealer in second-hand businesses" (Hawley 1955, 212) makes no bones about the fact that he only "buy[s] them to sell" (Hawley 1955, 212), explicitly hoping to avoid being involved with company operations. Austen and McCall are presented as engaging in two different kinds of economic activity that, although defined in contrast to one another, present their differences more as complementary alternatives than as a form of opposition. If Austen's sale of Suffolk is a way to avoid dealing with uncertainty, then McCall's purchase of the company is a way of accepting precisely that same problem. In arranging to sell Suffolk, Austen does solve the problem of uncertainty about his own financial future, but he does so precisely by removing himself from any responsibility for the problem of Suffolk's financial future, which has not changed in any visible way.

Austen's response to the difficult decisions about Suffolk's financial future, coupled with a still emergent vision of some kind of division of labor, is where the novel introduces two divergent, competing accounts of the nature of an economic problem. Austen's response to uncertainty is to immediately seek out corporate consultants, bankers, and other financial experts. Part of his rejection of the work of coordinating production under uncertainty is to turn to someone who, by virtue of their expertise, can give him definitive answers. It is not clear until the end of the novel, however, just what this means or what is at stake in Austen's rejection of uncertainty. In order to fully produce that account, Hawley first uses Austen's sale of Suffolk to McCall to shift the problem to McCall and uses his process of arranging a subsequent sale to construct an account of how uncertainty is dealt with as part of the market process.

When Hawley sets up McCall to play the role of entrepreneur by searching for a way to resolve the uncertainty surrounding Suffolk's financial future, he faces what is perhaps the most difficult task of narrating economic ideas: telling a story about spontaneous order. Because narrative is, by definition, a way of selecting, filtering, ordering, and arranging events that lead to a specific outcome, it is difficult to imagine stories that don't convey a sense of their own intentionality and design. The idea that stories are in some way incompatible with the idea of spontaneous order is, in fact, a point that Tyler Cowen took up specifically in his 2009 TEDx talk entitled "Be Suspicious of Simple Stories."

> You can't make a movie and say, "It was all a big accident." No, it has to be a conspiracy, people plotting together, because a story is about intention. A story is not about spontaneous order or complex human institutions which are the product of human action but not of human design. No, a story is about evil people plotting together.

Cowen is certainly right that the vast majority of our stories in television, literature, and film tend to portray complex systems as a result of intention, especially when it comes to economic systems. Although I myself will shortly go on to point out a number of different narrative tropes that Hawley evokes that are problematic precisely because they fail to distinguish between storytelling patterns and patterns of economic behavior, I think that it is a mistake to be suspicious of stories because they are simple. Despite the fact that I've presented much of *Cash McCall* in fairly straightforward terms, stripped down to the essential moments as suggested by its formal structure, the novel is, in many ways, a highly complex narrative, driven by the implications of numerous overlapping and interconnected revelations about who knew what and when they knew it. The story unfolds as an entire network of people connected to Suffolk learn, perceive, and transmit information (and misinformation). When it comes to describing how McCall functions as an entrepreneur, however, Hawley doesn't proceed by deepening the complexity. Instead, Hawley presents McCall's process of discovery, the problem of dispersed knowledge, and the spontaneous emergence of order by making that part of the story as simple as possible. The danger of stories conveying economic ideas is not that they are a simple and therefore an unreliable means of describing complex systems. The danger is that they are simplistic.

In order to construct a simple account of how McCall at once sells Suffolk and resolves the problem of uncertainty about the company's financial future, Hawley begins by having McCall do nothing. After agreeing to buy the company, McCall leaves town for a few days and is completely out of touch with everyone associated with Suffolk. The transitional manager, Gil Clark, tasked with facilitating the transfer of ownership and operations out of Austen's hands is frantic with worry because McCall hasn't yet learned about the demand from the company's largest customer, Andscott Instrument Corporation, to invest or lose their business. When McCall does return and finalizes the paperwork for purchasing the company, he hardly has time to worry about the problem because the owner of Andscott comes to visit him personally. Andscott's owner is upset that, as an important supplier for his company, Suffolk has been sold without him knowing about it. He somewhat carelessly reveals that he only demanded that Suffolk buy new equipment because his company was suffering from its own financial difficulties and wasn't sure that he could cover the expense himself. Alerted to the fact that there was some kind of difficulty between Suffolk and Andscott, McCall begins to make a few rapid but discrete inquiries and discovers that Suffolk has some unique productive resources that could benefit Andscott greatly. It is only at this point that McCall approaches the owner of Andscott and negotiates a deal to sell Suffolk to him for $3 million worth of shares in the new, combined company.

Although there are many other business dealings surrounding this series of events that are quite complex, this process of finding out about the opportunity for and arranging what is, in effect, the merger of the two companies is very rapid and fairly straightforward. In a way, Hawley describes the merger of these two companies almost as if it happens by itself. There is, of course, a lot of information that has to come out about which company has the most efficient process, whose engineers are best suited for meeting particular design challenges, and who owns which patents, but all of this is revealed only after McCall is alerted to the fact that Suffolk has heretofore unrealized potential. Even though all of that information does have to be brought together in order for it to make financial sense to merge the two companies— that is, even though the information necessary to realize this deal is dispersed among a number of different people at different companies who aren't all aware that they hold information relevant to coordinating production, the process of bringing all of this information together is fairly spontaneous. The owner of Andscott hears about the sale and delivers some key information to McCall. McCall then goes out and gathers a bit more information that completes the picture based on what he has been told, and now it makes sense to solve Andscott's problems by giving the company access to all of Suffolk's productive resources and to solve Suffolk's problem by ensuring that it has all the orders it needs to remain profitably productive.

In arranging this alignment of productive needs and resources, Hawley also manages to create the conditions for demonstrating one of the most conceptually difficult aspects of thinking about the market as a process that solves coordination problems spontaneously. When, near the end of the novel, Austen finds out that McCall has arranged to sell Suffolk for a million-dollar price increase in less the forty-eight hours, he is extremely upset, in part because he didn't get the higher price but also because he assumes that McCall must have worked out the deal before hand in order to pull off such a large price increase so quickly. This accusation that the price difference must arise from an illegitimate or unethical form of information asymmetry says something about Austen's views on uncertainty (more on that later), but it emphasizes a somewhat counterintuitive way of thinking about inefficiency in signaling and the cost of discovery. Hawley makes it clear to the reader that, despite Austen's accusation, McCall had absolutely no prior knowledge about the possibility of selling Suffolk to Andscott. In fact, contrary to his normal discovery practices, McCall has effectively no current information on Suffolk at all when he buys the company, so there is no way he could have preplanned the sale to Andscott. What's more, the reason that Andscott hadn't made a serious effort to buy Suffolk already was he thought it wasn't possible and, in an important way, it wasn't. Austen never listened to any purchase offers until after Andscott's demands. And an essential requirement of his decision to sell was that he would only accept payment in cash. Andscott, because it was in a difficult financial situation, would have been unable to buy for cash. In a very real sense, Andscott didn't know it could buy Suffolk from Austen because it couldn't. And, in a very real and not just symbolic sense, it was precisely the fact that McCall bought the company for $2 million that created the conditions to sell it for $3 million. Or, in terms of the market process, $2 million dollars was the cost to discover the opportunity to sell Suffolk for $3 million.

There is a certain kind of elegance in the way that Hawley is able to at once demonstrate the complexity and messiness of the contingent and changing market conditions that are constantly making and unmaking opportunities, revealing information that can help coordinate or further complicate problems of coordination, while at the same time reducing the most conceptually difficult moments to some of the simplest moments in the story. It is a surprisingly detailed and conceptually thorough description of how the market operates that parallels market process theory to an impressive degree. That is not to say that there is any evidence that Hawley had any familiarity with the formal economic theories that describe the market as a process, especially given the fact that a number of central texts would not be published for years to come. I think, more than anything, this demonstrates the degree to which *Cash McCall*, as a procedural narrative that tries to faithfully follow the ins and outs of how businessmen actually go about discovering, arranging, and concluding deals in the market, suggests that there is some kind of overlap between the way that the market operates as a process and the act of trying to narrate the market as a process; they both tend to hit upon exactly the same kind of events and draw the same kind of relationships between them. At the very least, *Cash McCall* demonstrates the possibility that there are ways to pair particular kinds of narrative and particular economic theories that are compatible in order to communicate economic ideas in a form that is accessible to the general public without necessarily sacrificing any essential ideas or conceptual robustness.

## MISUNDERSTANDING UNCERTAINTY EXACERBATES UNCERTAINTY

Despite the fact that *Cash McCall* contrasts Austen à la producer with McCall à la entrepreneur, the relationship is much more in the sense of complementary alternatives than binary opposites. McCall's work as an entrepreneur isn't superior to Austen's manufacturing work and vice versa because Austen can't effectively coordinate production without the kind of work that McCall does and McCall doesn't have anything to coordinate without Austen's kind of productive work. Both Austen and McCall fill necessary functions in meeting demand under conditions of uncertainty. And yet, when it comes to the problem of what people believe about uncertainty, McCall and Austen are oriented precisely in opposition to one another. Austen's desire to withdraw from the problem of uncertainty isn't a problem per se because production and discovery are to some degree separable functions. His desire is not, however, simply a matter of preference; his desire grows out of his beliefs about the nature of the problem he faces. Hawley uses Austen's aversion to uncertainty to illustrate the nature and implications of a particular way of misunderstanding uncertainty. To that end, McCall's sale of Suffolk for $3 million marks the discovery of a new opportunity for utilizing the company's productive capacity as well as providing a moment of narrative tension that renders visible the problem arising from Austen's mistaken belief about the nature of economic uncertainty. Austen's visceral reaction to the news of Suffolk's resale price and his allegations of fraud are the means by which Hawley both evokes and deconstructs existing accounts of market prices as a problem of injustice, unfairness, or inequality based on a failure to recognize the problem of coordination.

There is a certain narrative familiarity and plausibility to Austen's position that present a rhetorical challenge for Hawley. Anyone who, like Grant Austen, sells their company for a price 50 percent lower than the price it sells for one day later would experience at least some degree of seller's remorse. Given the rapidity of the second sale, it wouldn't be entirely unreasonable to at least wonder if the second sale was in the works before the first was completed. In that sense, it's hard to blame Austen for either the intensity of his emotional reaction or for entertaining the possibility of conspiracy and fraud. When all of this is added to the fact that, from a storytelling perspective, pitting the hardworking, productive businessman in a battle for survival against the slick, predatory capitalist is a common trope in business narratives, the difference between the two sales prices of Suffolk seems a sufficient problem in itself to serve as the driving tension of the entire novel. In this sense, Hawley uses Austen to construct a narrative account that has the potential to perpetuate a mistaken belief about the nature of an economic problem.

By the time Austen learns about the resale of Suffolk and in a fit of rage, charges off to find an attorney willing to bring a lawsuit against McCall for fraud and theft, however, it's already been made clear that there is no way McCall could be guilty of any such thing. And, in fact, Hawley has already set up several circumstances that would demonstrate that if anything, the opposite of what Austen believes is true. Hawley uses Austen's accusations against McCall to evoke then dismiss a whole series of ways to interpret the sales of Suffolk according to a mistaken idea of uncertainty. Hawley evokes the idea that McCall was able to buy low and sell high because he had some kind of special information about Suffolk and Andscott. But, not only does McCall admit to buying Suffolk without calling his normal team of investigators to assemble a thorough file on the company, but also, during negotiations, Austen makes a conscious and deliberate choice not to tell McCall that his company is in danger of losing over half its revenue. Even if the sales prices were to be seen as a problem of unequal access to information, the information is running clearly in Austen's rather than in McCall's favor.

Hawley evokes the idea that McCall is able to extract such a large profit margin because he is some kind of financial genius. Hawley builds into the narrative descriptions of several companies that McCall owns expressly for the purpose of investigating and analyzing the financial potential of companies. And yet, when McCall meets Austen to discuss the possibility of buying the company, he agrees to a deal on the spot with consulting any documentation or employing his information-gathering mechanisms. If he had put some kind of financial genius to work calculating how to get the best deal, the financial investigation would have revealed that Suffolk was on the verge of losing its biggest customer and, consequently, it wouldn't be a good purchase without a significant price reduction. In other words, Hawley gives McCall all the trappings of the highly calculating financial expert and then makes sure that he doesn't use them. Furthermore, he arranges so that if he had put those skills to work, he would have tried to bargain Austen down if he had been

willing to buy at all. The upshot is that Hawley makes it impossible to think
of McCall's million-dollar profit as a matter of his ability to empirically judge
the value of the company.

Hawley also evokes the idea that it is a problem that McCall simply got so
much more than Austen. Austen however, in his anger, manages to gloss over
several important facts. When Austen learns about the price that McCall gets
for Suffolk he is informed of both the amount and the manner of purchase
in detail. He is informed directly that McCall received a certain number of
shares from the sale that have a certain price on the market currently that,
when multiplied together, add up to $3 million. There is, however, no reason
to assume that McCall could dump that many shares of stock on the market
all at once for full price. And, in an important sense, McCall won't know
how much he actually sold for in a dollar amount until he actually sells those
shares. Perhaps most arithmetically simple but all the subtler for it is the fact
that Austen feels cheated because he got a "hell of a lot less" (Hawley 1955,
376), but if you do a simple comparison of their immediate net gain, McCall
only comes away with $1 million and Austen with $2 million.

If you look at all of the mistaken reasons that Austen devises to
explain McCall's million-dollar profit—fraud, financial genius, unequal
distribution—they are all one form or another of the same mistake: thinking
that there is some kind of correct or ideal price that can be rationally and reliably determined by sufficiently skilled or knowledgable individuals. In other
words, Hawley works to challenge the myth that the economy is subject to
economic calculation.

The final, ironic reiteration of this problem is in a very subtle element of
the novel. In several places throughout the novel, Hawley interjects brief
discussions of tax rates into the business negotiations. He emphasizes the
fact that Austen's company is subject to a "90 percent excess profit tax"
(Hawley 1955, 8). Hawley presents the tax rates as an indirect form of price
control, meaning, it doesn't matter how much money you make, your profits
after clearing expenses are always going to be reduced by an entire order
of magnitude. Any gains you make to combat that reduction are themselves
subject to the same level of reduction. The irony is in the fact that Austen
increasingly buys into a notion of economic expertise as a way to escape
uncertainty, whether that be through hiring knowledgable consultants to
outsource entrepreneurial work or in seeking a resolution to price difference
through the courts, but the main reason he has any of these problems is that
his business has, for years, been subject to a form of economic calculation
that presumes to determine with a simple formula what constitutes excess
profits. Although it is a fairly simple matter to determine what constitutes
today's profits based on today's expenses, a more realistic understanding of
profit requires thinking about the relationship of profits and expenses across

longer periods of time in relation to changes in consumer demand. Austen never realizes that selling his company is a way to correct distortions in prices and production that slowly built up over years until it made his business unsustainable without a major reorganization of productive assets across more than one firm. His increasing commitment to the idea of economic calculation was a realignment of his view of the market, accepting an institutional framework of a mixed economy that actually lessened his ability to respond to uncertainty.

That isn't just the greatest irony of the book, but of the idea of economic calculation as well. Acting as if the economy is subject to calculation in order to eliminate uncertainty merely exacerbates the selfsame problem. And it is by way of narrative that Hawley uses irony to deliver a description of the economic calculation problem in a *New York Times* best-selling novel. Economists haven't always done a particularly good job of translating their disciplinary knowledge into such forms that are accessible to the general public. Certainly our culture is saturated with stories that emphasize sentiment and sympathy before all else. And certainly such stories are highly compatible with the kind of folk economics that can't distinguish poverty from scarcity and assumes that good intentions lead to good outcomes. The fact that there are, however, powerful stories full of bad economic thinking should steer us toward rather than away from using narrative. On the one hand, the fact that stories can be so powerful should tell us that we have a popular, accessible, and highly effective form of communication already available to us. And on the other hand, the fact that people will mold their understanding of the economy to fit the stories they hear should tell us that we need to make sure there are stories full of good economics. Speaking from my own introduction to the economic way of thinking, I can attest that there is something compelling about the power and elegance of economic theory. But from a position outside the discipline, I can also attest that there is nothing more likely to promote real understanding or to reconcile sometimes complex and counterintuitive ideas with the experience of the real world than a good story. Because people understand the world they live in through stories, they need stories that narrate the market process.

## REFERENCES

Boettke, Peter J. 2005. "Teaching Economics through Ayn Rand: How the Economy Is Like a Novel and How the Novel Can Teach Us about Economics." *Journal of Ayn Rand Studies* 6 (2): 445–65.

Cowen, Tyler. 1998. *In Praise of Commercial Culture*. Cambridge, MA: Harvard University Press.

————. November 2009. "Be Suspicious of Simple Stories" [Video file]. Retrieved from https://www.ted.com/talks/tyler_cowen_be_suspicious_of_stories.

Hawley, Cameron. 1955. *Cash McCall*. Boston: Houghton-Mifflin.

Hirschman, Albert O. (1977) 2003. *The Passion and the Interests*. Princeton, NJ: Princeton University Press.

Kirzner, Israel M. (1992) 1996. *The Meaning of Market Process: Essays in the Development of Modern Austrian Economics*. London: Routledge.

Lavoie, Don, and Emily Chamlee-Wright. 2000. *Culture and Enterprise: The Development, Representation, and Morality of Business*. New York: Routledge.

McCloskey, Deirdre. (1982) 1998. *The Rhetoric of Economics*. Madison: University of Wisconsin Press.

Storr, Virgil, and Bridget Butkevich. 2007. "Subalternity and Entrepreneurship: Tales of Marginalized but Enterprising Characters, Oppressive Settings and Haunting Plots." *International Journal of Entrepreneurship and Innovation* 8 (4): 251–60.

*Chapter 10*

# The Market Process in Health Care

## Jerrod Anderson

Consumer shopping is a key ingredient to encouraging market competition. Markets in which consumers can effectively shop incentivize producers to offer goods at lower prices, higher qualities, or both. Where consumers cannot effectively shop, competition is diminished. The health care market in the United States seems to be characterized by consumers that cannot effectively shop for health care. This could be for any number of reasons: consumers do not fully understand the product they are consuming, prices are hidden behind layers of bureaucracy, restrictions exist on the type of competition providers and insurers can engage in, and so on.

In this chapter I explore how private institutions can structure exchange to support a well-functioning market, even in the face of potential market imperfections. Since as early as Arrow (1963), economists have viewed the health care market as fundamentally dysfunctional, mainly due to asymmetric information issues. Asymmetric information is viewed as a problem in many other markets, such as auto mechanic, lawyer, and tax accountant services, but these markets tend to have only one relationship characterized by asymmetric information. Health care, on the other hand, because of the insurance component, has multiple relationships characterized by asymmetric information: adverse selection may affect who buys insurance and what insurance is offered, moral hazard can encourage insured individuals to overconsume health care, the doctor's superior medical knowledge incentivizes overtreatment and over-diagnosis, and there is a potential moral component that is inevitably attached to the issue (Arrow 1963). I use the historical example of "lodge doctors" (those hired by mutual aid societies and other organizations beginning in the nineteenth century) to demonstrate how these groups supported a well-functioning health care market. I then use the characteristics of the lodge doctor arrangement to understand how modern insurance companies could serve as institutional cornerstones for a well-functioning health care market today.

Three general attributes characterize how the lodge doctor institution enhanced consumer shopping and strengthened competitive forces. First, information about provider quality must be truthfully and publicly revealed. Mutual aid societies that employed lodge doctors achieved this by choosing the lodge doctor through election. Medical tourism can achieve this through data collection on outcomes by insurers in the course of normal business activity.

Second, health care providers must have the incentive to provide the service at a low cost. Both mutual aid societies and insurers providing medical tourism policies do this by contracting a fixed salary with the provider determined annually via a bidding process (in the case of the lodge doctor) and a fixed fee for a procedure decided before the procedure begins (in the case of medical tourism). By offering alternative means of obtaining health care, these practices also have the added benefit of putting downward pressure on prices of providers that are not subject to those contracts.

Third, the payment arrangement must incentivize the provider to maintain quality. In the case of the lodge doctor, this was achieved through the fixed salary, which channeled the doctor's efforts toward effective prevention and early treatment, and through the yearly election, which incentivized the doctor to provide high-quality care in order to keep his job. In the case of insured medical tourism, insurance companies have the incentive to contract with high-quality providers because those insurers bear the cost of complications of postoperative care upon the patients' return home.

In the first section, I describe the role of the consumer in the market process and how we should view what are often termed market imperfections, which can potentially blunt market competition. This is followed by a review of the literature on consumer shopping in order to show that under most current arrangements, consumers cannot effectively shop for medical care. The next section describes lodge doctor practices and how they aided in increasing competition in the health care market. I discuss limitations of this model in the present day. I then describe medical tourism, how it can enhance competition in the health care market, and what the impediments to increasing its use are. The chapter concludes with a brief discussion of the findings.

## CONSUMER SOVEREIGNTY AND ITS IMPEDIMENTS

Mises puts the consumer at the heart of the market process. He notes that, while entrepreneurs take the helm, the consumers are the captains of the ship and exercise consumer sovereignty over the market (Mises [1949] 2007,

269).[1] Successful entrepreneurs are those who fulfill the wants and desires of consumers. If an entrepreneur brings to market a product that is anathema to consumer preferences, that entrepreneur's business career is not long for this world.

As many other market process theorists, including Hayek (1948) and Kirzner (1973, 1997), have noted (with varying degrees of emphasis), producers' success is a derivative of their ability to satisfy consumer demand. If a producer does not satisfy consumers' desires for a low enough price, consumers are free to buy from another purveyor of goods and services, conditional on that other producer being in the market. The combination of free entry in the market for producers and the consumers' ability to buy from any producer should satisfy consumer preferences with profits tending toward zero. In Kirzner's view, this process is driven by the entrepreneurial role of both producers and consumers (Kirzner 1973). The entrepreneurial role of the producer is to be alert to profit opportunities afforded by gaps in supply that either lower the cost of an existing product or fulfill the desires of consumers with a new product. The entrepreneurial role of the consumer is to be alert to price differences among producers and to new products that fulfill their desires better than older products.

This process toward equilibrium may, however, be impeded if consumers are unable to effectively shop based on price or quality. This could be due to several factors: cognitive limitations of consumers, high search costs, high cost of switching from one producer to another, consumers not bearing the full marginal cost of buying the product, and so on. All these factors reduce the relative benefit a consumer gains from being alert. If a consumer is considering switching doctors, the consumer may not have access to information about quality, and if the consumer has access to quality measures, those measures may be incomplete and fail to address doctor characteristics like bedside manner. As noted by Mises (2007, 270), only a few sellers of goods and services directly interact with consumers, but the buying decisions of consumers trickle all the way up the supply chain to determine the prices of the most minute input. When consumers face impediments to shopping, this relay of information becomes distorted. I will describe how each of the factors listed above can limit the equilibrating effects of market competition. Because all those factors are present in the health care market, this exercise will provide a general way of viewing the market process in the health care market.

In general, the medical market is characterized by asymmetric information. This is a situation in which one party to an exchange has more information than the other about the product being sold. I will focus mostly on the issue of moral hazard. This is characterized by one party's action being hidden from the other. An example from the medical context is the service that a doctor provides. A patient may visit a doctor and present certain symptoms. Because the patient is not a medical expert, she is not sure whether the condition is serious or mild and does not know what action should be taken to treat the condition. The doctor may choose the treatment that maximizes his benefit rather than the patient's. Take the example of a stomachache and assume that the doctor knows the condition will resolve itself with no action on his part. In the extreme case, the doctor could recommend the removal of the appendix, and the patient would not know that this was a completely unnecessary procedure.[2] This type of information asymmetry makes service quality hard to ascertain.

When consumers face cognitive or informational limitations[3] in understanding the product for sale, the role of consumer alertness is necessarily dulled and, therefore, ex ante profit opportunities that benefit the consumer are reduced. If consumers do not understand a product, such as health insurance,[4] the alertness consumers exercise may only reveal false profit opportunities, since the consumers may choose a cost-increasing option without realizing their mistake. Given the cognitive and informational limitations of consumers, it may then not be in the producers' best interest to introduce a product that provides the consumer with a lower-cost option. This is often the case with consuming doctors' services, in which case the provider has much more information than the consumer, but if this is the case, we should ask why it may be difficult to get a second opinion.

High search costs and high switching costs are often blamed to some extent for why the health care market is different from other markets. On the one hand, thinking on these two particular topics tends to be plagued by the nirvana fallacy in the form of assuming that these costs should not exist and that the government should regulate these costs away.[5]

On the other hand, it can sometimes be a beneficial exercise to consider a market in which things are not as they currently are; in this case, a market with lower search and switching costs. The important thing to remember is that we must understand why those costs are present, and if we think a world in which those costs are lower is possible, the next issue to consider is what is impeding the reduction of those costs through competition. If there are rules that impede entrepreneurs from providing cost-reducing services to consumers, then we can fruitfully analyze the implications of removing those impediments. If the issue is search cost, then we must ask why an information aggregator has not emerged to provide consumers with the relevant information (more on this topic below). If the issue is switching cost, we should ask why there may not be enough doctors in an area to make switching relatively easier. It may be that there are restrictions on entry into the health care market, and restrictions on market entry or on certain uses of price and quality of information forestall entrepreneurial activity on the supplier side.

Lastly, most of the marginal cost of health care is not borne by the consumer of health care due to current payment models, which tend to be fee-for-service arrangements in which the provider is paid for each service rendered. These payment models not only allow consumers to face a lower marginal cost at the point of care through a system of premiums, co-pays, and coinsurances, but most of these payment models also separate the financing decisions from treatment decisions. Taking these in turn, if consumers do not bear the full marginal cost of care, then the relative profit from their alertness decreases, thus reducing consumers' incentives to be aware of lower-cost alternatives. Because of the separation of financing and treatment decisions, doctors have less of an incentive to control costs than if they were also in charge of financing the care.[6] With this fee-for-service payment, the doctor faces no incentive to provide a particular quality of care at the lowest cost and has an incentive to overtreat the patient because she benefits with each procedure performed. With capitation payment (fee per patient), the doctor has an incentive to undertreat the patient given that the payment is the same independent of quality. As in the cases above, these payment structures only impede the market process if there is some restriction on alternative payment methods.[7]

## HEALTH CARE AND CONSUMER SHOPPING

Much of the rhetoric about the health care market today is about the soaring cost and the increasing share of GDP of medical care. Regarding the second point, we should not care about the share of GDP going to any particular product market. If consumers and producers are engaging in voluntary exchange and there are relatively few impediments to the types of contracting in which consumers can engage, then the amount of consumption in that product market reflects the fulfillment of consumers' desires, and there is no necessary share that one product market should have of GDP. It is the soaring costs that may reflect that all may not be well in the medical care market. Here I provide an overview of empirical findings related to consumer shopping behavior in both health care and health insurance markets.

In analyzing consumer shopping behavior in the health care market, we must remember that consumers' incentives to shop may be attenuated, depending on the type of insurance coverage a consumer has. Many studies on consumer shopping utilize differences in the behavior of those with a high-deductible health plan (HDHP)[8] and those with traditional health plans. The idea is that high deductibles give consumers "skin in the game." In HDHPs, insurance does not begin to cover the costs of health as soon as traditional insurance plans, which increases the marginal cost a consumer faces each time she seeks medical attention. This should incentivize the consumer, at the margin, to consider shopping before deciding on a particular health care provider. Sinaiko, Mehrotra, and Sood (2016) report findings from a survey of approximately two thousand health care consumers. The consumer demographics were broadly similar, with HDHP consumers having slightly higher incomes, and beliefs and attitudes toward health care were also similar. When consumers were asked whether they would use price information if it were available, there was no statistical difference in the percent of "very likely" and "likely" responses between the consumers, with HDHPs (56 percent) and consumers with traditional health plans (50 percent). When asked about their most recent use of medical care, only 10 percent of traditional health plan consumers and 11 percent of HDHP consumers responded that they had considered other health care professionals, and only 4 percent of HDHP consumers and 3 percent of traditional health plan consumers responded that they considered other health professionals and compared costs of those health professionals.

From these findings, it does not appear that consumers who face higher marginal costs engage in different shopping behavior than those who face lower marginal costs. Several factors could explain these findings. Search cost may be too great. Shopping for price requires calling different providers, asking whether they take a particular insurance, then waiting for the care provider to respond with what the price of the care will be, which depends on the negotiated contract between the insurer and the provider. Also, given that the consumers with HDHPs have higher incomes, the relative search costs for the HDHP group are somewhat higher. However, the fact that only half of each group would use price information if it were available suggests that there is a low level of interest in shopping around.

Brot-Goldberg et al. (2015) compare the behavior of health care consumers from a large employer that switched from a plan with no cost sharing to an HDHP. As would be expected, spending decreased substantially, approximately 12 percent over a two-year period. The authors decompose this spending reduction to measure the effect that comes from price shopping, quantity reduction, and quantity substitution. The price shopping effect is found by comparing whether consumers shifted toward a lower-cost provider, conditional on a given procedure. The total quantity effect is measured as the total change in health care expenditure minus the change in expenditure caused by provider price inflation and consumer shopping. Quantity reduction is just the measured change in the number of procedures, and quantity substitution is the part of the total quantity effect not explained by quantity reduction. They find that 90 percent of the spending reduction in the first year after the switch comes from quantity reduction, with the remainder coming mostly from quantity substitutions. The mix of procedures chosen by consumers suggests that consumers, overall, chose higher-priced providers after switching to the HDHP. The authors also estimate the potential reduction in medical expenditure if those consumers who choose providers with higher than median prices choose providers with median prices.[9] This would reduce expenditure by approximately 20 percent.

These findings do not necessarily suggest that consumers are acting irrationally. The analysis does not account for the quality of the provider, and depending on the correlation between price and quality, reducing expenditures solely through quantity reductions may be optimal. That quantity reduction accounts for almost the entire reduction in expenditure may be a sign that moral hazard was driving previous health care consumption decisions. This analysis also only considers the effect of the decisions of a subset of consumers on provider prices. If the quantity reduction were market wide, we would expect providers to reduce prices. That the mix of providers whom consumers chose became more expensive after the switch does, however, suggest that consumers may not be shopping effectively.

These studies suggest that consumer shopping for medical providers may not be effective in enhancing competition in health care markets. There are factors that are not taken into account: search costs incurred every time a consumer shops for a provider, the quality of the doctor, and the switching cost of choosing a new provider. These are difficulties that economists encounter when analyzing the shopping behavior of consumers in the health care market. We may be able to avoid these difficulties by analyzing how consumers choose prescription drug plans (PDPs).

Several studies show that upon enrollment in Medicare Part D, consumers choose PDPs that are not optimal by not choosing the lowest-cost alternative. Abaluck and Gruber (2011) show that only 12 percent of consumers chose the lowest-cost plan in their state (with a mean savings of 30 percent possible), and if only plans with non-increasing variance in expenditure are analyzed, 70 percent of consumers did not choose the lowest cost plan, conditional on realized expenses. These authors also found that consumers put more weight on plan premiums than on expected out-of-pocket costs.

This may be a somewhat unfair test, since consumers cannot perfectly foresee their prescription usage throughout the year. Heiss et al. (2013) provide benchmarks for various types of consumers: perfect foresight, rational expectations (using past data plus current information to forecast costs), adaptive expectations (assuming next period's cost will equal last period's cost) minimum premium, and random. The authors calculate the optimal plans for individuals using these benchmarks and compare them to consumers' actual choices and find that only compared to randomly choosing a prescription drug plan do more than half of consumers choose a lower cost plan than the benchmark. The percent of consumers choosing a plan with total higher costs than the benchmark varies from 66 percent when compared to the cheapest premium benchmark to 93 percent with the perfect-foresight benchmark.[10] So even when compared to rules-of-thumb behavior, consumers overspend.

Zhou and Zhang (2012) and Patel et al. (2015) find similar results of consumer overspending and non-enrollment in lowest-cost plans, and Ho, Hogan, and Morton (2015) find that consumers' inattention blunts competition to reduce prices among plan providers. Evidence on consumer learning is mixed with Ketcham et al. (2012), finding significant learning, with 81 percent of the sample benefiting from reduced overspending, while Abaluck and Gruber (2016) find little evidence of learning. When provided with information about potential savings, many consumers switch to the lower cost plan (Patel et al. 2009).

There is some evidence that consumers can effectively shop under different payment contracts. Robinson and Brown (2013) examine a change in payment arrangements for knee and hip replacement surgery within the California Public Employee's Retirement System (CalPERS). CalPERS switched to a reference price system in which CalPERS set a maximum amount it would pay for knee and hip replacements. Patients could choose any number of hospitals to receive the knee or hip replacement. If the negotiated price was higher than the reference price, the patients had to cover the difference. Before CalPERS put this payment arrangement into effect, high-cost (priced above the reference price) hospitals served 52 percent of CalPERS knee and hip replacement patients. After the change, high-priced hospitals operated on only 37 percent of CalPERS patients. In addition, those high-priced hospitals reduced their prices by an average of 26 percent after CalPERS switched to reference pricing. This suggests that for certain procedures, increasing the marginal cost the consumer faces may lead to increased shopping. I should note that, in addition to switching to reference pricing, CalPERS also provided patients a list of hospitals that charged less than the reference and were of sufficiently high quality. Without this information, it is unclear how well patients would have been able to shop for the procedure.

This brings up the idea that consumers will be able to shop better for some health care based on the urgency of treatment. If consumers can shop for some services, such as hip and knee replacements, we may expect that prices are less variable. Frost and Newman (2016) analyze a nationally representative data set of health insurance claims and categorize the services into shoppable and non-shoppable.[11] They find that shoppable services have a smaller variation in prices than non-shoppable services. This is crude evidence that shopping does occur in the health care market. The authors also calculate that about 43 percent of health expenditure is on shoppable services and that only 7 percent of out-of-pocket spending is on shoppable services.

This suggests that under current institutional arrangements the range of shopping (whatever the effectiveness) in the health care market is rather limited.

This review of the literature suggests that health care consumers face difficulties in shopping for health care. This could be because there are switching costs involved in changing providers, high search costs due to the Rube-Goldberg nature of the health care system, cognitive limitations that impede proper calculation, or consumers not bearing the full marginal cost of care.[12] While there is some evidence to suggest that health care consumers can effectively shop for health care services, under most institutional arrangements we see today, shopping remains marginal and muted. There are, however, historical examples of various institutions, such as mutual aid societies, and contemporary arrangements, for example, medical tourism, that provide insights into how exchange in the health care market can be structured to allow for beneficial competition. These show that increasing the range of exchange relationships, rather than constraining them, can lead to a more well-functioning market.

## LODGE DOCTORS

Two alternative payment arrangements are for an organization to hire a doctor on contract (practiced by mutual aid societies, unions, and some employers) or for an individual to have a prepaid plan with a particular group practice (Chapin 2015). These arrangements have essentially the same incentive structure for both consumers and doctors. If an organization hires a doctor on a fixed salary contract, the doctor benefits himself the most by treating the patients as minimally as possible, possibly given some minimum quality threshold. Because the patient faces zero (or near zero) marginal cost for seeing the doctor, the patient benefits the most from visiting the doctor more than if he faced the full marginal cost of the visit. This contrasts with the fee for service where the doctor has the incentive to overtreat.

These different types of pay contracts open up new avenues of competition, but the potential impediments to consumer shopping are still inherent in the market. Consumers may not have enough information about the quality of the doctor or fully understand the prepayment contract, and search and switching cost are not mitigated by these contracts, per se. The main benefit of this model is that, even though consumers still do not face the full marginal cost of seeing the doctor, the doctor's incentive is to minimize the amount of care, which reduces the cost of service. This leaves more room for the possibility of price reducing competition, but even if two prepaid group practices open up next to each other, the consumer still faces impediments to shopping effectively. We can still imagine a scenario in which consumers face lower search and switching costs and can counteract the incentive of the doctor to undertreat them. We will examine how mutual aid societies' contracts with doctors solved the problems of search costs and informational asymmetries.

Mutual aid societies (or lodges) hired doctors on a fixed salary basis and generally charged members a $2 annual fee that covered doctor's services but not the cost of medicine (Beito 2000, 111–12). This fee was approximately a day's wages for a laborer and was around the same price as one nighttime house call from a non-lodge doctor. Lodge doctors were elected by members of mutual aid societies on a yearly basis, which meant that every year they had to compete with other doctors to get the lodge contract.

The fixed salary contract paired with the hiring through election provided the main benefit of the structure of lodge doctor contracts. With access provided through membership in the lodge plus the annual fee, the price the consumer faced for seeing the doctor was near certain. Hiring by election acted to publicly reveal the quality of the lodge doctor, so at least the quality of the incumbent doctor was more easily verified than if the consumer were to shop for a doctor on his own. Thus the informational asymmetry between doctor and patient was substantially reduced,[13] and the bidding process reduced the cost of searching for another physician. Because this was a yearly process, the doctors were never far removed from competition. Additionally, lodges also competed for members by having lower mortality rates (119). They would advertise the mortality rate of lodge members compared to the mortality rate of the local population, so there was at least some incentive to hire doctors of at least a minimum sufficient quality.

The social aspect of the mutual aid society encouraged discussion of the lodge doctor among members. Thus, when it was time to elect the lodge doctor, the information obtained by members who sought care during the year and the information gathered by those who talked to those patients during the year is aggregated in the outcome of the vote (Arrow 1951). There are potential drawbacks to this way of choosing the doctor. Someone may start rumors to discourage the rehiring of the current doctor in order to facilitate the hiring of another doctor, or a lodge leader may manipulate the choice of alternatives in order to obtain a particular desired result.

While the hire-by-election system may be imperfect, due to who nominates the doctors and whether the doctor has personal relationships with the lodge members, the question remains as to whether it is better than the relevant alternatives. One alternative is hiring-by-appointment (rather than election). This option is potentially just as prone to manipulation as election, but it does not have the same beneficial information revelation potential. Another alternative is to not hire a lodge doctor and have members purchase medical care individually. While an individual patient could consult his social network for recommendations, having a yearly assessment of one particular doctor by a large group may yield more information. This alternative also abandons the benefit of bargaining as a large group, which lowers the cost to the individual patient.[14]

Due to the fixed salary payment scheme, extra doctor's visits did not impose additional costs on the lodge or its members, and the hiring-by-election system incentivized the doctors to respond in a timely manner to requests from lodge members. Not only did the fixed salary payment encourage members to contact the doctor at the onset of an ailment, leading to quicker treatment, but it also encouraged doctors to practice preventative medicine. Because doctors incurred a personal cost and no extra revenue every time they saw a patient, it was in the doctors' best interest to do his best to cure the patient as quickly as possible.

Both the practice of lodge doctors and prepaid groups were competitive threats to existing solo practice physicians. Local medical societies led the way in the fight against the practice of lodge doctors. Because of the fixed salary payment, lodge members could see the lodge doctor for much less than seeing a non-lodge doctor. This put downward pressure on prices that non-lodge doctors could charge. To give an idea of the reach of the lodge practice, Beito (2000, 111) notes that in Seattle about 20 percent of males over age twenty-one had access to a lodge doctor. Lodge doctors represented a significant competitive threat to doctors outside of mutual aid societies. In the second decade of the twentieth century, local medical societies not only withdrew some lodge doctors' memberships but also led boycotts against the lodge doctors. Revoking a doctor's membership or not admitting the doctor altogether impeded a doctor's ability to obtain malpractice insurance (Chapin 2015, 23). These boycotts took the form of not aiding or consulting with the lodge doctor. This would reduce the ability of a lodge doctor to provide good-quality service, especially for a difficult medical case. Medical society members also colluded to have lodge doctors admitting privileges to local hospitals revoked. This further reduced the lodge doctor's ability to provide a high quality of service to lodge members. State medical societies also charged lodge doctors and doctors in prepaid group practices with various ethics violations, leading to some doctors losing their licenses.

The efforts of local medical societies were successful in part due to the increasing restriction on the supply of doctors and due to the monopolies the state medical societies had over certification of doctors. With a monopoly over granting licenses to doctors, state medical societies could credibly threaten doctors who engaged in the various alternative payment arrangements discussed above. The ever tighter certification requirements on doctors and medical schools led to a much lower rate of doctors in the population, from 164 per 100,000 people in 1910 to 125 per 100,000 in 1930 (Beito 2000,

128). This increased the cost of hiring a lodge doctor and enabled local medical societies to have a tighter grip on the market for doctors' services.

Given the reduction in the membership in mutual aid societies and the fragmentation and price inflation of health care, the type of arrangement provided by the mutual aid societies may be infeasible today. The benefits of mutual aid societies in the health care market were largely dependent on the social nature of those groups. Individuals who were embedded in particular social networks[15] collectively made the choice of doctor. The market for doctor services has changed dramatically since the beginning of the 1900s due, in part, to increased regulation of licensing and increased specialization that comes with increased knowledge. The lodge doctor practice does, however, provide us with general lessons of how payment contracts for health care that enhance consumers' shopping capabilities can be structured. In order to reduce information asymmetries, there must be some way to aggregate data on the doctor. The threat of the consumer exiting the doctor-patient relationship must be credible. This ensures that the doctor is under competitive pressure. Mutual aid societies achieved these goals through yearly elections of the lodge doctor. The doctor also faced cost minimization incentives while still maintaining sufficient quality, which was achieved through the combining of a fixed salary with the yearly election. While there is now less opposition to fixed-fee contracts with the success of companies like Kaiser Permanente and Geiringer Health System, the ease of consumer switching and lower search costs remain pertinent goals. In the next section I discuss the example of medical tourism and how this may provide a way of translating the lessons from mutual aid societies to the present day.

## MEDICAL TOURISM

Medical tourism is the act of traveling away from one's local health care market to receive medical care, both domestic and foreign. The promise of medical tourism is that patients can choose to have a procedure performed at a lower cost hospital while still receiving a sufficient level of quality, and this in turn increases the competitive pressure on higher-cost hospitals to lower prices. Medical tourism can take place internationally and domestically, and while domestic tourism may not have as great a cost-saving function, the easier enforcement of liability laws may serve as a greater incentive to maintain quality. Medical tourism can take place either through insurance policies or independent of insurance. While any medical tourism can serve to increase competitive pressure on high-cost hospitals, I will show that tourism through insurance policies provides the greatest enhancement to consumer shopping. I apply the term medical tourism to both domestic and international travel.

Let's look at the case of the noninsured medical tourist. The procedures that consumers usually purchase are one-offs, so competition may be blunted because the consumer cannot switch providers. Once the procedure is performed and the consumer returns to her home country, the relationship is over. Foreign hospitals can develop a reputation for being high quality, but this can be difficult for the consumer to verify. The consumer can search for quality information from the Joint Commission International (JCI), which rates and accredits hospitals internationally (Labonte 2013). JCI ratings improve a consumer's ability to shop for health care internationally, but it does have limitations. At face value, JCI does give consumers more information about hospital quality, but rather than relying on what hospitals say about their own quality, now the consumer is relying on JCI to be truthful about the quality of the hospitals it rates. In a sense, by suggesting that consumers can take JCI at its word we are just pushing the asymmetric information problem up a level. Because JCI gains revenue for certifying hospitals, not all of its incentives are necessarily aligned with truthful revelation, though reputation concerns (supported through Internet ratings sites or message boards) may strengthen truth-telling incentives. The foreign hospital can also partner with a high-quality institution in America to signal its own high quality, but the correlation between the partner quality and the quality of the foreign hospital remains uncertain because the oversight of the partner institution may be lax (Cohen 2015).

Facilitators also serve as an information aggregator for medical tourism. These middleman organizations help potential patients plan their medical tourism trip, with many offering packages that include flight and hotel reservations, recommending destination hospitals, scheduling the procedure, and even organizing sightseeing excursions while the patient is in the destination country. This dramatically cuts down the transaction costs incurred by the patient, yet many of the same difficulties of the patient performing all these functions still apply. Many medical tourism facilitators gain revenue from referral fees paid by foreign hospitals (Spece 2010). Just like in the case of JCI accreditation, having a facilitator vouch for a provider's quality shifts the principal agent problem from the patient-hospital relationship to the patient-facilitator relationship.

One may suggest that liability enforcement can mitigate many of these issues. With regard to accreditors and facilitators, the body of case law has not found the connection between treatments and these third parties to be close enough to justify finding them liable for postoperative complications or malpractice (Cohen 2015).[16] Because the consumer's relationship with the foreign hospital ends upon the consumer's return to her home country, the foreign hospital is not responsible for any complications that may arise from the procedure. While bringing a malpractice lawsuit against a foreign hospital could mitigate incentives to skimp on care quality, in reality, there are many logistical obstacles of, for example, a US citizen bringing a lawsuit against a Thai provider (Cohen 2015). These liability and malpractice issues are either reduced or completely absent when medical tourism occurs within the domestic market. So while medical tourism independent of insurers can provide competitive pressure on high-cost providers and enhance the effectiveness of consumer shopping, difficulties remain that may be resolved by medical tourism through insurers.

Medical tourism facilitated by health insurers holds the possibility of overcoming some of the difficulties involved with individuals engaging in tourism on their own. We must first note that for insured medical tourism to effectively aid in consumer search, consumers must be able to shop effectively for those insurance policies. This comes with all the caveats mentioned in above in the section "Health Care and Consumer Shopping." In the case of insured medical tourism, health insurers, like the various accrediting agencies, can act as data aggregators for the price and quality of foreign hospitals, but in this case insurers have an advantage because they will have the ability to constantly monitor the quality of these hospitals. This can occur through the use of the data health insurers have on their customers. If the insurer has customers who suddenly show signs of increasing morbidity or mortality after visiting a particular destination hospital, the insurer is in a position to either stop sending patients to that facility or to aid that facility in correcting any failings. With the accrediting agencies, data on quality may be updated every few years (at most, annually). The insurer's role as data aggregator reduces any search cost or informational asymmetry that may exist. This allows consumers to shop much more effectively. The prices of medical tourism for both insured and uninsured patients are generally negotiated as a fixed fee and are known to the patient before undergoing the procedure (Herrick 2007).

Even though insurers cannot generally be held liable for medical malpractice, insured medical tourism has an advantage over uninsured in that the insurer has the incentive to verify and enforce quality standards of destination hospitals. This is because the insurer bears the cost of procedures that result from postoperative complications upon the patient's return home. This is not the case in uninsured medical tourism, in which accreditors and facilitators bear no burden of the cost of complications that arise upon the patient's return home.

The role of the insurer is to essentially act as a well-informed consumer. The same attributes for successful consumer shopping that characterized the practice of lodge doctors are also potentially available to insurers. The doctor does not have the incentive to overtreat due to the fixed fee transaction. As with lodge doctors, this reduces the doctor's incentive (at the margin) to prescribe unnecessary procedures and incentivizes the doctor to reduce cost. The quality of care can be sustained by the insurer channeling customers only to high-quality destination hospitals and threatening to exit from the relationship if quality becomes too low. The credibility of threatening exit from these relationships also increases with the available alternatives, and medical tourism is nothing if not a way of increasing the number of available alternatives.

Because the insurer has the data on diagnosis, treatment, and outcome for all of its customers, the insurer can determine the quality of the doctors that the customers choose. This is one of the main characteristics that allow the medical tourism model to scale. Whereas the lodge doctor model relied on relatively tight social networks to ascertain quality, today's insurers can determine quality from the data they obtain as routine business procedure. The insurer has the incentive to maintain relationships with high-quality hospitals because the insurer bears the cost of postoperative complications when the patient returns home. This expansion of the number of relevant substitutes also puts downward pressure on prices of the local high-priced facilities. So long as the cost savings to consumers are sufficiently high, they will participate in the practice of medical tourism. But if medical tourism holds such promise, we must ask why we see so little of it.

There are several impediments to insurers offering these types of services.[17] Federal and state regulations on geographic coverage and accessibility prevent insurers from selling insurance policies based solely on medical tourism. For HMOs these laws require that medically necessary services be available twenty-four hours a day and seven days a week. They also require that services "within the area served by the health maintenance organization be available and accessible to each of its members . . . and in a manner which assures continuity" (Cohen 2015, 142). The assurance of continuity seems to forestall the ability of an HMO to provide medical tourism coverage policies. State regulations on the distance that defines accessibility for preferred provider organizations similarly prevent PPOs from offering stand-alone medical tourism policies.

The main impediments to selling insurance with medical tourism coverage are laws limiting the financial incentives insurers can offer to or the financial disincentives insurers can impose upon their customers. By limiting the deductible, co-pay, or coinsurance difference between a preferred and non-preferred provider (commonly between 20 and 25 percent), these regulations impede the main promise of medical tourism of substantial savings reaped through providing competition with hospitals that have dramatically lower costs.[18]

## CONCLUSION

When describing perceived market imperfections, many researchers lament how these are inherent in the market being studied before calling for one regulation or another. A more fruitful line of inquiry sees market imperfections and asks what restrictions on the market process are hindering entrepreneurs from competing away available profits from correcting these imperfections. If these are truly market imperfections, then the researcher can identify (readily or with some imagination) a restriction on the market process. If the researcher cannot identify a restriction on the market process, then perhaps that is an inherent feature of the market that cannot be legislated away.

As seen in the section on lodge doctors, consumers were able to enter into many types of contracts with medical providers, whether it was as an individual paying for a prepaid plan or as a group of individuals negotiating their own contract with a provider. By allowing a diversity of modes of exchange, individuals were able to experiment with different types of contracts. I showed how these types of arrangements resulted in contracts that improved quality and lowered costs, at the margin. Once the type of person who could be hired as a doctor was restricted and the types of contracts patients and doctors could enter into was decreased, the issues of information asymmetry, such as the ascertaining of quality, predictably emerged.

As of today, self-insured employers have provided most of the insured medical tourism, mainly due to their exemptions through ERISA.[19] So in the space that is less regulated we see experimentation with different types of contracting in the medical care market. As mentioned, one of the reasons there is less medical tourism in the insured space is because of the restrictions on contracting that current regulations impose on health care consumers. As with the practice of lodge doctors, if insurers were allowed more leeway in the types of contracts they can offer to their consumers, we should expect to see a multiplicity of contracts to serve the different ends of a heterogeneous consumer population.

As presented in Cohen (2015), much of the discussion about insured medical tourism is in terms of its potential while much of the discussion about non-insured medical tourism is in terms of current practice. Again, the reason is due to the restrictions on insurers to offer contracts, which a subset of the health care market currently seeks. Even in this noninsured context, institutions emerged to facilitate exchange. The experimentation indicative of the market process is absent due to the restrictions on exchange. Where we see this experimentation, we also see institutions arising to mitigate the issues of information asymmetry, for example, accreditors used by noninsured medical tourists.

What this chapter highlights is that where exchange faces fewer restrictions, more types of exchange occur in the marketplace. Not only do more types of exchange occur, but these types of exchange solve problems that are considered by many to be endemic to a particular market; in this case, asymmetric information in the health care market. Rather than seeing market failures as a situation in which exchange should be restricted, using the lens of the market process allows the researcher to see how expanding the possibilities of exchange enables alert entrepreneurs to mitigate the problems that characterize situations of market failure.

## NOTES

The views expressed in this chapter are the views of the author and do not represent the position of the Agency for Healthcare Research and Quality or any department or division of the US government.

1. There is some controversy over Mises's use of "consumer sovereignty" and whether it is meant as just a metaphor, which is ironic, since Mises points to the convention of calling successful businessmen kings and dukes as a harmful metaphor. Rothbard ([1962] 2009, 561), among others, notes that the term is unsuitable for a description of a true market economy, as sovereign implies some sort of power backed by force. The reference to monopoly prices as an "infringement on the sway of consumers" also neglects the consumer role of entrepreneurs to consume/use their resources as they see fit (Mises [1949] 2007). I will view this term as metaphorical and focus on the role of consumer behavior in the market process.

2. This is a general issue in the market for expert services. See Dulleck and Kerschbamer (2006) for an extensive review.

3. These limitations are potentially due to making decisions in states of heightened emotions and drastic circumstances, such as life-and-death situations associated with medical conditions.

4. See Bhargava et al. (2015) and Johnson et al. (2013) for experimental evidence that consumers have trouble distinguishing objectively better health insurance plans from strictly dominated ones.

5. Just run an Internet search for price transparency laws to see how state governments have handled the issue of search cost.

6. Examples of doctors being in charge of financing medical care include prepaid plans that were popular in the early 1900s and some integrated care firms of today (Chapin 2015, 18–20).

7. I address this topic below in the discussion of the lodge doctor.

8. $1,250 for individual and $2,500 for family. See Internal Revenue Service, High-Deductible Health Plan Definition for 2014. http://www.irs.gov/pub/irs-drop/rp-13-25.pdf.

9. This obviously does not control for increases in prices that would occur for those median-priced doctors when they see an increase in demand for their services, but it also does not control for the reduction in the prices of those providers with higher-than-median prices.

10. Average overspending relative to benchmark ranges from $115 (lowest premium) to $315 (perfect foresight).

11. Shoppable services are both the highest spending and able to be scheduled in advance. This is a crude measure, and it is unclear as to why the actual price would make it more or less shoppable.

12. See Bhargava et al. (2015) and Johnson et al. (2013) for experimental evidence that consumers have trouble distinguishing objectively better health insurance plans from strictly dominated ones.

13. Medical society ethics enforcement provides only a roundabout way of regulating quality and the feedback is generally only sensitive to extreme cases of malfeasance.

14. By revealed preference, those who joined the mutual aid society thought that buying doctors' services on the open market was an inferior alternative. We should keep in mind that while the price mechanism is a great allocator of resources, it is only an imperfect information conduit. As noted in Hayek (1945), the consumer does not necessarily know why the price is what it is. It is just a datum the consumer uses to make a choice. In the world of Yelp and Trip Advisor, it should not surprise us that the price does not reveal all the information a consumer may desire. The mutual aid society is an institution that arose, at least in part, to aid consumers in their health care consumption choices.

15. See Chalupnicek and Dvorak (2009) for a discussion of British friendly societies and social capital.

16. While I have not seen it discussed in the literature, it is unclear why facilitators cannot credibly offer a money-back guarantee or voluntarily choose a contract that transfers liability from the foreign provider to the facilitator. It may be that the terms of these types of contracts are unobservable or hard to verify, but this remains an underexplored topic with regard to medical tourism.

17. All these examples are discussed in Cohen (2015, 141–44).

18. Because many policies provided by self-insured employers are exempt from state insurance laws, we see greater uptake of policies augmented by medical tourism.

19. See Cohen (2015) for a brief discussion of ERISA. Also see http://www.amednews.com/article/20121029/business/310299966/4/ for examples of self-insured employers sponsoring medical tourism.

## REFERENCES

Abaluck, Jason, and Jonathan Gruber. 2011. "Choice Inconsistencies among the Elderly: Evidence from Plan Choice in the Medicare Part D Program." *American Economic Review* 101 (4): 1180–210.

———. 2016. "Evolving Choice Inconsistencies in Choice of Prescription Drug Insurance." *American Economic Review* 106 (8): 2145–84.

Arrow, Kenneth. 1951. *Social Choice and Individual Values*. New Haven, CT: Yale University Press.

———. 1963. "Uncertainty and the Welfare Economics of Medical Care." *American Economic Review* 53 (5): 941–73.

Beito, David T. 2000. *From Mutual Aid to the Welfare State*. Chapel Hill: University of North Carolina Press.

Bhargava, Saurabhg, George Loewenstein, and Justin Sydnor. 2015. "Do Individuals Make Sensible Health Insurance Decisions? Evidence from a Menu with Dominated Options." NBER Working Paper No. 21160.

Brot-Goldberg, Zarek C., Amitabh Chandra, Benjamin R. Handel, and Jonathan T. Kolstad. 2015. "What Does a Deductible Do? The Impact of Cost-Sharing on Health Care Prices, Quantities, and Spending Dynamics." NBER Working Paper No. 21632.

Chalupnicek, Pavel, and Luka Dvorak. 2009. "Health Insurance before the Welfare State." *Independent Review* 13 (3): 367–87.

Chapin, Christy Ford. 2015. *Ensuring America's Health: The Public Creation of the Corporate Health Care System.* Cambridge: Cambridge University Press.

Cohen, I. Glenn. 2015. *Patients with Passports: Medical Tourism, Law, and Ethics.* Oxford: Oxford University Press.

Dulleck, Uwe, and Rudolf Kerschbamer. 2006. "On Doctors, Mechanics, and Computer Specialists: The Economics of Credence Goods." *Journal of Economic Literature* 44 (1): 5–42.

Frost, Amanda, and David Newman. 2016. "Spending on Shoppable Services in Health Care." Issue Brief 11, Health Care Cost Institute.

Hayek, Friedrich A. 1945. "Use of Knowledge in Society." *American Economic Review* 35 (4): 519–30.

———. 1948. "The Meaning of Competition." In *Individualism and Economic Order.* Chicago: University of Chicago Press.

Heiss, Florian, Adam Leive, Daniel McFadden, and Joachim Winter. 2013. "Plan Selection in Medicare Part D: Evidence from Administrative Data." *Journal of Health Economics* 32 (6): 1325–44.

Herrick, Devon M. 2007. "Medical Tourism: Global Competition in Health Care." NCPA Policy Report No. 304.

Ho, Kate, Joseph Hogan, and Fiona Scott Morton. 2015. "The Impact of Consumer Inattention on Insurer Pricing in the Medicare Part D Program." NBER Working Paper No. 21028.

Johnson, Eric J., Ran Hassin, Tom Baker, Allison T. Bajger, and Galen Treuer. 2013. "Can Consumers Make Affordable Care Affordable? The Value of Choice Architecture." *PLOS ONE* 8 (12). doi:10.1371/journal.pone.0081521.

Ketcham, Jonathan D., Claudio Lucarelli, Eugenio J. Miravete, and M. Christopher Roebuck. 2012. "Sinking, Swimming, or Learning to Swim in Medicare Part D." *American Economic Review* 102 (6): 2639–73.

Kirzner, Israel M. 1973. *Competition and Entrepreneurship.* Chicago: University of Chicago Press.

———. 1997. "Entrepreneurial Discovery and the Competitive Market Process: An Austrian Approach." *Journal of Economic Literature* 35 (1): 60–85.

Labonte, Ronald. 2013. "Overview: Medical Tourism Today: What, Who, Why and Where?" In *Travelling Well: Essays in Medical Tourism,* edited by Ronald Labonte, Vivien Runnels, Corinne Packer, and Raywat Deonandan. Ottawa: Institute of Population Health, University of Ottawa.

Mises, Ludwig von. [1949] 2007. *Human Action: A Treatise on Economics,* vol. 2. Indianapolis: Liberty Fund.

Patel, Rajul, Helene Lipton, Timothy Cutler, Amanda Smith, Shirley Tsunoda, and Marilyn Stebbins. 2009. "Cost Minimization of Medicare Part D Prescription Drug Plan Expenditures." *American Journal of Managed Care* 15 (8): 545–53.

*Jerrod Anderson*

Patel, Rajul, Mark Walberg, Yvonne Mai, Nataliya McElroy, Anil Mallya, Kim Aesun, Justin Seo, and Joseph Woelfel. 2015. "Medicare Part D Optimization: Potential Out-of-Pocket Savings through Plan Reexamination." *American Journal of Pharmacy Benefits* 7 (2): 84–91.

Robinson, James C., and Timothy T. Brown. 2013. "Increases in Consumer Cost Sharing Redirect Patient Volumes and Reduce Hospital Prices for Orthopedic Surgery." *Health Affairs* 32 (8): 1392–97.

Rothbard, Murray N. [1962] 2009. *Man, Economy, and State.* Auburn, AL: Ludwig von Mises Institute.

Sinaiko, Anna D., Ateev Mehrotra, and Neeraj Sood. 2016. "Cost-Sharing Obligations, High-Deductible Health Plan Growth, and Shopping for Health Care." *Jama Internal Medicine* 176 (3): 395–97.

Spece, Roy G. 2010. "Medical Tourism: Protecting Patients from Conflicts of Interest in Broker's Fees Paid by Foreign Providers." *Journal of Health and Biomedical Law* 6 (1): 1–36.

Zhou, Chao, and Yuting Zhang. 2012. "The Vast Majority of Medicare Part D Beneficiaries Still Don't Choose the Cheapest Plans that Meet their Medication Needs." *Health Affairs* 31 (10): 2259–65.

*Chapter 11*

# This Is Your Entrepreneurial Alertness on Drugs

## *Prohibition and the Market Process*

### Audrey Redford

Markets for prohibited goods exist, despite extensive efforts to suppress them. The intention of prohibitionist policies is to eliminate the market for a particular good(s). In order to accomplish this goal, laws and their enforcement are usually directed at the supply side, the production and distribution, of these illegal goods. When economists model the markets of illegal goods, prohibition is taken into account not through the elimination of supply (because we know that the supply of illegal goods, like drugs, still exists). Instead, economists frequently model prohibition as a tax or as an additional cost of doing business (Thornton 1991). This additional cost of doing business includes the costs required to evade law enforcement and consideration of the cost and likelihood of punishment (Thornton 1991; Becker, Murphy, and Grossman 2006). However, understanding how entrepreneurs respond and try to cope with prohibition policies is restricted under this framework. Market process theory, as it focuses on entrepreneurial action in the pursuit of profit, couples nicely with these insights to provide a more complete picture.

In order to remain in the market, prohibition entrepreneurs have the incentive to figure out ways of minimizing these costs of doing illegal business, as well as establishing and maintaining institutions that promote cooperation. Beyond these costs, entrepreneurs and firms within illegal markets are still concerned with increasing their profitability. How do these new profit opportunities emerge, and how do illegal firms innovate? Furthermore, how do these additional costs associated with doing illegal business shape the ability and the context within which these prohibition entrepreneurs come upon and implement new innovations?

In order to tease out what market process theory can tell us about markets for prohibited goods, we must unpack what "prohibition" means in practice. A key, but by no means exclusive, component of prohibition is that formal (legal) property rights are not afforded to prohibited goods and services. Established, observable, and enforceable property rights are necessary for economic calculation (Mises [1949] 2007) and the market process (Kirzner 1992, 2000). One of the many roles assumed by governments is the formal provision of property rights. However, other methods of informal property rights protection exist. There is an extensive literature on the informal provision of property rights through nongovernmental and private governance (see "Drug Prohibition—a Market (?) without Formal Rules" below). These provisions can and do exist in the absence of, as supplements to, and as alternatives to formal property rights provided by the government. Informal governance is frequently present within illegal markets. This helps to explain why we observe order in the exchange of illegal goods, despite the absence of formal rules.

Another key feature of prohibition is that government-sanctioned law enforcement actively seeks to arrest and punish individuals involved in the production, distribution, and trade of prohibited goods and services. This feature not only raises the cost to individuals participating in illegal markets, but it also undermines the informal institutional structures that exist in the absence of formal protection. If prohibition simply meant that individuals involved in activities deemed illegal were not privy to protection, resources, and adjudication provided by the government's property rights system, then the differences between legal and illegal markets could be explained by the differences in the formal and informal sets of rules that govern each, respectively. Therefore, in order to fully explain the differences in entrepreneurial options and outcomes between legal and illegal markets, the government's role in significantly raising the costs of participating in illegal markets must be taken into consideration. These costs are created and raised when the actors working within illegal markets are not extended formal property rights and when prohibition policies and law enforcement initiatives are utilized by the government as tools to undermine the informal governing institutions.

This chapter suggests that because illegal goods are forced outside of the traditional property rights–based institutional arrangement and are faced with continuing efforts on the part of the government and law enforcement to stifle and eliminate these illegal markets, entrepreneurial efforts within illegal markets will be channeled toward protective innovations that allow these entrepreneurs to remain in business. Throughout this chapter, I refer to entrepreneurs engaging in these activities that create or enforce protection of informal property rights as "protective entrepreneurs." In an effort to evade law enforcement and maintain governance in the face of government intervention, both of which are necessary in order to remain in business, illegal entrepreneurs must trade off against productive entrepreneurial endeavors when they act as protective entrepreneurs. In order to describe these ideas more clearly, I will use the market for illegal drugs as an example of a market for a prohibited good.

By using market process theory and digging deeper into the interaction between the institutional framework and the market for illegal drugs, this chapter contributes several extensions to the broader prohibition literature. Past literature, as referenced in the opening paragraphs, has offered a limited distinction between legal markets and the markets for prohibited goods, in the form of the "cost of doing illegal business." This chapter extends our understanding of the cost of doing illegal business by differentiating between the costs of creating an informal governance structure and the costs of constantly adapting that structure to endure changes in the enforcement of prohibition. The argument in the pages that follow also emphasizes how these costs directly impact not only the incentives of illegal entrepreneurs, but also the channels within which they focus their entrepreneurial efforts. Finally, this chapter advances the literature by emphasizing how prohibition policies shape specialization opportunities for illegal entrepreneurs. These subtle, but crucial, distinctions create considerable leverage for explaining the divergence in qualities of legal and illegal markets, such as the use of violence and product safety.

In this chapter, the first section will discuss the literature on the impact of rules (formal and informal) on entrepreneurship and the market process. Next, using illegal drug markets as an illustrative example, I will show that thriving markets for prohibited goods exist and describe some examples of the entrepreneurial innovations within these illegal markets. In the third section I will outline problems that we see with illegal markets and differentiate which problems are associated with the lack of formal rights versus the presence of law enforcement. The final section will briefly explain how insights from illegal markets can inform the discussion of other markets without formal rules, specifically developing economies, and offer conclusions.

## FORMAL VS. INFORMAL RULES AND THE MARKET PROCESS

Market process theory and the study of entrepreneurial activity in response to economic and institutional conditions can enhance our understanding of how markets evolve. Israel Kirzner, in "The Market: Its Structure and Operation," rather simply defines the market process as "what goes on when potential buyers and potential sellers are in mutual contact" (2011, 24). At first glance, this seems applicable to almost any circumstance. Kirzner is clear in other places, however, that what can be considered a market process is far more attenuated. Elsewhere, Kirzner states, "We have emphasized the importance of entrepreneurial entry as the driving force in the market process. But, more generally, this process depends on individual freedom to pursue perceived opportunities, within the limits of property rights, without arbitrary obstacles being placed in one's path" (1992, 53). Property rights, as it turns out, are crucial to the market process. In "The Limits of the Market: The Real and Imagined," Kirzner expands this emphasis on property rights when he states, "[The] limits on the market are imposed by its institutional prerequisites. Without these institutional prerequisites—primarily, private property rights and freedom and enforceability of contract—the market cannot operate" (2000, 83).

Formal property rights, upheld by the government, are frequently taken as a starting point for the market process to function. As Mises notes in *Human Action*, "The state creates and preserves the environment in which the market economy can safely operate" (Mises [1949] 2007, 257). In describing Kirzner's approach to analyzing the market process, Boettke writes, "The economist first assumes the moral norms, ethical rules, and the legal institutions that define and enforce private property and ensure the freedom of contract are in place; he then examines the processes of exchange and production that emerge within the market economy that exhibit the strong tendency to realize all the gains from trade and technological innovation" (2014, 235). However, it is unclear from this literature if formal property rights are necessary or just sufficient for the market process to take place.

Yoram Barzel ([1989] 1997) provides us with an important distinction between *economic (property) rights* and *legal (property) rights* in the analysis of property rights. *Economic rights* refer to "the individual's ability, in expected terms, to consume the good (or the services of the asset) directly or to consume it indirectly through exchange" ([1989] 1997, 3). It is important to note that there is nothing given about the protection of economic rights in this definition. *Legal rights*, by contrast, "are the rights recognized and enforced, in part, by the government" (Barzel [1989] 1997, 4). Barzel continues by saying, "These [legal] rights, as a rule, enhance economic rights, but the former are neither necessary nor sufficient for the existence of the latter" (4). The literature on the role and success of private governance suggests that other options beyond legal protection are available for the enforcement of property rights.

There is a significant literature on the role of informal institutions and private governance in overcoming collective action problems as well as establishing, maintaining, and enforcing property rights in the absence of the state (see Benson 1989, 1990; Ostrom 1990; Greif 1993; Greif, Milgrom, and Weingast 1994; Dixit 2009; Leeson 2014; Stringham 2015). In many of these situations, government has been unsuccessful in enforcing property rights to the satisfaction of market participants and these participants establish alternative rules to facilitate exchange and solve problems. Informal governance structures apply a variety of methods, such as social norms, contractual agreements, and written constitutions, to achieve order such that trade and cooperation can take place. There is evidence, in fact, that informal institutions are what really matter for securing private property. Williamson and Kerekes (2011) find that after controlling for informal institutions, formal institutions have no impact on securing property. In their introduction, they state, "Our paper challenges conventional beliefs that formal institutions are the driving force establishing property rights. Instead, we contend that informal mechanisms are crucially important but are often underestimated . . . while the benefits of codification are typically overstated" (2011, 538–39). Given such evidence, it is unclear why activity within markets whose property rights are enforced by exclusively informal mechanisms would be considered any less of a market process that those markets whose disciplinary mechanisms are both formally codified and informal.

Markets for illegal goods present an additional puzzle for the application of market process theory. In describing prohibition in *Man, Economy, and State*, Rothbard states, "In many cases of product prohibition, of course, inevitable pressure develops . . . for the re-establishment of the market illegally, i.e., a 'black market.' A black market is always in difficulties because of its illegality" ([1962] 2009, 901). Consequently, as Boettke and Coyne (2004), in summarizing Rothbard's discussion of prohibition and property rights under socialism, note, "Individuals within this prohibition environment still pursue their plans, but they are forced to do so in a manner that is different from what would take place in an unhampered market environment" (83). "Illegal underground markets arise," as Benson and Baden (1985) describe, "when the institutional structure precludes private owners from allocating their resources in a competitive market" (393). It is an empirical reality that markets (or at least things that look an awful lot like markets) for illegal goods exist despite policies enacted to eradicate them. In these environments, as Boettke, Coyne, and Leeson (2004) state, "there is a strong disconnect between *de jure* rules and *de facto* realities" (74). They argue further that "[d]ue to the fact that the *de facto* realities were not recognized by the legal and political system, market participants [were] forced to undertake transactions outside the formal legal system" (2004, 75).

The literature on extralegal governance suggests that not only do markets for illegal goods not shut down in the face of prohibition, but that governance is actually sought out in order to better facilitate trade, even among criminals (see Leeson 2009, 2014; Skarbek 2011, 2014). Similar to legal markets with insufficient formal property rights protection, informal institutional entrepreneurs step in to create a system of governance to establish and maintain order. This is the role that organized crime syndicates, drug trafficking organizations, drug gangs, and prison gangs play within the illegal goods trade when they establish and protect property rights (Gambetta 1993, Fiorentini and Peltzman 1995, Skaperdas 2001, Sobel and Osoba 2009, Leeson and Skarbek 2010). Anderson (1995, 33–34) explains that when organized crime groups engage in illegal activity, they act like mafias, and she describes one of the key characteristics of mafias as "performing governmental functions—law enforcement and criminal justice—in that sphere were the legal judicial system refuses to exercise power."

Illegal governance structures use a variety of methods to maintain order. David Skarbek, in his book, *The Social Order of the Underworld: How Prison Gangs Govern the American Penal System*, provides a detailed account of how prison gangs provide a governance structure such that the trade of contraband, including illicit drugs, can take place even in an environment where such activity is strictly forbidden. Gangs facilitate trade by establishing and protecting private property rights to contraband. They also establish order to incentivize cooperation, thus allowing prisoners to trade and evade detection by prison guards. In similar fashion to Leeson (2007a, 2007b, 2009), Skarbek presents a "hard case" for informal governance by showing how individuals who have previously proven that they have little regard for formal rules (as they have been incarcerated for breaking the law), are confined to small proximities living among enemies, and are constantly under the supervision of law enforcement are able to find a set of rules by which they can live in order to facilitate cooperation and commerce. Additionally, Leeson and Skarbek (2010) and Skarbek (2011) emphasize how criminal organizations utilize constitutions because they generate information and methods of punishment that can align private behavior with group incentives. Leeson and Rogers (2012) highlight the importance of organizational structure for illegal governance in aligning incentives based on the contestability of the industry. Skarbek (2012) describes how norms and the creation of organizations or groups can both be used to establish governance over prison populations. As the size and heterogeneity of the population increases, norms are less desirable and the role of organizations increases. These smaller groups are better able to transmit information, delineate insiders and outsiders, and enforce rules among one another.

Governance is not the only hurdle for the application of market process theory in illegal markets. Unlike in legal markets governed by informal institutions, the government is actively enforcing laws and policies that undermine the property rights of illegal goods in prohibition markets. In legal markets, as Barzel ([1989] 1997) describes it, "Assuming that ownership is not attenuated, the legal owners of commodities are free to exercise their rights over their commodities in any (legal) way they choose" (92). This is not the case when the good in question is illegal. Thus, problems of governance within illegal markets arise when the informal rules are insufficient in protecting property rights against the government. Individuals working within these markets must, therefore, participate in entrepreneurial innovations that make them more successful in evading law enforcement, protecting their informal rights against law enforcement, and reestablishing order after the government has undermined the governance structure. Put differently, in the absence of legal rights, entrepreneurs will have to alter the methods by which they informally provide protection for the economic rights, to use Barzel's term, of individuals involved in illegal markets. It is the task of this chapter to use market process theory to analyze how illegal entrepreneurs cope with law enforcement that seeks to undermine their rights.

Kirzner, as documented above, makes it clear, in no uncertain terms, that the institutional framework of the market must be taken as given. Furthermore, he is cautious about social scientists explaining the emergence of the framework within which the market process takes place. He states, "It follows that those institutions cannot be created by the market itself. The institutions upon which the market must depend must have been created or have evolved through processes different from those spontaneous coordinative processes which we have seen to constitute the essence of the market's operation" (Kirzner 2000, 83). Boettke (2014) reemphasizes Kirzner's apprehension toward the application of market process theory to explain the evolution of institutional frameworks. Boettke writes, "But [Kirzner] raises a caution to those who indiscriminately want to stretch spontaneous order explanations from the market within a given institutional framework to the explanation of that evolution of that framework itself" (2014, 241). Boettke, commenting on Kirzner's explanation of language as a spontaneous order, states that "Kirzner is making the very sensible point that in social evolution, without recourse to the mechanisms provided by property rights, freely adjusting prices, and the lure of profit and the discipline of loss, all we can say is that practices that evolve serve as focal points of action" (2014, 241).

Barzel ([1989] 1997), too, approaches the emergence of property rights with caution. He states, "It might be tempting to trace the pattern of currently existing property rights holding to its point of origin to determine how and why it came out, yet such an effort would be futile. The ability to consume commodities, including those necessary to sustain life, implies the possession of rights over them. Once this is understood, it becomes clear that one cannot expect to discover any evidence of a pre-property rights state, since it is not possible to endow a pre-property rights state of affairs with meaning" (85). A few sentences later, he continues, "Once some rights are already in existence, it is possible to explore their evolution with respect to changes in economic conditions and legal constraints" (Barzel [1989] 1997, 85). This is why he is very clear in differentiating economic rights from legal rights.

It is clear from this discussion that the institutional framework is of utmost importance in explaining how market outcomes manifest. Boettke also states that "[w]hile the entrepreneurial element of human action is ever present, the entrepreneurial market process and the efficiency properties it exhibits are institutionally contingent. Against the appropriate institutional backdrop, entrepreneurial action will tend to realize the gains from trade and the gains from innovation. Absent that framework, however, entrepreneurial action can run in a variety of directions, and without any guarantee of social desirability" (2014, 243).

We can reconcile Kirzner's warning against using market process theory as a method to explain the emergence of property rights by saying that the informal institutional entrepreneurs working within illegal markets take the economic property rights of illegal goods as given (where the government does not). However, they have the additional task of acting as protective entrepreneurs in *how* they choose to enforce and protect those rights. Thus market process theory can help to explain how these entrepreneurs alter their methods of property rights protection and tactics of law enforcement evasion in response to changes in economic conditions as well as changes in law enforcement.

In the sections that follow, I will use the market for illegal drugs as a test case for this application. To do so, I will provide examples of changes in evasion and protection tactics within illegal drug markets in response to changes in drug policy to illustrate how these entrepreneurs adapt. I will then explain how government enforcement of such drug policies exacerbates negative outcomes and violence associated with the drug war by limiting the number of illegal drug market participants which decreases specialization, limits entrepreneurial alertness to other methods of protection, and reinforces the criminal presence and violence associated with drug markets.

## DRUG PROHIBITION—A MARKET (?) WITHOUT FORMAL RULES

Despite the intentions of policy makers over the past century and a half, the market for illegal drugs is alive and thriving. Between 2000 and 2010, US drug users are estimated to have spent roughly $100 billion annually on heroin, cocaine, marijuana, and methamphetamine (RAND Corporation 2014, 2). This is more than double the estimated annual expenditure, roughly $41.3 billion (as calculated by Miron and Waldock (2010)), of US state and federal governments on prohibition enforcement. Illegal drug markets manage to thrive despite the lack of formal property rights afforded to them and in direct opposition to formal law enforcement tactics aimed at shutting them down. The lack of formal rights and law enforcement efforts, however, significantly impacts the trajectory and profitable opportunities available in these markets. Entrepreneurs working within these markets must operate within the constraints they face due to law enforcement and must find new ways to innovate in order to remain profitable.

As a result of these constraints, many of the entrepreneurial discoveries that are profitable in illegal drugs markets are centered around how to remain in business without being caught by the police. These discoveries are innovative in the sense that entrepreneurs have found new ways to decrease the risk of capture, but they are not innovative in the same product-improving sense that is associated with legal goods, as they are often associated with socially undesirable outcomes. Innovations in illegal markets are frequently unintended by policy makers and are often only profitable because of the presence of law enforcement. Altering drug-trafficking routes, involving women and children in drug smuggling, recruiting children to sell drugs, increasing the potency of drugs, and developing designer drugs are all innovations geared toward increasing profitability by lowering the risk of detection.

Since the first federal law targeted at drug smuggling was enacted in 1914 (Redford and Powell 2016), the US government has been involved in a variety of drug interdiction operations. Much in the same way a legal shipping company would find the cheapest route by which to ship cargo from one location to another such that it arrives to its final destination with as little damage as possible, illegal drug trafficking organizations (DTOs) do the same. Although they do not pay tariffs or a variety of other costs that are involved with legally shipping a good from one country to another, DTOs incur significant costs to avoid detection, evade capture, and ensure that no one steals the product at any step along the distribution chain. Kostelnik and Skarbek (2013) emphasize that this requires several layers of governance and an intricate reward and punishment system to elicit cooperation. Additional problems and costs can arise for these DTOs, however, when law enforcement discovers a drug trafficking route. In his chapter in *Ending the Drug Wars: Report of the LSE Expert Group on the Economics of Drug Policy*, Peter Reuter utilizes the "balloon effect" metaphor to describe how interdiction along one drug smuggling route can redirect trafficking activity to a different drug smuggling route (2014, 33). Reuter (2014, 40) notes that while the data that is necessary to test his hypothesis effectively does not exist, it is a helpful, albeit incomplete, metaphor that captures the incentives that smugglers face—"Smugglers, like other profit-making enterprises, have incentives to respond to changes in costs."

Daniel Mejia and Pascual Restrepo (2014), in their chapter of the same LSE Expert Group volume, also provide evidence of entrepreneurial responses to interdiction operations on the part of individuals involved in DTOs. They comment that "[a]ll in all, the recent Latin American experience shows that when a country is (locally) successful in the fight against drug production and trafficking—which is the exception rather than the rule—DTOs are displaced to other countries where they find more favourable environments to run their operations. The displacement of drug trafficking activities to other countries after successful interdiction strategies are implemented in one country leads to cycles of violence and instability in the receiving countries" (2014, 29). Since evasion is of utmost importance to the business of drug trafficking, the use of routes known to law enforcement poses significant costs and risks. Entrepreneurs working within these DTOs respond to the discovery of a trafficking route by law enforcement by no longer using that route and seeking out alternative routes. DTOs incur significant costs in rerouting drug smuggling operations, as it frequently requires them to do business with new people and cross terrain with which they are less familiar. Despite these costs of transition, these new locations are still preferred and are more profitable than attempting to do business along a trafficking route that is known to law enforcement, as doing so would result in capture and a significant cost to continuing (if not a shutdown of) business.

In addition to altering routes of drug smuggling, interdiction efforts also frequently change the methods by which the drug is transported (especially if alternative routes are not available). Entrepreneurs working within DTOs must be alert to ways of smuggling drugs without law enforcement detection, and sometimes this includes very creative and clever methods. Although by definition all reports by law enforcement and the media regarding seizures of smuggled drugs are unsuccessful attempts, they do provide us with evidence that trafficking entrepreneurs are testing out different methods to avoid detection. In one such seizure, in January 2016, US Customs and Border Protection intercepted 2,493 pounds of marijuana hidden in carrots (US Customs and Border Protection 2016). In April 2011, *USA Today* reported,

> In the past two months alone, inventory confiscated at New York-area airports and ports included opium concealed in porcelain cat figurines, cocaine in bags of freeze-dried coffee, drugs built into the railings of a suitcase, sewn into pants, molded into sneakers, concealed in clothing hangers or packed into the console of a Nintendo Wii video game system. . . . Drugs have been hidden in electrical cords, in a computer mouse, a child's Mr. Potato Head doll, baby diapers, drug-soaked clothing, toothpaste, cosmetics, fruit that is expertly sliced, gutted, filled with drugs and resealed to look untouched, or in live animals—such as puppies—and of course, in people.

Not only are drugs smuggled in other goods, but they are also ingested by people in order to bypass additional security measures brought on by law enforcement. According to Silverberg, Menes, and Kim (2006), the practice of "body packing," swallowing or inserting packets of wrapped drugs into one's person, was first documented in 1975 (541). As the Council on Hemispheric Affairs (2011) reported, "Government efforts to impede drug smuggling have only increased the level of women's participation in the business because women were less likely to be associated with drug trafficking and, therefore, could sneak past security with relatively small amounts of narcotics in their chests, or swallow pellets containing drugs." Such tactics can be viewed as innovations on the part of trafficking entrepreneurs to find new methods to get drugs over the border undetected. These methods become entrepreneurial alternatives to help DTOs remain in business when other methods are compromised.

Children are also recruited to work as smugglers. Like women, children are less frequently associated with illegal drug activity compared to men. A crucial difference, however, is that children are not subjected to the same punishments as adults for breaking the law. They are also cheaper labor because children are typically less skilled and have less experience compared to adults. Booth and Fainaru (2009) report that "[a]lthough the exploitation of children by criminals is timeless, authorities say the cartels [in Mexico] are responding to new realities here. They have stepped up recruiting to replace tens of thousands of members who have been killed or arrested during President Felipe Calderón's U.S.-backed war against the traffickers." Booth and Fainaru (2009) quote Martin Barron Cruz, a researcher at the National Institute of Criminal Science in Mexico, saying, "These days, youths are joining the drug cartels at an ever-younger age because they're cheap. . . . It is a question of the market. A kid of 15 ends up doing the same job as a 20-year-old, but for half the money. It is easier for the cartels to dispose of them when they are no longer needed. . . . I say 'dispose' because, sadly, there's no other word for it. They eliminate them, often using another kid of the same age."

Child involvement is not just isolated to smuggling. Lamar (2001) describes how, during the 1990s, teenagers became significantly more involved in the crack market. He states that "[w]ith the advent of crack, juvenile arrests in New York City tripled, from 386 in 1983 to 1,052 [in 2000]. Detroit-area police busted 647 youths [in 2000], almost twice as many as in 1986. A staggering increase in juvenile drug arrests has occurred in Washington, jumping from 483 in 1983 to 1,894 in 1987." Lamar's article supports the idea that drug entrepreneurs respond to law enforcement and adjust tactics to evade punishment, maintain protection, and keep costs low. "There is no provision under our law to mandate restrictive custody for these youths," describes George Robinson, an Atlanta-based assistant district attorney, in Lamar (2001). Robinson continues, "They're selling drugs, and we're just spanking them on the hands."

Increases in drug potency can also be categorized as entrepreneurial innovations. Since drug punishments are delineated by law enforcement based on
drug type and quantity, drug entrepreneurs face strong incentives to traffic
and distribute smaller quantities to decrease punishment. Drug entrepreneurs
also face an incentive to traffic and distribute smaller amounts of drugs
because it decreases the likelihood of detection. However, the smaller the
quantity, the less revenue that the entrepreneur can earn, ceteris paribus. This
presents the entrepreneur with a trade-off, unless she is able to find a way to
alter the drug to increase a consumer or lower-level supplier's willingness to
pay. Increasing the potency is one such way.

Thornton (1998) presents a theoretical framework for, as well as empirical
evidence on, the impact of prohibition of goods such as drugs and alcohol
during Prohibition. Thornton finds that the average observed potency of marijuana between 1974 and 1984 increased by 800 percent (1998, 733). Since
this article, more recent data has been made available. According to ElSohly
(2009), the Director of the National Institute on Drug Abuse Marijuana
Project, the percentage of Delta-9 THC (the psychoactive ingredient in marijuana), which is used to measure marijuana potency, increased from .74 percentage points in 1975 to 8.49 percentage points in 2008 (8). This is a greater
than an eleven-fold increase in the potency of marijuana in thirty-three years.
Thornton's article also documents the impact of Prohibition on alcohol consumption. This data is especially useful as it provides information on alcohol
potency during the years, but it also highlights what happened to alcohol
potency and consumer behavior after Prohibition was repealed. This allows
us to tease out how market behavior was altered as a result of prohibitionist
policies. Thornton (1998, 732) documents that distilled spirit consumption
as a percentage of total alcohol consumption was on the decline prior to
Prohibition, dropping from roughly 80 percent to 40 percent between 1840
and 1920. After Prohibition began in January 1920, Thornton shows that this
percentage dramatically rose to roughly 90 percent and remained above 80
percent until the mid-1930s. After Prohibition was repealed, the percentage
of distilled spirit consumption as a percentage of total alcohol consumption
declined rapidly to around 50 percent.

One final example of entrepreneurial innovation within the illegal drug
market is the evolution of designer drugs through malnovation (Redford,
forthcoming). Malnovation refers to the induced drug discovery process
created by drug scheduling laws. According to Redford (forthcoming, 4),
these laws created "new incentives for drug entrepreneurs to: find recre-
ational uses of lower scheduled drugs, seek out and create entirely new or
previously unscheduled drugs, and slightly modify the chemical structure
of existing, scheduled drugs." In the instance of designer drug malnovation,
illegal drug entrepreneurs, in an effort to avoid legal punishment, operate in

a gray area by producing drugs that are not technically illegal because their chemical formulas are slightly altered such that they are no longer the same chemical substance specified on the scheduling list. Redford uses this method of malnovation to explain the evolution of synthetic cathinones (bath salts) in the 2000s and fentanyl variants in the 1980s. This process frequently results in socially undesirable outcomes such as overdose and death epidemics as the variants within the larger drug family are sold under the same street names despite their chemical differences. By using the same street name, drug entrepreneurs are able to sell technically legal forms of drugs in established consumer groups. Over time, however, this can become dangerous and unprofitable as further chemical manipulation takes place, in response to the older variants being added to the scheduling list, thus increasing the heterogeneity in the variants sold under the same street name.

Playing devil's advocate, without a realistic counterfactual, it is impossible to know whether or not these specific instances of increasing potency, creating designer drugs, hiring women to body pack drugs for smuggling, recruiting and coercing children to smuggle and sell drugs, and altering trafficking routes could have taken place in the absence of Prohibition. We could concoct scenarios in which a legal drug entrepreneur would make similar innovations in response to market conditions, thus making them productive. Legal shipping companies alter trade routes all the time, and shipping smaller quantities of goods is cheaper because they require fewer resources. However, risking a person's life by forcing them to swallow condoms full of heroin to smuggle over the Mexican border into the United States or coercing a child into selling heroin on a street corner seem unrealistic in a market where such goods could be flown on a parcel plane and sold in a retail store. It also begs the question of why we do not see such things in markets for goods such as marijuana in Colorado, distilled spirits, sandwich bread, or economics textbooks.

## LAW ENFORCEMENT AND INFORMAL ENTREPRENEURIAL RESPONSE

The entrepreneurial innovations within illegal drug markets described in the previous section are examples that highlight how Prohibition policies incentivize and facilitate outcomes that help individuals in the illegal drug trade to evade and protect themselves against law enforcement but do not yield positive sum outcomes. Recall that productive entrepreneurship, the form of entrepreneurship that facilitates economic growth, takes place when the pursuit of profit is aligned with positive sum outcomes.

The shift away from productive entrepreneurship does not imply that these entrepreneurs are (irrationally) engaging in activities that yield themselves or their customers less benefit than the costs they incur. Instead it is a way to describe entrepreneurship that does not lead to economic progress and positive-sum outcomes. In "The Substance of Entrepreneurship and the Entrepreneurship of Substances," March, Martin, and Redford (2016) describe specific forms of entrepreneurship that are either welfare destroying (nonproductive and destructive entrepreneurship) or only welfare enhancing due to an existing institutional impediment (superfluous entrepreneurship). In each of the examples of nonproductive entrepreneurship mentioned in the above section, economic progress is stunted due to the institutional structure.

A necessary condition for individuals involved in the illegal drug trade, including those involved in the drug trade within prison, is to remain in business and not get caught by law enforcement. This strongly incentivizes entrepreneurs to remain alert to and invest resources into methods of law enforcement evasion and protection against law enforcement. As prohibitionist policies are enforced, the institutional framework protecting the rights of illegal goods is consistently undermined, and entrepreneurs must continuously find ways to alter informal rights provisions to keep illegal drug trade flowing in ways that they would not have to in the absence of Prohibition. Time, effort, and resources that could be spent on productive entrepreneurial activities (such as ensuring product safety, quality control, effective advertising, developing new drugs that better fulfill consumer wants than previous drugs, etc.) are instead directed at protective and evasive activities, as these are prerequisites for the drug trade to function at all.

Not only does Prohibition limit productive entrepreneurship and innovations such as drug safety, but it also encourages and exacerbates the very violence that it seeks to eliminate. Violence, however, is not a necessary condition for markets operating within informal institutions. Violence and the credible threat of violence is useful in maintaining order within a governance system, but not all systems of private governance require it in order to be effective (see the discussion in the section above on "Drug Prohibition"). Something else has to explain the persistence of violence in illegal markets that is not observed in legal markets. I argue that the enforcement of Prohibition creates an environment in which violence is a useful tool for protection.

The goal of prohibitionist policies is to decrease the overall number of would-be illegal substance users, traffickers, producers, and sellers by increasing the cost of doing illegal business. This cost of participation also changes the relative makeup and desirable qualities of market participants. As a result, markets for illegal goods are frequently populated by individuals who have demonstrated their comparative advantage in evading law enforcement and effectively using violence as well as those individuals whose marginal cost of committing an additional crime is very low. As Miron notes, "Thus, prohibition enriches the segment of society willing to evade the law"

(2001, 841). Existing criminals and those involved in organized crime and illegal enterprises have demonstrated both qualities.

Drug gangs and organized crime groups devise ways to establish and maintain rights primarily through the threat of violence. One of the main ways this is done is through the delineation of territory. The threat of violence and other extralegal forms of punishment are used as a means to enforce or to predate on territory for selling or distributional purposes (Levitt and Venkatesh 2000; Reuter 2009). Drug-selling gangs provide protection for their members engaging in illegal drug transactions. Therefore, gangs and criminal networks with the highest capacity for violence will succeed, so long as their use of violence is not sufficiently high to scare off consumers that are averse to violence and to warrant additional police attention. This provides context not only for why violence is initially useful to groups operating in illegal markets, but also has implications for how protective entrepreneurship evolves over time and to which opportunities entrepreneurs working within this environment are alert.

Knowledge, as we know from Hayek (1945), is dispersed throughout the economy, frequently in tacit form, and can never be known to a single mind. Linking the role of knowledge and ignorance and their role in the market process, Kirzner (1992, 52–53) writes, "The existence of unknown ignorance manifests itself in markets as unnoticed opportunities for pure profits. Such opportunities attract the alertness of entrepreneurs. It is the series of discoveries stimulated by such alertness that constitutes the market process." These discoveries allow entrepreneurs to cope with the world around them, and in the case of illegal markets, protective entrepreneurs, in the pursuit of profit, are alert to new methods of facilitating governance, protecting rights, and evading law enforcement.

Individuals, however, are not alert to all opportunities always and equally. As Baumol (1990) explains, entrepreneurship is shaped by the institutional framework within which it takes place. As Martin (2011) informs us, entrepreneurial alertness, too, is shaped by the environment, including the institutions, within which the entrepreneur is operating. Martin writes, "One key feature of alertness is that it is not a *general* ability to perceive profit opportunities. . . . Alertness is specialized to a context of action. If we make the plausible assumption that experience in a 'line of endeavor' specializes individuals' alertness to the context of that endeavor, then we can explain how discoveries can lead to further discoveries. A discovery can lead to further discoveries when it allows an entrepreneur's alertness to be further specialized" (2011, 75–76). In illegal drug markets, entrepreneurs already possess an initial skill set in the efficient use of violence and law enforcement evasion, thus they will be alert to new methods by which they can use these skills in order to achieve a profit. As these discoveries manifest into profit opportunities, illegal drug entrepreneurs' alertness to violent methods of protection and law enforcement evasion is further specialized. Just like in legal markets with formal rights, once a previously unseen profit opportunity is recognized, the entrepreneur executes a plan that reallocates scarce resources toward their newly discovered higher-valued uses. Real resources are allocated toward more productive ways of evading law enforcement and violent methods of informally protecting rights.

Empirical evidence supports the argument that law enforcement is a primary driver of violence within illegal drug markets. Miron (1999, 79) finds that "the homicide rate is currently [as of 1999] 25 percent–75 percent higher than it would be in the absence of drug prohibition." Reuter (2009) cites the intensity of law enforcement as a proximate cause for increased violence throughout his article, "Systemic Violence in Drug Markets." Two examples he provides are through the means of arresting high-level illegal gang officials such that turnover in the organization is higher, leading to greater conflict (2009, 278) and fear of the trading partner being a possible informant (2009, 281). Reuter (2009) also discusses how violence is not only used as a method of rights protection, but that individuals use violence in illegal drug enterprises to move up in the organizational chain of command, as a disciplinary device to hedge against being informed on, and to gain access to transportation routes (275–77). In the absence of Prohibition and the enforcement thereof, concerns about being informed on to the police would not be a concern. Furthermore, if the costs of punishment and the need to evade law enforcement associated with participating in the drug trade were to dissipate in the absence of Prohibition, this would increase the extent of the market, allow for greater specialization, and widen the realm of entrepreneurial alertness to other methods of informal property rights protection. Private methods of arbitration, contract enforcement, and conflict resolution that have worked well in legal industries would now be accessible to the drug industry, providing substitutes for organized crime, drug gangs, and other violent methods of enforcement that were previously relied upon.

## CONCLUSION

Markets for illegal goods are insightful case studies for examining entrepreneurship and applying market process theory because they are not easy cases. Because there are multiple factors within prohibition and rights' enforcement, such an exercise can show the robustness as well as highlight the shortcomings of theory application. By providing a detailed account of what is required for the market process to operate and introducing a market in which the rights in question are not provided formally, this chapter takes steps to reconcile what the formality of property rights does vis-à-vis entrepreneurship.

The goal of this chapter is not to suggest that informal property rights protection and extralegal governance within illegal drug markets increase violence. This chapter seeks to shed light on why violence still exists in markets for prohibited goods and why productive entrepreneurship is stifled in favor of nonproductive forms of entrepreneurship in markets for prohibited goods in ways that we do no observe in markets for legal goods. Gangs and organized crime provide order in an otherwise chaotic market. Their presence actually decreases overall violence by using controlled acts of violence to maintain structure and order. This chapter wishes to add to this literature by suggesting that where we do still see violence in the markets for illegal goods, it is a result not of the failure of these extralegal forms of governance, but instead is because the government does not recognize the informal rights established within these markets, thus limiting specialization and the space for entrepreneurial alertness.

This lack of informal rights recognition through prohibition and law enforcement also encourages innovations in evasion instead of productive forms of entrepreneurship. In markets in which the government does not undermine or ignore the rights (formally or informally established) of the participants, productive forms of entrepreneurship that capture the interests of consumers are what earn entrepreneurs profit and keep them in business. In prohibited markets, however, productive entrepreneurship can only take place once protection of informal rights is established and law enforcement has been avoided. Since law enforcement is constantly intervening within illegal drug markets, entrepreneurship is constantly channeled toward evasion and protection and away from productive innovations.

The analysis from this chapter can be applied to other markets for illegal goods, but it also has implications for the discussion on rights and entrepreneurship in developing economies. The conclusions from this paper are consistent with some of the findings within the literature on developing economies. In a discussion on the political infrastructure of economic development, Boettke (2001, 242) states that "[i]ndividuals tend to get around the lack of *de jure* property rights through: (1) tacit acceptance of *de facto rights*, which is self-enforced because of the discipline of repeated dealings; (2) the use of extensive family networks (kinship); and (3) the employment of extra-legal contract enforcement." Leeson and Boettke (2009) find there are significant similarities between illegal markets as described in this chapter and developing economies. They "argue there are two tiers of entrepreneurship important for economic development. The lower one, which we call the 'productive tier,' is concerned with investments in productive technologies that improve productivity (innovation) and better service consumer needs (arbitrage). The higher one, which we call the 'protective tier,' is concerned with the creation of protective technologies that secure citizens' private property rights vis-à-vis one another (governance)" (Leeson and Boettke 2009, 253).

The conclusions of this chapter are in line with Boettke (2001) and Leeson and Boettke (2009), but these conclusions shed light on additional inquiries for research. The success of the informal enforcement of rights is going to depend on whether or not the government utilizes resources to undermine them. If this is the case, the informal governance structure will be limited in its ability to continuously facilitate productive entrepreneurship because evasive and protective entrepreneurship will take precedence. Methods of adapting the informal institutions will also be limited if there are punishments associated with participating in markets governed by de facto rights. Another line of future research could investigate whether violence is as persistent in informally governed economies where the governing norms are not supported by the government but the market activity is not prohibited. Such an investigation could also call on insights from Boettke, Coyne, and Leeson's (2008) paper, "Institutional Stickiness and New Development Economics." Developing economies where the informal norms and governance of the populace is inconsistent with the formal rules (as would be the case in countries where democracy is exported instead of homegrown) would make for an interesting case study to see if violence or other methods of enforcement would prove more effective in reducing predation on the part of the government while encouraging market cooperation.

## NOTE

I thank the participants of the 2015–2016 Adam Smith Fellowship research program for their helpful comments on previous drafts. I also thank Peter Boettke, Christopher Coyne, and Virgil Storr for insightful comments, scholarly advice, mentorship, and support during this process. I would also like to thank the Mercatus Center for generously funding and facilitating this edited volume. Any remaining errors are my own.

## REFERENCES

Anderson, Annelise. 1995. "Organised Crime, Mafia and Governments." In *The Economics of Organised Crime*, by Gianluca Fiorentini and Sam Peltzman, 33–53. Cambridge: Cambridge University Press.

Barzel, Yoram. (1989) 1997. *Economic Analysis of Property Rights*. Second edition. New York: Cambridge University Press.

Baumol, William J. 1990. "Entrepreneurship: Productive, Unproductive, and Destructive." *Journal of Political Economy* 98 (5): 893–21.

Becker, Gary S., Kevin M. Murphy, and Michael Grossman. 2006. "The Market for Illegal Goods: The Case of Drugs." *Journal of Political Economy* 114 (1): 38–60.

Benson, Bruce L. 1989. "The Spontaneous Evolution of Commercial Law." *Southern Economic Journal* 55 (3): 165–76.

———. 1990. *The Enterprise of Law: Justice without the State.* Oakland, CA: Pacific Research Institute for Public Policy.

Benson, Bruce L., and John Baden. 1985. "The Political Economy of Corruption: The Logic of Underground Government." *Journal of Legal Studies* 14 (2): 391–410.

Boettke, Peter J. 2001. "The Political Infrastructure of Economic Development." In *Calculation and Coordination: Essays on Socialism and Transitional Political Economy*, by Peter J. Boettke, 234–47. London: Routledge.

———. 2014. "Entrepreneurship, and the Entrepreneurial Market Process: Israel M. Kirzner and the Two Levels of Analysis in Spontaneous Order Studies." *Review of Austrian Economics* 27: 233–47.

Boettke, Peter J., and Christopher J. Coyne. 2004. "The Forgotten Contribution: Murray Rothbard on Socialism in Theory and in Practice." *Quarterly Journal of Austrian Economics* 7 (2): 71–89.

Boettke, Peter J., Christopher J. Coyne, and Peter T. Leeson. 2004. "The Many Faces of the Market." *Journal des Economistes et det Etudes Humaines* 14 (2): 71–86.

———. 2008. "Institutional Stickiness and the New Development Economics." *American Journal of Economics and Sociology* 67 (2): 331–58.

Booth, William, and Steve Fainaru. 2009. "Mexican Drug Cartels Increasingly Recruit the Young." *Washington Post*, November 3.

Council on Hemispheric Affairs. 2011. *The Rise of Femicide and Women in Drug Trafficking.* October 28. Accessed July 20, 2016. http://www.coha.org/the-rise-of-femicide-and-women-in-drug-trafficking/.

Dixit, Avinash. 2009. "Governance Institutions and Economic Activity." *American Economic Review* 99 (1): 3–24.

ElSohly, Mahmoud A. 2009. *Potency Monitoring Project Quarterly Report 104.* Oxford: NIDA Marijuana Project, University of Mississippi,

Fiorentini, Gianluca, and Sam Peltzman. 1995. *The Economics of Organised Crime.* Cambridge: Cambridge University Press.

Gambetta, Diego. 1993. *The Sicilian Mafia: The Business of Private Protection.* Cambridge, MA: Harvard University Press.

Greif, Avner. 1993. "Contract Enforceability and Economic Institutions in Early Trade: The Maghribi Traders' Coalition." *American Economic Review* 83 (3): 525–48.

Greif, Avner, Paul Milgrom, and Barry R. Weingast. 1994. "Coordination, Commitment, and Enforcement: The Case of the Merchant Guild." *Journal of Political Economy* 102 (4): 745–76.

Hayek, F. A. 1945. "The Use of Knowledge in Society." *American Economic Review* 35 (4): 519–30.

Kirzner, Israel M. 1992. "The Meaning of Market Process." In *The Meaning of Market Process: Essays in the Development of Modern Austrian Economics*, by Israel M. Kirzner, 38–54. London: Routledge.

———. 2000. "The Limits of the Market: The Real and the Imagined." In *The Driving Force of the Market: Essays in Austrian Economics*, by Israel M. Kirzner, 77–87. New York: Routledge.

————. 2011. "The Market: Its Structure and Operation." In *Market Theory and the Price System*, by Israel M. Kirzner, edited by Peter J. Boettke and Frederic Sautet, 14–34. Indianapolis: Liberty Fund.

Kostelnik, James, and David Skarbek. 2013. "The Governance Institutions of a Drug Trafficking Organization." *Public Choice* 156 (1–2): 95–103.

Lamar, Jacob V. 2001. "Kids Who Sell Crack." *Time*, June 24.

Leeson, Peter T. 2007a. "Trading with Bandits." *Journal of Law and Economics* 50 (2): 303–21.

————. 2007b. "An-arrrgh-chy: The Law and Economics of Pirate Organization." *Journal of Political Economy* 115 (6): 1049–94.

————. 2009. "The Law of Lawlessness." *Journal of Legal Studies* 38: 471–503.

————. 2014. *Anarchy Unbound: Why Self-Governance Works Better Than You Think*. New York: Cambridge University Press.

Leeson, Peter T., and David Skarbek. 2010. "Criminal Constitutions." *Global Crime* 11 (3): 279–97.

Leeson, Peter T., and Douglas Bruce Rogers. 2012. "Organizing Crime." *Supreme Court Economic Review* 20 (1): 89–123.

Leeson, Peter T., and Peter J. Boettke. 2009. "Two-Tiered Entrepreneurship and Economic Development." *International Review of Law and Economics* 29: 252–59.

Levitt, Steven D., and Sudhir Alladi Venkatesh. 2000. "An Economic Analysis of a Drug-Selling Gang's Finances." *Quarterly Journal of Economics* 115 (3): 755–89.

March, Raymond J., Adam G. Martin, and Audrey Redford. 2016. "The Substance of Entrepreneurship and the Entrepreneurship of Substances." *Journal of Entrepreneurship and Public Policy* 5 (2): 201–20.

Martin, Adam. 2011. "Discovering the Gains from Trade: Alertness and the Extent of the Market." *The Annual Proceedings of the Wealth and Well-Being of Nations* 3: 65–85.

Mejia, Daniel, and Pascual Restrepo. 2014. "Why Is Strict Prohibition Collapsing? A Perspective from Producer and Transit Countries." In *Ending the Drug War: Report of the LSE Expert Group on the Economics of Drug Policy*, 26–32. London: LSE IDEAS.

Miron, Jeffrey A. 1999. "Violence and the U.S. Prohibitions of Drugs and Alcohol." *American Law and Economics Review* 1 (1–2): 78–114.

————. 2001. "Violence, Guns, and Drugs: A Cross-Country Analysis." *Journal of Law and Economics* 44 (2): 615–33.

Miron, Jeffrey A., and Katherine Waldock. 2010. "The Budgetary Impact of Ending Drug Prohibition." Cato Institute. Accessed March 1, 2016. http://object.cato.org/sites/cato.org/files/pubs/pdf/DrugProhibitionWP.pdf.

Mises, Ludwig. (1949) 2007. *Human Action: A Treatise on Economics*. Indianapolis, IN: Liberty Fund.

Ostrom, Eilnor. 1990. *Governing the Commons: The Evolution of Institutions for Collective Action*. New York: Cambridge University Press.

RAND Corporation. 2014. "How Big Is the U.S. Market for Illegal Drugs?" Accessed March 25, 2016. http://www.rand.org/content/dam/rand/pubs/research_briefs/RB9700/RB9770/RAND_RB9770.pdf.

Redford, Audrey. Forthcoming. "Don't Eat the Brown Acid: Induced Malnovation in Drug Markets." *Review of Austrian Economics.*

Redford, Audrey, and Benjamin Powell. 2016. "The Dynamics of Intervention in the War on Drugs: The Build-Up to the Harrison Act of 1914." *Independent Review* 20 (4): 509–30.

Reuter, Peter. 2009. "Systemic Violence in Drug Markets." *Crime, Law, and Social Change* 52 (3): 275–84.

———. 2014. "The Mobility of Drug Trafficking." In *Ending the Drug Wars: Report of the LSE Expert Group on the Economics of Drug Policy*, 33–40. London: LSE IDEAS.

Rothbard, Murray N. (1962) 2009. *Man, Economy, and State.* Second edition. Auburn, AL: Ludwig won Mises Institute.

Silverberg, Daniel, Tehillah Menes, and Unsup Kim. 2006. "Surgery for 'Body Packers': A 15-Year Experience." *World Journal of Surgery* 30 (4): 541–46.

Skaperda, Stergio. 2001. "The Political Economy of Organized Crime: Providing Protection When the State Does Not." *Economics of Governance* 2 (3): 173–202.

Skarbek, David. 2011. "Governance and Prison Gangs." *American Political Science Review* 105 (4): 702–16.

———. 2012. "Prison Gangs, Norms, and Organizations." *Journal of Economic Behavior and Organization* 82 (1): 96–109.

———. 2014. *The Social Order of the Underworld: How Prison Gangs Govern the American Penal System.* New York: Oxford University Press.

Sobel, Russell S., and Brian J. Osoba. 2009. "Youth Gangs as Pseudo-Governments: Implications for Violent Crime." *Southern Economic Journal* 75 (4): 996–1018.

Stringham, Edward Peter. 2015. *Private Governance: Creating Order in Economic and Social Life.* New York: Oxford University Press.

Thornton, Mark. 1991. *The Economics of Prohibtion.* Salt Lake City: University of Utah Press.

———. 1998. "The Potency of Illegal Drugs." *Journal of Drug Issues* 28 (3): 725–40.

US Customs and Border Protection. 2016. *CBP Detects Over One Ton of Marijuana at the Pharr International Bridge.* January 13. Accessed July 28, 2016. https://www.cbp.gov/newsroom/local-media-release/2016-01-13-000000/cbp-detects-over-one-ton-marijuana-pharr.

*USA Today.* 2011. "Smugglers Find Creative Ways to Move Contraband." April 16.

Williamson, Claudia R., and Carrie B. Kerekes. 2011. "Securing Private Property: Formal versus Informal Institutions." *Journal of Law & Economics* 54 (3): 537–72.

# Index

# About the Authors

**Mr. Jerrod Anderson**, Statistician, Agency for Healthcare Research and Quality, 5600 Fishers Lane, 07 N 180B, Rockville MD 20857, jerrodfanderson@gmail.com

**Dr. Peter J. Boettke**, University Professor of Economics and Philosophy, George Mason University, and Director, F. A. Hayek Program for Advanced Study in Philosophy, Politics and Economics, Mercatus Center at George Mason University, Mason Hall D101, 4400 University Drive, Fairfax VA 22030, pboettke@gmu.edu

**Dr. Nicholas Cowen**, Fellow, New York University School of Law, 110 West Third Street, Room 230, New York NY 10012, ncowen@uclmail.net

**Dr. Christopher J. Coyne**, F. A. Harper Professor of Economics, George Mason University, and Associate Director, F. A. Hayek Program for Advanced Study in Philosophy, Politics and Economics, Mercatus Center at George Mason University, Mason Hall D101, 4400 University Drive, Fairfax VA 22030, ccoyne3@gmu.edu

**Mr. Jason Douglas**, PhD Candidate, University of Illinois at Chicago, English Department, 128 S. Heather Drive, Crystal Lake IL 60014, jgdoug@gmail.com

**Ms. Crystal A. Dozier**, Graduate Teaching Assistant, Texas A&M University, Department of Anthropology, MS 4352 TAMU, College Station TX 77843-4352, cdozier@tamu.edu

**Mr. Frank Garmon Jr.**, Instructor of History; PhD candidate, Christopher Newport University; University of Virginia, McMurran Hall 313, 1 Avenue of the Arts, Newport News VA 23606, fwg3gc@virginia.edu

**Dr. Bryan Leonard**, Assistant Professor, Arizona State University, School of Sustainability, PO Box 875502, Tempe AZ 85287, bryan.leonard@asu.edu

**Mr. Nicholas O'Neill**, PhD Student, University of Chicago, History Department, 655 Goodpasture Island Road, Apt. 141, Eugene OR 97401, oneilln@uchicago.edu

**Dr. Audrey Redford**, Assistant Professor of Economics, Western Carolina University, Forsyth 226i, 1 University Drive, Cullowhee NC 28723, amredford@email.wcu.edu

**Dr. Nathan Sawatzky**, Postdoctoral Fellow in Classics, University of California, Berkeley, 1929 Rose Street, Berkeley CA 94709, npsawatzky@gmail.com

**Mr. Dan C. Shahar**, Visiting Assistant Professor, University of Arizona, Philosophy Department, 3681 E. Camino de Jaime, Tucson AZ 85718, dcshahar@email.arizona.edu

**Dr. Virgil Henry Storr**, Research Associate Professor of Economics, George Mason University, and Don C. Lavoie Senior Fellow, F. A. Hayek Program for Advanced Study in Philosophy, Politics and Economics, Mercatus Center at George Mason University, Mason Hall D101, 4400 University Drive, Fairfax VA 22030, vstorr@mercatus.gmu.edu

**Ms. Brianne Wolf**, PhD Candidate, University of Wisconsin–Madison, Political Science Department, 110 North Hall, 1050 Bascom Mall, Madison WI 53706, bwolf@wisc.edu